A Reader's Guide to Contemporary Literary Theory

FIFTH EDITION

Raman Selden
Peter Widdowson
Peter Brooker

PEARSON
Longman

Harlow, England • London • New York • Boston • San Francisco • Toronto
Sydney • Tokyo • Singapore • Hong Kong • Seoul • Taipei • New Delhi
Cape Town • Madrid • Mexico City • Amsterdam • Munich • Paris • Milan

PEARSON EDUCATION LIMITED

Edinburgh Gate
Harlow CM20 2JE
United Kingdom
Tel: +44 (0)1279 623623
Fax: +44 (0)1279 431059
Website: www.pearsoned.co.uk

Fifth edition published in Great Britain in 2005

© Prentice Hall Europe 1985, 1997
© Pearson Education Limited 2005

The rights of Raman Selden, Peter Widdowson and
Peter Brooker to be identified as authors
of this work has been asserted in accordance
with the Copyright, Designs and Patents Act 1988.

ISBN: 978-0-582-89410-5

British Library Cataloguing in Publication Data
A CIP catalogue record for this book can be obtained from the British Library

Library of Congress Cataloging in Publication Data
Selden, Raman.
   A reader's guide to contemporary literary theory / Raman Selden, Peter Widdowson,
Peter Brooker.— 5th ed.
      p. cm.
   Includes bibliographical references and index.
   ISBN 0-582-89410-7 (pbk.)
      1. Criticism—History—20th century. I. Widdowson, Peter. II. Brooker, Peter. III. Title.

PN94.S45 2005
801'.95'0904—dc22

                                                                        2004063377

10 9 8 7 6 5
09

Set in 9/13.5pt Stone Serif by 35
Printed and bound in Malaysia, PJB (CTP)

The Publishers' policy is to use paper manufactured from sustainable forests.

A Reader's Guide to
Contemporary Literary Theory

In memory of Raman Selden, as always.

Contents

Preface to the Fifth Edition

R aman Selden's original *A Reader's Guide to Contemporary Literary Theory* (1985) now appears in a new fifth edition. Some little while after revising the second edition in 1989, Raman prematurely and tragically died of a brain tumour. He was much loved and highly respected – not least for the remarkable achievement of producing a short, clear, informative and unpolemical volume on a diverse and difficult subject. A third edition appeared in 1993, brought up-to-date by Peter Widdowson, and in 1997 he was joined by Peter Brooker in an extensive reworking of the fourth edition (debts to other advisers who assisted them on those occasions are acknowledged in previous Prefaces). Now, in 2005, and as witness to its continuing success and popularity, the moment for further revision of *A Reader's Guide* has arrived once more.

Twenty years is a long time in contemporary literary theory, and the terrain, not surprisingly, has undergone substantial change since Raman Selden first traversed it. As early as the third edition, it was noted that, in the nature of things, the volume was beginning to have two rather more clearly identifiable functions than it had when the project was initiated. The earlier chapters were taking on a historical cast in outlining movements from which newer developments had received their impetus but had then superseded, while the later ones attempted to take stock of precisely those newer developments, to mark out the coordinates of where we live and practise theory and criticism now. This tendency was strengthened in the reordering and restructuring of the fourth edition, and the present version continues to reflect it, so that the last five chapters – including a new concluding one on what it might mean to be 'Post-Theory' – now comprise half the book. The Introduction reflects, amongst other things, on the issues which lie behind the current revisions, and the reading lists have, of course, again been extensively updated.

Introduction

I t is now twenty years since Raman Selden undertook the daunting task of writing a brief introductory guide to contemporary literary theory, and it is salutary to consider how much has changed since the initial publication of *A Reader's Guide* in 1985. In his Introduction to that first edition, it was still possible for Raman to note that,

> until recently ordinary readers of literature and even professional literary critics had no reason to trouble themselves about developments in literary theory. Theory seemed a rather rarefied specialism which concerned a few individuals in literature departments who were, in effect, philosophers pretending to be literary critics. . . . Most critics assumed, like Dr Johnson, that great literature was universal and expressed general truths about human life . . . [and] talked comfortable good sense about the writer's personal experience, the social and historical background of the work, the human interest, imaginative 'genius' and poetic beauty of great literature.

For good or ill, no such generalizations about the field of literary criticism could be made now. Equally, in 1985 Raman would rightly point to the end of the 1960s as the moment at which things began to change, and comment that 'during the past twenty years or so students of literature have been troubled by a seemingly endless series of challenges to the consensus of common sense, many of them deriving from European (and especially French and Russian) intellectual sources. To the Anglo-Saxon tradition, this was a particularly nasty shock.' But he could also still present 'Structuralism' as a newly shocking 'intruder in the bed of Dr Leavis's *alma mater*' (Cambridge), especially a structuralism with 'a touch of *Marxism* about [it]', and note the even more *outré* fact that there was already 'a *poststructuralist* critique of structuralism', one of the main influences on which was the '*psychoanalytic* structuralism' of the French writer, Jacques Lacan. All of which, he could say at the time, 'only confirmed ingrained prejudices'. No criticism of Raman, of course – indeed, that he *could* say this is to make the very point – but such a conjuncture within 'English' or Literary Studies now seems to belong irrevocably to the dim and distant past. As later pages of the present introduction attest, over the last twenty years a seismic change has taken place which has transformed the contours of 'contemporary literary theory', and which has therefore required a reconfiguration of *A Reader's Guide* to match.

Nevertheless, we retain – along with, it is only fair to note, a good proportion of what Raman originally wrote in the first editions of the book – a commitment to many of his founding beliefs about the need for a concise, clear, introductory guide to the field. We might add that the constant fissurings and reformations of contemporary theory since seem to reconfirm the continuing need for some basic mapping of this complex and difficult terrain, and the *Guide*'s widespread adoption on degree courses throughout the English-speaking world also appears to bear this out.

It goes without saying, of course, that 'theory' in the fullest generic sense is not a unique product of the late twentieth century – as its Greek etymology, if nothing else, clearly indicates. Nor, of course, is Literary or Critical Theory anything new, as those will confirm who studied Plato, Aristotle, Longinus, Sidney, Dryden, Boileau, Pope, Burke, Coleridge and Arnold in their (traditional) 'Literary Theory' courses. Indeed, one of Raman Selden's other (edited) books is entitled *The Theory of Criticism from Plato to the Present: A Reader* (1988). Every age has its theoretical definitions of the nature of literature and its theorized principles on which critical approaches to the analysis of literature are premised. But in the 1980s, Fredric Jameson made a telling observation in his essay, 'Postmodernism and Consumer Society' (in Kaplan (ed.), 1988: see 'Further reading' for Chapter 8); he wrote: 'A generation ago, there was still a technical discourse of professional philosophy . . . alongside which one could still distinguish that quite different discourse of the other academic disciplines – of political science, for example, or sociology or literary criticism. Today, increasingly, we have a kind of writing simply called "theory" which is all or none of these things at once.' This 'theoretical discourse', he goes on, has marked 'the end of philosophy as such' and is 'to be numbered among the manifestations of postmodernism'. The kinds of originary theoretical texts Jameson had in mind were those from the 1960s and 1970s by, for example, Barthes, Derrida, Foucault, Lacan, Althusser, Kristeva, together with earlier 'remobilized' texts by, among others, Bakhtin, Saussure, Benjamin and the Russian Formalists. Through the

1980s and 1990s, this process seemed to compound itself in self-generating fashion, with 'Theory' (now adorned by a tell-tale capital 'T') being put on the syllabus by a plethora of Readers, Guides and introductory handbooks. Certainly in 'English' – plunged into a permanent state of 'crisis' (but only, it appeared, for those who did not want to countenance change) – 'Theory' courses became *de rigueur*, prompting one of the central and unresolved debates in that discipline at least: 'How to Teach Theory' (more on this later). This period (*c.*late 1960s to late 1990s), we may call 'Theorsday' – or, more recognizably, 'The Moment of Theory' – a historically and culturally specific phenomenon coterminous with Poststructuralism, Postmodernism and the sidelining of materialist politics, a period which, it now seems, has been superseded by one declared 'post-Theory' (see below and the Conclusion to the present volume).

But back in 1985, Raman Selden's impetus in writing *A Reader's Guide* was because he believed that the questions raised by contemporary literary theory were important enough to justify the effort of clarification, and because many readers by then felt that the conventional contemptuous dismissal of theory would no longer do. If nothing else, they wanted to know exactly what they were being asked to reject. Like Raman, we too assume that the reader is interested by and curious about this subject, and that s/he requires a sketch-map of it as a preliminary guide to traversing the difficult ground of the theories themselves. Apropos of this, we also firmly hold that the 'Selected Reading' sections at the end of each chapter, with their lists of 'Basic Texts' and 'Further Reading', are an integral part of our project to familiarize the reader with the thinking which has constructed their present field of study: the *Guide*, in the beginning and in the end, is no substitute for the original theories.

Inevitably, any attempt to put together a brief summation of complex and contentious concepts, to say much in little, will result in over-simplifications, compressions, generalizations and omissions. For example, we made the decision when revising the fourth edition that approaches premised on pervasive linguistic and psychoanalytic theories were best dispersed throughout the various chapters rather than having discrete sections devoted to them. 'Myth criticism', which has a long and varied history and includes the work of Gilbert Murray, James Frazer, Carl Jung, Maud Bodkin and Northrop Frye, was omitted because it seemed to us that it had not entered the mainstream of academic or popular culture, and had not challenged received ideas as vigorously as the theories we do examine. The chapter on New Criticism and F. R. Leavis comes before the one on Russian Formalism when even a cursory glance will indicate that chronologically the latter *precedes* the former. This is because Russian Formalism, albeit mainly *produced* in the second two decades of the twentieth century, did not have widespread impact until the late 1960s and the 1970s, when it was effectively rediscovered, translated and given currency by Western intellectuals who were themselves part of the newer Marxist and structuralist movements of that period. In this respect, the Russian Formalists 'belong' to that later moment of their *reproduction* and were mobilized by the new left critics in their assault, precisely, on established literary criticism represented most centrally, in the Anglo-Saxon cultures, by New Criticism and Leavisism. Hence, we present the latter as *anterior* to Formalism in terms of critical theoretical ideology, because they represent the traditions of criticism, from the outset and principally, with which contemporary critical theory had to engage. In any event, while the *Reader's Guide* does not pretend to give a comprehensive picture of its field, and cannot be anything other than selective and partial (in both senses), what it does offer is a succinct overview of the most challenging and prominent trends within the theoretical debates of the last forty years.

But more generally, and leaving aside for the moment the fact that in 2005, if not in 1985, the effects of these theoretical debates have so marked literary studies that it is unthinkable to ignore them, why should we trouble ourselves about theory? How, after all, does it affect our experience and understanding of reading literary texts? One answer would be that some familiarity with theory tends to undermine reading as an *innocent* activity. If we begin to ask ourselves questions about the construction of meaning in fiction, the presence of ideology in poetry, or how we measure the *value* of a literary work, we can no longer naïvely accept the 'realism' of a novel, the 'sincerity' of a poem, or the 'greatness' of either. Some readers may cherish their illusions and mourn the loss of innocence, but if they are serious, they must confront the problematical issues raised about 'Literature' and its social relations by major theorists in recent years. Other readers again may believe that theories and concepts will only deaden the spontaneity of their response to literary works, but they will thereby fail to realize that *no* discourse about literature is theory-free, that even apparently 'spontaneous' discussion of literary texts is dependent on the *de facto* (if less self-conscious) theorizing of older generations. Their talk of 'feeling', 'imagination', 'genius', 'sincerity' and 'reality' is full of dead theory which is sanctified by time and has become part of the naturalized language of common sense. A second answer might be, then, that far from having a sterile effect on our reading, new ways of seeing literature can revitalize our engagement with texts; that if we are to be adventurous and exploratory in our reading *of* literature, we must also be adventurous in our thinking *about* literature.

One simple way of demonstrating the effect of theorizing literature is to see how different theories raise different questions about it from different foci of interest. The following diagram of linguistic communication, devised by Roman Jakobson, helps to distinguish some possible starting-points:

CONTEXT
ADDRESSER > MESSAGE > ADDRESSEE
CONTACT
CODE

An addresser sends a message to an addressee; the message uses a code (usually a language familiar to both addresser and addressee); the message has a context (or 'referent') and is transmitted through a contact (a medium such as live speech, the telephone or writing). For the purposes of discussing literature, the 'contact' is usually now the printed word (except, say, in drama or performance-poetry); and so we may restate the diagram thus:

CONTEXT
WRITER > WRITING > READER
CODE

If we adopt the addresser's viewpoint, we draw attention to the *writer*, and his or her 'emotive' or 'expressive' use of language; if we focus on the 'context', we isolate the 'referential' use of language and invoke its historical dimension at the point of the work's production; if we are principally interested in the addressee, we study the *reader*'s reception of the 'message', hence introducing a different historical context (no longer the moment of a text's production but of its *reproduction*), and so on. Different literary theories also tend to place the emphasis upon one function rather than another; so we might represent some major earlier ones diagrammatically thus:

MARXIST
ROMANTIC > FORMALIST   > READER-
HUMANIST   STRUCTURALIST   ORIENTED

Romantic-humanist theories emphasize the *writer*'s life and mind as expressed in his or her work; 'reader' theories (phenomenological criticism) centre themselves on the *reader*'s, or 'affective', experience; formalist theories concentrate on the nature of the *writing* itself; Marxist criticism regards the social and historical *context* as fundamental; and structuralist poetics draws attention to the *codes* we use to construct meaning. At their best, of course, none of these approaches totally ignores the other dimensions of literary communication: for example, Western Marxist criticism does not hold a strictly referential view of language, and the writer, the audience and the text are all included within the overall sociological perspective. However, it is noteworthy in what we have outlined above that none of the examples is taken from the more contemporary theoretical fields of feminism, poststructuralism, postmodernism, postcolonialism and gay, lesbian or queer theory. This is because all of these, in their different ways, disturb and disrupt the relations between the terms in the original diagram, and it is these movements which account for the disproportionate scale of the twenty-year gap between the moment when Raman Selden began the book and the moment of its revision now.

Developments in critical theory and practice have diversified in geometric progression since 1985, and the shape and composition of the present version of *A Reader's Guide* attempt to take account of this and are witness to it. Although not overtly structured to indicate such a change, the book is now in two distinct halves. Those theories which comprised the entirety of the earlier editions have been reduced and pressed back into Chapters 1–6, or just about half of the whole volume. It is clear that these are now part of the *history* of contemporary literary theory, but are not accurately described as 'contemporary literary theory' themselves. This is not to say that they are now redundant, sterile or irrelevant – their premises, methodologies and perceptions remain enlightening, and may yet be the source of still more innovative departures in theorizing literature – but in so far as they were the pace-makers for the new leaders of the field, they have dropped back and are out of the current race. A difficult decision in this context was how to deal with the chapter on feminist theories. In earlier editions, this had concluded the book – signalling that this was where the action was; but the chronology of the chapter, often paralleling other theories of the 1960s and 1970s, came to make it look like a gestural afterthought: 'and then there is feminism'. In the fourth edition, therefore, we returned the chapter comprising that time-frame, with its largely 'white' Anglo-American and French focus, to its more appropriate place at the end of the 'historical' half of the book, and dispersed accounts of the newer feminisms, taking account especially of their pivotal non-Eurocentric energies, throughout the later 'contemporary' chapters. The long chapter on poststructuralism now contains rather more on psychoanalytic theories and an updating of the treatment of New Historicism and Cultural Materialism. A previous single chapter on postmodernism and postcolonialism was split in the fourth edition into two separate chapters, with new sections which introduced both theorists who had only more recently begun to make a major mark on the field and the impact of work around gender, sexuality, race and ethnicity. In addition, there was an entirely new chapter on gay, lesbian and queer theories, which brought the book's coverage of the most dynamic areas of activity up-to-date. Most of the above has been retained in the present fifth edition, although revised and refined where necessary. The most significant addition here, however, is the concluding chapter on 'Post-Theory', which takes stock of the various emergent tendencies and debates regarding aesthetics and politics which are occurring under its banner. Finally, the 'Selected Reading' sections have again been recast to make them more accessible and up-to-date. One notable change in these is the inclusion (in square brackets) of dates of first publication for many of the founding texts of contemporary literary theory in order to indicate how much earlier they often are than the modern editions by which they subsequently made their impact. Equally, the date of translation into English of seminal European texts is included for the same reason.

So what has been the turbulence between 1985 and 2005 in the field of 'contemporary literary theory'; what is the context which explains the continuous need to revise *A Reader's Guide*? For a start, 'Theory', even 'literary theory', can no longer usefully be regarded as a progressively emerging body of work, evolving through a series of definable phases or 'movements' – of delivery, critique, advancement, reformulation, and so on. This appeared to be the case in the later 1970s and early 1980s – although no doubt it was never entirely true – when the 'Moment of Theory' seemed to have arrived and there was an anxiety, even to those enthusiastically participating in it, that a new academic subject, worse a new scholasticism – radical and subversive, yes, but also potentially exclusive in its abstraction – was coming into being. Books poured from the presses, conferences abounded, 'Theory' courses at undergraduate and postgraduate level proliferated, and any residual notions of 'practice' and of 'the empirical' became fearsomely problematical. Such a 'Moment of Theory' no longer obtains – whether, paradoxically, because it coincided with the rise to political power of the new right, whether because, by definition in a postmodern world, it could not survive in a more or less unitary state, or whether it contained, as itself a postmodern creature, the catalysing agents for its own dispersal, are beyond confident assertion. But a change *has* occurred – a change producing a situation very different to that of the increasingly abstract and self-obsessed intellectual field which the original edition of this book felt itself just about able to describe and contain. First, the singular and capitalized 'Theory' has devolved rapidly into 'theories' – often overlapping and mutually generative, but also in productive contestation. The 'Moment of Theory', in other words, has spawned a hugely diverse tribe of *praxes*, or theorized practices, at once self-conscious about their projects and representing radical forms of political action, at least in the cultural domain. This has been particularly the case with critical theories and practices which focus on gender and sexuality and with those which seek to deconstruct Euro- and ethnocentricity. Second, given the postmodern theoretical fission we have suggested above, there has been a turn in some quarters to ostensibly more traditional positions and priorities. The verdict here is that 'Theory Has Failed': that, in an ironic postmodern twist, the 'End of Theory' is now with us. This is by no means the Lazarus-like spasms of the old guard come back from the dead, but the view of younger academics who have gone through the theory mill and who wish to challenge the dominance of theoretical discourse in literary studies on behalf of literature itself – to find a way of talking about literary texts, about the experience of reading and evaluating them. As the concluding chapter in the present edition makes clear, this aspect of 'post-theory' is most perceptible in the tendency towards a so-called 'New Aesthetics'. The question of 'practice' in the present theoretical context we will return to briefly below.

Other related effects of developments in contemporary theory over the past decades may be adduced as follows. Perhaps the most notable has been the deconstruction of notions of a given literary canon – of an agreed selection of 'great works' which are the benchmark for the discrimination of 'literary value', and without exposure to which no literary education can be complete. The theoretical challenging of the criteria on which the canon is established, together with the arrival on the agenda of many more marginal kinds of literary and other cultural production hitherto excluded from it, has at once caused a withering of the old verities and an explosion of new materials for serious study. While the canon retains some prestigious defenders (for example, Harold Bloom and George Steiner), the more pervasive tendency has been to push literary studies towards forms of cultural studies, where a much larger and uncanonized range of cultural production is under analysis. Indeed, it might more accurately be said that this tendency represents a form of feedback, since it was precisely the earlier initiatives of Cultural Studies proper which were among the agents that helped to subvert naturalized notions of 'Literature' and literary criticism in the first place. In the context of contemporary literary theory, however, the more telling recent shift has been to the development of 'Cultural Theory' as the umbrella term for the whole field of enquiry. Most of the significant work outlined in the later chapters of this *Reader's Guide*, it is important to note – on postmodernism, postcolonialism, gay, lesbian and queer theories, in particular – is always *more than literary* in orientation. Such theories promote a global reinterpretation and redeployment of all forms of discourse as part of a radical cultural politics, among which 'the literary' may be merely one more or less significant form of representation. The present volume recognizes this, but in turn and given its brief, it attempts to retain a literary focus within the broad and constantly mutating processes of cultural history.

Despite the complexity and diversity of the field as we have presented it, however, there are a number of fundamental lessons that the theoretical debates of the past thirty years have thrown up – ones learnt not only by radicals but also by those who wish to defend more conventional or traditionally humanistic positions and approaches. They are: that *all* literary-critical activity is *always* underpinned by theory; that the theory, whatever it may be, represents an ideological – if not expressly political – position; that it is more effective, if not more honest, to have a praxis which is explicitly theorized than to operate with naturalized and unexamined assumptions; that such a praxis may be tactical and strategic rather than seemingly philosophically absolute; that 'Theory' is no longer apparently monolithic and awesome (although still 'difficult'); and that it is to be *put to use* and critiqued rather than studied in the abstract and for its own sake.

It is at this point, then, that we might reflect for a moment on the notion that 'Theory Has Failed' and that an age of 'post-theory' has dawned (to be revisited more substantively in our Conclusion). What is meant by 'The Failure of Theory'? In Literary Studies, the crucial issue seems to be the relation between Theory and Criticism. But what, after all, is Theory in this context? What distinguishes it from 'practice', and how then does it impact on 'empirical' textual analysis? The answers lie in a number of fallacies which traverse the notion of the failure of theory. First, it implies that theory has a privileged role in a hierarchy of conceptual, creative and critical discourses, rather than recognizing the dialectical relationship between theory and practice in which they test and transform each other. Second, it assumes that theory somehow exists outside the kinds of assumptions and ideologies it discloses, that it is not itself a socio-cultural practice (Terry Eagleton once put the converse: 'just as all social life is theoretical, so all theory is a real social practice' (Eagleton, 1990)). Third, as a consequence, it seems to set up a stark choice at a specious crossroads between a cul-de-sac of autonomous and impenetrable theory and a through-road of critical practice, accessible language and direct encounter with literary texts. The first we might call 'Metaphysics', the second 'New Criticism' – and we have been there before. In reality, of course, there is no crossroads: theory shadows criticism as a questioning and interiorized companion, and the conversation between them goes on, whatever their apparent separation. The function of literary/critical theory is to reveal and debate the assumptions of literary form and identity and to disclose the interleaved criteria of aesthetic, moral and social values on which critical modes depend and which their procedures enact and confirm. No justification should be needed, therefore, to encourage this conversation further, to make criticism's theoretical assumptions explicit, to assess one theory by another, to ask how a theoretical framework influences the interpretation of literary texts. But perhaps the most insistent fallacy is the judgement that the 'radical' Theory of the post-1960s period failed to produce a criticism which matched its radicalizing intentions; that instead of a theoretically aware, interventionist and socially purposive criticism which could be deployed in the empirical analysis of texts came work of wayward or leaden abstraction and of self-promoting dogma. Now we would be the first to admit that the academic world has supped full of the ritualistic trotting-out of major theorists' names and theoretical clichés; of wooden Foucauldian or Bakhtinian 'readings' of this, that or the other; of formulaic gesturing towards the 'theoretical underpinnings' of this or that thesis – often seriously disjunct from what are, in effect, conventional literary-critical analyses. In the present context, then, we might want to recast 'post-theory' as 'post-Theoreticism', where '-eticism' is shorthand for an arcane, hermetic scholasticism, but 'theory' properly remains the evolving matrix in which new critical practices are shaped. In a sense, as the introduction to a collection of essays on the subject suggests, 'post-theory' is to flag no more than 'theory "yet to come"' (McQuillan et al. (eds), 1999: see 'References' for Conclusion).

In the event, the demystification of theory, which has resulted in the great plurality of theorized praxes for specific interests and purposes, should allow us to be rather more self-questioning and critical about it. For example, in the context of 'post-theory', is one implication that we would no longer have to face that overwhelming question which has haunted our profession since the 1970s: 'How to Teach Theory'? Would grateful students no longer have to 'do Theory'? The answer must surely be No; but a principal anxiety about the term 'post-theory' is that it might seem to legitimate such 'end of Theory' fantasies. To restate the obvious, occupying a theory-free zone is a fundamental impossibility, and to allow our students to think that it is not would be a dereliction of intellectual duty. But if we do continue to teach theory, familiar questions abound. Given that 'the

Theory course' is usually taught independently of those on the familiar literary genres, and so becomes boxed off from what are still seen as the central components of a literature degree, we might want to ask: whether it is indeed appropriate to place the autonomous study of literary/critical theory on every undergraduate literature degree; whether such theory is something which can be usefully studied as though it were a separate philosophical genre; where historically such a theory course might start, and wherever it does, how far the student needs to comprehend the informing philosophical antecedents of any critical position or practice before taking it up (must you know Marx to engage with marxist critical theory)? Should students be introduced to theory via abstruse, perplexing and intimidating theoretical essays which are conceptually and stylistically far removed from their own experience of studying literature? Can students engage in meaningful seminar discussion when they have limited grasp of the debates the theory is addressing and scant knowledge of the literary texts to which it may do no more than allude in passing? Are particular theories actually tied to particular kinds of text or to particular periods (is the same theory usefully applied, for example, to a novel and to a poem, to Renaissance and to Romantic literature); how far and with what justification does a theoretical position 'rewrite' its object of study? Is there any meaningful use, finally, in simply *lecturing* on theory? All such questions are, in effect, a reflex of the pressing central questions: how to get beyond a passive engagement with theory or, conversely, a loose pluralism in which students shop around for those theories which most appeal to them (i.e. the ones they find easiest to grasp), and what, crucially, is theory's relation to critical practice?

These questions are at the heart of a pragmatic and strategic politics in the general field of cultural study in the early 2000s, and they urgently demand answers if theory is not to be seen by students as yet another example of arid scholasticism (some such answers are more or less convincingly proposed by the 'post-theory' texts surveyed in our concluding chapter). Students need to be able to make informed and engaged *choices* about the theories they encounter, to take a critical stance towards them, and to deploy the resulting insights in their own critical practice. Perhaps, as Mikko Lehtonen argued in 2001, since there can be no such thing as '"untheoretical" criticism versus "theoretical" theory', since 'teaching literature is always already teaching theory', and since students 'are always already inside theory', 'Theory can be taught best as *theorising*'. Without in any sense denying the importance of ingesting the theoretical work itself or appearing to promote once more a simplistic empiricism, this new edition of *A Reader's Guide* seeks to facilitate the process of becoming theorized by making the plethora of theoretical positions now available accessible to students. The fundamental belief behind the book is that to be in a position to understand and mobililize theory – to be able to theorize *one's own practice* – is to enfranchise oneself in the cultural politics of the contemporary period.

Selected reading
Anthologies of literary theory

Brooker, Peter and Widdowson, Peter (eds), *A Practical Reader in Contemporary Literary Theory* (Prentice Hall/Harvester Wheatsheaf, Hemel Hempstead, 1996).

Davis, Robert Con and Schleifer, Ronald (eds), *Contemporary Literary Criticism: Literary and Cultural Studies: 1900 to the Present* (4th edn, Longman, London and New York, 1998).

Lodge, David (ed.), *Twentieth-Century Literary Criticism: A Reader* (Longman, London and New York, 1977).

Lodge, David and Wood, Nigel (eds), *Modern Criticism and Theory: A Reader* (2nd edn, Pearson Education, Harlow, 1999).

Newton, K. M. (ed.), *Twentieth-Century Literary Theory: A Reader* (2nd edn, Macmillan, Basingstoke, 1997).

Rice, Philip and Waugh, Patricia (eds), *Modern Literary Theory: A Reader* (4th edn, Arnold, London, 2001).

Rivkin, Julie and Ryan, Michael (eds), *Literary Theory: An Anthology* (2nd edn, Blackwell, Oxford, 2004).

Rylance, Rick (ed.), *Debating Texts: A Reader in Twentieth-Century Literary Theory and Method* (Open University Press, Milton Keynes, 1987).

Selden, Raman (ed.), *The Theory of Criticism from Plato to the Present: A Reader* (Longman, London and New York, 1988).

Tallack, Douglas (ed.), *Critical Theory: A Reader* (Prentice Hall/Harvester Wheatsheaf, Hemel Hempstead, 1995).

Walder, Dennis (ed.), *Literature in the Modern World: Critical Essays and Documents* (2nd edn, Oxford University Press with the Open University, Oxford, 2003).

Further reading and reference works

Barry, Peter, *Beginning Theory: An Introduction to Literary and Cultural Theory* (Manchester University Press, Manchester, 2002).

Bennett, Andrew and Royle, Nicholas, *An Introduction to Literature, Criticism and Theory* (3rd edn, Pearson Education, Harlow, 2004).

Bergonzi, Bernard, *Exploding English: Criticism, Theory, Culture* (Clarendon Press, Oxford, 1991).

Bertens, Hans, *Literary Theory: The Basics* (Routledge, London, 2001).

Bloom, Harold, *The Western Canon* (Macmillan, London, 1995).

Brooker, Peter, *A Glossary of Cultural Theory* (2nd edn, Arnold, London, 2002).

Coyle, Martin, Garside, Peter, Kelsall, Malcolm and Peck, John (eds), *Encyclopaedia of Literature and Criticism* (Routledge, London, 1990).

'Critical Theory in the Classroom' issue, *Critical Survey*, 4, 3 (1992).

Eaglestone, Robert, *Doing English: A Guide for Literature Students* (2nd edn, Routledge, London, 2002).

Eagleton, Terry, *Literary Theory: An Introduction* [1983] (2nd edn, Blackwell, Oxford, 1996).

Eagleton, Terry, *The Significance of Theory* (Blackwell, Oxford, 1990).

Earnshaw, Steven, *The Direction of Literary Theory* (Macmillan, Basingstoke, 1996).

Easthope, Antony, *Literary into Cultural Studies* (Routledge, London, 1991).

Green, Keith and Le Bihan, Jill, *Critical Theory and Practice: A Coursebook* (Routledge, London, 1995).

Hawthorn, Jeremy (ed.), *A Glossary of Contemporary Literary Theory* (3rd edn, Arnold, London, 1998. *A Concise Glossary of Contemporary Literary Theory* is also available in paperback).

Knellwolf, Christa and Norris, Christopher (eds), *The Cambridge History of Literary Criticism*, vol. IX, *Twentieth-Century Historical, Philosophical and Psychological Perspectives* (Cambridge University Press, Cambridge, 2001).

Lehtonen, Mikko, 'Seven Theses on Theory', *The European English Messenger* (Spring, 2001).

Milne, Drew (ed.), *Modern Critical Thought: An Anthology of Theorists Writing on Theorists* (Blackwell, Oxford, 2003).

Murray, Chris (ed.), *Encyclopedia of Literary Critics and Criticism*, 2 vols (Routledge, London, 1999).

Newton, K. M. (ed.), *Theory into Practice: A Reader in Modern Criticism* (Macmillan, Basingstoke, 1992).

Payne, Michael (ed.), *A Dictionary of Cultural and Critical Theory* (Blackwell, Oxford, 1996).

Selden, Raman, *Practising Theory and Reading Literature: An Introduction* (Harvester Wheatsheaf, Hemel Hempstead, 1989).

Showalter, Elaine, *Teaching Literature* (Blackwell, Oxford, 2002).

Sim, Stuart (ed.), *The A–Z Guide to Modern Literary and Cultural Theorists* (Prentice Hall/Harvester Wheatsheaf, Hemel Hempstead, 1995).

Simons, Jon (ed.), *Contemporary Critical Theorists: From Lacan to Said* (Edinburgh University Press, Edinburgh, 2004).

Wolfreys, Julian (ed.), *Literary Theories: A Reader and Guide* (Edinburgh University Press, Edinburgh, 1999).

Wolfreys, Julian, Womak, Kenneth and Roberts, Ruth (eds), *The Edinburgh Encyclopaedia of Modern Criticism and Theory* (Edinburgh University Press, Edinburgh, 2002).

CHAPTER 1

New Criticism, moral formalism and F. R. Leavis

Origins: Eliot, Richards, Empson

The origins of the dominant Anglo-American traditions of criticism in the mid-twentieth century (roughly from the 1920s to the 1970s) are of course complex and often apparently contradictory – as are their theoretical and critical positions and practices. But we may crudely say that the influence of the British nineteenth-century poet and literary and cultural critic Matthew Arnold is strongly perceptible in them – especially the Arnold who proposed that philosophy and religion would be 'replaced by poetry' in modern society and who held that 'Culture' – representing 'the best that has been known and thought in the world' – could mount a humanistic defence against the destructive 'Anarchy' (Arnold's word) of what F. R. Leavis was later to call the 'technologico-Benthamite' civilization of urban, industrialized societies. The principal twentieth-century mediator of Arnold into the new critical movements, and himself the single most influential common figure behind them – British or American – was the American (and then naturalized English) poet, dramatist and critic, T. S. Eliot (see below).

To over-simplify, what is central to all the diverse inflections of the Anglo-American tradition – and itself derived from the two sources mentioned above – is a profound, almost reverential regard for literary works themselves. This may manifest itself as an obsessive concern with 'the text itself', 'the words on the page', nothing more nor less; with literary works as icons of human value deployed against twentieth-century cultural barbarism; or as an 'objective', 'scientific', 'disinterested' (Arnold's word) criticism of the text – but at heart it represents the same aesthetico-humanist idealization of works of Literature. We capitalize 'Literature' because one of the most influential

– and later most crucially deconstructed – effects of this critical tradition was the elevation of some literary works over others by way of close and 'disinterested' textual analysis ('scrutiny' leading to 'discrimination', both key Leavisite terms). Only some literary writing, in other words, was 'Literature' (the best that has been thought and *written*), and could become part of the 'tradition' (Eliot's key term and then Leavis's, as in *The Great Tradition*) or, more recognizably these days, of *the canon*. By its nature, the canon is exclusive and hierarchical, and would clearly be seen to be artificially constructed by choices and selections made by human agency (critics) were it not for its endemic tendency to naturalize itself as, precisely, *natural*: self-evidently, unarguably *given*, *there*, and not created by critical 'discrimination', by taste, preference, partiality, etc. This is its great danger; and of course it disenfranchises huge tracts of literary writing from serious study and status. It is why, in the post-1960s critical revolution, it had to be demystified and dismantled, so that all the writing which had been 'hidden from criticism' – 'gothic' and 'popular' fiction, working-class and women's writing, for example – could be put back on the agenda in an environment relatively free from pre-emptive evaluation.

T. S. Eliot was central to many of the tendencies sketched in so far, and his early essay 'Tradition and the Individual Talent' (1919) has been perhaps the single most influential work in Anglo-American criticism. In it, Eliot does two things in particular: he emphasizes that writers must have 'the historical sense' – that is, a sense of the tradition of writing in which they must situate themselves; and that this process reinforces the necessary 'depersonalization' of the artist if his or her art is to attain the 'impersonality' it must have if it is 'to approach the condition of science'. Famously, he wrote: 'Poetry is not a turning loose of emotion, but an escape from emotion; it is not the expression of personality, but an escape from personality', while characteristically adding that, 'of course, only those who have personality or emotions know what it means to want to escape from those things'. The poet (and we may note Eliot's privileging of poetry as the dominant genre, for this was to become the main focus of much New Criticism – and an instance therefore of the way particular theories relate most closely to particular kinds of writing: see Introduction, p. 11) becomes a kind of impersonal 'catalyst' of experience, a 'medium' not of his or her 'consciousness' or 'personality' but of that which in the end makes up the 'medium' itself – the poem – and our sole object of interest. In another famous phrase from his essay on 'Hamlet' (1919), Eliot describes the work of art as an 'objective correlative' for the experience which may have engendered it: an impersonal re-creation which is the autonomous object of attention. (It is closely related to the notion of the 'image' which is central to the poetics of Ezra Pound, Imagism and Eliot's own poetic practice.) What emerges from all this in the context of the diverse developments of New Criticism is the (seemingly) anti-romantic thrust of Eliot's thinking (a new 'classicism'); the emphasis on 'science', 'objectivity', 'impersonality', and the 'medium' as the focal object of analysis; and the notion of a 'tradition' of works which most successfully hold an 'essence' of human experience in their constituent 'medium'.

In the immediate post-First World War period when Eliot was developing these ideas, 'English' was emerging (most particularly at Cambridge University) as a (some would say *the*) central subject in the Arts higher-education syllabus, and with it a new, younger generation of academics determined to transcend the older 'bellettrist' critical tradition which had dominated English hitherto. In a sense, they can be regarded as the first proponents of a 'professional' criticism working from within the academy, and it was to them that Eliot's critical precepts appealed most strongly. It is worth registering – both in the present context and in the later one of contemporary critical theory's assault on the earlier tradition, and of *its* consonance with *post*modernism – that this new criticism had a thoroughly symbiotic relationship with literary modernism, finding its premises borne out in such works and using these as its model texts for analysis. To put it over simply, perhaps: this new critical movement *was* 'modernist' criticism.

I. A. Richards, William Empson and, slightly later, F. R. Leavis (see below) were the main proponents of the new English at Cambridge. Richards, whose background was in philosophy (aesthetics, psychology and semantics), produced his widely influential *Principles of Literary Criticism* in 1924. In it he innovatively attempted to lay down an explicit theoretical base for literary study. Arguing that criticism should emulate the precision of science, he attempted to articulate the special character of literary language, differentiating the 'emotive' language of poetry from the 'referential' language of non-literary discourse (his *Science and Poetry* was to follow in 1926). Even more influential – certainly in terms of its title and the praxis it enunciates – was *Practical Criticism* (1929), in which Richards included examples of his students' attempts to analyse short, unidentified poems, showed how slack their reading equipment was, and attempted to establish basic tenets for the close reading of poetry. Practical Criticism became, in both the United States and England, the central compulsory critical and pedagogic tool of the higher-education (and then secondary) English syllabus – rapidly and damagingly becoming untheorized, and thus naturalized, as *the* fundamental critical practice. Its virtues were, however – and we may yet come to regret its obloquy in the demystifying theoretical initiatives of the past thirty years – that it encouraged attentive close reading of texts and, in its intellectual and historical abstraction, a kind of democratization of literary study in the classroom, in which nearly everyone was placed on an equal footing in the face of a 'blind' text – a point we will re-emphasize in the context of American New Criticism. Indeed Richards left Cambridge in 1929, later settling at Harvard University, and his influence, particularly through *Practical Criticism*, substantially underpinned native developments in the States which were moving in similar directions.

William Empson, who transferred from mathematics to English as an undergraduate and became Richards's pupil, is most important in our context here for his first, famously precocious and astoundingly quickly produced work (written when he was Richards's student), *Seven Types of Ambiguity* (1930). It would be inaccurate to characterize Empson as purely a New Critic (his later work and career constantly refused easy labelling or placing) but that first book, with its emphasis on 'ambiguity' as the defining characteristic of poetic language, its virtuoso feats of close, creative 'practical criticism' in action, and its apparent tendency to detach literary texts from their contexts in the process of 'reading' their ambiguities was particularly influential on New Criticism.

The American New Critics

American New Criticism, emerging in the 1920s and especially dominant in the 1940s and 1950s, is equivalent to the establishing of the new professional criticism in the emerging discipline of 'English' in British higher education during the inter-war period. As always, origins and explanations for its rise – in its heyday to almost hegemonic proportions – are complex and finally indefinite, but some suggestions may be sketched in. First, a number of the key figures were also part of a group called the Southern Agrarians, or 'Fugitives', a traditional, conservative, Southern-oriented movement which was hostile to the hard-nosed industrialism and materialism of a United States dominated by 'the North'. Without stretching the point too far, a consanguinity with Arnold, Eliot and, later, Leavis in his opposition to modern 'inorganic' civilization may be discerned here. Second, New Criticism's high point of influence was during the Second World War and the Cold War succeeding it, and we may see that its privileging of literary texts (their 'order', 'harmony' and 'transcendence' of the historically and ideologically determinate) and of the 'impersonal' analysis of what makes them great works of art (their innate value lying in their superiority to material history: see below Cleanth Brooks's essay about Keats's 'Ode on a Grecian Urn') might represent a haven for alienated intellectuals and, indeed, for whole generations of quietistic students. Third, with the huge expansion of the student population in the States in this period, catering for second-generation products of the American 'melting pot', New Criticism with its 'practical criticism' basis was at once pedagogically economical (copies of short texts could be distributed equally to everyone) and also a way of coping with masses of individuals who had no 'history' in common. In other words, its ahistorical, 'neutral' nature – the study only of 'the words on the page' – was an apparently equalizing, democratic activity appropriate to the new American experience.

But whatever the socio-cultural explanations for its provenance, New Criticism is clearly characterized in premise and practice: it is not concerned with *context* – historical, biographical, intellectual and so on; it is not interested in the 'fallacies' of 'intention' or 'affect'; it is concerned solely with the 'text in itself', with its language and organization; it does not seek a text's 'meaning', but how it 'speaks itself' (see Archibald MacLeish's poem 'Ars Poetica', itself a synoptic New Critical document, which opens: 'A poem must not mean/But be'); it is concerned to trace how the parts of the text relate, how it achieves its 'order' and 'harmony', how it contains and resolves 'irony', 'paradox', 'tension', 'ambivalence' and 'ambiguity'; and it is concerned essentially with articulating the very 'poem-ness' – the formal quintessence – of the poem itself (and it usually *is* a poem – but see Mark Schorer and Wayne Booth, below).

An early, founding essay in the self-identification of New Criticism is John Crowe Ransom's 'Criticism, Inc.' (1937). (His book on Eliot, Richards and others, entitled *The New Criticism*, 1941, gave the movement its name.) Ransom, one of the 'Fugitives' and editor of the *Kenyon Review* 1939–59, here lays down the ground rules: 'Criticism, Inc.' is the 'business' of professionals – professors of literature in the universities in particular; criticism should become 'more scientific, or precise and systematic'; students should 'study literature, and not merely about literature'; Eliot was right to denounce romantic literature as 'imperfect in objectivity, or "aesthetic distance"'; criticism is *not* ethical, linguistic or historical studies, which are merely 'aids'; the critic should be able to exhibit not the 'prose core' to which a poem may be reduced but 'the differentia, residue, or tissue, which keeps the object poetical or entire. The character of the poem resides for the good critic in its way of exhibiting the residuary quality.'

Many of these precepts are given practical application in the work of Cleanth Brooks, himself also a 'Fugitive', professional academic, editor of

the *Southern Review* (with Robert Penn Warren) 1935–42, and one of the
most skilled and exemplary practitioners of the New Criticism. His and
Warren's textbook anthologies, *Understanding Poetry* (1938) and *Understanding Fiction* (1943), are often regarded as having spread the New Critical
doctrine throughout generations of American university literature students,
but his most characteristic book of close readings is the significantly titled
The Well-Wrought Urn: Studies in the Structure of Poetry (1947), in which the
essay on the eponymous urn of Keats's Ode, 'Keats's Sylvan Historian: History
Without Footnotes' (1942), is in our view the best exemplification, explicitly and implicitly, of New Critical practice one could hope to find. Brooks
at once quotes the opening of MacLeish's 'Ars Poetica' (see above); refers
to Eliot and his notion of the 'objective correlative'; rejects the relevance
of biography; reiterates throughout the terms 'dramatic propriety', 'irony',
'paradox' (repeatedly) and 'organic context'; performs a bravura reading
of the poem which leaves its 'sententious' final dictum as a dramatically
organic element of the whole; constantly admires the poem's 'history'
above the 'actual' histories of 'war and peace', of 'our time-ridden minds',
of 'meaningless' 'accumulations of facts', of 'the scientific and philosophical generalisations which dominate our world'; explicitly praises the
poem's 'insight into essential truth'; and confirms the poem's value to us
(in 1942, in the midst of the nightmare of wartime history) precisely
because, like Keats's urn, it is 'All breathing human passion far above' – thus
stressing 'the ironic fact that all human passion *does* leave one cloyed; hence
the superiority of art' (our italics).

As New Criticism is, by definition, a praxis, much of its 'theory' occurs
along the way in more specifically practical essays (as with Brooks above)
and not as theoretical writing (see below, also, for Leavis's refusal to theorize his position or engage in 'philosophical' extrapolation). But there are
two New Critical essays in particular which are overtly theoretical and which
have become influential texts more generally in modern critical discourse:
'The Intentional Fallacy' (1946) and 'The Affective Fallacy' (1949), written
by W. K. Wimsatt – a professor of English at Yale University and author of
the symptomatically titled book, *The Verbal Icon: Studies in the Meaning of
Poetry* (1954) – in collaboration with Monroe C. Beardsley, a philosopher
of aesthetics. Both essays, influenced by Eliot and Richards, engage with the
'addresser' (writer) –'message' (text) –'addressee' (reader) nexus outlined in
the Introduction, in the pursuit of an 'objective' criticism which abjures both
the personal input of the writer ('intention') and the emotional effect on
the reader ('affect') in order purely to study the 'words on the page' and
how the artefact 'works'. The first essay argues that 'the design or intention

of the author is neither available nor desirable as a standard for judging the success of a work of literary art'; that a poem 'goes about the world beyond [the author's] power to intend about it or control it' – it 'belongs to the public'; that it should be understood in terms of the 'dramatic *speaker*' of the text, not the author; and be judged only by whether it 'works' or not. Much critical debate has since raged about the place of intention in criticism, and continues to do so: Wimsatt and Beardsley's position strikes a chord, for example, with poststructuralist notions of the 'death of the author' (see below, pp. 149–50) and with deconstruction's freeing of the text from 'presence' and 'meaning'. But there the resemblance ends, for the New Critics still basically insist that there is a determinate, ontologically stable 'poem itself', which is the ultimate arbiter of its own 'statement', and that an 'objective' criticism is possible. This runs quite counter to deconstruction's notion of the 'iterability' of a text in its multiplex 'positioned' rereadings.

This difference becomes very much clearer in the second essay, which argues that the 'affective fallacy' represents 'a confusion between the poem and its *results*': 'trying to derive the standard of criticism from the psychological effects of the poem . . . ends in impressionism and relativism'. Opposing the 'classical objectivity' of New Criticism to 'romantic reader psychology', it asserts that the outcome of both fallacies is that 'the poem itself, as an object of specifically critical judgement, tends to disappear'. And the importance of a poem in classic New Critical terms is that by 'fixing emotions and making them more permanently perceptible', by the 'survival' of 'its clear and nicely interrelated meanings, its completeness, balance, and tension', it represents 'the most precise emotive report on customs': 'In short, though cultures have changed, poems remain and explain.' Poems, in other words, are our cultural heritage, permanent and valuable artefacts; and therein lies the crucial difference from more contemporary theoretical positions.

As we have noted, New Criticism focused principally on poetry, but two essays by Mark Schorer, 'Technique as Discovery' (1948) and 'Fiction and the Analogical Matrix' (1949), mark the attempt to deploy New Critical practice in relation to prose fiction. In the first of these, Schorer notes: 'Modern criticism has shown us that to speak of content as such is not to speak of art at all, but of experience; and that it is only when we speak of the *achieved* content, the form, the work of art as a work of art, that we speak as critics. The difference between content, or experience, and achieved content, or art, is technique.' This, he adds, has not been followed through in regard to the novel, whose own 'technique' is language, and whose own 'achieved content' – or 'discovery' of what it is saying – can only, as with a poem, be analysed in terms of that 'technique'. In the second essay, Schorer extends his analysis of the language of fiction by revealing the unconscious patterns of imagery and symbolism (way beyond the author's 'intention') present in all forms of fiction and not just those which foreground a 'poetic' discourse. He shows how the author's 'meaning', often contradicting the surface sense, is embedded in the matrix of linguistic analogues which constitute the text. In this we may see connections with later poststructuralist theories' concern with the sub-texts, 'silences', 'ruptures', 'raptures' and 'play' inherent in all texts, however seemingly stable – although Schorer himself, as a good New Critic, does not deconstruct modern novels, but reiterates the coherence of their 'technique' in seeking to capture 'the whole of the modern consciousness . . . the complexity of the modern spirit'. Perhaps it is, rather, that we should sense an affinity between the American New Critic, Schorer, and the English moral formalist, F. R. Leavis (see below), some of whose most famous criticism of fiction in the 1930s and beyond presents 'the Novel as Dramatic Poem'.

Finally, we should notice another American 'movement' of the mid-twentieth century which was especially influential in the study of fiction: the so-called 'Chicago School' of 'Neo-Aristotelians'. Theoretically offering a challenge to the New Critics but in fact often seen as only a New Critical 'heresy' in their analysis of formal structure and in their belief, with T. S. Eliot, that criticism should study 'poetry as poetry and not another thing', the Neo-Aristotelians were centred, from the later 1930s through the 1940s and 1950s, on R. S. Crane at the University of Chicago. Establishing a theoretical basis derived principally from Aristotle's *Rhetoric* and *Poetics*, Crane and his group sought to emulate the logic, lucidity and scrupulous concern with evidence found there; were worried by the limitations of New Critical practice (its rejection of historical analysis, its tendency to present subjective judgements as though they were objective, its concern primarily with poetry); and attempted therefore to develop a more inclusive and catholic criticism which would cover all genres and draw for its techniques, on a 'pluralistic and instrumentalist' basis, from whatever method seemed appropriate to a particular case. The anthology *Critics and Criticism: Ancient and Modern* (1952; abridged edition with Preface by Crane, 1957) contains many examples of their approach, including Crane's own exemplary reading of Fielding's *Tom Jones*, 'The Concept of Plot and the Plot of *Tom Jones*'.

In effect, the Neo-Aristotelians were most influential in the study of narrative structure in the novel, and most particularly by way of the work of a slightly later critic, Wayne C. Booth, who nevertheless acknowledged that he was a Chicago Aristotelian. His book *The Rhetoric of Fiction* (1961) has been widely read and highly regarded, although latterly contemporary critical theory has demonstrated its limitations and inadequacies (by Fredric Jameson, see Chapter 5, p. 105, and implicitly by much 'reader-oriented' theory, see Chapter 3). Booth's project was to examine 'the art of communicating with readers – the rhetorical resources available to the writer of epic, novel or short story as he tries, consciously or unconsciously, to impose his fictional world upon the reader'. Although accepting in New Critical terms that a novel is an 'autonomous' text, Booth develops a key concept with the notion that it nevertheless contains an authorial 'voice' – the 'implied author' (his or her 'official scribe' or 'second self') – whom the reader invents by deduction from the attitudes articulated in the fiction. Once this distinction between author and the 'authorial voice' is made, the way is open to analyse, in and for themselves, the many and various forms of narration which construct the text. A major legacy of Booth's is his separating out of 'reliable' and 'unreliable' narrators – the former, usually in the third person, coming close to the values of the 'implied author'; the latter, often a character within the story, a deviant from them. What Booth did was at once to enhance the formal equipment available for analysis of the 'rhetoric of fiction' and, paradoxically perhaps, to promote the belief that authors *do* mean to 'impose' their values on the reader and that 'reliability' is therefore a good thing. We may see here a consonance with the 'moral formalism' of Leavis, and the reason why poststructuralist narratology has gone beyond Booth.

Moral formalism: F. R. Leavis

Despite, or rather because of, the fact that F. R. Leavis (and 'Leavisite criticism' more generally, flowing from the journal *Scrutiny* (1932–53)) became the major single target for the new critical theory of the 1970s and beyond in the British context at least, both Raymond Williams in *Politics and Letters* (1979) and Terry Eagleton in *Literary Theory: An Introduction* (1983) bear witness to his enormous, ubiquitous influence in English Studies from the 1930s onwards. Apropos of Leavis's *The Great Tradition* (1948), Williams remarks that by the early 1970s, in relation to the English novel, Leavis 'had completely won. I mean if you talked to anyone about [it], including people who were hostile to Leavis, they were in fact reproducing his sense of the shape of its history.' And more generally, Eagleton writes: 'Whatever the "failure" or "success" of *Scrutiny* . . . the fact remains that English students in England today [1983] are "Leavisites" whether they know it or not, irremediably altered by that historic intervention.'

Leavis, profoundly influenced by Matthew Arnold and by T. S. Eliot (Leavis's *New Bearings in English Poetry* (1932) in effect first taught the English how to 'read' *The Waste Land*), was, like Richards and Empson above, one of the new academics in Cambridge in the late 1920s and early 1930s who turned the English syllabus away from the bellettrism of Sir Arthur Quiller-Couch and others, and put it at the centre of arts education in the university. His *Education and the University* (1943) – in part made up of essays published earlier, including the widely influential 'A Sketch for an "English School"' and 'Mass Civilization and Minority Culture' – bears witness to the fact that Leavis was an *educator* as much as he was a critic, and to the practical, empirical, strategically anti-theoretical nature of his work (as also do later works like *English Literature in Our Time and the University*, 1969, *The Living Principle: English as a Discipline of Thought*, 1975, and *Thought, Words and Creativity*, 1976). In a famous exchange with the American critic René Wellek, for example (see Leavis's essay 'Literary Criticism and Philosophy', 1937, in *The Common Pursuit*, 1952), he defends his refusal to theorize his work by saying that criticism and philosophy are quite separate activities and that the business of the critic is to 'attain a peculiar completeness of response [in order] to enter into possession of the given poem . . . in its concrete fullness'.

In addition to editing *Scrutiny*, Leavis taught generations of students – many of whom themselves became teachers and writers; was the informing presence behind, for example, the widely selling, ostensibly neutral but evidently Leavisite *Pelican Guide to English Literature* (1954–61) edited by Boris Ford in seven volumes; and produced many volumes of criticism and cultural commentary. All of these are indelibly imbued with his 'theory' – although resolutely untheorized in abstract terms – a theory which is dispersed throughout his work, therefore, and has to be extrapolated from it along the way.

Following Richards, Leavis is a kind of 'practical critic', but also, in his concern with the concrete specificity of the 'text itself', the 'words on the page', a kind of New Critic too: '[the critic] is concerned with the work in front of him as something that should contain within itself the reason why it is so and not otherwise' ('The Function of Criticism' in *The Common Pursuit*, 1952 – note the sideways reference to both Arnold and Eliot in the essay's title). But to regard Leavis simply in this way, with its implication of inherent formalism and ahistoricism, is a mistake; for his close address to the text is only ever to establish the vitality of its 'felt life', its closeness to 'experience', to prove its moral force, and to demonstrate (by close *scrutiny*) its excellence. The passage from Eliot which gave Leavis his title for *The Common Pursuit* speaks of the critic's task as engaging in 'the common pursuit of true judgement', and *Revaluation* (1936) is an Eliot-like sorting-out of the 'true' tradition of English poetry, just as *The Great Tradition* (1948) itself opens with the classic Leavisian 'discrimination' that 'The great English novelists are' Jane Austen, George Eliot, Henry James and Joseph Conrad – a dogmatic and exclusive list which immediately suggests just how tendentious Leavis's 'true judgement' may, in fact, be. A major plank in Leavis's platform, in other words, is to identify the 'great works' of literature, to sift out the dross ('mass' or 'popular' fiction, for example), and to establish the Arnoldian and Eliotian 'tradition' or 'canon'. This is necessary because these are the works which should be taught in a university English course as part of the process of cultural filtering, refining and revitalizing which such courses undertake on behalf of the nation's cultural health. In particular, such works will promote the values of 'Life' (the crucial Leavisian word, never defined: 'the major novelists . . . are significant in terms of that human awareness they promote; awareness of the possibilities of life') against the forces of materialism, barbarism and industrialism in a 'technologico-Benthamite' society: they represent a 'minority culture', in other words, embattled with a 'mass civilisation'.

Just as Leavis's *moral* fervour distinguishes him from the more abstract or aesthetic formalism of the New Critics, so too does his emphatically sociological and historical sense. Literature is a weapon in the battle of cultural politics, and much of the 'great' literature of the past (especially but not exclusively, from before Eliot's 'dissociation of sensibility' in the seventeenth century) bears witness to the 'organic' strength of pre-industrial cultures. The past and past literature, as for Arnold and Eliot once more, act as a measure of the 'wasteland' of the present age – although the work of the 'great' moderns (Eliot and D. H. Lawrence, for example), in its 'necessary' difficulty, complexity and commitment to cultural values, is also mobilized on 'Life's' behalf in the inimical world of the twentieth century. As for the New Critics, too, great works of literature are vessels in which humane values survive; but for Leavis they are also to be actively deployed in an ethico-sociological cultural politics. Paradoxically then, and precisely because of this, Leavis's project is both elitist and culturally pessimistic. It is perhaps not surprising, therefore, that in the twentieth century it became so profoundly popular and influential; had indeed until quite recently become naturalized *as* 'Literary Studies'. (In this context, see Perry Anderson's critique of Leavisism in 'Components of the National Culture', 1968, in which he asserts that Leavisian literary criticism, in mid-century Britain, filled the vacuum left by the failure to develop a British Marxism or sociology.) Hence the absence of theory. Not *being* a theory, but merely 'true judgement' and common sense based on lived experience ('"This – doesn't it? – bears such a relation to that; this kind of thing – don't you find it so? – wears better than that"', for the essay 'Literary Criticism and Philosophy' see above p. 24), Leavisian criticism had no need of theory – could not in fact be theorized. Paradoxically, and for many years, that was its greatest strength.

Selected reading

Key texts

Arnold, Matthew, *Culture and Anarchy* [1869], ed. J. Dover Wilson (Cambridge University Press, Cambridge [1932], 1971).

Arnold, Matthew, *Essays in Criticism*, Second Series, 1888.

Booth, Wayne C., *The Rhetoric of Fiction* (University of Chicago Press, Chicago, 1961).

Brooks, Cleanth, *The Well-Wrought Urn: Studies in the Structure of Poetry* [1947] (Methuen, London, 1968).

Brooks, Cleanth and Warren, Robert Penn (eds), *Understanding Poetry: An Anthology for College Students* (Henry Holt, New York, 1938).

Brooks, Cleanth and Warren, Robert Penn (eds), *Understanding Fiction* (Appleton-Century-Crofts, New York, 1943).

Crane, R. S. (ed.), *Critics and Criticism: Ancient and Modern* (Chicago University Press, Chicago, 1952; abridged, with Crane's Preface, 1957).

Eliot, T. S., *Notes Towards the Definition of Culture* (Faber, London, 1948).

Eliot, T. S., *Selected Essays* [1932] (Faber, London, 1965).

Empson, William, *Seven Types of Ambiguity* [1930] (Penguin, Harmondsworth, 1961).

Empson, William, *Some Versions of Pastoral* [1935] (Penguin, Harmondsworth, 1966).

Leavis, F. R., *New Bearings in English Poetry* [1932] (Penguin, Harmondsworth, 1963).

Leavis, F. R., *Revaluation* [1936] (Penguin, Harmondsworth, 1978).

Leavis, F. R., *Education and the University* [1943] (Cambridge University Press, Cambridge, 1962).

Leavis, F. R., *The Common Pursuit* [1952] (Penguin, Harmondsworth, 1978).

Leavis, F. R., *D. H. Lawrence: Novelist* [1955] (Penguin, Harmondsworth, 1964).

Ransom, John Crowe, *The New Criticism* (New Directions, Norfolk, Conn., 1941).

Ransom, John Crowe, 'Criticism, Inc.' [1937] in *The World's Body* [1938] (Kennikat Press, New York, 1964).

Richards, I. A., *Principles of Literary Criticism* [1924] (Routledge, London, 2001).

Richards, I. A., *Practical Criticism* [1929] (Routledge, London, 1964).

Richards, I. A., *I. A. Richards: Selected Writings 1919–1938*, 10 vols, ed. with intro. by John Constable (Routledge, London, 2001).

Schorer, Mark, 'Technique as Discovery', *The Hudson Review* (1948).

Schorer, Mark, 'Fiction and the Analogical Matrix', *Kenyon Review* (1949).

Williams, R., *Politics and Letters* (Verso, London, 1979).

Wimsatt, W. K., Jr and Beardsley, Monroe C., 'The Intentional Fallacy' [1946], reprinted in Wimsatt, *The Verbal Icon: Studies in the Meaning of Poetry* [1954] (Methuen, London, 1970).

Wimsatt, W. K., Jr and Beardsley, Monroe C., 'The Affective Fallacy' [1949], reprinted in Wimsatt, *The Verbal Icon: Studies in the Meaning of Poetry* [1954] (Methuen, London, 1970).

Further reading

Baldick, Chris, *The Social Mission of English Criticism* (reprint edn, Oxford University Press, Oxford, 1988).

Doyle, Brian, *English and Englishness* (Routledge, London, 1989).

Eagleton, Terry, *Literary Theory: An Introduction* (1983) (2nd edn, Blackwell, Oxford, 1996).

Fekete, John, *The Critical Twilight: Explorations in the Ideology of Anglo-American Literary Theory from Eliot to McLuhan* (Routledge, London, 1977).

Graff, Gerald, *Professing Literature: An Institutional History* (Chicago University Press, Chicago, 1987).

Lentricchia, Frank, *After the New Criticism* [1980] (Methuen, London, 1983).

MacCullum, Patricia, *Literature and Method: Towards a Critique of I. A. Richards, T. S. Eliot and F. R. Leavis* (Gill & Macmillan, Dublin, 1983).

MacKillop, I. D., *F. R. Leavis: A Life in Criticism* (Allen Lane, The Penguin Press, Harmondsworth, 1995).

Mulhern, Francis, *The Moment of 'Scrutiny'* (Verso, London, 1979).

Newton, K. M., *Interpreting the Text: A Critical Introduction to the Theory and Practice of Literary Interpretation* (Harvester Wheatsheaf, Hemel Hempstead, 1990).

Norris, Christopher, *William Empson and the Philosophy of Literary Criticism* (Athlone Press, London, 1978).

Parrinder, Patrick, *Authors and Authority: English and American Criticism, 1750–1990* (2nd edn, Macmillan, Basingstoke, 1991).

Rylance, Rick, 'The New Criticism', in *Encyclopaedia of Literature and Criticism*, Martin Coyle, Peter Garside, Malcolm Kelsall and John Peck (eds) (Routledge, London, 1990).

Samson, Anne, *F. R. Leavis* (Harvester Wheatsheaf, Hemel Hempstead, 1992).

CHAPTER 2

Russian formalism and the Bakhtin School

S tudents of literature brought up in the tradition of Anglo-American New Criticism with its emphasis on 'practical criticism' and the organic unity of the text might expect to feel at home with Russian Formalism. Both kinds of criticism aim to explore what is specifically *literary* in texts, and both reject the limp spirituality of late Romantic poetics in favour of a detailed and empirical approach to reading. That being said, it must be admitted that the Russian Formalists were much more interested in 'method', much more concerned to establish a 'scientific' basis for the theory of literature. As we have seen, the New Critics combined attention to the specific verbal ordering of texts with an emphasis on the *non-conceptual* nature of literary meaning: a poem's complexity embodied a subtle response to life, which could not be reduced to logical statements or paraphrases. Their approach, despite the emphasis on close reading of texts, remained fundamentally humanistic. For example, Cleanth Brooks (see Chapter 1, pp. 19–20) insisted that Marvell's 'Horatian Ode' is not a political statement of Marvell's position on the Civil War but a dramatization of opposed views, unified into a poetic whole. Brooks concluded his account by arguing that like all 'great poetry' the poem embodies 'honesty and insight and whole-mindedness'. The first Russian Formalists on the other hand considered that human 'content' (emotions, ideas and 'reality' in general) possessed no literary significance in itself, but merely provided a context for the functioning of literary 'devices'. As we shall see, this sharp division of form and content was modified by the later Formalists, but it remains true that the Formalists avoided the New Critics' tendency to endow aesthetic form with moral and cultural significance. They aimed rather to outline models and hypotheses (in a scientific spirit) to explain how aesthetic effects are produced by literary devices, and how the 'literary' is distinguished from and related to the 'extra-literary'. While the New Critics regarded literature as a form of human understanding, the Formalists thought of it as a special use of language.

Peter Steiner (1984) has argued convincingly against a monolithic view of Russian Formalism, himself discriminating between formalisms in highlighting three metaphors which act as generative models for three phases in its history. The model of the 'machine' governs the first phase, which sees literary criticism as a sort of mechanics and the text as a heap of devices. The second is an 'organic' phase which sees literary texts as fully functioning 'organisms' of interrelated parts. The third phase adopts the metaphor of 'system' and tries to understand literary texts as the products of the entire literary system and even of the meta-system of interacting literary and non-literary systems.

Shklovsky, Mukařovský, Jakobson

Formalist studies were well established before the 1917 Revolution – in the Moscow Linguistic Circle, founded 1915, and in Opojaz (the letters stand for 'The Society for the Study of Poetic Language'), started in 1916. The leading figures of the former group were Roman Jakobson and Petr Bogatyrev, who both later helped to found the Prague Linguistic Circle in 1926. Viktor Shklovsky, Yury Tynyanov and Boris Eikhenbaum were prominent in Opojaz. The initial impetus was provided by the Futurists, whose artistic efforts before the First World War were directed against 'decadent' bourgeois culture and especially against the anguished soul-searching of the Symbolist movement in poetry and the visual arts. They derided the mystical posturing of poets such as Briusov who insisted that the poet was 'the guardian of the mystery'. In place of the 'absolute', Mayakovsky, the extrovert Futurist poet, offered the noisy materialism of the machine age as the home of poetry. However, it should be noted that the Futurists were as opposed to realism as the Symbolists had been: their slogan of the 'self-sufficient word' placed a stress on the self-contained sound patterning of words as distinct from their ability to refer to things. The Futurists threw themselves behind the Revolution and emphasized the artist's role as (proletarian) producer of crafted objects. Dmitriev declared that 'the artist is now simply a constructor and technician, a leader and foreman'. The Constructivists took these arguments to their logical extreme and entered actual factories to put into practice their theories of 'production art'.

From this background the Formalists set about producing a theory of literature concerned with the writer's *technical* prowess and *craft* skill. They avoided the proletarian rhetoric of the poets and artists, but they retained a somewhat mechanistic view of the literary process. Shklovsky was as vigorously materialistic in his attitudes as Mayakovsky. The former's famous definition of literature as 'the sum total of all stylistic devices employed in it' sums up well this early phase of formalism.

At first, the Formalists' work developed freely, especially between 1921 and 1925 when the weary USSR was emerging from 'War Communism'. Non-proletarian economics and literature were allowed to flourish during this breathing space, and by 1925 formalism was the dominant method in literary scholarship. Trotsky's sophisticated criticisms of formalism in *Literature and Revolution* (1924) ushered in a defensive phase, culminating in the Jakobson/Tynyanov theses (1928). Some regard the later developments as signalling the defeat of pure formalism and a capitulation to the Communist 'social command'. We would argue that, before official disapproval brought an end to the movement in about 1930, the need to take account of the sociological dimension produced some of the best work of the period, especially in the writings of the 'Bakhtin School' which drew on formalist and Marxist traditions in fruitful ways that anticipated later developments. The more structuralist type of formalism, initiated by Jakobson and Tynyanov, was continued in Czech formalism (notably by the Prague Linguistic Circle), until Nazism brought it to an end. Some of this group, including René Wellek and Roman Jakobson, emigrated to the United States where they helped shape the development of New Criticism during the 1940s and 1950s.

The Formalists' technical focus led them to treat literature as a special use of language which achieves its distinctness by deviating from and distorting 'practical' language. Practical language is used for acts of communication, while literary language has no practical function at all and simply makes us *see* differently. One might apply this fairly easily to a writer such as Gerard Manley Hopkins, whose language is 'difficult' in a way which draws attention to itself as 'literary', but it is also easy to show that there is no intrinsically literary language. Opening Hardy's *Under the Greenwood Tree* at random, we read the exchange '"How long will you be?" "Not long. Do wait and talk to me".' There is absolutely no linguistic reason to regard the words as 'literary'. We read them as literary rather than as an act of communication only because we read them in what we take to be a literary work. As we shall see, Tynyanov and others developed a more dynamic view of 'literariness' as a functioning system, which avoids this problem.

What distinguishes literature from 'practical' language is its *constructed* quality. Poetry was treated by the Formalists as the quintessentially literary use of language: it is 'speech organized in its entire phonic texture'. Its most important constructive factor is rhythm. Consider a line from Donne's 'A Nocturnall upon St Lucies Day', stanza 2:

> For I am every dead thing

A Formalist analysis would draw attention to an underlying iambic impulse (laid down in the equivalent line in the first stanza: 'The Sunne is spent, and now his flasks'). In the line from stanza 2, our anticipation is frustrated by a dropped syllable between 'dead' and 'thing'; we perceive a deviation from the norm, and this is what produces aesthetic significance. A Formalist would also note finer differences of rhythm produced by syntactical differences between the two lines (for example, the first has a strong caesura, the second none). Poetry exercises a controlled violence upon practical language, which is thereby deformed in order to compel our attention to its constructed nature.

The earlier phase of Formalism was dominated by Viktor Shklovsky, whose theorizing, influenced by the Futurists, was lively and iconoclastic. While the Symbolists had viewed poetry as the expression of the Infinite or some unseen reality, Shklovsky adopted a down-to-earth approach, seeking to define the techniques which writers use to produce specific effects. Shklovsky called one of his most attractive concepts 'defamiliarization' (*ostranenie*: 'making strange'). He argued that we can never retain the freshness of our perceptions of objects; the demands of 'normal' existence require that they must become to a great extent 'automatized' (a later term). That Wordsworthian innocent vision through which Nature retains 'the glory and the freshness of a dream' is not the normal state of human consciousness. It is the special task of art to give us back the awareness of things which have become habitual objects of our everyday awareness. It must be stressed that the Formalists, unlike the Romantic poets, were not so much interested in the perceptions themselves as in the nature of the devices which produce the effect of 'defamiliarization'. The purpose of a work of art is to change our mode of perception from the automatic and practical to the artistic. In 'Art as Technique' (1917), Shklovsky makes this clear:

> The technique of art is to make objects 'unfamiliar', to make forms difficult, to increase the difficulty and length of perception because the process of perception is an aesthetic end in itself and must be prolonged. *Art is a way of experiencing the artfulness of an object; the object is not important.* (Lemon and Reis, 1965, p. 12; Shklovsky's emphasis)

The Formalists were fond of citing two English eighteenth-century writers, Laurence Sterne and Jonathan Swift. Boris Tomashevsky shows how devices of defamiliarization are used in *Gulliver's Travels*:

> In order to present a satirical picture of the European social-political order, Gulliver . . . tells his master (a horse) about the customs of the ruling class in human society. Compelled to tell everything with the utmost accuracy, he removes the shell of euphemistic phrases and fictitious traditions which justify such things as war, class strife, parliamentary intrigue and so on. Stripped of their verbal justification and thus defamiliarized, these topics emerge in all their horror. Thus criticism of the political system – nonliterary material – is artistically motivated and fully involved in the narrative.
> (Lemon and Reis, 1965, p. 86)

At first this account seems to stress the content of the new perception itself ('horror' at 'war' and 'class strife'). But in fact, what interests Tomashevsky is the artistic transformation of 'non-literary material'. Defamiliarization changes our response to the world but only by submitting our habitual perceptions to a processing by literary form.

In his monograph on Sterne's *Tristram Shandy*, Shklovsky draws attention to the ways in which familiar actions are defamiliarized by being slowed down, drawn out or interrupted. This technique of delaying and protracting actions makes us attend to them, so that familiar sights and movements cease to be perceived automatically and are thus 'defamiliarized'. Mr Shandy, lying despondently on his bed after hearing of his son Tristram's broken nose, might have been described conventionally ('he lay mournfully upon his bed'), but Sterne chose to defamiliarize Mr Shandy's posture:

> The palm of his right hand, as he fell upon the bed, receiving his forehead, and covering the greatest part of both his eyes, gently sunk down with his head (his elbow giving way backwards) till his nose touch'd the quilt; – his left arm hung insensible over the side of the bed, his knuckles reclining upon the handle of the chamber pot . . .

The example is interesting in showing how often defamiliarization affects not a perception as such but merely the presentation of a perception. By slowing down the description of Mr Shandy's posture, Sterne gives us no new insight into grief, no new perception of a familiar posture, but only a heightened verbal presentation. It is Sterne's very lack of concern with perception in the non-literary sense which seems to attract Shklovsky's admiration. This emphasis on the actual process of presentation is called 'laying bare' one's technique. Many readers find Sterne's novel irritating for its continual references to its own novelistic structure, but 'laying bare' its own devices is, in Shklovsky's view, the most essentially *literary* thing a novel can do.

'Defamiliarization' and 'laying bare' are notions which directly influenced Bertolt Brecht's famous 'alienation effect' (see Chapter 5, pp. 88–91, for further treatment of this). The classical ideal that art should *conceal* its own processes (*ars celare artem*) was directly challenged by the Formalists and by Brecht. For literature to present itself as a seamless unity of discourse and as a natural representation of reality would be deceitful and, for Brecht, politically regressive – which is why he rejected realism and embraced modernism (for the Lukács/Brecht debate about this, see Chapter 5, pp. 86–91 *passim*). For example, in a Brechtian production a male character may be played by an actress in order to destroy the naturalness and familiarity of the role and by defamiliarizing the role to make the audience attend to its specific maleness. The possible political uses of the device were not foreseen by the Formalists, since their concerns were purely technical.

Theories of narrative – especially the distinction between 'story' and 'plot' – have a prominent place in Russian Formalism. The Greek tragedians had drawn upon traditional stories which consisted of a series of incidents. In section 6 of the *Poetics*, Aristotle defines 'plot' ('mythos') as the 'arrangement of the incidents'. A 'plot' is clearly distinguished from a story upon which a plot may be based. A plot is the artful disposition of the incidents which make up a story. A Greek tragedy usually starts with a 'flashback', a recapitulation of the incidents of the story which occurred prior to those which were selected for the plot. In Virgil's *Aeneid* and in Milton's *Paradise Lost*, the reader is plunged *in medias res* ('into the middle of things'), and earlier incidents in the story are introduced artfully at various stages in the plot, often in the form of retrospective narration: Aeneas narrates the Fall of Troy to Dido in Carthage, and Raphael relates the War in Heaven to Adam and Eve in Paradise.

The Russian Formalists, however, stress that only 'plot' (*sjuzet*) is strictly literary, while 'story' (*fabula*) is merely raw material awaiting the organizing hand of the writer. As Shklovsky's essay on Sterne reveals, the Formalists had a more revolutionary concept of plot than Aristotle. The plot of *Tristram Shandy* is not merely the arrangement of story-incidents but also all the 'devices' used to interrupt and delay the narration. Digressions, typographical games, displacement of parts of the book (preface, dedication, etc.) and extended descriptions are all devices to make us attend to the novel's form. In a sense, 'plot', in this instance, is actually the violation of the expected formal arrangements of incidents. By frustrating familiar plot arrangement, Sterne draws attention to plotting itself as a literary object. In this way, Shklovsky is not at all Aristotelian. In the end, a carefully ordered Aristotelian 'plot' should give us the essential and familiar truths of human life; it should be plausible and have a certain inevitability. The Formalists, on the other hand, often linked theory of plot with the notion of defamiliarization: the plot *prevents* us from regarding the incidents as typical and familiar. Instead, we are made constantly aware how artifice constructs or forges (makes/counterfeits) the 'reality' presented to us. In its display of *poiesis* ('poet' = 'maker') rather than *mimesis* ('copying' = realism), this looks forward, as does Sterne, to postmodernist self-reflexivity.

A further concept within Russian Formalist narrative theory is 'motivation'. Tomashevsky called the smallest unit of plot a 'motif', which we may understand as a single statement or action. He makes a distinction between 'bound' and 'free' motifs. A bound motif is one which is required by the story, while a 'free' motif is inessential from the point of view of the story. However, from the literary point of view, the 'free' motifs are potentially the focus of art. For example, the device of having Raphael relate the War in Heaven is a 'free' motif, because it is not part of the story in question. However, it is formally *more* important than the narration of the War itself, because it enables Milton to insert the narration artistically into his overall plot.

This approach reverses the traditional subordination of formal devices to 'content'. The Formalists rather perversely seem to regard a poem's ideas, themes, and references to 'reality' as merely the external excuse the writer required to justify the use of formal devices. They called this dependence on external, non-literary assumptions 'motivation'. According to Shklovsky, *Tristram Shandy* is remarkable for being totally without 'motivation'; the novel is entirely made up of formal devices which are 'bared'.

The most familiar type of 'motivation' is what we usually call 'realism'. No matter how formally constructed a work may be, we still often expect it to give us the illusion of the 'real'. We expect literature to be 'life-like', and may be irritated by characters or descriptions which fail to match our common-sense expectations of what the real world is like. 'A man in love wouldn't behave like that' and 'people of that class wouldn't talk like that' are the kind of remarks we might make when we notice a failure of realistic motivation. On the other hand, as Tomashevsky pointed out, we become accustomed to all kinds of absurdities and improbabilities once we learn to accept a new set of conventions. We fail to notice the improbable way in which heroes are always rescued just before they are about to be killed by the villains in adventure stories. Indeed, realism's central strategy is to disguise its artificiality, to pretend there is no art between it and the reality it shows us; in this respect, it does the exact opposite of 'baring its device'.

The theme of 'motivation' turned out to be important in a great deal of subsequent literary theory. Jonathan Culler summed up the general theme neatly when he wrote: 'To assimilate or interpret something is to bring it within the modes of order which culture makes available, and this is usually done by talking about it in a mode of discourse which a culture takes as natural' (1975: see 'Key texts' for Chapter 4). Human beings are endlessly inventive in finding ways of making sense of the most random or chaotic utterances or inscriptions. We refuse to allow a text to remain alien and outside our frames of reference; we insist on 'naturalizing' it, and effacing its textuality. When faced with a page of apparently random images, we prefer to naturalize it by attributing the images to a disordered mind or by regarding it as a reflection of a disordered world, rather than to accept its disorder as strange and inexplicable. The Formalists anticipated structuralist and poststructuralist thought by attending to those features of texts which resist the relentless process of naturalization. Shklovsky refused to reduce the bizarre disorder of *Tristram Shandy* to an expression of Tristram's quirky mind, and instead drew attention to the novel's insistent literariness which checks naturalization.

We have already noted in passing the shift from Shklovsky's notion of the text as a heap of devices to Tynyanov's of the text as a functioning system. The high point of this 'structural' phase was the series of statements known as the Jakobson–Tynyanov theses (1928). The theses reject a mechanical formalism and attempt to reach beyond a narrowly literary perspective by trying to define the relationship between the literary 'series' (system) and other 'historical series'. The way in which the literary system develops historically cannot be understood, they argue, without understanding the way in which other systems impinge on it and partly determine its evolutionary path. On the other hand, they insist, we must attend to the 'immanent laws' of the literary system itself if we are to understand correctly the correlation of the systems.

The Prague Linguistic Circle, founded in 1926, continued and developed the 'structural' approach. Mukařovský, for example, developed the formalist concept of 'defamiliarization' into the more systematic 'foregrounding' which he defined as 'the aesthetically intentional distortion of the linguistic components'. He also underlined the folly of excluding extra-literary factors from critical analysis. Taking over Tynyanov's dynamic view of aesthetic structures, he placed great emphasis on the dynamic tension between literature and society in the artistic product. Mukařovský's most powerful argument concerned the 'aesthetic function', which proves to be an ever-shifting boundary and not a watertight category. The same object can possess several functions: a church may be both a place of worship and a work of art; a stone may be a door-stop, a missile, building material and an object of artistic appreciation. Fashions are especially complex signs and may possess social, political, erotic and aesthetic functions. The same variability of function can be seen in literary products. A political speech, a biography, a letter and a piece of propaganda may or may not possess aesthetic value in different societies and periods. The circumference of the sphere of 'art' is always changing, and always dynamically related to the structure of society.

Mukařovský's insight has been taken up by Marxist critics to establish the social bearings of art and literature. We can never talk about 'literature' as if it were a fixed canon of works, a specific set of devices, or an unchanging body of forms and genres. To endow an object or artifact with the dignity of aesthetic value is a *social* act, ultimately inseparable from prevailing ideologies. Modern social changes have resulted in certain artifacts, which once had mainly non-aesthetic function, being regarded as primarily art-objects. The religious function of icons, the domestic functions of Greek vases, and the military function of breastplates have been subordinated in modern times to a primarily aesthetic function. What people choose to regard as 'serious' art or 'high' culture is also subject to changing values. Jazz, for example, once 'popular' music in brothels and bars, has become serious art, although its 'low' social origins still give rise to conflicting evaluations. From this perspective, art and literature are not eternal verities but are always open to new definitions – hence the increasing presence, as the literary canon is deconstructed, of 'popular' writing on 'Cultural Studies' (rather than 'Literature') courses. The dominant class in any historical era will have an important influence on definitions of art, and where new trends arise will normally wish to incorporate them into its ideological world.

It gradually became apparent, then, that literary devices were not fixed pieces that could be moved at will in the literary game. Their value and meaning changed with time and also with context. With this realization, 'device' gave way to 'function' as the leading concept. The effect of this shift was far-reaching. Formalists were no longer plagued by an unresolved rejection of 'content', but were able to internalize the central principle of 'defamiliarization'; that is to say, instead of having to talk about literature defamiliarizing reality, they could begin to refer to the defamiliarizing of literature itself. Elements *within* a work may become 'automatized' or may have a positive aesthetic function. The same device may have different aesthetic functions in different works or may become totally automatized.

For example, archaisms and Latinate word order may have an 'elevating' function in an epic poem, or an ironic function in a satire, or even become totally automatized as general 'poetic diction'. In the last case, the device is not 'perceived' by the reader as a functional element, and is effaced in the same way as ordinary perceptions become automatized and taken for granted. Literary works are seen as *dynamic systems* in which elements are structured in relations of foreground and background. If a particular element is 'effaced' (perhaps archaic diction), other elements will come into play as dominant (perhaps plot or rhythm) in the work's system. Writing in 1935, Jakobson regarded 'the dominant' as an important late Formalist concept, and defined it as 'the focusing component of a work of art: it rules, determines and transforms the remaining components'. He rightly stresses the non-mechanistic aspect of this view of artistic structure. The dominant provides the work with its focus of crystallization and facilitates its unity or *gestalt* (total order). The very notion of defamiliarization implied *change* and historical development. Rather than look for eternal verities which bind all great literature into a single canon, the Formalists were disposed to see the history of literature as one of permanent revolution. Each new development is an attempt to repulse the dead hand of familiarity and habitual response. This dynamic notion of the dominant also provided the Formalists with a useful way of explaining literary history. Poetic forms change and develop not at random but as a result of a 'shifting dominant': there is a continuing shift in the mutual relationships among the various elements in a poetic system. Jakobson added the interesting idea that the poetics of particular periods may be governed by a 'dominant' which derives from a non-literary system. The dominant of Renaissance poetry was derived from the visual arts; Romantic poetry oriented itself towards music; and Realism's dominant is verbal art. But whatever the dominant may be, it organizes the other elements in the individual work, relegating to the background of aesthetic attention elements which in works of earlier periods might have been 'foregrounded' as dominant. What changes is not so much the elements of the system (syntax, rhythm, plot, diction, etc.) but the *function* of particular elements or groups of elements. When Pope wrote the following lines satirizing the antiquarian, he could rely on the dominance of the values of prose clarity to help him achieve his purpose:

> But who is he, in closet close y-pent,
> Of sober face, with learned dust besprent?
> Right well mine eyes arede the myster wight,
> On parchment scraps y-fed, and Wormius hight.

The Chaucerian diction and archaic word order are immediately treated by the reader as comically pedantic. In an earlier period Spenser was able to hark back to Chaucer's style without calling up the satiric note. The shifting dominant operates not only within particular texts but within particular literary periods.

The Bakhtin School

The so-called Bakhtin School arose in the later period of formalism, although it was never, in fact, part of that movement. The authorship of several key works of the group is disputed and we are compelled simply to refer to the names which appear on the original title pages – Mikhail Bakhtin, Pavel Medvedev and Valentin Voloshinov. These works have been differently interpreted and employed in liberal and left criticism. Medvedev had begun his career as an orthodox Marxist whose earliest essays were anti-formalist, and his *The Formal Method in Literary Scholarship: A Critical Introduction to Social Poetics* (1929) was a thoroughgoing critique of formalism, while seeing it as a worthy opponent. However, the School may be considered formalist in its concern for the linguistic structure of literary works, although works authored by Voloshinov, particularly, were deeply influenced by Marxism in the belief that language could not be separated from ideology. This intimate connection between language and ideology, discussed in Voloshinov's *Marxism and the Philosophy of Language* (1973), immediately drew literature into the social and economic sphere, the homeland of ideology. This approach departs from classical Marxist assumptions about ideology by refusing to treat it as a purely mental phenomenon which arises as a reflex of a material (real) socio-economic substructure. Ideology is not separable from its medium – language. As Voloshinov put it, 'consciousness itself can arise and become a viable fact only in the material embodiment of signs'. Language, a socially constructed sign-system, is itself a material reality.

The Bakhtin School was not interested in abstract linguistics of the kind which later formed the basis of structuralism. They were concerned with language or discourse as a social phenomenon. Voloshinov's central insight was that 'words' are active, dynamic social signs, capable of taking on different meanings and connotations for different social classes in different social and historical situations. He attacked those linguists (including Saussure) who treated language as a synchronic (unhistorical) and abstract system. He rejected the whole notion of 'The isolated, finished, monologic utterance, divorced from its verbal and actual context and standing open not to any possible sort of active response but to passive understanding'. The Russian *slovo* may be translated 'word' but is used by the Bakhtin School with a strongly social flavour (nearer to 'utterance' or 'discourse'). Verbal signs are the arena of continuous class struggle: the ruling class will always try to narrow the meaning of words and make social signs 'uni-accentual', but in times of social unrest the vitality and basic 'multi-accentuality' of linguistic signs becomes apparent as various class interests clash and intersect upon the ground of language. 'Heteroglossia' is a fundamental concept, most clearly defined in Bakhtin's 'Discourse in the Novel' (written 1934–5). The term refers to the basic condition governing the production of meaning in all discourse. It asserts the way in which *context* defines the meaning of utterances, which are heteroglot in so far as they put in play a multiplicity of social voices and their individual expressions. A single voice may give the impression of unity and closure, but the utterance is constantly (and to some extent unconsciously) producing a plenitude of meanings, which stem from social interaction (dialogue). 'Monologue' is, in fact, a forcible imposition on language, and hence a distortion of it.

It was Mikhail Bakhtin who developed the implications of this dynamic view of language for literary texts. However, he did not, as one might have expected, treat literature as a direct reflection of social forces, but retained a formalist concern with literary structure, showing how the dynamic and active nature of language was given expression in certain literary traditions. He stressed not the way texts reflect society or class interests, but rather the way language is made to disrupt authority and liberate alternative voices. A libertarian language is entirely appropriate in describing Bakhtin's approach, which is very much a celebration of those writers whose work permits the freest play of different value systems and whose authority is not imposed upon the alternatives. Bakhtin is profoundly un-Stalinist. His classic work is *Problems of Dostoevsky's Poetics* (1929), in which he developed a bold contrast between the novels of Tolstoy and those of Dostoevsky. In the former, the various voices we hear are strictly subordinated to the author's controlling purpose, his 'truth'. In contrast to this 'monologic' type of novel, Dostoevsky developed a new 'polyphonic' (or dialogic) form, whose orchestration is non-author/itarian in its refusal to unify the various points of view expressed in the various characters. The consciousness of the various characters does not merge with the author's nor do they become subordinated to the author's viewpoint; they retain an integrity and independence, and are 'not only objects of the author's word, but subjects of their own directly significant word as well'. In this book and in his later one on Rabelais, Bakhtin explores the liberating and often subversive use of various dialogic forms in classical satire and in medieval and Renaissance cultural forms.

Bakhtin's discussion of 'Carnival' has important applications both to particular texts and to the history of literary genres. The festivities associated with Carnival are collective and popular; hierarchies are turned on their heads (fools become wise, kings become beggars); opposites are mingled (fact and fantasy, heaven and hell); the sacred is profaned. The 'jolly relativity' of all things is proclaimed. Everything authoritative, rigid or serious is subverted, loosened and mocked. This essentially popular and libertarian social phenomenon has a formative influence on literature of various periods, but becomes especially dominant in the Renaissance. 'Carnivalization' is the term Bakhtin uses to describe the shaping effect of Carnival on literary genres. The earliest carnivalized literary forms are the Socratic dialogue and the Menippean satire. The former is in its origins close to the immediacy of oral dialogue, in which the discovery of truth is conceived as an unfolding exchange of views rather than as an authoritative monologue. The Socratic dialogues come down to us in the sophisticated literary forms devised by Plato. Some of the 'jolly relativity' of Carnival survives in the written works, but there is also, in Bakhtin's view, some dilution of that collective quality of enquiry in which points of view collide without a strict hierarchy of voices being established by the 'author'. In the last Platonic dialogues, argues Bakhtin, the later image of Socrates as the 'teacher' begins to emerge and to replace the carnivalistic image of Socrates as the grotesque hen-pecked provoker of argument, who was midwife to rather than author of truth.

In Menippean satire, the three planes of Heaven (Olympus), the Underworld, and Earth are all treated to the logic of Carnival. For example, in the underworld earthly inequalities are dissolved; emperors lose their crowns and meet on equal terms with beggars. Dostoevsky brings together the various traditions of carnivalized literature. The 'fantastic tale' *Bobok* (1873) is almost pure Menippean satire. A scene in a cemetery culminates in a weird account of the brief 'life outside life' of the dead in the grave. Before losing their earthly consciousness completely, the dead enjoy a period of a few months when they are released from all the obligations and laws of normal existence and are able to reveal themselves with a stark and unlimited freedom. Baron Klinevich, 'king' of the corpses, declares, 'I just want everyone to tell the truth . . . On earth it is impossible to live without lying, because life and lie are synonyms; but here we will tell the truth just for fun.' This contains the seed of the 'polyphonic' novel, in which voices are set free to speak subversively or shockingly, but without the author stepping between character and reader.

Bakhtin raises a number of themes developed by later theorists. Both Romantics and Formalists (including the New Critics) regarded texts as organic unities, as integrated structures in which all loose ends are finally gathered up into aesthetic unity by the reader. Bakhtin's emphasis on Carnival breaks up this unquestioned organicism and promotes the idea that major literary works may be multi-levelled and resistant to unification. This leaves the author in a much less dominant position in relation to his or her writings. The notion of individual identity is left problematic: 'character' is elusive, insubstantial and quirky. This anticipates a major concern of recent poststructuralist and psychoanalytic criticism, although one should not exaggerate this, or forget that Bakhtin still retains a firm sense of the writer's controlling artistry. His work does not imply the radical questioning of the role of author which arises in the work of Roland Barthes and other poststructuralists. However, Bakhtin does resemble Barthes in his 'privileging' of the polyphonic novel. Both critics prefer liberty and pleasure to authority and decorum. There is a tendency among recent critics to treat polyphonic and other kinds of 'plural' text as normative rather than as eccentric; that is, they treat them as more truly literary than more univocal (monologic) kinds of writing. This may appeal to modern readers brought up on Joyce and Beckett, but we must also recognize that both Bakhtin and Barthes are indicating *preferences* which arise from their own social and ideological predispositions. Nevertheless, it remains true that, in asserting the openness and instability of literary texts, Bakhtin, or rather the readings of Bakhtin, have confirmed that such preferences have a central place in the inescapable 'politics' of criticism.

The work of Mukařovský, the Jakobson–Tynyanov theses, and the theories of Bakhtin pass beyond the 'pure' Russian Formalism of Shklovsky, Tomashevsky and Eikhenbaum and form an apt prelude to our later chapter on Marxist critical theories, which in any case influenced their more sociological interests. The Formalists' isolation of the literary system is evidently at odds with the Marxist subordination of literature to society, but we shall discover that not all Marxist critics follow the harsh antiformalist line of the official, socialist-realist Soviet tradition. However, first, we will survey another school of critical theory which primarily situates the differential nature of the 'aesthetic function' with the 'addressee' or 'reader' of literary texts (see Jakobson's diagram in the Introduction, p. 5).

Selected reading

Key texts

Bakhtin, Mikhail, *The Dialogic Imagination: Four Essays* [1975], ed. by Michael Holquist, trans. by C. Emerson and M. Holquist (University of Texas Press, Austin, 1981).

Bakhtin, Mikhail, *Problems of Dostoevsky's Poetics* [1929; revd edn, 1963], trans. and ed. by Caryl Emerson, intro. by Wayne C. Booth (Manchester University Press, Manchester, 1984).

Bakhtin, Mikhail, *Rabelais and His World* [1965; 1st Eng. trans. 1968], trans. by Hélène Iswolsky (Indiana University Press, Bloomington, 1984).

Bakhtin, Mikhail and Medvedev, P. N., *The Formal Method in Literary Scholarship: A Critical Introduction to Sociological Poetics* [1928], trans. by A. J. Wehrle (Harvard University Press, Cambridge, Mass., 1985).

Garvin, Paul L. (trans.), *A Prague School Reader* (Georgetown University Press, Washington, DC, 1964).

Lemon, Lee T. and Reis, Marion J. (eds and trans.), *Russian Formalist Criticism: Four Essays* (Nebraska University Press, Lincoln, 1965). Includes Viktor Shklovsky's essays 'Art as Technique' [1917] and 'Laurence Sterne' [1921].

Mukařovský, Jan, *Aesthetic Function, Norm and Value as Social Facts* [1936], trans. by M. E. Suino (Michigan University Press, Ann Arbor, 1970).

Voloshinov, Valentin, *Marxism and the Philosophy of Language* [1929], trans. by L. Matejka and I. R. Titunik (Seminar Press, New York, 1973; reprint Harvard University Press, Cambridge, Mass., 1986).

Further reading

Bennett, Tony, *Formalism and Marxism* (2nd edn, Routledge, London, 2003).

Clark, Katerina and Holquist, Michael, *Mikhail Bakhtin* (Harvard University Press, Cambridge, Mass. and London, 1984).

Dentith, Simon, *Bakhtinian Thought: An Introductory Reader* (Routledge, London, 1995).

Erlich, Victor, *Russian Formalism: History, Doctrine* (3rd edn, Yale University Press, New Haven and London, 1981).

Gardiner, Michael, *The Dialogics of Critique: M. M. Bakhtin and the Theory of Ideology* (Routledge, London, 1992).

Hirschkop, Ken, *Mikhail Bakhtin: An Aesthetic for Democracy* (Oxford University Press, Oxford, 1999).

Hirschkop, Ken and Shepherd, David (eds), *Bakhtin and Cultural Theory* (Manchester University Press, Manchester, 1991).

Holquist, Michael, *Dialogism: Bakhtin and His World* (2nd edn, Routledge, London, 2002).

Jameson, Fredric, *The Prison-House of Language: A Critical Account of Structuralism and Russian Formalism* (Princeton University Press, Princeton, NJ and London, 1972).

Jefferson, Ann, 'Russian Formalism', in *Modern Literary Theory: A Comparative Introduction*, Ann Jefferson and David Robey (eds) (2nd edn, Batsford, London, 1986).

Lodge, David, *After Bakhtin: Essays on Fiction and Criticism* (Routledge, London, 1990).

Morson, Gary Saul and Emerson, Caryl, *Mikhail Bakhtin: Creation of a Prosaics* (Stanford University Press, Stanford, 1990).

Pearce, Lynne, *Reading Dialogics* (Arnold, London, 1994).

Selden, Raman, *Criticism and Objectivity* (Allen & Unwin, London, Boston, Sydney, 1984), ch. 4, 'Russian Formalism, Marxism and "Relative Autonomy"'.

Shepherd, David, Brandist, Craig and Tihanov, Galin (eds), *The Bakhtin Circle: In the Master's Absence* (Manchester University Press, Manchester, 2003).

Stallybrass, Peter and White, Allon, *The Politics and Poetics of Transgression* (Routledge, London, 1986).

Steiner, Peter, *Russian Formalism: a Metapoetics* (Ithaca: Cornell U.P., 1984).

Thompson, Ewa M., *Russian Formalism and Anglo-American New Criticism: A Comparative Study* (Mouton, The Hague, 1971).

Trotsky, Leon, *Literature and Revolution* (Michigan University Press, Ann Arbor, 1960).

Womack, Kenneth and Davis, Todd F., *Formalist Criticism and Reader-Response Theory* (Palgrave Macmillan, Basingstoke, 2002).

Young, Robert, 'Back to Bakhtin', *Cultural Critique*, vol. 2 (1985/6), 71–92.

CHAPTER 3

Reader-oriented theories

The twentieth century has seen a steady assault upon the objective certainties of nineteenth-century science. Einstein's theory of relativity alone cast doubt on the belief that objective knowledge was
simply a relentless and progressive accumulation of facts. The philosopher
T. S. Kuhn has shown that what emerges as a 'fact' in science depends upon
the frame of reference which the scientific observer brings to the object of
understanding. *Gestalt* psychology argues that the human mind does not
perceive things in the world as unrelated bits and pieces but as *configurations* of elements, themes, or meaningful, organized wholes. Individual items
look different in different contexts, and even within a single field of vision
they will be interpreted according to whether they are seen as 'figure' or
'ground'. These approaches and others have insisted that the perceiver
is active and not passive in the act of perception. In the case of the
famous duck–rabbit puzzle (see p. 46), only the perceiver can decide how
to orient the configuration of lines. Is it a duck looking left, or a rabbit
looking right?

How does this modern emphasis on the observer's active role affect literary theory? Consider once more (see Introduction, p. 5) Jakobson's model
of linguistic communication:

$$\begin{array}{c} \text{CONTEXT} \\ \text{ADDRESSER} \quad > \quad \text{MESSAGE} \quad > \quad \text{ADDRESSEE} \\ \text{CONTACT} \\ \text{CODE} \end{array}$$

Jakobson believed that literary discourse is different from other kinds of
discourse by having a 'set to the message'; a poem is about itself (its form,

its imagery, its literary meaning) before it is about the poet, the reader, or the world. However, if we reject formalism and adopt the perspective of the reader or audience, the whole orientation of Jakobson's diagram changes. From this angle, we can say that the poem has no real existence until it is read; its meaning can only be discussed by its readers. We differ about interpretations only because our ways of reading differ. It is the reader who applies the code in which the message is written and in this way *actualizes* what would otherwise remain only potentially meaningful. If we consider the simplest examples of interpretation, we see that the addressee is often actively involved in constructing a meaning. For example, consider the system used to represent numerals in electronic displays. The basic configuration consists of seven segments ⊟. One might regard this figure as an imperfect square (⊡) surmounted by three sides of a similar square (ⁿ), or as the reverse. The viewer's eye is invited to interpret this shape as an item in the familiar numerical system, and has no difficulty in 'recognizing' an 'eight'. The viewer is able to construct the numerals without difficulty from variations of this basic configuration of segments, even though the forms offered are sometimes poor approximations: ⧄ is 2, ⧅ is 5 (not 'S'), and ⧆ is 4 (not a defective 'H'). The success of this piece of communication depends on (1) the viewer's knowledge of the number system and (2) the viewer's ability to complete what is incomplete, or select what is significant and ignore what is not. Seen in this way the addressee is not a passive recipient of an entirely formulated meaning, but an active agent in the making of meaning. However, in this case, the addressee's task is very simply performed, because the message is stated within a completely closed system.

But take the following poem by Wordsworth:

A slumber did my spirit seal;
I had no human fears;
She seemed a thing that could not feel
The touch of earthly years.

No motion has she now, no force;
She neither hears nor sees;
Rolled round in earth's diurnal course,
With rocks, and stones, and trees.

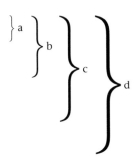

Leaving aside many preliminary and often unconscious steps which readers must make to recognize that they are reading a lyric poem, and that they accept the speaker as the authentic voice of the poet and not as a dramatic persona, we can say that there are two 'statements' made, one in each stanza: (1) I thought she could not die; (2) She is dead. As readers we ask ourselves what sense we make of the *relationship* between the statements. Our interpretation of every phrase will turn on the answer to this question. How are we to regard the speaker's attitude towards his earlier thoughts about the female (baby, girl, or woman)? Is it good and sensible to have 'no human fears', or is it naïve and foolish? Is the 'slumber' which sealed his spirit a sleep of illusion or an inspired reverie? Does 'she seemed' suggest that she had all the visible marks of an immortal being, or that the speaker was perhaps mistaken? Does the second stanza suggest that she has no spiritual existence in death and is reduced to mere inanimate matter? The first two lines of the stanza invite this view. However, the last two lines open another possible interpretation – that she has become part of a natural world and partakes of an existence which is in some sense greater than the naïve spirituality of stanza 1; her individual 'motion' and 'force' are now subsumed in the grand motion and force of Nature.

From the perspective of reader-oriented criticism the answers to these questions cannot simply be derived from the text. The meaning of the text is never self-formulated; the reader must act upon the textual material in order to produce meaning. Wolfgang Iser (see below, pp. 52–4) argues that literary texts always contain 'blanks' which only the reader can fill. The 'blank' between the two stanzas of Wordsworth's poem arises because the relationship between the stanzas is unstated. The act of interpretation requires us to fill this blank. A problem for theory centres on the question of whether or not the text itself triggers the reader's act of interpretation, or whether the reader's own interpretative strategies impose solutions upon the problems thrown up by the text. Even before the growth of reader-response theory, semioticians had developed the field with some sophistication. Umberto Eco's

The Role of the Reader (1979, comprising essays dating from 1959) argues that some texts are 'open' (Joyce's *Finnegans Wake*, atonal music) and invite the reader's collaboration in the production of meaning, while others are 'closed' (comics, detective fiction) and predetermine the reader's response. He also speculates on how the codes available to the reader determine what the text means as it is read.

But before we survey the various ways in which the reader's role in constructing meaning has been theorized, we must pose the question: *who is* 'the reader'? The narratologist Gerald Prince asks why, when we study novels, do we take such pains to discriminate between the various kinds of narrator (omniscient, unreliable, implied author, etc.), but never ask questions about the different kinds of person to whom the narrator addresses the discourse. Prince calls this person the 'narratee'. We must not confuse the narratee with the reader. The narrator may specify a narratee in terms of sex ('Dear Madam . . .'), class ('gentlemen'), situation (the 'reader' in his armchair), race (white) or age (mature). Evidently actual readers may or may not coincide with the person addressed by the narrator. An actual reader may be a black, male, young factory-worker reading in bed. The narratee is also distinguished from the 'virtual reader' (the sort of reader whom the author has in mind when developing the narrative) and the 'ideal reader' (the perfectly insightful reader who understands the writer's every move).

How do we learn to identify narratees? When the novelist Anthony Trollope writes 'Our archdeacon was worldly – who among us is not so?', we understand that the narratees here are people who, like the narrator, recognize the fallibility of all human beings, even the most pious. There are many 'signals', direct and indirect, which contribute to our knowledge of the narratee. The assumptions of the narratee may be attacked, supported, queried or solicited by the narrator who will thereby strongly imply the narratee's character. When the narrator apologizes for certain inadequacies in the discourse ('I cannot convey this experience in words'), this indirectly tells us something of the narratee's susceptibilities and values. Even in a novel which appears to make no direct reference to a narratee we pick up tiny signals even in the simplest of literary figures. The second term of a comparison, for example, often indicates the kind of world familiar to the narratee ('the song was as sincere as a TV jingle'). Sometimes the narratee is an important character. For example, in *A Thousand and One Nights* the very survival of the narrator, Scheherazade, depends on the continued attention of the narratee, the caliph; if he loses interest in her stories, she must die. The effect of Prince's elaborated theory is to highlight a dimension of narration which had been understood intuitively by readers but which had remained shadowy and undefined. He contributes to reader-oriented theory by drawing attention to ways in which narratives produce their own 'readers' or 'listeners', who may or may not coincide with actual readers. Many of the writers discussed in the following pages ignore this distinction between reader and narratee.

Phenomenology: Husserl, Heidegger, Gadamer

A modern philosophical tendency which stresses the perceiver's central role in determining meaning is known as 'phenomenology'. According to Edmund Husserl the proper object of philosophical investigation is the contents of our consciousness and not objects in the world. Consciousness is always of something, and it is the 'something' which appears to our consciousness which is truly real to us. In addition, argued Husserl, we discover in the things which appear in consciousness ('phenomena' in Greek, meaning 'things appearing') their universal or essential qualities. Phenomenology claims to show us the underlying nature both of human consciousness and of 'phenomena'. This was an attempt to revive the idea (eclipsed since the Romantics) that the individual human mind is the centre and origin of all meaning. In literary theory this approach did not encourage a purely subjective concern for the critic's mental structure but a type of criticism which tries to enter into the world of a writer's works and to arrive at an understanding of the underlying nature or essence of the writings as they appear to the critic's consciousness. The early work of J. Hillis Miller, the American (later deconstructionist – see Chapter 7, pp. 176–7) critic, was influenced by the phenomenological theories of the so-called 'Geneva School' of critics, who included Georges Poulet and Jean Starobinski. For example, Miller's first study of Thomas Hardy, *Thomas Hardy: Distance and Desire* (1970; he wrote further 'deconstructive' studies later), uncovers the novels' pervasive mental structures, namely 'distance' and 'desire'. The act of interpretation is possible because the texts allow the reader access to the author's consciousness, which, says Poulet, 'is open to me, welcomes me, lets me look deep inside itself, and . . . allows me . . . to think what it thinks and feel what it feels'. Derrida (see Chapter 7) would consider this kind of thinking 'logocentric' for supposing that a meaning is centred on a 'transcendental subject' (the author) and can be recentred on another such subject (the reader).

  The shift towards a reader-oriented theory is prefigured in the rejection of Husserl's 'objective' view by his pupil Martin Heidegger. The latter argued that what is distinctive about human existence is its *Dasein* ('givenness'): our consciousness both *projects* the things of the world and at the same time *is subjected to* the world by the very nature of existence in the world. We find ourselves 'flung down' into the world, into a time and place we did not choose, but simultaneously it is our world in so far as our consciousness projects it. We can never adopt an attitude of detached contemplation, looking down upon the world as if from a mountain top. We are inevitably merged with the very object of our consciousness. Our thinking is always in a situation and is therefore always *historical*, although this history is not external and social but personal and inward. It was Hans-Georg Gadamer who, in *Truth and Method* (1975), applied Heidegger's situational approach to literary theory. Gadamer argued that a literary work does not pop into the world as a finished and neatly parcelled bundle of meaning; rather meaning depends on the historical situation of the interpreter. Gadamer influenced 'reception theory' (see Jauss below).

Hans Robert Jauss and Wolfgang Iser

Jauss, an important German exponent of 'reception' theory (*Rezeption-ästhetik*), gave a historical dimension to reader-oriented criticism. He tried to achieve a compromise between Russian Formalism which ignores history, and social theories which ignore the text. Writing during a period of social unrest at the end of the 1960s, Jauss and others wanted to question the old canon of German literature *and* to show that it was perfectly reasonable to do so. The older critical outlook had ceased to make sense in the same way that Newton's physics no longer seemed adequate in the early twentieth century. He borrows from the philosophy of science (T. S. Kuhn) the term 'paradigm' which refers to the scientific framework of concepts and assumptions operating in a particular period. 'Ordinary science' does its experimental work within the mental world of a particular paradigm, until a new paradigm displaces the old one and throws up new problems and establishes new assumptions. Jauss uses the term 'horizon of expectations' to describe the criteria readers use to judge literary texts in any given period. These criteria will help the reader decide how to judge a poem as, for example, an epic or a tragedy or a pastoral; it will also, in a more general way, cover what is to be regarded as poetic or literary as opposed to unpoetic or non-literary uses of languages. Ordinary writing and reading will work within such a horizon. For example, if we consider the English Augustan period, we might say that Pope's poetry was judged according to criteria which were based upon values of clarity, naturalness and stylistic decorum (the words should be adjusted according to the dignity of the subject). However, this does not establish once and for all the value of Pope's poetry. During the second half of the eighteenth century, commentators began to question whether Pope was a poet at all and to suggest that he was a clever versifier who put prose into rhyming couplets and lacked the imaginative power required of true poetry. Leapfrogging the nineteenth century, we can say that modern readings of Pope work within a changed horizon of expectations: we now often value his poems for their wit, complexity, moral insight and their renewal of literary tradition.

The original horizon of expectations only tells us how the work was valued and interpreted when it appeared, but does not establish its meaning finally. In Jauss's view it would be equally wrong to say that a work is universal, that its meaning is fixed forever and open to all readers in any period: 'A literary work is not an object which stands by itself and which offers the same face to each reader in each period. It is not a monument which reveals its timeless essence in a monologue.' This means, of course, that we will never be able to survey the successive horizons which flow from the time of a work down to the present day and then, with an Olympian detachment, to sum up the work's final value or meaning. To do so would be to ignore our own historical situation. Whose authority are we to accept? That of the first readers? The combined opinion of readers over time? Or the aesthetic judgement of the present? The first readers may have been incapable of seeing the revolutionary significance of a writer (for example, William Blake), and the same objection must also apply to succeeding readers' judgements, including our own.

Jauss's answers to these questions derive from the philosophical 'hermeneutics' of Hans-Georg Gadamer, a follower of Heidegger (see above). Gadamer argues that all interpretations of past literature arise from a dialogue between past and present. Our attempts to understand a work will depend on the questions which our own cultural environment allows us to raise. At the same time, we seek to discover the questions which the work itself was trying to answer in its own dialogue with history. Our present perspective always involves a relationship to the past, but at the same time the past can only be grasped through the limited perspective of the present. Put in this way, the task of establishing a *knowledge* of the past seems hopeless. But a hermeneutical notion of 'understanding' does not separate knower and object in the familiar fashion of empirical science; rather it views understanding as a 'fusion' of past and present: we cannot make our journey into the past without taking the present with us. 'Hermeneutics' was a term originally applied to the interpretation of sacred texts; its modern equivalent preserves the same serious and reverent attitude towards the secular texts to which it tries to gain access.

Jauss recognizes that a writer may directly affront the prevailing expectations of his or her day. Indeed, reception theory itself developed in Germany during the 1960s in a climate of literary change: writers such as Rolf Hochhuth, Hans Magnus Enzenberger and Peter Handke were challenging accepted literary formalism by increasing the direct involvement of reader or audience. Jauss himself examines the case of the French poet Baudelaire whose *Les Fleurs du mal* had in the late nineteenth century created uproar and attracted legal prosecution by offending the norms of bourgeois morality *and* the canons of romantic poetry. However, the poems also immediately produced a new aesthetic horizon of expectations; the literary *avant-garde* saw the book as a trail-blazing work of decadence, and the poems were 'concretized' (Iser's term – see below) as expressions of the aesthetic cult of nihilism. Jauss assesses later psychological, linguistic and sociological interpretations of Baudelaire's poems, but often disregards them, thus casting doubt upon a method which recognizes its own historical limitations while still feeling able to regard certain other interpretations as raising 'falsely posed or illegitimate questions'. The 'fusion of horizons' is not, it seems, a total merging of all the points of view which have arisen but only those which to the hermeneutical sense of the critic appear to be part of the gradually emerging totality of meanings which make up the true unity of the text.

A leading exponent of German reception theory, and a member of the so-called 'Constance School' of such, is Wolfgang Iser, who draws heavily on the phenomenological aesthetician Roman Ingarden and on the work of Gadamer (see above). Unlike Jauss, Iser decontextualizes and dehistoricizes text and reader. A key work, building on an earlier book, *The Implied Reader* (1974), is his *The Act of Reading: A Theory of Aesthetic Response* (1978), in which, as elsewhere, he presents the text as a potential structure which is 'concretized' by the reader in relation to his or her extra-literary norms, values and experience. A sort of oscillation is set up between the power of the text to control the way it is read and a reader's 'concretization' of it in terms of his or her own experience – an experience which will itself be modified in the act of reading. 'Meaning', in this theory, lies in the adjustments and revisions to expectations which are brought about in the reader's mind in the process of making sense of his or her dialectical relationship to the text. Iser himself does not entirely resolve the relative

weight of the text's determinacy and the reader's experience in this relationship, although it would seem that his emphasis falls more heavily on
the latter.

In Iser's view the critic's task is to explain not the text as an object
but rather its effects on the reader. It is in the nature of texts to allow a
spectrum of possible readings. The term 'reader' can be subdivided into
'implied reader' and 'actual reader'. The first is the reader whom the text
creates for itself and amounts to 'a network of response-inviting structures'
which predispose us to read in certain ways. The 'actual reader' receives
certain mental images in the process of reading; however, the images will
inevitably be coloured by the reader's 'existing stock of experience'. If
we are atheists we will be affected differently by the Wordsworth poem
above (p. 47) than if we are Christians. The experience of reading will
differ according to our past experiences.

The words we read do not represent actual objects but human speech
in fictional guise. This fictional language helps us to construct in our minds
imaginary objects. To take one of Iser's own examples: in *Tom Jones* Fielding
presents two characters, Allworthy (the perfect man) and Captain Blifil (the
hypocrite). The reader's imaginary object, 'the perfect man', is subject to
modification: when Allworthy is taken in by Blifil's feigned piety, we adjust
the imaginary object in view of the perfect man's lack of judgement. The
reader's journey through the book is a continuous process of such adjustments. We hold in our minds certain expectations, based on our memory
of characters and events, but the expectations are continually modified,
and the memories transformed as we pass through the text. What we grasp
as we read is only a series of changing viewpoints, not something fixed and
fully meaningful at every point.

While a literary work does not represent objects, it does refer to the extra-
literary world by selecting certain norms, value systems or 'world-views'.
These norms are concepts of reality which help human beings to make
sense of the chaos of their experience. The text adopts a 'repertoire' of such
norms and suspends their validity within its fictional world. In *Tom Jones*,
various characters embody different norms: Allworthy (benevolence), Squire
Western (ruling passion), Square (the eternal fitness of things), Thwackum
(the human mind as a sink of iniquity), Sophia (the ideality of natural
inclinations). Each norm asserts certain values at the expense of others, and
each tends to contract the image of human nature to a single principle or
perspective. The reader is therefore impelled by the unfinished nature of
the text to relate the values of the hero (good nature) to the various norms

which are violated by the hero in specific incidents. *Only the reader* can actu-alize the degree to which particular norms are to be rejected or questioned. *Only the reader* can make the complex moral judgement on Tom, and see that, while his 'good nature' disrupts the restrictive norms of other characters, it does so partly because Tom lacks 'prudence' and 'circum-spection'. Fielding does not tell us this, but as readers we insert this into the interpretation in order to fill a 'gap' or 'blank' (key terms in Iser's theory) in the text. In real life we sometimes meet people who appear to represent certain world-views ('cynicism', 'humanism'), but we assign such descriptions ourselves on the basis of received ideas. The value systems we encounter are met at random: no author selects and predetermines them and no hero appears in order to test their validity. So, even though there are 'gaps' in the text to be filled, the text is much more definitely struc-tured than life.

If we apply Iser's method to our Wordsworth poem, we see that the reader's activity consists in first adjusting his or her viewpoint ((a), (b), (c), then (d)), and secondly in filling a 'blank' between the two stanzas (between transcendent spirituality and pantheistic immanence). This application may seem rather unwieldy because a short poem does not require the reader to make the long sequence of adjustments necessary when reading a novel. However, the concept of 'gaps' remains valid.

As we have suggested, it remains unclear whether Iser wishes to grant the reader the power to fill up at will the blanks in the text or whether he regards the text as the final arbiter of the reader's actualizations. Is the gap between 'the perfect man' and 'the perfect man's lack of judgement' filled by a freely judging reader or by a reader who is *guided* by the text's instructions? Iser's emphasis is ultimately phenomenological: the reader's experience of reading is at the centre of the literary process. By resolv-ing the contradictions between the various viewpoints which emerge from the text or by filling the 'gaps' between viewpoints in various ways, the readers take the text into their consciousnesses and make it their own *experience*. It seems that, while texts do set the terms on which the reader actualizes meanings, the reader's own 'store of experience' will take some part in the process. The reader's existing consciousness will have to make certain internal adjustments in order to receive and process the alien viewpoints which the text presents as reading takes place. This situ-ation produces the possibility that the reader's own 'world-view' may be modified as a result of internalizing, negotiating and realizing the partially indeterminate elements of the text: to use Iser's words, reading 'gives us the chance to formulate the unformulated'.

Fish, Riffaterre, Bleich

Other (diverse) inflections of reader-oriented theory are represented by the three critics surveyed here (see also Jonathan Culler in Chapter 4). Stanley Fish, the American critic of seventeenth-century English literature, developed a perspective called an 'affective stylistics'. Like Iser, he concentrates on the adjustments of expectation to be made by readers as they pass along the text, but considers this at the immediately local level of the sentence. He separates his approach very self-consciously from all kinds of formalism (including American New Criticism) by denying literary language any special status; we use the same reading strategies to interpret literary and non-literary sentences. His attention is directed to the developing responses of the reader in relation to the words of sentences as they succeed one another in time. Describing the fallen angels' state of awareness, having plummeted from heaven to hell, Milton wrote in *Paradise Lost*: 'Nor did they not perceive the evil plight'. This cannot be treated as a statement equivalent to 'they perceived the evil plight'. We must attend, argues Fish, to the sequence of words which creates a state of suspension in the reader, who hangs between two views of the fallen angels' awareness. His point is weakened though not refuted by the fact that Milton was evidently imitating the double negative in the style of classical epic. But the following sentence by Walter Pater receives an especially sensitive analysis by Fish: 'This at least of flame-like, our life has, that it is but the concurrence, renewed from moment to moment, of forces parting sooner or later on their ways.' He points out that by interrupting 'concurrence of forces' with 'renewed from moment to moment' Pater prevents the reader from establishing a definite or stable image in the mind, and at each stage in the sentence forces the reader to make an adjustment in expectation and interpretation. The idea of 'the concurrence' is disrupted by 'parting', but then 'sooner or later' leaves the 'parting' temporally uncertain. The reader's expectation of meaning is thus continuously adjusted: the meaning is the total movement of reading.

Jonathan Culler (see also Chapter 4) has lent general support to Fish's aims, but has criticized him for failing to give us a proper theoretical formulation of his reader criticism. Fish believes that his readings of sentences simply follow the natural practice of informed readers. In his view a reader is someone who possesses a 'linguistic competence', has internalized the syntactic and semantic knowledge required for reading. The 'informed reader' of literary texts has also acquired a specifically 'literary competence' (knowledge of literary conventions). Culler makes two trenchant criticisms of Fish's position:

1 He fails to theorize the conventions of reading: that is, he fails to ask the question 'What conventions do readers follow when they read?'

2 His claim to read sentences word by word in a temporal sequence is misleading: there is no reason to believe that readers actually do take in sentences in such a piecemeal and gradual way. Why does he assume, for example, that the reader, faced with Milton's 'Nor did they not perceive', will experience a sense of being suspended between two views?

There is something factitious about Fish's continual willingness to be surprised by the next word in a sequence. Also, Fish himself admits that his approach tends to privilege those texts which proceed in a self-undermining way (*Self-Consuming Artifacts* (1972) is the title of one of his earlier books). Elizabeth Freund points out that in order to sustain his reader orientation Fish has to suppress the fact that the actual experience of reading is not the same thing as a verbal rendering of that experience. By treating his own reading experience as itself an act of interpretation he is ignoring the gap between experience and the understanding of an experience. What Fish gives us, therefore, is not a definitive account of the nature of reading but Fish's understanding of his own reading experience.

In *Is There a Text in This Class?* (1980) Fish acknowledges that his earlier work treated his own experience of reading as the norm, and goes on to justify this position by introducing the idea of 'interpretative communities'. This meant that he was trying to persuade readers to adopt 'a set of community assumptions so that when they read they would do what I did'. Of course, there may be many different groups of readers who adopt particular kinds of reading strategies, but in this later phase of his work the strategies of a particular interpretative community determine the entire process of reading – the stylistic facts of the texts and the experience of reading them. If we accept the category of interpretative communities, we no longer need to choose between asking questions about the text or about the reader; the whole problem of subject and object disappears. However, the price that must be paid for this solution is high: by reducing the whole process of meaning-production to the already existing conventions of the interpretative community, Fish seems to abandon all possibility of deviant interpretations or resistances to the norms which govern acts of interpretation. As Elizabeth Freund points out: 'The appeal to the imperialism of agreement can chill the spines of readers whose experience of the community is less happily benign than Fish assumes.'

The French semiotician Michael Riffaterre agrees with the Russian Formalists in regarding poetry as a special use of language. Ordinary language is practical and is used to refer to some sort of 'reality', while poetic language focuses on the message as an end in itself. He takes this formalist view from Jakobson, but in a well-known essay he attacks Jakobson's and Lévi-Strauss's interpretation of Baudelaire's 'Les Chats'. Riffaterre shows that the linguistic features they discover in the poem could not possibly be perceived even by an informed reader. All manner of grammatical and phonemic patterns are thrown up by their structuralist approach, but not all the features they note can be part of the poetic structure for the reader. In a telling example he objects to their claim that by concluding a line with the word *volupté* (rather than, say, *plaisir*) Baudelaire is making play with the fact that a feminine noun (*la volupté*) is used as a 'masculine' rhyme, thus creating sexual ambiguity in the poem. Riffaterre rightly points out that a reasonably practised reader may well never have heard of the technical terms 'masculine' and 'feminine' rhyme. However, Riffaterre has some difficulty in explaining why something perceived by Jakobson does not count as evidence of what readers perceive in a text.

Riffaterre developed his theory in *Semiotics of Poetry* (1978), in which he argues that competent readers go beyond surface meaning. If we regard a poem as a string of statements, we are limiting our attention to its 'meaning', which is merely what it can be said to represent in units of information. If we attend only to a poem's 'meaning' we reduce it to a (possibly nonsensical) string of unrelated bits. A true response starts by noticing that the elements (signs) in a poem often appear to depart from normal grammar or normal representation: the poem seems to be establishing significance only *indirectly* and in doing so 'threatens the literary representation of reality'. It requires only ordinary linguistic competence to understand the poem's 'meaning', but the reader requires 'literary competence' (for more on this term, see Culler, Chapter 4, pp. 75–7) to deal with the frequent 'ungrammaticalities' encountered in reading a poem. Faced with the stumbling-block of ungrammaticalness the reader is forced, during the process of reading, to uncover a second (higher) level of significance which will explain the ungrammatical features of the text. What will ultimately be uncovered is a structural 'matrix', which can be reduced to a single sentence or even a single word. The matrix can be deduced only indirectly and is not actually present as a word or statement in the poem. The poem is connected to its matrix by actual versions of the matrix in the form of familiar statements, clichés, quotations, or conventional associations. These versions are called 'hypograms'. It is the matrix which ultimately gives a poem unity. This reading process can be summarized as follows:

1   try to read for ordinary 'meaning';

2   highlight those elements which appear ungrammatical and which obstruct an ordinary mimetic interpretation;

3   discover the 'hypograms' (or commonplaces) which receive expanded or unfamiliar expression in the text;

4   derive the 'matrix' from the 'hypograms'; that is, find a single statement or word capable of generating the 'hypograms' and the text.

If we tried, hesitantly, to apply this theory to the Wordsworth poem 'A slumber did my spirit seal' (see above, p. 47), we might finally arrive at the matrix 'spirit and matter'. The 'hypograms' which are reworked in the text appear to be (1) death is the end of life; (2) the human spirit cannot die; (3) in death we return to the earth from which we came. The poem achieves unity by reworking these commonplaces in an unexpected way from a basic matrix. No doubt Riffaterre's theory would look stronger if we had given one of his own examples from Baudelaire or Gautier, for his approach seems much more appropriate as a way of reading difficult poetry which goes against the grain of 'normal' grammar or semantics. As a general theory of reading it has many difficulties, not least that it disallows several kinds of reading that you or I might think perfectly straightforward (for example, reading a poem for its political message).

An American critic who has derived approaches to reader theory from psychology is David Bleich. His *Subjective Criticism* (1978) is a sophisticated argument in favour of a shift from an objective to a subjective paradigm in critical theory. He argues that modern philosophers of science (especially T. S. Kuhn) have correctly denied the existence of an objective world of facts. Even in science, the perceiver's mental structures will decide what counts as an objective fact: 'Knowledge is made by people and not found [because] the object of observation appears changed by the act of observation.' He goes on to insist that the advances of 'knowledge' are determined by the *needs of the community*. When we say that 'science' has replaced 'superstition', we are describing not a passage from darkness to light, but a change in paradigm which occurs when certain urgent needs of the new community come into conflict with old beliefs and demand new beliefs.

'Subjective criticism' is based on the assumption that 'each person's most urgent motivations are to understand himself'. In his classroom experiments,

Bleich was led to distinguish between (1) the reader's spontaneous 'response' to a text and (2) the 'meaning' the reader attributed to it. The latter is usually presented as an 'objective' interpretation (something offered for negotiation in a pedagogic situation), but is necessarily developed from the *subjective response* of the reader. Whatever system of thought is being employed (moralist, Marxist, structuralist, psychoanalytic, etc.), interpretations of particular texts will normally reflect the subjective individuality of a personal 'response'. Without a grounding in 'response', the application of systems of thought will be dismissed as empty formulae derived from received dogma. Particular interpretations make more sense when critics take the trouble to explain the growth and origin of their views.

Reader-oriented theories have no single or predominant philosophical starting-point; the writers we have considered belong to quite different traditions of thought; and there are few common terms or positions among them. The German writers, Jauss and Iser, draw upon phenomenology and hermeneutics in their attempts to describe the process of reading in terms of the reader's consciousness. Riffaterre presupposes a reader who possesses a specifically *literary* competence, while Fish believes that readers respond to the sequence of words in sentences whether or not the sentences are literary. Bleich regards reading as a process which depends upon the subjective psychology of the reader. And in Chapter 7 we will see how Roland Barthes celebrates the end of structuralism's reign by granting the reader the power to create meanings by 'opening' the text to the interminable play of 'codes'. Whatever else one may take from these reader-oriented theories, there is no doubt that they fundamentally challenge the predominance of the text-oriented theories associated with New Criticism and Formalism: we can no longer talk about the meaning of a text without taking into account the reader's contributions to it.

Selected reading

Key texts

Bleich, David, *Subjective Criticism* (Johns Hopkins University Press, Baltimore and London, 1978).

Eco, Umberto, *The Role of the Reader: Explorations in the Semiotics of Texts* [1979] (reprint edn, Indiana University Press, Bloomington, 1984).

Fish, Stanley, *Self-Consuming Artifacts: The Experience of Seventeenth-Century Literature* (California University Press, Berkeley, 1972).

Fish, Stanley, *Is There a Text in This Class? The Authority of Interpretative Communities* (Harvard University Press, Cambridge, Mass., 1980).

Fish, Stanley, *Doing What Comes Naturally: Changes, Rhetoric, and the Practice of Theory in Literary and Legal Studies* (Clarendon Press, Oxford, 1990).

Ingarden, Roman, *The Literary Work of Art* [1931], trans. by George G. Grabowicz (Northwestern University Press, Evanston, Ill., 1973).

Iser, Wolfgang, *The Implied Reader* [1972] (Johns Hopkins University Press, Baltimore, 1974).

Iser, Wolfgang, *The Act of Reading: A Theory of Aesthetic Response* [1976] (Johns Hopkins University Press, Baltimore, 1978).

Iser, Wolfgang, *Prospecting: From Reader Response to Literary Anthropology* (Johns Hopkins University Press, Baltimore, 1989).

Jauss, Hans R., *Toward an Aesthetic of Reception*, trans. by T. Bahti (Harvester Wheatsheaf, Hemel Hempstead, 1982).

Miller, J. Hillis, *Thomas Hardy: Distance and Desire* (Oxford University Press, Oxford, 1970).

Miller, J. Hillis, *Theory Now and Then* (Harvester Wheatsheaf, Hemel Hempstead, 1991).

Prince, Gerald, 'Introduction to the Study of the Narratee', in Jane P. Tompkins (ed.), below.

Riffaterre, Michael, 'Describing Poetic Structures: Two Approaches to Baudelaire's *Les Chats*', in *Structuralism*, J. Ehrmann (ed.) (Doubleday, Garden City, New York, 1970).

Riffaterre, Michael, *Semiotics of Poetry* (Indiana University Press, Bloomington; Methuen, London, 1978).

Riffaterre, Michael, *Text Production* [1979], trans. by Terese Lyons (Columbia University Press, New York, 1983).

Suleiman, Susan and Crosman, Inge (eds), *The Reader in the Text: Essays on Audience and Interpretation* (Princeton University Press, Princeton, NJ, 1980).

Tompkins, Jane P. (ed.), *Reader-Response Criticism: From Formalism to Post-Structuralism* (Johns Hopkins University Press, Baltimore and London, 1980).

Further reading

Cf. 'Introductions' to Suleiman and Crosman (eds), *The Reader in the Text*, and Tompkins (ed.), *Reader-Response Criticism* (above).

Eagleton, Terry, *Literary Theory: An Introduction* (2nd edn, Blackwell, Oxford, 1996), ch. 2.

Freund, Elizabeth, *The Return of the Reader: Reader-Response Criticism* (Methuen, London and New York, 1987).

Holub, Robert C., *Reception Theory: A Critical Introduction* (Methuen, London and New York, 1984).

McGregor, Graham and White, R. S. (eds), *Reception and Response: Hearer Creativity and the Analysis of Spoken and Written Texts* (Routledge, London, 1990).

Sutherland, John, 'Production and Reception of the Literary Book', in *Encyclopaedia of Literature and Criticism*, Martin Coyle, Peter Garside, Malcolm Kelsall and John Peck (eds) (Routledge, London, 1990).

Wolfreys, Julian (ed.), *The J. Hillis Miller Reader* (Edinburgh University Press, Edinburgh, 2004).

Womack, Kenneth and Davis, Todd F., *Formalist Criticism and Reader-Response Theory* (Palgrave Macmillan, Basingstoke, 2002).

CHAPTER 4

Structuralist theories

New ideas often provoke baffled and anti-intellectual reactions, and this was especially true of the reception accorded the theories which go under the name of 'structuralism'. Structuralist approaches to literature challenged some of the most cherished beliefs of the ordinary reader. The literary work, we had long felt, is the child of an author's creative life, and expresses the author's essential self. The text is the place where we enter into a spiritual or humanistic communion with an author's thoughts and feelings. Another fundamental assumption which readers often make is that a good book tells the truth about human life – that novels and plays try to 'tell things as they really are'. However, structuralists have tried to persuade us that the author is 'dead' and that literary discourse has no truth function. In a review of a book by Jonathan Culler, John Bayley spoke for the anti-structuralists when he declared, 'but the sin of semiotics is to attempt to destroy our sense of truth in fiction . . . In a good story, truth precedes fiction and remains separable from it.' In a 1968 essay, Roland Barthes put the structuralist view very powerfully, and argued that writers only have the power to mix already existing writings, to reassemble or re-deploy them; writers cannot use writing to 'express' themselves, but only to draw upon that immense dictionary of language and culture which is 'always already written' (to use a favourite Barthesian phrase). It would not be misleading to use the term 'anti-humanism' to describe the spirit of structuralism. Indeed the word has been used by structuralists themselves to emphasize their opposition to all forms of literary criticism in which the human subject is the source and origin of literary meaning.

The linguistic background

The work of the Swiss linguist Ferdinand de Saussure, compiled and published after his death in a single book, *Course in General Linguistics* (1915), has been profoundly influential in shaping contemporary literary theory. Saussure's two key ideas provide new answers to the questions 'What is the object of linguistic investigation?' and 'What is the relationship between words and things?' He makes a fundamental distinction between *langue* and *parole* – between the language *system*, which pre-exists actual examples of language, and the individual *utterance*. *Langue* is the social aspect of language: it is the shared system which we (unconsciously) draw upon as speakers. *Parole* is the individual realization of the system in actual instances of language. This distinction is essential to all later structuralist theories. The proper object of linguistic study is the system which underlies any particular human signifying practice, not the individual utterance. This means that, if we examine specific poems or myths or economic practices, we do so in order to discover what system of rules – what grammar – is being used. After all, human beings use speech quite differently from parrots: the former evidently have a grasp of a system of rules which enables them to produce an infinite number of well-formed sentences; parrots do not.

Saussure rejected the idea that language is a word-heap gradually accumulated over time and that its primary function is to refer to things in the world. In his view, words are not symbols which correspond to referents, but rather are 'signs' which are made up of two parts (like two sides of a sheet of paper): a mark, either written or spoken, called a 'signifier', and a concept (what is 'thought' when the mark is made), called a 'signified'. The view he is rejecting may be represented thus:

SYMBOL = THING

Saussure's model is as follows:

$$\text{SIGN} = \frac{\text{signifier}}{\text{signified}}$$

'Things' have no place in the model. The elements of language acquire meaning not as the result of some connection between words and things, but only as parts of a system of relations. Consider the sign-system of traffic lights:

red – amber – green

$$\frac{\text{signifier ('red')}}{\text{signified (stop)}}$$

The sign signifies only within the system 'red = stop / green = go / amber = prepare for red or green'. The relation between signifier and signified is arbitrary: there is no natural bond between red and stop, no matter how natural it may *feel*. When the British joined the EEC they had to accept new electrical colour codings which seemed unnatural (brown not red = live; blue not black = neutral). Each colour in the traffic system signifies not by asserting a positive univocal meaning but by marking a *difference*, a distinction within a system of opposites and contrasts: traffic-light 'red' is precisely 'not-green'; 'green' is 'not-red'.

Language is one among many sign-systems (some believe it is the fundamental system). The science of such systems is called 'semiotics' or 'semiology'. It is usual to regard structuralism and semiotics as belonging to the same theoretical universe. Structuralism, it must be added, is often concerned with systems which do not involve 'signs' as such (kinship relations, for example, thus indicating its equally important origins in anthropology – see the references to Lévi-Strauss below, pp. 65, 68) but which can be treated in the same way as sign-systems. The American philosopher C. S. Peirce made a useful distinction between three types of sign: the 'iconic' (where the sign *resembles* its referent, e.g. a picture of a ship or a road-sign for falling rocks); the 'indexical' (where the sign is *associated*, possibly causally, with its referent, e.g. smoke as a sign of fire, or clouds as a sign of rain); and the 'symbolic' (where the sign has an *arbitrary* relation to its referent, e.g. language).

The most celebrated modern semiotician was Yury Lotman of the then USSR. He developed the Saussurean and Czech types of structuralism in works such as *The Analysis of the Poetic Text* (1976). One of the major differences between Lotman and the French structuralists is his retention of evaluation in his analyses. Literary works, he believes, have more value because they have a 'higher information load' than non-literary texts. His approach brings together the rigour of structuralist linguistics and the close reading techniques of New Criticism. Maria Corti, Caesare Segre, Umberto Eco (for a brief discussion of him as postmodern novelist, see Chapter 8, p. 199) in Italy and Michael Riffaterre (see Chapter 3) from France are the leading European exponents of literary semiotics.

The first major developments in structuralist studies were based upon advances in the study of phonemes, the lowest-level elements in the language system. A phoneme is a meaningful sound, one that is recognized or perceived by a language user. Hundreds of different 'sounds' may be made by the speakers of particular languages, but the number of phonemes will be limited. The word 'spin' may be pronounced within a wide range of phonetic difference, so long as the essential phoneme remains recognizable as itself. One must add that the 'essential phoneme' is only a mental *abstraction*: all actually occurring sounds are *variants* of phonemes. We do not recognize sounds as meaningful bits of noise in their own right, but register them as different in some respects from other sounds. Roland Barthes draws attention to this principle in the title of his most celebrated book, *S/Z* (see Chapter 7, pp. 151–3), which picks out the two sibilants in Balzac's *Sarrasine* (Sä-rä-zēn), which are differentiated phonemically as *voiced* (*z*) and *unvoiced* (*s*). On the other hand there are differences of raw sound at the phonetic (not phonemic) level which are not 'recognized' in English: the /p/ sound in 'pin' is evidently different from the /p/ sound in 'spin', but English speakers do not recognize a difference: the difference is not recognized in the sense that it does not 'distribute' meaning between words in the language. Even if we said 'sbin', we would probably hear it as 'spin'. The essential point about this view of language is that underlying our use of language is a *system*, a pattern of paired opposites, *binary oppositions*. At the level of the phoneme, these include nasalized/non-nasalized, vocalic/non-vocalic, voiced/unvoiced, tense/lax. In a sense, speakers appear to have internalized a set of rules which manifests itself in their evident *competence* in operating language.

We can observe 'structuralism' of this type at work in the anthropology of Mary Douglas. She examines the abominations of Leviticus, according to which some creatures are clean and some unclean on an apparently random principle. She solves the problem by constructing the equivalent of a phonemic analysis, according to which two rules appear to be in force:

1   'Cloven-hoofed, cud-chewing ungulates are the model of the proper kind of food for a pastoralist'; animals which only half conform (pig, hare, rock badger) are unclean.

2   Another rule applies if the first is not relevant: each creature should be in the element to which it is biologically adapted. So fish without fins are unclean, and so on.

At a more complex level, the anthropology of Claude Lévi-Strauss develops a 'phonemic' analysis of myths, rites, kinship structures. Instead of asking questions about the origins or causes of the prohibitions, myths or rites, the structuralist looks for the system of differences which underlies a particular human practice.

As these examples from anthropology show, structuralists try to uncover the 'grammar', 'syntax', or 'phonemic' pattern of particular human systems of meaning, whether they be those of kinship, garments, *haute cuisine*, narrative discourse, myths or totems. The liveliest examples of such analyses can be found in the earlier writings of Roland Barthes, especially in the wide-ranging *Mythologies* (1957) and *Système de la mode* (1967). The theory of these studies is given in *Elements of Semiology* (1967; see Chapter 7, p. 149).

The principle – that human performances presuppose a received system of differential relations – is applied by Barthes to virtually all social practices; he interprets them as sign-systems which operate on the model of language. Any actual 'speech' (*parole*) presupposes a system (*langue*) which is being used. Barthes recognizes that the language system may change, and that changes must be initiated in 'speech'; nevertheless, at any given moment there exists a working system, a set of rules from which all 'speeches' may be derived. To take an example, when Barthes examines the wearing of garments, he sees it not as a matter of personal expression or individual style, but as a 'garment system' which works like a language. He divides the 'language' of garments between 'system' and 'speech' ('syntagm').

System	*Syntagm*
'Set of pieces, parts or details which cannot be worn at the same time on the same part of the body, and whose variation corresponds to a change in the meaning of the clothing: toque-bonnet-hood, etc.'	'Juxtaposition in the same type of dress of different elements: skirt-blouse-jacket.'

To make a garment 'speech', we choose a particular ensemble (syntagm) of pieces each of which could be replaced by other pieces. An ensemble (sports jacket/grey-flannelled trousers/white open-necked shirt) is equivalent to a specific sentence uttered by an individual for a particular purpose; the elements fit together to make a particular kind of utterance and to evoke a meaning or style. No one can actually perform the system itself, but their selection of elements from the sets of garments which make up the system expresses their *competence* in handling the system. Here is a representation of a culinary example Barthes provides:

System	*Syntagm*
'Set of foodstuffs which have affinities or differences, within which one chooses a dish in view of a certain meaning: the types of entrée, roast or sweet.'	'Real sequence of dishes chosen during meal; menu.'

(A restaurant *à la carte* menu has both levels: entrée and examples.)

Structuralist narratology

When we apply the linguistic model to literature, we appear to be in a methodological loop. After all, if literature is already linguistic, what is the point of examining it in the light of a linguistic model? Well, for one thing, it would be a mistake to identify 'literature' and 'language'. It is true that literature *uses* language as its medium, but this does not mean that the structure of literature is identical with the structure of language. The units of literary structure do not coincide with those of language. This means that when the Bulgarian narratologist Tzvetan Todorov (see below, p. 70) advocates a new poetics which will establish a general 'grammar' of literature, he is talking about the underlying rules governing literary practice. On the other hand, structuralists agree that literature has a special relationship with language: it draws attention to the very nature and specific properties of language. In this respect structuralist poetics are closely related to Formalism.

Structuralist narrative theory develops from certain elementary linguistic analogies. Syntax (the rules of sentence construction) is the basic model of narrative rules. Todorov and others talk of 'narrative syntax'. The most elementary syntactic division of the sentence unit is between subject and predicate: 'The knight (subject) slew the dragon with his sword (predicate).' Evidently this sentence could be the core of an episode or even an entire tale. If we substitute a name (Launcelot or Gawain) for 'the knight', or 'axe' for 'sword', we retain the same essential structure. By pursuing this analogy between sentence structure and narrative, Vladimir Propp developed his theory of Russian fairy stories.

Propp's approach can be understood if we compare the 'subject' of a sentence with the typical characters (hero, villain, etc.) and the 'predicate' with the typical actions in such stories. While there is an enormous profusion of details, the whole corpus of tales is constructed upon the same basic set of thirty-one 'functions'. A function is the basic unit of the narrative 'language' and refers to the significant actions which form the narrative. These follow a logical sequence, and although no tale includes them all, in every tale the functions always remain in sequence. The last group of functions is as follows:

25   A difficult task is proposed to the hero.

26   The task is resolved.

27   The hero is recognized.

28   The false hero or villain is exposed.

29   The false hero is given a new appearance.

30   The villain is punished.

31   The hero is married and ascends the throne.

It is not difficult to see that these functions are present not just in Russian fairy tales or even non-Russian tales, but also in comedies, myths, epics, romances and indeed stories in general. However, Propp's functions have a certain archetypal simplicity which requires elaboration when applied to more complex texts. For example, in the Oedipus myth, Oedipus is set the task of solving the riddle of the sphinx; the task is resolved; the hero is recognized; he is married and ascends the throne. However, Oedipus is also the false hero and the villain; he is exposed (he murdered his father on the way to Thebes and married his mother, the queen), and punishes himself. Propp had added seven 'spheres of action' or roles to the thirty-one functions: villain, donor (provider), helper, princess (sought-after person) and her father, dispatcher, hero (seeker or victim), false hero. The tragic myth of Oedipus requires the substitution of 'mother/queen and husband' for 'princess and her father'. One character can play several roles, or several characters can play the same role. Oedipus is both hero, provider (he averts Thebes' plague by solving the riddle), false hero, and even villain.

Claude Lévi-Strauss, the structuralist anthropologist, analyses the Oedipus myth in a manner which is truly structuralist in its use of the linguistic model. He calls the units of myth 'mythemes' (compare phonemes and morphemes in linguistics). They are organized in binary oppositions (see above, p. 65) like the basic linguistic units. The general opposition underlying the Oedipus myth is between two views of the origin of human beings: (1) that they are born from the earth; (2) that they are born from coition. Several mythemes are grouped on one side or the other of the anti-thesis between (1) the *over*valuation of kinship ties (Oedipus marries his mother; Antigone buries her brother unlawfully); and (2) the *under*valuation of kinship (Oedipus kills his father; Eteocles kills his brother). Lévi-Strauss is not interested in the narrative *sequence*, but in the structural *pattern* which gives the myth its meaning. He looks for the 'phonemic' structure of myth. He believes that this linguistic model will uncover the basic structure of the human mind – the structure which governs the way human beings shape all their institutions, artefacts and forms of knowledge.

A. J. Greimas, in his *Sémantique Structurale* (1966), offers an elegant streamlining of Propp's theory. While Propp focused on a single genre, Greimas aims to arrive at the universal 'grammar' of narrative by applying to it a semantic analysis of sentence structure. In place of Propp's seven 'spheres of action' he proposes three pairs of binary oppositions which include all six roles (*actants*) he requires:

Subject/Object

Sender/Receiver

Helper/Opponent

The pairs describe three basic patterns which perhaps recur in all narrative:

1 Desire, search, or aim (subject/object).

2 Communication (sender/receiver).

3 Auxiliary support or hindrance (helper/opponent).

If we apply these to Sophocles' *Oedipus the King*, we arrive at a more penetrating analysis than when using Propp's categories:

1 O searches for the murderer of Laius. Ironically he searches for himself (he is both subject and object).

2 Apollo's oracle predicts O's sins. Teiresias, Jocasta, the messenger and the herdsman all, knowingly or not, confirm its truth. The play is about O's misunderstanding of the message.

3 Teiresias and Jocasta try to prevent O from discovering the murderer. The messenger and the herdsman unwittingly assist him in the search. O himself obstructs the correct interpretation of the message.

It can be seen at a glance that Greimas' reworking of Propp is in the direction of the 'phonemic' patterning we saw in Lévi-Strauss. In this respect Greimas is more truly 'structuralist' than the Russian Formalist Propp, in that the former thinks in terms of *relations* between entities rather than of the character of entities in themselves. In order to account for the various narrative sequences which are possible he reduces Propp's thirty-one functions to twenty, and groups them into three structures (syntagms): 'contractual', 'performative' and 'disjunctive'. The first, the most interesting, is concerned with the establishing or breaking of contracts or rules. Narratives may employ either of the following structures:

contract (or prohibition) > violation > punishment

lack of contract (disorder) > establishment of contract (order)

The Oedipus narrative has the first structure: he violates the prohibition against patricide and incest, and punishes himself.

The work of Tzvetan Todorov is a summation of Propp, Greimas and others. All the syntactic rules of language are restated in their narrative guise – rules of agency, predication, adjectival and verbal functions, mood and aspect, and so on. The minimal unit of narrative is the 'proposition', which can be either an 'agent' (e.g. a person) or a 'predicate' (e.g. an action). The propositional structure of a narrative can be described in the most abstract and universal fashion. Using Todorov's method, we might have the following propositions:

X is king   X marries Y

Y is X's mother   X kills Z

Z is X's father

These are some of the propositions which make up the narrative of the Oedipus myth. For X read Oedipus; for Y, Jocasta; for Z, Laius. The first three propositions denominate agents, the first and the last two contain predicates (to be a king, to marry, to kill). Predicates may work like adjectives and refer to static states of affairs (to be a king), or they may operate dynamically like verbs to indicate transgressions of law, and are therefore the most dynamic types of proposition. Having established the smallest unit (proposition), Todorov describes two higher levels of organization: the *sequence* and the *text*. A group of propositions forms a sequence. The basic sequence is made up of five propositions which describe a certain state which is disturbed and then re-established albeit in altered form. The five propositions may be designated thus:

Equilibrium^1 (e.g. Peace)

Force^1 (Enemy invades)

Disequilibrium (War)

Force^2 (Enemy is defeated)

Equilibrium^2 (Peace on new terms)

Finally a succession of sequences forms a text. The sequences may be organized in a variety of ways, by embedding (story within a story, digression, etc.), by linking (a string of sequences), or by alternation (interlacing of sequences), or by a mixture of these. Todorov provides his most vivid examples in a study of Boccaccio's *Decameron* (*Grammaire du Décaméron*, 1969). His attempt to establish the universal syntax of narrative has all the air of a scientific theory. As we shall see, it is precisely against this confidently objective stance that the poststructuralists react.

STRUCTURALIST THEORIES   71

Gérard Genette developed his complex and powerful theory of discourse in the context of a study of Proust's *À la recherche du temps perdu*. He refines the Russian Formalist distinction between 'story' and 'plot' (see Chapter 2, p. 34) by dividing narrative into three levels: story (*histoire*), discourse (*récit*), and *narration*. For example, in *Aeneid* II Aeneas is the story-teller addressing his audience (*narration*); he presents a verbal *discourse*; and his discourse represents events in which he appears as a character (*story*). These dimensions of narrative are related by three aspects, which Genette derives from the three qualities of the verb: *tense*, *mood* and *voice*. To take just one example, his distinction between 'mood' and 'voice' neatly clarifies problems which can arise from the familiar notion of 'point-of-view'. We often fail to distinguish between the voice of the narrator and the perspective (mood) of a character. In Dickens's novel *Great Expectations*, Pip presents the perspective of his younger self through the narrative voice of his older self.

Genette's essay on 'Frontiers of Narrative' (1966) provided an overview of the problems of narration which has not been bettered. He considers the problem of narrative theory by exploring three binary oppositions. The first, 'diegesis and mimesis' (narrative and representation), occurs in Aristotle's *Poetics* and presupposes a distinction between simple narrative (what the author says in his or her own voice as author) and direct imitation (when the author speaks in the person of a character). Genette shows that the distinction cannot be sustained, since if one *could* have direct imitation involving a pure representation of what someone actually said, it would be like a Dutch painting in which actual objects were included on the canvas. He concludes: 'Literary representation, the *mimesis* of the ancients, is not, therefore, narrative plus "speeches": it is narrative and only narrative.' The second opposition, 'narration and description', presupposes a distinction between an active and a contemplative aspect of narration. The first is to do with actions and events, the second with objects or characters. 'Narration' appears, at first, to be essential, since events and actions are the essence of a story's temporal and dramatic content, while 'description' appears to be ancillary and ornamental. 'The man went over to the table and picked up a knife' is dynamic and profoundly narrativistic. However, having established the distinction, Genette immediately dissolves it by pointing out that the nouns and verbs in the sentence are also descriptive. If we change 'man' to 'boy', or 'table' to 'desk', or 'picked up' to 'grabbed', we have altered the description. Finally, the opposition 'narrative and discourse' distinguishes between a pure telling in which 'no one speaks' and a telling in which we are aware of the person who is speaking. Once again,

Genette cancels the opposition by showing that there can never be a pure narrative devoid of 'subjective' coloration. However transparent and unmediated a narrative may appear to be, the signs of a judging mind are rarely absent. Narratives are nearly always impure in this sense, whether the element of 'discourse' enters via the voice of the narrator (Fielding, Cervantes) or a character-narrator (Sterne), or through epistolary discourse (Richardson). Genette believes that narrative reached its highest degree of purity in Hemingway and Hammett, but that with the *nouveau roman* narrative began to be totally swallowed up in the writer's own discourse. In our later chapter on poststructuralism, we shall see that Genette's theoretical approach, with its positing and cancellation of oppositions, opens the door to the 'deconstructive' philosophy of Jacques Derrida.

At this point, the reader may well object that structuralist poetics seems to have little to offer the practising critic, and it is perhaps significant that fairy stories, myths and detective stories often feature as examples in structuralist writings. Such studies aim to define the *general principles* of literary structure and not to provide interpretations of individual texts. A fairy story will provide clearer examples of the essential narrative grammar of all stories than will *King Lear* or *Ulysses*. Tzvetan Todorov's lucid 'The Typology of Detective Fiction' (1966) distinguishes the narrative structures of detective fiction into three chronologically evolving types: the 'whodunit', the 'thriller' and the 'suspense novel'. He makes a virtue of the fact that the narrative structures of popular literature can be studied much more systematically than those of 'great' literature, because they readily conform to the rules of popular genres.

Metaphor and metonymy

There are some instances when a structuralist theory provides the practical critic with a fertile ground for interpretative applications. This is true of Roman Jakobson's study of 'aphasia' (speech defect) and its implications for poetics. He starts by stating the fundamental distinction between horizontal and vertical dimensions of language, a distinction related to that between *langue* and *parole*. Taking Barthes' garments system as an example, we note that in the vertical dimension we have an inventory of elements that may be substituted for one another: toque-bonnet-hood; in the horizontal dimension, we have elements chosen from the inventory to form an actual sequence (skirt-blouse-jacket). Thus a given sentence may be viewed either vertically or horizontally:

1 Each element is *selected* from a set of possible elements and could be substituted for another in the set.

2 The elements are *combined* in a sequence, which constitutes a *parole*.

This distinction applies at all levels – phoneme, morpheme, word, sentence. Jakobson noticed that aphasic children appeared to lose the ability to operate one or other of these dimensions. One type of aphasia exhibited 'contiguity disorder', the inability to combine elements in a sequence; the other suffered 'similarity disorder', the inability to substitute one element for another. In a word-association test, if you said 'hut', the first type would produce a string of synonyms, antonyms, and other *substitutions*: 'cabin', 'hovel', 'palace', 'den', 'burrow'. The other type would offer elements which *combine* with 'hut', forming potential sequences: 'burnt out', 'is a poor little house'. Jakobson goes on to point out that the two disorders correspond to two figures of speech – metaphor and metonymy. As the foregoing example shows, 'contiguity disorder' results in substitution in the vertical dimension as in metaphor ('den' for 'hut'), while 'similarity disorder' results in the production of parts of sequences for the wholes as in metonymy ('burnt out' for 'hut'). Jakobson suggested that normal speech behaviour also tends towards one or other extreme, and that literary style expresses itself as a leaning towards either the metaphoric or the metonymic. The historical development from romanticism through realism to symbolism can be understood as an alternation of style from the metaphoric to the metonymic back to the metaphoric. David Lodge, in *The Modes of Modern Writing* (1977), applied the theory to modern literature, adding further stages to a cyclical process: modernism and symbolism are essentially metaphoric, while anti-modernism is realistic and metonymic.

An example: in its broad sense, metonymy involves the shift from one element in a sequence to another, or one element in a context to another: we refer to a *cup* of something (meaning its *contents*); the *turf* (for *racing*), a fleet of a hundred *sails* (for *ships*). Essentially metonymy requires a *context* for its operation; hence Jakobson's linking of realism with metonymy. Realism speaks of its object by offering the reader aspects, parts, and contextual details, in order to evoke a whole. Consider the passage near the opening of Dickens's *Great Expectations*. Pip begins by establishing himself as an identity in a landscape. Reflecting on his orphaned condition, he tells us that he can describe his parents through the only visual remains – their graves: 'As I never saw my father or my mother . . . my first fancies regarding what they were like were *unreasonably* [our italics] derived from their tombstones. The shapes of the letters on my father's, gave me an odd idea that he was a square stout man....' This initial act of identification is metonymic in that Pip links two parts of a context: his father and his father's tombstone. However, this is not a 'realistic' metonymy but an 'unrealistic' derivation, 'an odd idea', although suitably childlike (and in that sense psychologically realistic). Proceeding to the immediate setting on the evening of the convict's appearance, the moment of truth in Pip's life, he gives the following description:

> Ours was the marsh country, down by the river, within, as the river wound, twenty miles of the sea. My first most vivid and broad impression of the *identity of things* [our italics], seems to me to have been gained on a memorable raw afternoon towards evening. At such a time I found out for certain, that this bleak place overgrown with nettles was the churchyard; and that Philip Pirrip, late of this parish, and also Georgiana wife of the above, were dead and buried; and that . . . the dark flat wilderness beyond the churchyard, intersected with dykes and mounds and gates, with scattered cattle feeding on it, was the marshes; and that the low leaden line beyond, was the river; and that the distant savage lair from which the wind was rushing was the sea; and that the small bundle of shivers growing afraid of it all and beginning to cry, was Pip.

Pip's mode of perceiving the 'identity of things' remains metonymic and not metaphoric: churchyard, graves, marshes, river, sea and Pip are conjured up, so to speak, from contextual features. The whole (person, setting) is presented through selected aspects. Pip is evidently more than a 'small bundle of shivers' (he is also a bundle of flesh and bones, thoughts and feelings, social and historical forces), but here his identity is asserted through metonymy, a significant detail offered as his total self at this moment.

In a useful elaboration of Jakobson's theory David Lodge rightly points out that 'context is all-important'. He shows that changing context can change the figures. Here is Lodge's amusing example:

> Those favourite filmic metaphors for sexual intercourse in the prepermissive cinema, skyrockets and waves pounding on the shore, could be disguised as metonymic background if the consummation were taking place on a beach on Independence Day, but would be perceived as overtly metaphorical if it were taking place on Christmas Eve in a city penthouse.

The example warns us against using Jakobson's theory too inflexibly.

Structuralist poetics

Jonathan Culler made the first attempt to assimilate French structuralism to an Anglo-American critical perspective in *Structuralist Poetics* (1975). He accepts the premise that linguistics affords the best model of knowledge for the humanities and social sciences. However, he prefers Noam Chomsky's distinction between 'competence' and 'performance' to Saussure's between '*langue*' and '*parole*'. The notion of 'competence' has the advantage of being closely associated with the *speaker* of a language; Chomsky showed that the starting-point for an understanding of language was the native speaker's ability to produce and comprehend well-formed sentences on the basis of an unconsciously assimilated knowledge of the language system. Culler brings out the significance of this perspective for literary theory: 'the real object of poetics is not the work itself but its intelligibility. One must attempt to explain how it is that works can be understood; the implicit knowledge, the conventions that enable readers to make sense of them, must be formulated. . . .' His main endeavour is to shift the focus from the text to the reader. He believes that we can determine the rules that govern the interpretation of texts, but not those rules that govern the writing of texts. If we begin by establishing a range of interpretations which seem acceptable to skilled readers, we can then establish what norms and procedures led to the interpretations. To put it simply, skilled readers, when faced with a text, seem to know how to make sense of it – to decide what is a possible interpretation and what is not. There seem to be rules governing the sort of sense one might make of the most apparently bizarre literary text. Culler sees the structure not in the system underlying the text but in the system underlying the reader's act of interpretation. To take a bizarre example, here is a three-line poem:

> Night is generally my time for walking;
> It was the best of times, it was the worst of times;
> Concerning the exact year there is no need to be precise.

When we asked a number of colleagues to read it, a variety of interpretative moves were brought into play. One saw a *thematic* link between the lines ('Night', 'time', 'times', 'year'); another tried to envisage a *situation* (psychological or external); another tried to see the poem in terms of formal patternings (a past tense – 'was' – framed by present tenses – 'is'); another saw the lines as adopting three different attitudes to time: specific, contradictory, and non-specific. One colleague recognized that line two comes from the opening of Dickens's *A Tale of Two Cities*, but still accepted it as a 'quotation' which served a function within the poem. We finally had to reveal that the other lines were also from the openings of Dickens's novels (*The Old Curiosity Shop* and *Our Mutual Friend*). What is significant from a Cullerian point of view is not that the readers were caught out but that they followed recognizable procedures for making sense of the lines.

We all know that different readers produce different interpretations, but while this has led some theorists to despair of developing a theory of reading at all, Culler later argues, in *The Pursuit of Signs* (1981), that it is this variety of interpretation which theory has to explain. While readers may differ about meaning, they may well follow the same set of interpretative conventions, as we have seen. One of his examples is New Criticism's basic assumption – that of unity; different readers may discover unity in different ways in a particular poem, but the basic forms of meaning they look for (forms of unity) may be the same. While we may feel no compulsion to perceive the unity of our experiences in the real world, in the case of poems we often expect to find it. However, a variety of interpretations can arise because there are several models of unity which one may bring to bear, and within a particular model there are several ways of applying it to a poem. It can certainly be claimed for Culler's approach that it allows a genuine prospect of a theoretical advance; on the other hand, one can object to his refusal to examine the *content* of particular interpretative moves. For example, he examines two political readings of Blake's 'London' and concludes: 'The accounts different readers offer of what is wrong with the social system will, of course, differ, but the formal interpretative operations that give them a structure to fill in seem very similar.' There is something limiting about a theory which treats interpretative moves as substantial and the content of the moves as immaterial. After all, there may be historical grounds for regarding one way of applying an interpretative model as more valid or plausible than another, while readings of different degrees of plausibility may well share the same interpretative conventions.

As we have noted, Culler holds that a theory of the structure of texts or genres is not possible because there is no underlying form of 'competence' which produces them: all we can talk about is the competence of readers to make sense of what they read. Poets and novelists write on the basis of this competence: they write what can be read. In order to read texts as literature we must possess a 'literary competence', just as we need a more general 'linguistic competence' to make sense of the ordinary linguistic utterances we encounter. We acquire this 'grammar' of literature in educational institutions. Culler recognized that the conventions which apply to one genre will not apply to another, and that the conventions of interpretation will differ from one period to another, but as a structuralist he believed that theory is concerned with static, synchronic systems of meaning and not diachronic historical ones.

The main difficulty about Culler's approach surrounds the question of how systematic one can be about the interpretative rules used by readers. He does not allow for the profound *ideological* differences between readers which may undermine the institutional pressures for conformity in reading practices. It is hard to conceive of a single matrix of rules and conventions which would account for the diversity of interpretations which might be produced in a single period about individual texts. At any rate, we cannot simply take for granted the existence of any entity called a 'skilled reader', defined as the product of the institutions we term 'literary criticism'. However, in his later work – *On Deconstruction: Theory and Criticism after Structuralism* (1983), and more particularly *Framing the Sign* (1988) – Culler moved away from such purist structuralism and towards a more radical questioning of the institutional and ideological foundations of literary competence. In the latter book, for instance, he explores and challenges the powerful tendency in post-war Anglo-American criticism, sustained by its institutionalization in the academy, to promote crypto-religious doctrines and values by way of the authority of 'special texts' in the literary tradition.

Structuralism attracted some literary critics because it promised to introduce a certain rigour and objectivity into the impressionistic realm of literature. This rigour is achieved at a cost. By subordinating *parole* to *langue* the structuralist neglects the specificity of actual texts, and treats them as if they were like the patterns of iron filings produced by an invisible force. The most fruitful applications of the Saussurean model have been those which treat structuralist concepts as *metaphors* – as heuristic devices for analysing texts. Attempts to found a 'scientific' literary structuralism have not produced impressive results. Not only the text but also the author is cancelled as the structuralist places in brackets the actual work and the person who wrote it, in order to isolate the true object of enquiry – the system. In Romantic thought on literature, the author is the sentient being who precedes the work and whose experience nourishes it; the author is the origin of the text, its creator and progenitor. According to structuralists, writing has no origin. Every individual utterance is preceded by language: in this sense, every text is made up of the 'already written'.

By isolating the system, structuralists also cancel history, since the structures discovered are either universal (the universal structures of the human mind) and therefore timeless, or arbitrary segments of a changing and evolving process. Historical questions characteristically are about *change* and *innovation*, whereas structuralism has to exclude them from consideration in order to isolate a system. Therefore structuralists are interested not in the development of the novel or the transition from feudal to Renaissance literary forms, but in the structure of narrative as such and in the system of aesthetics governing a period. Their approach is necessarily static and ahistorical: they are interested in neither the moment of the text's production (its historical context, its formal links with past writing, etc.) nor the moment of its reception or 'reproduction' (the interpretations imposed on it subsequent to its production – see Chapter 3, for theories to do with this).

There is no doubt that structuralism represented a major challenge to the dominant New Critical, Leavisite, and generally humanist types of critical practice. They all presupposed a view of language as something capable of *grasping* reality. Language had been thought of as a reflection of either the writer's mind or the world as seen by the writer. In a sense the writer's language was hardly separable from his or her personality; it expressed the author's very being. However, as we have seen, the Saussurean perspective draws attention to the pre-existence of language. In the beginning was the word, and the word created the text. Instead of saying that an author's language reflects reality, the structuralists argue that the structure of language produces 'reality'. This represents a massive 'demystification' of literature. The source of meaning is no longer the writer's or the reader's *experience* but the operations and oppositions which govern language. Meaning is determined no longer by the individual but by the system which governs the individual.

At the heart of structuralism is a *scientific* ambition to discover the codes, the rules, the systems, which underlie all human social and cultural practices. The disciplines of archaeology and geology are frequently invoked as the models of structuralist enterprise. What we see on the surface are the traces of a deeper history; only by excavating beneath the surface will we discover the geological strata or the ground plans which provide the true explanations for what we see above. One can argue that all science is structuralist in this respect: we see the sun move across the sky, but science discovers the true structure of the heavenly bodies' motion.

Readers who already have some knowledge of the subject will recognize that we have presented only a certain classical type of structuralism in this chapter – one whose proponents suggest that definite sets of relations (oppositions, sequences of functions or propositions, syntactical rules) underlie particular practices, and that individual performances derive from structures in the same way as the shape of landscapes derives from the geological strata beneath. A structure is like a centre or point of origin, and replaces other such centres of origins (the individual or history). However, our discussion of Genette showed that the very definition of an opposition within narrative discourse sets up a *play* of meaning which resists a settled or fixed structuration. For example, the opposition between 'description' and 'narration' tends to encourage a 'privileging' of the second term ('description' is ancillary to 'narration'; narrators describe incidentally, as they narrate). But if we interrogate this now hierarchized pair of terms, we can easily begin to reverse it by showing that 'description' is after all dominant because all narration implies description. In this way we begin to undo the structure which had been centred upon 'narration'. This process of 'deconstruction' which can be set in motion at the very heart of structuralism is one of the major elements in what we call poststructuralism (see Chapter 7).

Selected reading

Key texts

[For later works by and about Roland Barthes, see Chapter 7, 'Selected Reading'.]

Barthes, Roland, *Writing Degree Zero* [1953], trans. by Annette Lavers and Colin Smith (Jonathan Cape, London, 1967).

Barthes, Roland, *Elements of Semiology* [1964], trans. by Annette Lavers and Colin Smith (Jonathan Cape, London, 1967).

Barthes, Roland, *Critical Essays* [1964], trans. by Richard Howard (Northwestern University Press, Evanston, Ill., 1972).

Barthes, Roland, *Selected Writings* [1982, as *A Barthes Reader* (Jonathan Cape)], trans. ed. and intro. by Susan Sontag (Fontana, London, 1983).

Blonsky, Marshall (ed.), *On Signs: A Semiotic Reader* (Basil Blackwell, Oxford, 1985).

Culler, Jonathan, *Structuralist Poetics: Structuralism, Linguistics and the Study of Literature* [1975] (Routledge, London, 2002).

Culler, Jonathan, *The Pursuit of Signs: Semiotics, Literature, Deconstruction* [1981] (Routledge, London, 2001).

Culler, Jonathan, *On Deconstruction: Theory and Criticism After Structuralism* (Routledge, London, 1983).

Culler, Jonathan, *Framing the Sign* (Basil Blackwell, Oxford, 1988).

de Saussure, Ferdinand, *Course in General Linguistics* [1915], trans. by Wade Baskin; intro. by Jonathan Culler (Fontana/Collins, London, 1974).

Genette, Gérard, *Narrative Discourse* [1972], trans. by Jane E. Lewin; foreword by Jonathan Culler (Basil Blackwell, Oxford, 1980).

Genette, Gérard, *Figures of Literary Discourse* [1966], trans. by Alan Sheridan (Basil Blackwell, Oxford, 1982).

Greimas, A. J., *Sémantique Structurale* [1966], trans. by Daniele McDowell, Ronald Schleifer and Alan Velie (University of Nebraska Press, Lincoln, 1983).

Innes, Robert E. (ed.), *Semiotics: An Introductory Reader* (Hutchinson, London, 1986).

Jakobson, Roman, 'Linguistics and Poetics', in T. Sebeok (ed.), *Style in Language* (MIT Press, Cambridge, Mass., 1960), pp. 350–77.

Jakobson, Roman (with Morris Halle), *Fundamentals of Language* [1956; revd edn, 1971] (Mouton, The Hague and Paris, 1975).

Lane, Michael (ed.), *Structuralism: A Reader* (Jonathan Cape, London, 1970).

Lévi-Strauss, Claude, *Structural Anthropology* [1958], trans. [1963] by Claire Jacobson and Brook G. Schoepf (Allen Lane, London, 1968).

Lodge, David, *The Modes of Modern Writing: Metaphor, Metonymy, and the Typology of Modern Literature* (Arnold, London, 1977).

Lotman, Yury, *The Analysis of the Poetic Text* [1972], ed. and trans. by D. Barton Johnson (Ardis, Ann Arbor, 1976).

Propp, Vladimir, *The Morphology of the Folktale* [1958; trans. by Laurence Scott; intro. by Svatava Pirkova-Jakobson] (revd edn, Texas University Press, Austin and London, 1968).

Todorov, Tzvetan, *The Fantastic: A Structural Approach to a Literary Genre* [1970], trans. by Richard Howard (Cornell University Press, Ithaca, 1973).

Todorov, Tzvetan, *The Poetics of Prose* [1971], trans. by Richard Howard (Cornell University Press, Ithaca, 1977). Includes 'The Typology of Detective Fiction'.

Further reading

Connor, Steven, 'Structuralism and Post-Structuralism: From the Centre to the Margin', in *Encyclopedia of Literature and Criticism*, Martin Coyle, Peter Garside, Malcolm Kelsall and John Peck (eds), (Routledge, London, 1990).

Culler, Jonathan, *Saussure* (Fontana, London, 1976).

Harland, Richard, *Superstructuralism: The Philosophy of Structuralism and Post-Structuralism* (Routledge, London, 1987).

Hawkes, Terence, *Structuralism and Semiotics* [1977] (2nd edn, Routledge, London, 2003).

Jackson, Leonard, *The Poverty of Structuralism: Literature and Structuralist Theory* (Longman, London, 1991).

Jameson, Fredric, *The Prison-House of Language: A Critical Account of Structuralism and Russian Formalism* (Princeton University Press, Princeton, NJ and London, 1972).

Lodge, David, *Working with Structuralism* (Routledge, London, 1986).

Rimmon-Kenan, Shlomith, *Narrative Fiction: Contemporary Poetics* (2nd edn, Routledge, London and New York, 2002).

Scholes, Robert, *Structuralism in Literature: An Introduction* (Yale University Press, New Haven and London, 1974).

Sturrock, John, *Structuralism* (2nd edn, with intro. by Jean-Michel Rabaté, Blackwell, Oxford, 2003).

[NB. Most of the subsequent theoretical work related to this area constitutes, by definition, the 'Selected Reading' for '*Post*structuralist theories' (see Chapter 7).]

CHAPTER 5

Marxist theories

Of the kinds of criticism represented in this guide, Marxist criticism has the longest history. Karl Marx himself made important general statements about culture and society in the 1850s. Even so, it is correct to think of Marxist *criticism* as a twentieth-century phenomenon.

The basic tenets of Marxism are no easier to summarize than the essential doctrines of Christianity, but two well-known statements by Marx provide a sufficient point of departure:

> It is not the consciousness of men that determines their being, but, on the contrary, their social being that determines their consciousness.

> The philosophers have only *interpreted* the world in various ways; the point is to *change* it.

Both statements were intentionally provocative. By contradicting widely accepted doctrines, Marx was trying to put people's thought into reverse gear. First, philosophy has been merely airy contemplation; it is time that it engaged with the real world. Secondly, Hegel and his followers in German philosophy have persuaded us that the world is governed by thought, that the process of history is the gradual dialectical unfolding of the laws of Reason, and that material existence is the expression of an immaterial spiritual essence. People have been led to believe that their ideas, their cultural life, their legal systems, and their religions were the creations of human and divine reason, which should be regarded as the unquestioned guides to human life. Marx reverses this formulation and argues that all mental (ideological) systems are the products of real social and economic existence. The material interests of the dominant social class determine how people see human existence, individual and collective. Legal systems, for example, are not the pure manifestations of human or divine reason, but ultimately reflect the interests of the dominant class in particular historical periods.

In one account, Marx described this view in terms of an architectural metaphor: the 'superstructure' (ideology, politics) rests upon the 'base' (socio-economic relations). To say 'rests upon' is not quite the same as saying 'is caused by'. Marx was arguing that what we call 'culture' is not an independent reality but is inseparable from the historical conditions in which human beings create their material lives; the relations of exploitation and domination which govern the social and economic order of a particular phase of human history will in some sense 'determine' the whole cultural life of the society.

In its crudest formulations, the theory is evidently far too mechanical. For example, in *The German Ideology* (1846) Marx and Engels talk about morality, religion and philosophy as 'phantoms formed in the brains of men', which are the 'reflexes and echoes' of 'real life-processes'. On the other hand, in a famous series of letters written in the 1890s Engels insists that, while he and Marx always regarded the economic aspect of society as the *ultimate* determinant of other aspects, they also recognized that art, philosophy and other forms of consciousness are 'relatively autonomous' and possess an independent ability to alter men's existence. After all, how else do Marxists expect to alter people's awareness except by political discourse? Were we to examine the novels of the eighteenth century or the philosophy of the seventeenth century in Europe, we would recognize, if we were Marxists, that these writings arose at particular phases in the development of early capitalist society. The conflict of social classes establishes the ground upon which ideological conflicts arise. Literature and art belong to the ideological sphere, but possess a relationship to ideology which is often less direct even than is found in the case of religious, legal and philosophical systems.

The special status of literature is recognized by Marx in a celebrated passage in his *Grundrisse*, in which the problem of an apparent discrepancy between economic and artistic development is discussed. Greek tragedy is considered a peak of literary development and yet it coincides with a social system and a form of ideology (Greek myth) which are no longer valid for modern society. The problem for Marx was to explain how an art and literature produced in a long-obsolete social organization can still give us aesthetic pleasure and be regarded as 'a standard and unattainable ideal'. He seems to be accepting reluctantly a certain 'timelessness' and 'universality' in literature and art; reluctantly, because this would be a major concession to one of bourgeois ideology's premises. However, it is now possible to see that Marx was simply falling back on received (Hegelian) ways of think-ing about literature and art. Our discussion of Mukařovský in Chapter 2 established what can now be regarded as a Marxist view: that canons of great literature are socially generated. The 'greatness' of Greek tragedy is not a universal and unchanging fact of existence, but a *value* which must be reproduced from generation to generation.

Even if we reject a privileged status for literature, there remains the question of how far literature's historical development is independent of historical development in general. In his attack on the Russian Formalists in *Literature and Revolution*, Trotsky conceded that literature had its own principles and rules. 'Artistic creation', he admits, is 'a changing and a transformation of reality in accordance with the peculiar laws of art.' He still insists that the 'reality' remains the crucial factor and not the formal games which writers play. Nevertheless, his remarks point forward to a continuing debate in Marxist criticism about the relative importance of literary form and ideological content in literary works.

Soviet Socialist Realism

Marxist criticism written in the West has often been adventurous and exhil-arating, but Socialist Realism, as the official Communist 'artistic method', seemed drab and blinkered to Western readers. The doctrines expounded by the Union of Soviet Writers (1932–4) appealed to certain of Lenin's pre-Revolutionary statements as these were interpreted during the 1920s. The theory addressed certain major questions about the evolution of literature, its reflection of class relations and its function in society.

As we have seen, when the Revolution of 1917 encouraged the Formal-ists to continue developing a revolutionary theory of art, there emerged at the same time an orthodox Communist view, which frowned upon formalism and regarded the nineteenth-century tradition of Russian realism as the only suitable foundation for the aesthetics of the new Communist society. The 'modernist' revolutions in European art, music and literature which occurred around 1910 (Picasso, Stravinsky, Schoenberg, Joyce, Woolf, T. S. Eliot) were to be regarded by Soviet critics as the decad-ent products of late capitalist society. The modernist rejection of traditional realism paradoxically left Socialist Realism as the leading custodian of bour-geois aesthetics. In Tom Stoppard's play *Travesties* (1975), the Dadaist poet Tzara is made to complain that 'the odd thing about revolution is that the further left you go politically, the more bourgeois they like their art'. The combination of nineteenth-century aesthetics and revolutionary politics remained the essential recipe of Soviet theory.

The principle of *partinost'* (commitment to the working-class cause of the Party) is derived almost exclusively from Lenin's essay 'Party Organisation and Party Literature' (1905), and there remains some doubt about Lenin's intentions in arguing that, while all writers were free to write what they liked, they could not expect to be published in Party journals unless they were committed to the Party's political line. While this was a reasonable demand to make in the precarious circumstances of 1905, it took on a much more despotic significance after the Revolution, when the Party controlled publishing.

The quality of *narodnost'* ('popularity') is central to both the aesthetics and the politics. A work of art of any period achieves this quality by expressing a high level of social awareness, revealing a sense of the true social conditions and feelings of a particular epoch. It will also possess a 'progressive' outlook, glimpsing the developments of the future in the lineaments of the present, and giving a sense of the ideal possibilities of social development from the point of view of the mass of working people. In the 1844 'Paris Manuscripts', Marx argues that the capitalist division of labour destroyed an earlier phase of human history in which artistic and spiritual life were inseparable from the processes of material existence, and craftsmen still worked with a sense of beauty. The separation of mental and manual work dissolved the organic unity of spiritual and material activities, with the result that the masses were forced to produce commodities without the joy of creative engagement in their work. Only folk art survived as the people's art. The appreciation of high art was professionalized, dominated by the market economy and limited to a privileged section of the ruling class. The truly 'popular' art of socialist societies, argued Soviet critics, will be accessible to the masses and will restore their lost wholeness of being.

The theory of the class nature of art (*klassovost'*) is a complex one. In the writings of Marx, Engels and the Soviet tradition, there is a double emphasis – on the writer's commitment or class interests on the one hand, and the social realism of the writer's work on the other. Only the crudest forms of Socialist Realism treat the class nature of art as a simple matter of the writer's explicit class allegiance. In his letter (1888) to Margaret Harkness on her novel *City Girl*, Engels praises her for not writing an explicitly socialist novel. He argues that Balzac, a reactionary supporter of the Bourbon dynasty, provides a more penetrating account of French society in all its economic details than 'all the professed historians, economists and statisticians of the period together'. Balzac's insights into the downfall of the nobility and the rise of the bourgeoisie compelled him to 'go against his own class sympathies and political prejudices'. Realism transcends class sympathies. This argument was to have a powerful influence not only on the theory of Socialist Realism but on later Marxist criticism.

Socialist Realism was considered to be a continuation and development of bourgeois realism at a higher level. Bourgeois writers are judged not according to their class origins or explicit political commitment, but by the extent to which their writings reveal insights into the social developments of their time. The Soviet hostility to modernist novels can best be understood in this context. Karl Radek's contribution to the Soviet Writers' Congress in 1934 posed the choice 'James Joyce or Socialist Realism?' During a discussion Radek directed a vitriolic attack against another Communist delegate, Herzfelde, who had defended Joyce as a great writer. Radek regards Joyce's experimental technique and his 'petty bourgeois' content as all of a piece. Joyce's preoccupation with the sordid inner life of a trivial individual indicates his profound unawareness of the larger historical forces at work in modern times. For Joyce 'the whole world lies between a cupboard of medieval books, a brothel and a pot house'. He concludes, 'if I were to write novels, I would learn how to write them from Tolstoy and Balzac, not from Joyce.'

This admiration for nineteenth-century realism was understandable. Balzac, Dickens, George Eliot, Stendhal and others developed a sophisticated literary form which explores the individual's involvement in the complex network of social relations. Modernist writers abandoned this project and began to reflect a more fragmented image of the world, which was often pessimistic and introverted, exploring the alienated individual consciousness in retreat from the 'nightmare of history' which is modern society. Nothing could be further from the 'revolutionary romanticism' of the Soviet school, which wanted to project a heroic image. Andrey Zhdanov, who gave the keynote speech at the 1934 Congress, reminded writers that Stalin had called upon them to be the 'engineers of the human soul'. At this stage, the political demands upon writers became brutally insistent. Engels was clearly doubtful of the value of overly committed writing, but Zhdanov dismissed all such doubts: 'Yes, Soviet literature is tendentious, for in epochs of class struggle there is not and cannot be a literature which is not class literature, not tendentious, allegedly non-political.'

Lukács and Brecht

It is appropriate to consider next the first major Marxist critic, Georg Lukács, since his work is inseparable from orthodox Socialist Realism, and then the views of his 'opponent' in their debate about realism, the dramatist/theorist Bertolt Brecht. It can be argued that Lukács anticipated some of the Soviet doctrines, but, at any rate, he developed the realist approach with great subtlety. He inaugurated a distinctively Hegelian style of Marxist thought, treating literary works as reflections of an unfolding system. A realist work must reveal the underlying pattern of contradictions in a social order. His view is Marxist in its insistence on the material and historical nature of the structure of society.

Lukács' use of the term 'reflection' is characteristic of his work as a whole. Rejecting the 'naturalism' of the then recent European novel, he returns to the old realist view that the novel reflects reality, not by rendering its mere surface appearance, but by giving us 'a truer, more complete, more vivid and more dynamic reflection of reality'. To 'reflect' is 'to frame a mental structure' transposed into words. People ordinarily possess a reflection of reality, a consciousness not merely of objects but of human nature and social relationships. Lukács would say that a reflection may be more or less concrete. A novel may conduct a reader 'towards a more concrete insight into reality', which transcends a merely common-sense apprehension of things. A literary work reflects not individual phenomena in isolation, but 'the full process of life'. However, the reader is always aware that the work is not itself reality but rather 'a special form of reflecting reality'.

A 'correct' reflection of reality, therefore, according to Lukács, involves more than the mere rendering of external appearances. Interestingly, his view of reflection undermines at the same time both naturalism and modernism. A randomly presented sequence of images may be interpreted either as an *objective* and impartial reflection of reality (as Zola and the other exponents of 'naturalism' might be taken as saying) or as a purely *subjective* impression of reality (as Joyce and Virginia Woolf seem to show). The randomness can be seen as a property either of reality or of perception. Either way, Lukács rejects such merely 'photographic' representation. Instead, he describes the truly realistic work which gives us a sense of the 'artistic necessity' of the images presented; they possess an 'intensive totality' which corresponds to the 'extensive totality' of the world itself. Reality is not a mere flux, a mechanical collision of fragments, but possesses an 'order', which the novelist renders in an 'intensive' form. The writer does not impose an abstract order upon the world, but rather presents the reader with an image of the richness and complexity of life from which emerges a sense of the order within the complexity and subtlety of lived experience. This will be achieved if all the contradictions and tensions of social existence are realized in a formal whole.

Lukács is able to insist on the principle of underlying order and structure because the Marxist tradition borrowed from Hegel the 'dialectical' view of history. Development in history is not random or chaotic, nor is it a straightforward linear progression, but rather a dialectical development. In every social organization, the prevailing mode of production gives rise to inner contradictions which are expressed in class struggle. Capitalism developed by destroying the feudal mode of production and replacing it with one based on absolute private property and the market, which made possible far higher levels of productivity (commodity production). However, while the process of production was increasingly socialized, the ownership of the means of production became concentrated in private hands. Workers who had owned their looms or tools eventually had nothing to sell but their labour. The inherent contradiction is expressed in the conflict of interest between capitalist and worker. The private accumulation of capital was the foundation of factory working, and thus the contradiction (privatization/socialization) is a necessary unity, which is central to the nature of the capitalist mode of production. The 'dialectical' resolution of the contradiction is always already implied in the contradiction itself: if people are to re-establish control over their labour power, the ownership of the means of production must also be socialized. This brief excursus is intended to show how Lukács' whole view of realism is shaped by the nineteenth-century inheritance of Marxism.

In a series of brilliant works, especially *The Historical Novel* (1937) and *Studies in European Realism* (1950), Lukács refines and extends his theory, and in *The Meaning of Contemporary Realism* (1957) he advances the Communist attack on modernism. He refuses to deny Joyce the status of a true artist, but asks us to reject his view of history, and especially the way in which Joyce's 'static' view of events is reflected in an epic structure which is itself essentially static. For Lukács, this failure to perceive human existence as part of a dynamic historical environment infects the whole of contemporary modernism, as reflected in the works of writers such as Kafka, Beckett and Faulkner. These writers, he argues, are preoccupied with formal experiment – with montage, inner monologues, the technique of 'stream of consciousness', the use of reportage, diaries, etc. All this formalistic virtuosity is the result of a narrow concern for subjective impressions, a concern which itself stems from the advanced individualism of late capitalism. Instead of an objective realism we have an *angst*-ridden vision of the world. The fullness of history and its social processes are narrowed down to the bleak inner history of absurd existences. This 'attenuation of actuality' is contrasted to the dynamic and developmental view of society to be found in the great nineteenth-century novelists and in their latter-day heirs like Thomas Mann, who, though not 'socialist', achieve a genuinely 'Critical Realism'.

By divorcing the individual from the outer world of objective reality, the modernist writer, in Lukács' view, is compelled to see the inner life of characters as 'a sinister, inexplicable flux', which ultimately also takes on a timeless static quality. Lukács seems unable to perceive that in rendering the impoverished and alienated existence of modern subjects some modern writers achieve a kind of realism, or at any rate develop new literary forms and techniques which articulate modern reality. Insisting on the reactionary nature of modernist *ideology*, he refused to recognize the *literary* possibilities of modernist writings. Because he thought the *content* of modernism was reactionary, he treated modernist *form* as equally unacceptable. During his brief stay in Berlin during the early 1930s, he found himself attacking the use of modernist techniques of montage and reportage in the work of fellow radicals, including the outstanding dramatist Bertolt Brecht.

Bertolt Brecht's early plays were radical, anarchistic and anti-bourgeois, but not anti-capitalist. After reading Marx in about 1926, his youthful iconoclasm was converted to conscious political commitment, although he always remained a maverick and never a Party man. Around 1930 he was writing the so-called *Lehrstücke*, didactic plays intended for working-class audiences, but he was forced to leave Germany when the Nazis took power in 1933. He wrote his major plays in exile, mainly in Scandinavian countries. Later, in America, he was brought before the McCarthy Committee for un-American Activities and finally settled in East Germany in 1949. He had trouble too with the Stalinist authorities of the GDR, who regarded him as both an asset and a liability.

His opposition to Socialist Realism certainly offended the East German authorities. His best-known theatrical device, the alienation effect (*Verfremdungseffekt*), recalls the Russian Formalists' concept of 'defamiliarization' (see Chapter 2, pp. 32–4). Socialist Realism favoured realistic illusion, formal unity and 'positive' heroes. He called *his* theory of realism 'anti-Aristotelian', a covert way of attacking the theory of his opponents. Aristotle emphasized the universality and unity of the tragic action, and the identification of audience and hero in empathy which produces a 'catharsis' of emotions. Brecht rejected the entire tradition of 'Aristotelian' theatre. The dramatist should avoid a smoothly interconnected plot and any sense of inevitability or universality. The facts of social injustice needed to be presented as if they were shockingly unnatural and totally surprising.

It is all too easy to regard 'the price of bread, the lack of work, the declara-tion of war as if they were phenomena of nature: earthquakes or floods', rather than as the results of exploitative human agency.

To avoid lulling the audience into a state of passive acceptance, the illusion of reality must be shattered by the use of the alienation effect. The actors must not lose themselves in their roles or seek to promote a purely empathic audience identification. They must present a role to the audience as both recognizable and unfamiliar, so that a process of critical assessment can be set in motion. The situation, emotions and dilemmas of the char-acters must be understood from the outside and presented as strange and problematic. This is not to say that actors should avoid the use of emotion, but only the resort to empathy. This is achieved by 'baring the device', to use the Formalist term (see Chapter 2, pp. 33–4). The use of gesture is an important way of externalizing a character's emotions. Gesture or action is studied and rehearsed as a device for conveying in a striking way the specific social meaning of a role. One might contrast this with the Stanislavskian 'method acting', which encourages total identification of actor and role. Improvisation rather than calculation is encouraged in order to create a sense of 'spontaneity' and individuality. This foregrounding of a character's inner life allows its social meaning to evaporate. The gestures of a Marlon Brando or a James Dean are personal and idiosyncratic, while a 'Brechtian' actor (for example Peter Lorre or Jack Nicholson) performs rather like a clown or mimic, using diagrammatic gestures which *indicate* rather than reveal. In any case, Brecht's plays, in which the 'heroes' are so often ordinary, tough and unscrupulous, do not encourage the cult of personality. Mother Courage, Asdak and Sweik are boldly outlined on an 'epic' canvas: they are remarkably dynamic social beings, but have no focused 'inner' life.

Brecht rejected the kind of formal unity admired by Lukács. First, Brecht's 'epic' theatre, unlike Aristotle's tragic theatre, is composed of loosely linked episodes of the kind to be found in Shakespeare's history plays and eighteenth-century picaresque novels. There are no artificial constraints of time and place, and no 'well-made' plots. Contemporary in-spiration came from the cinema (Charlie Chaplin, Buster Keaton, Eisenstein) and modernist fiction (Joyce and Dos Passos). Second, Brecht believed that no model of good form could remain in force indefinitely; there are no 'eternal aesthetic laws'. To capture the living force of reality the writer must be willing to make use of every conceivable formal device, old and new: 'We shall take care not to ascribe realism to a particular historical form of novel belonging to a particular period, Balzac's or Tolstoy's, for instance, so as to set up purely formal and literary criteria of realism.' He considered

Lukács' desire to enshrine a particular literary form as the only true model for realism to be a dangerous kind of formalism. Brecht would have been the first to admit that, if his own 'alienation effect' were to become a formula for realism, it would cease to be effective. If we copy other realists' methods, we cease to be realists ourselves: 'Methods wear out, stimuli fail. New problems loom up and demand new techniques. Reality alters; to represent it the means of representation must alter too.' These remarks express clearly Brecht's undogmatic and experimental view of aesthetics. However, there is nothing in the least 'liberal' in his rejection of orthodoxy; his restless search for new ways of shaking audiences out of their complacent passivity into active engagement was motivated by a dedicated political commitment to unmasking every new disguise used by the deviously protean capitalist system.

The Frankfurt School and After: Adorno and Benjamin

While Brecht and Lukács held conflicting views of realism, the Frankfurt School of Marxist aesthetics rejected realism altogether. The Institute for Social Research at Frankfurt practised what it called 'Critical Theory', which was a wide-ranging form of social analysis grounded in Hegelian Marxism and including Freudian elements. The leading figures in philosophy and aesthetics were Max Horkheimer, Theodor Adorno and Herbert Marcuse. Exiled in 1933, the Institute was relocated in New York, but finally returned to Frankfurt in 1950 under Adorno and Horkheimer. They regarded the social system, in Hegelian fashion, as a totality in which all the aspects reflected the same essence. Their analysis of modern culture was influenced by the experience of fascism which had achieved hegemonic dominance at every level of social existence in Germany. In America they saw a similar 'one-dimensional' quality in the mass culture and the permeation of every aspect of life by commercialism.

Art and literature have a privileged place in Frankfurt thinking. In an early initiative in critical theory, Marcuse proposed the notion of 'affirmative culture', by which he sought to register the dialectical nature of culture as conformist (in its quietist cultivation of inner fulfilment) but also critical (in so far as it bore in its very form the image of an undamaged existence). Marcuse, while always insisting on the negative, transcendent power of 'the aesthetic dimension', adapted the revolutionary commitment of his youth to changed social and cultural circumstances. For the outstanding exponent of Critical Theory, Adorno, art – with philosophy – was the only theatre of resistance to 'the administered universe' of the twentieth century. Adorno criticized Lukács' view of realism, arguing that great literature does not, nor needs to, directly address social reality. In Adorno's view, art's detachment from dominant reality gives it its special significance and power. Modernist writings are particularly distanced from the reality to which they allude and this allows them the space to critique conformist trends in their world. While popular art forms are forced to collude with the economic system which shapes them, 'autonomous' works have the power to 'negate' the reality to which they relate. Because modernist texts reflect the alienated inner lives of individuals, Lukács attacked them as 'decadent' embodiments of late capitalist society and evidence of the writers' inability to transcend the atomistic and fragmented worlds in which they were compelled to live. Adorno argues that art cannot simply reflect the social system, but acts within that reality as an irritant which produces an indirect sort of knowledge: 'Art is the negative knowledge of the actual world.' This can be achieved, he believed, by writing 'difficult' experimental texts and not directly polemical or critical works – a position which not only separated him from Lukács but governed his view of the limitations of Brecht's art and ideas.

In Frankfurt School thinking, literary works did not aspire to the formal coherence and progressive content valued by Lukács, but sought rather, by distancing and estranging reality, to prevent the easy absorption of new insights or the co-option of the art work by consumer society. Modernists try to disrupt and fragment the picture of modern life rather than master its dehumanizing mechanisms. Lukács could see only symptoms of decay in this kind of art and could not recognize its power to *reveal* and 'defamiliarize' from its own antagonistic, non-conformist position. Proust's use of *monologue intérieur* does not just reflect an alienated individualism, but both grasps a 'truth' about modern society (the alienation of the individual) and enables us to see that the alienation is part of an objective social reality. In a complex essay on Samuel Beckett's *Endgame* Adorno meditates on the ways in which Beckett uses form to evoke the emptiness of modern culture. Despite the catastrophes and degradations of twentieth-century history, the play suggests, we persist in behaving as if nothing has changed. We persist in our foolish belief in the old truths of the unity and substantiality of the individual or the meaningfulness of language. The play presents characters who possess only the hollow shells of individuality and the fragmented clichés of a language. The absurd discontinuities of discourse, the pared-down characterization, and plotlessness, all contribute to the aesthetic effect of distancing the reality to which the play alludes, thereby giving us a 'negative' knowledge of modern society.

Marx believed that he had extracted the 'rational kernel' from the 'mystical shell' of Hegel's dialectic. What survives is the dialectical method of understanding the real processes of human history. The Frankfurt School's work has much of the authentic Hegelian subtlety in dialectical thought. The meaning of dialectic in the tradition of Hegel can be summed up as 'the development which arises from the resolution of contradictions inherent in a particular aspect of reality'. Adorno's *Philosophy of Modern Music*, for example, develops a dialectical account of the composer Schoenberg. The composer's 'atonal' revolution arose in a historical context in which the extreme commercialization of culture destroys the listener's ability to appreciate the formal unity of a classical work. The commercial exploitation of artistic techniques in cinema, advertising, popular music and so on forces the composer to respond by producing a shattered and fragmented music, in which the very grammar of musical language (tonality) is denied. Each individual note is cut off and cannot be resolved into meaning by the surrounding context. Adorno describes the content of this 'atonal' music in the language of psychoanalysis: the painfully isolated notes express bodily impulses from the unconscious. The new form is related to the individual's loss of conscious control in modern society. By allowing the expression of violent unconscious impulses, Schoenberg's music evades the censor, reason. The dialectic is completed when this new system is related to the new totalitarian organization of late capitalist imperialism, in which the autonomy of the individual is lost in the massive and monolithic market-system. That is to say, the music is at once a rebellion against a one-dimensional society and also a symptom of an inescapable loss of freedom. Adorno's dialectical view of the position of the arts under late capitalism has made his work a compelling influence in later debates on postmodern arts and society (Jameson, 1991) as well as on a movement such as the 'New Aestheticism' (see 'Conclusion' here), which sees itself as advancing beyond the commonplaces of postmodernism. Adorno continues in these contexts to inspire a belief in an uncompromising, critical and semi-autonomous literature and culture.

Walter Benjamin – a friend of Adorno but also of Brecht (to whom Adorno was antipathetic by temperament and outlook) and of Gershom Sholem (the great student of Judaic mysticism, who looked askance upon his old companion's conversion to materialist thought) – was the most idiosyncratic Marxist thinker of his generation. His association with the Frankfurt School was fleeting. He depended on its journal for a small income but had also to contend with Adorno's editorial strictures upon his ideas and writing. His early 'academic' criticism, devoted to Goethe and to German Baroque drama, is legendarily obscure, and much of his cultural journalism is tantalizingly enigmatic. His life's work and major achievement was the 'Arcades Project', a fascinating exploration of the emerging commercial culture of Paris, 'capital of the nineteenth century', which remained unfinished at his death (but was published in translation in the late 1990s). He was among the earliest and best interpreters of Brecht's theatre and a bold, intransigently materialist theorist of the new means of artistic production, yet his last essay, the 'Theses on the Philosophy of History', combined its Marxist dialectical materialism with the idiom of messianic theology. Benjamin's best-known essay, 'The Work of Art in the Age of Mechanical Reproduction', argues that modern technical innovations (above all, photography and cinema) have profoundly altered the status of the 'work of art'. Once, artistic works had an 'aura' deriving from their uniqueness. This was especially true of the visual arts, but was true also of literature. The new media shatter the quasi-religious ethos of the supposed uniquely original (as if 'sacred') work of art. To a greater and greater extent the *reproduction* of art objects (by means of photography or radio transmission) means that they are actually designed for reproducibility; and in the emergence of cinema we discover 'copies' without an 'original'. Here, Benjamin argued, was the technical basis of a new ethos of artistic production and consumption, one in which awe and deference would give way to a posture of analysis and relaxed expertise, in which art, no longer steeped in 'ritual', would be opened to politics. Arguments such as these on reproduction and the loss of originality have been taken up in debates on postmodernism and provide a materialist gloss on its themes of imitation and simulation. Adorno commented on the element of wishful thinking in Benjamin's essay, yet the latter remains exemplary in its attention to the specific historical and cultural effect of new technologies.

Benjamin's companion essay, 'The Author as Producer', on the politics of artistic practice, was written principally with Bertolt Brecht's theatre in mind, and has made its own distinctive, but probably now less regarded, contribution. Here Benjamin argued that while new technology might have revolutionary potential, there was no guarantee of its revolutionary effect. It was necessary for socialist writers and artists to realize this potential in their work. Benjamin rejects here too the idea that revolutionary art is achieved by attending to the correct subject-matter. (In this respect, his views are pitched against the realist orthodoxy of the day.) Instead of being concerned with a work of art's position within the social and economic relations of its time, he asks the question: what is 'the function of a work within the literary production relations of its time'? The artist needs to revolutionize the *artistic* forces of production of his or her time. And this is a matter of *technique*, although the correct technique will arise in response to a complex historical combination of social and technical changes.

A further, important, and highly influential concept – that of the urban *flaneur* (the stroller or window-shopper) – is derived from Benjamin's studies of the nineteenth-century poet Charles Baudelaire, which had formed part of the Arcades Project. Later commentary, by Janet Wolff, Elizabeth Wilson and others, has introduced the vital aspect of gender (in the figure of the female '*flaneuse*') into considerations of urban life and identity under modernity. In Literary Studies, Virginia Woolf has been a case in point. Subsequent criticism has also combined this with an interest in new technologies once more (the cinema and Internet, see Friedberg, 1994, and Donald, 2005) and with insights on urban 'psychogeography' derived from the French Situationist movement of the 1960s. A writer such as the London-based novelist-journalist Iain Sinclair draws eclectically on these sources. Critical trends in 'cultural' or 'literary geography' (Soja, 1996; Donald, 1999; Thacker, 2003) have also taken up and developed Benjamin's earlier insights on the modern city, often along with those of Michel Foucault (see Chapter 7) on space and place. Elsewhere, the publication through the 1990s of Benjamin's correspondence and other writings testifies to the continuing interest of his work across a wide field in the Humanities and Social Sciences.

'Structuralist' Marxism: Goldmann, Althusser, Macherey

The intellectual life of Europe during the 1960s was dominated by structuralism (see Chapter 4). Marxist criticism was not unaffected by this intellectual environment. Both traditions believe that individuals cannot be understood apart from their social existence. Marxists believe that individuals are 'bearers' of positions in the social system and not free agents. Structuralists consider that individual actions and utterances have no meaning apart from the signifying systems which generate them. However, structuralists tend to regard these underlying structures as timeless and self-regulating systems, but Marxists see them as historical, changeable and fraught with contradictions.

Lucien Goldmann, a Romanian theorist based in France, rejected the idea that texts are creations of individual genius and argued that they are based upon 'trans-individual mental structures' belonging to particular groups (or classes). These 'world-views' are perpetually being constructed and dissolved by social groups as they adjust their mental image of the world in response to the changing reality before them. Such mental images usually remain ill-defined and half-realized in the consciousness of social agents, but great writers are able to crystallize world-views in a lucid and coherent form.

Goldmann's celebrated *Le Dieu Caché* (*The Hidden God*) establishes connections between Racine's tragedies, Pascal's philosophy, a French religious movement (Jansenism) and a social group (the *noblesse de la robe*). The Jansenist world-view is tragic: it sees the individual as divided between a hopelessly sinful world and a God who is absent. God has abandoned the world but still imposes an absolute authority upon the believer. The individual is driven into an extreme and tragic solitude. The underlying structure of relationships in Racine's tragedies expresses the Jansenist predicament, which in turn can be related to the decline of the *noblesse de la robe*, a class of court officials who were becoming increasingly isolated and powerless as the absolute monarchy withdrew its financial support. The 'manifest' content of the tragedies appears to have no connection with Jansenism, but at a deeper structural level they share the same form: 'the tragic hero, equidistant from God and from the world, is *radically alone*'. In other words, the expressive relationship between social class and literary text was registered not in 'reflected' content but in a parallelism of form, or 'homology'. By means of the concept of homology, Goldmann was able to think beyond the confines of the dogmatic realist tradition (though he retained his admiration for Lukács' earlier work) and to develop a distinctive variety of Marxist literary and cultural analysis to which he gave the name 'genetic structuralism'.

His later work, especially *Pour une sociologie du roman* (1964), appears to resemble that of the Frankfurt School by focusing on the 'homology' between the structure of the modern novel and the structure of the market economy. He argues that by about 1910 the transition from the 'heroic' age of liberal capitalism to its imperialist phase was well under way. As a consequence the importance of the individual within economic life was drastically reduced. Finally, in the post-1945 period the regulation and management of economic systems by the state and by corporations brought to its fullest development that tendency which Lukács called 'reification' (this refers to the reduction of value to exchange value and the domination of the human world by objects). In the classic novel, objects only had significance in relation to individuals, but in the novels of Sartre, Kafka and Robbe-Grillet, the world of objects begins to displace the individual. This final stage of Goldmann's writing depended upon a rather crude model of 'superstructure' and 'base', according to which literary structures simply correspond to economic structures. It avoids the pessimism of the Frankfurt School, but lacks their rich dialectical insights.

Louis Althusser, the French Marxist philosopher, has had a major influence on Marxist literary theory especially in France and Britain. His work is clearly related to structuralism and has been claimed for poststructuralism (see also Chapter 7, p. 148). He rejects the Hegelian revival within Marxist philosophy, and argues that Marx's real contribution to knowledge stems from his 'break' with Hegel. He criticizes Hegel's account of 'totality', according to which the essence of the whole is expressed in all its parts. Althusser avoids terms such as 'social system' and 'order', because they suggest a structure with a centre which determines the form of all its emanations. Instead he talks of the 'social formation', which he regards as a 'decentred' structure. Unlike a living organism this structure has no governing principle, no originating seed, no overall unity. The implications of this view are arresting. The various elements (or 'levels') within the social formation are not treated as reflections of one essential level (the economic level for Marxists): the levels possess a 'relative autonomy', and are ultimately determined by the economic level only 'in the last instance' (this complex formulation derives from Engels). The social formation is a structure in which the various levels exist in complex relations of inner contradiction and mutual conflict; its contradictions are never 'simple' but 'overdetermined' in nature. This structure of contradictions may be dominated at any given stage by one or other of the levels, but which level it is to be is itself 'determined' ultimately by the economic level. For example, as Marx himself observed, in feudal social formations religion is structurally dominant, but this does not mean that religion is the essence or centre of the structure. Its leading role is itself determined by the economic level, though not directly.

Althusser refuses to treat art as simply a form of ideology. In 'A Letter on Art', he locates it somewhere between ideology and scientific knowledge. A great work of literature does not give us a properly conceptual understanding of reality but neither does it merely express the ideology of a particular class. He draws upon Engels' arguments about Balzac (see above, pp. 85–6) and declares that art 'makes us *see*', in a distanced way, 'the ideology from which it is born, in which it bathes, from which it detaches itself as art, and to which it alludes'. Althusser defines ideology as 'a representation of the imaginary relationship of individuals to their real conditions of existence'. The imaginary consciousness helps us to make sense of the world but also masks or represses our real relationship to it. For example, the ideology of 'freedom' promotes the belief in the freedom of all, including labourers, but it masks the real relations of liberal capitalist economy. A dominant system of ideology is accepted as a common-sense view of things by the dominated classes and thus the interests of the dominant class are secured. Art, however, achieves 'a retreat' (a fictional distance deriving from its formal composition) from the very ideology which feeds it. In this way a major literary work can transcend and critique the ideology in which it is nevertheless 'bathed'.

Pierre Macherey's *A Theory of Literary Production* (1966) was the first extended Althusserian discussion of art and ideology. Rather than treat the text as a 'creation' or a self-contained artefact, he regards it as a 'production' in which disparate materials are worked over and changed in the process. These materials are not 'free implements' to be used consciously to create a controlled and unified work of art. Irrespective of prevailing aesthetic norms and authorial intentions, the text, in working the pre-given materials, is never fully 'aware of what it is doing'. It has, so to speak, an 'unconscious' – a notion explored in terms of a text's repressed historical narrative in Fredric Jameson's *The Political Unconscious* (1981; see below, pp. 106–7). In effect, this is an account of the way ideology enters and deforms a would-be unified text. Ideology is normally lived as if it were totally natural, as if its imaginary and fluid discourse gives a perfect and unified explanation of reality. Once it is worked into a text, all its contradictions and gaps are exposed. The realist writer intends to unify all the elements in the text, but the work that goes on in the textual process inevitably produces certain lapses and omissions which correspond to the incoherence of the ideological discourse it uses: 'for in order to say anything, there are other things *which must not be said*'. The literary critic is not concerned to show how all the parts of the work fit together, or to harmonize and smooth over any apparent contradictions. Like a psychoanalyst, the critic attends to the text's unconscious – to what is unspoken and inevitably repressed.

How would this approach work? Consider Defoe's novel, *Moll Flanders*. In the early eighteenth century, bourgeois ideology smoothed over the contradictions between moral and economic requirements; that is, between on the one hand a providential view of human life which requires the deferment of immediate gratification for a long-term gain, and on the other an economic individualism which drains all value from human relations and fixes it solely in commodities. Set to work in *Moll Flanders* this ideological discourse is represented so that its contradictions are exposed. The operation of literary form on ideology produces this effect of incoherence. The literary use of Moll as narrator itself involves a double perspective. She tells her story prospectively and retrospectively: she is both a participant who relishes her selfish life as prostitute and thief, and a moralizer who relates her sinful life as a warning to others. The two perspectives are symbolically merged in the episode of Moll's successful business speculation in Virginia where she founds her enterprise upon the ill-gotten gains which were kept secured during her Newgate imprisonment. This economic success is *also* her reward for repenting of her evil life. In this way literary form 'congeals' the fluid discourse of ideology: by giving it formal substance the text shows up the flaws and contradictions in the ideology it uses. The writer does not *intend* this effect since it is produced so to speak 'unconsciously' by the text. The critic will therefore seek to disclose the rifts and silences (the 'not-said' of the text) in what Althusser termed a 'symptomatic' reading which reveals the limits of its determining ideology.

In a later, short – but, in its period, highly influential – study, 'On Literature as an Ideological Form' (1978), written with Etienne Balibar, Macherey departed more radically from the traditional notion of literature which the Frankfurt School defended and Althusser in part still entertained. The culture of 'the literary' was now rethought as a key practice within the education system, where it served to reproduce class-domination in language. This lent an expanded and more fully materialist notion of ideology to literary studies, understood as itself located within the education system which Althusser (1971) had named as one of the so-called 'Ideological State Apparatuses'.

'New Left' Marxism: Williams, Eagleton, Jameson

Marxist theory in the United States has been dominated by the Hegelian inheritance of the Frankfurt School (the journal *Telos* was the standard-bearer of this tradition). The revival of Marxist criticism in Britain (in decline since the 1930s) was fuelled by the 1968 'troubles' and by the ensuing influx of continental ideas (*New Left Review* was an important channel). A major theorist emerged in response to the specific conditions at work in each country. Fredric Jameson's *Marxism and Form* (1971) and *The Prison-House of Language* (1972) displayed dialectical skills worthy of a Marxist-Hegelian philosopher. Terry Eagleton's *Criticism and Ideology* (1976) built upon the anti-Hegelian Marxism of Althusser and Macherey, and produced an impressive critique of the British critical tradition and a radical revaluation of the development of the English novel. Later, Jameson and Eagleton were to respond inventively to the challenge of poststructuralism and postmodernism (see the section on 'Postmodernism and Marxism' in Chapter 8. For discussion of other subsequent inflections of Marxist critical theory, see the section on Marxist Feminism in Chapter 6 and that on New Historicism and Cultural Materialism in Chapter 7).

There was, of course, an outstanding presence already at work in the field: Raymond Williams. Beginning with a critical reassessment of the main English tradition of critical cultural thought (*Culture and Society 1780–1950*, 1958), Williams embarked on a radical theoretical construction of the whole domain of social meaning – 'culture' as 'a whole way of life'. This general perspective was developed in particular studies of drama, the novel, television, and historical semantics as well as further theoretical work. Williams's general project – the study of all forms of signification in their actual conditions of production – was always emphatically historical and materialist. Yet it was only in 1977, with the publication of a developed statement of his theoretical position, that he began to characterize his work as 'Marxist' (*Marxism and Literature*, 1977). What most importantly defined this position was the use of the concept of 'hegemony' developed by the Italian philosopher and political activist Antonio Gramsci (1891–1937). Hegemony, Williams explained, related the 'whole social process' to structures of power and influence and thus to patterns of domination, subordination and opposition. It went beyond the formal operation of ideology and beyond the idea of social control as manipulation or indoctrination to see relations of power as 'in effect a saturation of the whole procees of living', as operating by 'consent' and at such a depth that the hegemonic order of a class society passes as 'common sense' and 'the way things are'. As Williams puts it, hegemony 'constitutes a sense of reality for most people in the society . . . a "culture", but a culture which has to be seen as the lived dominance and subordination of particular classes'. This thinking placed Williams decisively in a Marxist tradition, if in one which rejected abstract, delimiting notions of ideology and materialism. In fact he had long since rejected the Communist orthodoxy of his student days. The powerful but idiosyncratic formulations he subsequently developed at a distance from available Marxist tenets in his earlier writings were sometimes construed by a younger generation of Marxists as a sign of theoretical and political weakness, and this partly accounts for the fact that Terry Eagleton launched his own theoretical intervention not merely as a rejection of the dominant Leavisian tradition but also as a revolutionary critique of his former mentor,

Williams. Eagleton was to revise this view later, most evidently at the time of Williams's death in 1988 (Eagleton, 1989). At this point Williams's unique status as a left public intellectual in British culture and his influence upon literary and cultual studies were clear – effectively summed up in the title of a posthumous collection of essays, *Resources of Hope* (1989). His major academic contribution was perhaps to help found the politicized histor-icist mode of analysis termed 'cultural materialism' (see Chapter 7, pp. 182, 184–5) which in the forms adopted in British cultural studies especially, pre-eminently in the work of Stuart Hall (see Hall, 1996) and in studies of popular culture, developed the Gramscian notion of hegemony, sketched above, and Williams's related distinction between 'dominant' 'residual' and 'emergent' aspects of culture (Williams, 1977).

In *Criticism and Ideology*, Eagleton, like Althusser, argued that criticism must break with its 'ideological prehistory' and become a 'science'. The cen-tral problem is to define the relationship between literature and ideology, because in his view texts do not reflect historical reality but rather work upon ideology to produce an *effect* of the 'real'. The text may appear to be free in its relation to reality (it can invent characters and situations at will), but it is not free in its use of ideology. 'Ideology' here refers not to formulated doctrines but to all those systems of representation (aesthetic, religious, judicial and others) which shape the individual's mental picture of lived experience. The meanings and perceptions produced in the text are a reworking of ideology's own working of reality. This means that the text works on reality at two removes. Eagleton goes on to deepen the theory by examining the complex layering of ideology from its most general pre-textual forms to the ideology of the text itself. He rejects Althusser's view that literature can distance itself from ideology; it is a complex reworking of already existing ideological discourses. However, following Macherey (see above, pp. 98–99), the literary result is not merely a reflection of other ideological discourses but a special *production* of ideology. For this reason criticism is concerned not with just the laws of literary form or the theory of ideology but rather with 'the laws of the production of ideological discourses as literature'.

Eagleton surveys a sequence of novels from George Eliot to D. H. Lawrence in order to demonstrate the interrelations between ideology and literary form. He argues that nineteenth-century bourgeois ideology blended a sterile utilitarianism with a series of organicist concepts of soci-ety (mainly deriving from the Romantic humanist tradition). As Victorian capitalism became more 'corporatist' it needed bolstering up by the sympathetic social and aesthetic organicism of the Romantic tradition.

Eagleton examines each writer's ideological situation and analyses the contradictions which develop in their thinking and the attempted resolutions of the contradictions in their writings. For example, he argues that Lawrence was influenced by Romantic humanism in his belief that the novel reflects the fluidity of life undogmatically, and that society too is ideally an organic order as against the alien capitalist society of modern England. After the destruction of liberal humanism in the First World War, Lawrence developed a dualistic pattern of 'female' and 'male' principles. This antithesis is developed and reshuffled in the various stages of his work, and finally resolved in the characterization of Mellors (*Lady Chatterley's Lover*), who combines impersonal 'male' power and 'female' tenderness. This contradictory combination, which takes various forms in the novels, can be related to a 'deep-seated ideological crisis' within contemporary society.

The impact of poststructuralist thought produced a radical change in Eagleton's work in the late 1970s. His attention shifted from the 'scientific' attitude of Althusser towards the revolutionary thought of Brecht and Benjamin. This shift had the effect of throwing Eagleton back towards the classic Marxist revolutionary theory of the *Theses on Feuerbach* (1845): 'The question whether objective truth can be attributed to human thinking is not a question of theory but is a *practical* question. . . . The philosophers have only *interpreted* the world in various ways; the point is to *change* it.' Eagleton believes that 'deconstructive' theories, as developed by Derrida, Paul de Man and others (see Chapter 7), can be used to undermine all certainties, all fixed and absolute forms of knowledge. On the other hand, he criticizes deconstruction for its petit-bourgeois denial of 'objectivity' and material 'interests' (especially class interests). This apparently contradictory view can be understood if we note that Eagleton was now espousing Lenin's and not Althusser's view of theory: correct theory 'assumes final shape only in close connection with the practical activity of a truly mass and truly revolutionary movement'. The tasks of Marxist criticism are now set up by politics and not by philosophy: the critic must dismantle received notions of 'literature' and reveal their ideological role in shaping the subjectivity of readers. As a socialist the critic must 'expose the rhetorical structures by which non-socialist works produce politically undesirable effects' and also 'interpret such works where possible "against the grain"', so that they work for socialism.

Eagleton's major book of this phase was *Walter Benjamin or Towards a Revolutionary Criticism* (1981). The odd materialist mysticism of Benjamin is read 'against the grain' to produce a revolutionary criticism. His view of history involves a violent grasping of historical meaning from a past which is always threatened and obscured by reactionary and repressive memory. When the right (political) moment comes, a voice from the past can be seized and appropriated to its 'true' purpose. Brecht's plays, admired by Benjamin, often reread history 'against the grain', breaking down the relentless narratives of history and opening the past to reinscription. For example, Shakespeare's *Coriolanus* and Gay's *Beggar's Opera* are 'rewritten' in order to expose their potential socialist meanings. (Brecht characteristically insisted that we must go beyond mere empathy with Shakespeare's self-regarding 'hero' and must be able to appreciate the tragedy not only of Coriolanus but also 'specifically of the plebs'.) Eagleton applauds Brecht's radical and opportunistic approach to meaning: 'a work may be realist in June and anti-realist in December'. Eagleton frequently alludes to Perry Anderson's *Considerations on Western Marxism* (1976), which shows how the development of Marxist theory always reflects the state of the working-class struggle. Eagleton believes, for example, that the Frankfurt School's highly 'negative' critique of modern culture was a response first to fascist domination in Europe, and then to the pervasive capitalist domination in the United States, but that it was also the result of the School's theoretical and practical divorce from the working-class movement. However, what makes Eagleton's revolutionary criticism distinctively *modern* is his tactical deployment of the Freudian theories of Lacan and the powerful deconstructive philosophy of Jacques Derrida (see Chapter 7); his *The Rape of Clarissa* (1982), a rereading of Richardson's novel inspired politically by both socialism and feminism, exemplifies the force of this revised critical strategy. Eagleton's work continues to develop and change. *The Ideology of the Aesthetic* (1990) recalls Frankfurtian rather than 'Parisian' antecedents: the culture of 'the aesthetic' in post-Enlightenment Europe is reviewed dialectically, seen both as a binding agent in the formation of 'normal' bourgeois subjectivity, and as the carrier of irrepressible, disruptive desire. One major work of recent years, inaugurating a trilogy of works on the literature and associated intellectual and political culture of Ireland, was *Heathcliff and the Great Hunger* (1995). Among other themes, Eagleton returns here to Emily Brontë's *Wuthering Heights*, which he sets now in the context of the Irish famine, and, again refocusing an earlier concern, considers the situation of Irish exiles, noticeably Oscar Wilde and George Bernard Shaw. *Heathcliff and the Great Hunger* was followed by *Crazy John and the Bishop and Other Essays on Irish Culture* (1998) and *Scholars and Rebels: Irish Cultural Thought from Burke to Yeats* (1999), both of which combine a broad cultural and historical sweep with the rediscovery of neglected writers and thinkers, amongst them, in *Scholars and Rebels*, the community of professional men (including

William Wilde, Charles Lever and Sheridan Le Fanu) centred upon the *Dublin University Magazine* and related to the Young Ireland movement. The trilogy might be described as a sustained example of 'cultural materialism'. As such, along with other work – for example, *The Idea of Culture* (2000) and *Sweet Violence: The Idea of the Tragic* (2002) – it expresses Eagleton's avowed debt since the late 1980s to Raymond Williams and to traditions of Western·Marxism while confirming his new-found political affiliation with the cause of Irish anti-colonial dissent. Both tendencies have dovetailed in a 'return home' to a life lived between Derry, Dublin and Manchester, where Eagleton has, since 2001, been Professor of Cultural Theory. A further related strand of writing appeared in the novel, *Saints and Scholars* (1987), in the script to Derek Jarman's film, *Wittgenstein* (1993), and in the TV and radio plays, *St Oscar* and *The White, The Gold and The Gangrene* (1997). In themselves, these artistic works brought a new breadth and dexterity, as well as a biting humour, to Eagleton's cultural project in an age when academic work and art are commonly divorced and satire is thought to be at an end. If writing in this mode is temporarily on hold – although the unexpected autobiographical *The Gatekeeper* (2003) certainly keeps up the comedy – one common aim around which the works increasingly cohere is a direct concern with the political role of the intellectual and the lasting value of dissenting traditions in the Western philosophical and literary tradition. This had led Eagleton to speak out himself publicly and regularly against the vapid claims of postmodernism (see Chapter 8, pp. 206–7) and, in one notable instance, against the compromised obscurantism of Gayatri Spivak's postcolonialism (in a 1999 review, 'The Gaudy Supermarket', of her *A Critique of Postcolonial Reason*. See Chapter 9, pp. 224–5). His *After Theory* (2003, and see 'Conclusion' to *The Reader's Guide*) continues in this same provocative, original and deeply committed vein.

In America, where the labour movement has been partially corrupted and totally excluded from political power, the appearance of a major Marxist theorist is an important event. On the other hand, if we keep in mind Eagleton's point about the Frankfurt School and American society, it is not without significance that Fredric Jameson's work has been deeply influenced by that School. In *Marxism and Form* (1971) he explores the dialectical aspect of Marxist theories of literature. After a fine sequence of studies (Adorno, Benjamin, Marcuse, Bloch, Lukács and Sartre) he presents the outline of a 'dialectical criticism'. Jameson believes that in the post-industrial world of monopoly capitalism the only kind of Marxism which has any purchase on the situation is a Marxism which explores the 'great themes of Hegel's philosophy – the relationship of part to whole, the opposition between concrete and abstract, the concept of totality, the dialectic of appearance and essence, the interaction between subject and object'. For dialectical thought there are no fixed and unchanging 'objects'; an 'object' is inextricably bound up with a larger whole, and is also related to a thinking mind which is itself part of a historical situation. Dialectical criticism does not isolate individual literary works for analysis; an individual is always part of a larger structure (a tradition or a movement) or part of a historical situation. The dialectical critic has no pre-set categories to apply to literature and will always be aware that his or her chosen categories (style, character, image, etc.) must be understood ultimately as an aspect of the critic's own historical situation. Jameson shows that Wayne Booth's *Rhetoric of Fiction* (1961: see Chapter 1, pp. 22–3) is lacking in a proper dialectical self-awareness. Booth adopts the concept of 'point of view' in the novel, a concept which is profoundly modern in its implied relativism and rejection of any fixed or absolute viewpoint or standard of judgement. However, by defending the specific point of view represented by the 'implied author', Booth tries to restore the certainties of the nineteenth-century novel, a move which reflects a nostalgia for a time of greater middle-class stability in an orderly class system. A Marxist dialectical criticism will always recognize the historical origins of its own concepts and will never allow the concepts to ossify and become insensitive to the pressure of reality. We can never get outside our subjective existence in time, but we *can* try to break through the hardening shell of our ideas 'into a more vivid apprehension of reality itself'.

A dialectical criticism will seek to unmask the inner form of a genre or body of texts and will work from the surface of a work inward to the level where literary form is deeply related to the concrete. Taking Hemingway as his example, Jameson contends that the 'dominant category of experience' in the novels is the process of writing itself. Hemingway discovered that he could produce a certain kind of bare sentence which could do two things well: denote the physical environment and suggest the tension of resentments between people (for example: 'They sat down at a table and the girl looked across at the hills on the dry side of the valley and the man looked at her and at the table', from 'Hills Like White Elephants', in *Men Without Women*, 1928). The achieved writing skill is linked conceptually with other human skills which are expressed in relation to the natural world (especially blood sports). The Hemingway cult of *machismo* reflects the American ideal of technical skill but rejects the alienating conditions of industrial society by transposing human skill into the sphere of leisure. Hemingway's laid-bare sentences cannot gain access to the complex fabric of American society and so his novels are directed to the thinned-down reality of foreign cultures in which individuals stand out with the 'cleanness of objects' and can therefore be contained in Hemingway's sentences. In this way Jameson shows how literary form is deeply engaged with a concrete reality.

His *The Political Unconscious* (1981) retains the earlier dialectical conception of theory but also assimilates various conflicting traditions of thought (structuralism, poststructuralism, Freud, Althusser, Adorno) in an impressive and still recognizably Marxist synthesis. Jameson argues that the fragmented and alienated condition of human society implies an original state of Primitive Communism in which both life and perception were 'collective'. When humanity suffered a sort of Blakean Fall, the very human senses themselves established separate spheres of specialization. A painter treats sight as a specialized sense; his or her paintings are a symptom of alienation. However, they are also a compensation for the loss of a world of original fullness: they provide colour in a colourless world.

All ideologies are 'strategies of containment' which allow society to provide an explanation of itself which suppresses the underlying contradictions of History; it is History itself (the brute reality of economic Necessity) which imposes this strategy of repression. Literary texts work in the same way: the solutions which they offer are merely symptoms of the suppression of History. Jameson cleverly uses A. J. Greimas' structuralist theory (the 'semiotic rectangle') as an analytic tool for his own purposes. Textual strategies of containment present themselves as formal patterns. Greimas' structuralist system provides a complete inventory of possible human relations (sexual, legal, etc.) which allows the critic to disclose those possibilities in a text that – in an echo of Pierre Macherey (1978; see above, pp. 98–9) – are *not said*. This 'not said' is, for Jameson, the repressed History.

Jameson also develops a powerful argument about narrative and interpretation. He believes that narrative is not just a literary form or mode but an essential 'epistemological category'; reality presents itself to the human mind only in the form of stories. Even a scientific theory is a form of story. Further, all narratives require interpretation. Here Jameson is answering the common poststructuralist argument against 'strong' interpretation. Deleuze and Guattari (in *Anti-Oedipus*; see Chapter 7, pp. 162–4) attack all 'transcendent' interpretation, allowing only 'immanent' interpretation which avoids imposing a strong 'meaning' on a text. Transcendent interpretation tries to master the text and in so doing *impoverishes* its true complexity. Jameson cunningly takes the example of New Criticism (a self-declared immanentist approach), and shows that it is in fact transcendent, its master code being 'humanism'. He concludes that all interpretations are necessarily transcendent and ideological. In the end, all we can do is to use ideological concepts as a means of transcending ideology.

Jameson's 'political unconscious' takes from Freud the essential concept of 'repression', but raises it from the individual to the collective level. The function of ideology is to repress 'revolution'. Not only do the oppressors need this political unconscious but so do the oppressed, who would find their existence unbearable if 'revolution' were not repressed. To analyse a novel we need to establish an absent cause (the 'not-revolution'). Jameson proposes a critical method which includes three 'horizons' (a level of immanent analysis, using Greimas for example; a level of social-discourse analysis; and an epochal level of Historical reading). The third horizon of reading is based upon Jameson's complex rethinking of Marxist models of society. Broadly, he accepts Althusser's view of the social totality as a 'decentred structure' in which various levels develop in 'relative autonomy' and work on different time-scales (the coexistence of feudal and capitalist time-scales, for example). This complex structure of antagonistic and out-of-key modes of production is the heterogeneous History which is mirrored in the heterogeneity of texts. Jameson is here answering the poststructuralists who would abolish the distinction between text and reality by treating reality itself as just more text. He shows that the textual heterogeneity can be understood only as it relates to social and cultural heterogeneity *outside* the text. In this he preserves a space for a Marxist analysis.

His reading of Joseph Conrad's *Lord Jim* shows that each of the various types of interpretation (impressionistic, Freudian, existential, and so on) which have been applied to the text actually expresses something in the text. Each mode of interpretation in turn reflects a development within modern society which serves the needs of capital. For example, impressionism is typified in the character Stein, the capitalist aesthete, whose passion for butterfly collecting Jameson regards as an allegory of Conrad's own 'passionate choice of impressionism – the vocation to arrest the living raw material of life, and by wrenching it from the historical situation . . . to preserve it beyond time in the imaginary'. This narrative response to History is both ideologically conditioned and utopian; it both represses History and envisages an ideal future.

Jameson's strong 'epistemological' understanding of narrative illuminates the political motivation of what remains his most important work to date, *Postmodernism, or the Cultural Logic of Late Capitalism* (1991). He maintains that postmodernism is not merely a style but rather the 'cultural dominant' of our time: a totalizing system which, in league with the operations of the global market under 'late capitalism', saturates all aspects of social, cultural and economic life, and so conditions, at the deepest levels, what we can know of the contemporary world (see Chapter 8, pp. 206–7 especially). He looks in particular to the strategy he terms 'cognitive mapping' (derived in part from critical urban geography and introduced in a celebrated discussion of the Bonaventure Hotel in Los Angeles) for the necessary understanding, critique and transcendence of the world capitalist system. Thus 'a pedagogical political culture', which would endow the individual subject with 'some heightened sense of place in the global system' and renew our capacity 'to act and struggle', will depend upon a 'new political art' committed to 'a global cognitive mapping'. At the same time, however, in a tension which has become characteristic of his thinking, Jameson muses gloomily some ten pages later 'on the impossible matter of the nature of a political art'. There is no progress or movement forward, only the consolation that reflection on this impossiblity 'may not be the worst way of marking time'. The implication is that the world space of multinational capital is in truth unmappable.

The bravura sweep of Jameson's work in this volume and other studies across the realms of theory, literature, art, film, architecture and the media remains an inspiration, but politically the outcome is a resilient but pessimistic 'late Marxism' indebted to Hegel and to Theodor Adorno (Jameson, 1991) which is bereft of a convincing social agency for change. Thus the political utopianism and faith in dialectical thinking apparent in earlier writings is diminished to the view that at present we can at best know what is impossible, becalmed as we are inside global capitalism. As he puts it more recently, in replying to the contemporary resurgence of the concept of 'modernity' and of 'alternative modernities' which aim to recognize cultural difference, the 'fundamental meaning of modernity is that of a world-wide capitalism itself. The standardisation projected by capitalist globalization in this third or late stage of the system casts considerable doubt on all these pious hopes for cultural variety in a future world colonised by a universal market order' (2002).

In the course of this chapter we have referred to 'structuralist' Marxism, and the economic writings of Karl Marx themselves have been regarded as essentially structuralist. However, it is worth emphasizing that the differences between Marxist and structuralist theories (see Chapter 4) are much greater than the similarities. For Marxism the ultimate ground of its theories is the material and historical existence of human societies; whereas for structuralists, the final bedrock is the nature of language. While Marxist theories are about the historical changes and conflicts which arise in society and appear indirectly in literary form, structuralism studies the internal working of systems in a textual emphasis which suspends their historical context and conditions.

Selected reading

Key texts

Adorno, Theodor W., *Prisms* [1955], trans. by Samuel and Shierry Weber (Neville Spearman, London, 1967).

Adorno, Theodor W. and Horkheimer, Max, *Dialectic of Enlightenment* [1944], trans. by John Cumming (Allen Lane, London, 1972).

Adorno, Theodor W., Benjamin, Walter, Bloch, Ernst, Brecht, Bertolt and Lukács, Georg, *Aesthetics and Politics*, trans. and ed. by Ronald Taylor; afterword by Fredric Jameson (New Left Books, London, 1977).

Althusser, Louis, *For Marx* [1965], trans. by Ben Brewster (Allen Lane, London, 1969).

Althusser, Louis, *Lenin and Philosophy and Other Essays* [1969], trans. by Ben Brewster (Verso, London, 1971). Includes 'Ideology and Ideological State Apparatuses' and 'A Letter on Art'.

Anderson, Perry, *Considerations on Western Marxism* (Verso, London, 1976).

Baxandall, Lee and Morawski, Stefan, *Marx and Engels on Literature and Art* (International General, New York, 1973).

Benjamin, Walter, *Illuminations* [1955; trans. by Harry Zohn, 1968], ed. and intro. by Hannah Arendt (Jonathan Cape, London, 1970).

Benjamin, Walter, *Charles Baudelaire: A Lyric Poet in the Era of High Capitalism* [1955], trans. by Harry Zohn (New Left Books, London, 1973).

Benjamin, Walter, *Understanding Brecht* [1966], trans. by Anna Bostock (New Left Books, London, 1973).

Benjamin, Walter, *Correspondence of Walter Benjamin, 1910–1940*, trans. by Manfred and Evelyn Jacobson; ed. by Gershom Schloem and Theodor Adorno (Chicago University Press, Chicago, 1994).

Benjamin, Walter, *Selected Writings* [original trans. by Edmund Jephcott *et al.*, 1972], 4 vols, ed. by Michael W. Jennings, Howard Eiland *et al.*, (Harvard University Press, Cambridge, Mass., 1996–2003). Especially vol. 2, 1927–34 (1999).

Benjamin, Walter, *The Arcades Project* [unfinished, posthumous: 1972], trans. by Howard Eiland and Kevin McLaughlin (Harvard University Press, Cambridge, Mass. and London, 1999).

Eagleton, Terry, *Criticism and Ideology* (New Left Books, London, 1976).

Eagleton, Terry, *Marxism and Literary Criticism* [1976] (2nd edn, Routledge, London, 2002).

Eagleton, Terry, *Walter Benjamin or Towards a Revolutionary Criticism* (New Left Books, London, 1981).

Eagleton, Terry, *The Rape of Clarissa* (Basil Blackwell, Oxford, 1982).

Eagleton, Terry, *Literary Theory: An Introduction* [1983] (2nd edn, Blackwell, Oxford, 1996).

Eagleton, Terry, *Against the Grain: Essays 1975–1985* (Verso, London, 1986).

Eagleton, Terry, *The Ideology of the Aesthetic* (Basil Blackwell, Oxford, 1990).

Eagleton, Terry, *Ideology: An Introduction* (Verso, London, 1991).

Eagleton, Terry, *Wittgenstein: The Terry Eagleton Script, The Derek Jarman Film* (BFI, London, 1993).

Eagleton, Terry, *Heathcliff and the Great Hunger* (Verso, London, 1995).

Eagleton, Terry, *The Illusions of Postmodernism* (Blackwell, Oxford, 1996).

Eagleton, Terry, *St Oscar and Other Plays* (Blackwell, Oxford, 1997).

Eagleton, Terry, *Crazy John and the Bishop and Other Essays on Irish Culture* (University of Notre Dame Press, Notre Dame, 1998).

Eagleton, Terry, *Scholars and Rebels: Irish Cultural Thought from Burke to Yeats* (Blackwell, Oxford, 1999).

Eagleton, Terry, 'The Gaudy Supermarket', *London Review of Books*, 21, 10 (1999), 3–6.

Eagleton, Terry, *The Idea of Culture* (Blackwell, Oxford, 2000).

Eagleton, Terry, *The English Novel: An Introduction* (Blackwell, Oxford, 2004).

Eagleton, Terry and Milne, Drew (eds), *Marxist Literary Theory: A Reader* (Basil Blackwell, Oxford, 1995).

Goldmann, Lucien, *The Hidden God* [1955], trans. by Philip Thody (Routledge & Kegan Paul, London, 1964).

Jameson, Fredric, *Marxism and Form: Twentieth-Century Dialectical Theories of Literature* (Princeton University Press, Princeton, NJ, 1971).

Jameson, Fredric, *The Prison-House of Language: A Critical Account of Structuralism and Russian Formalism* (Princeton University Press, Princeton, NJ, and London, 1972).

Jameson, Fredric, *The Political Unconscious: Narrative as a Socially Symbolic Act* [1981] (Routledge, London, 2002).

Jameson, Fredric, *The Ideologies of Theory. Vol. 1 Situations of Theory, Vol. 2 The Syntax of History* (Routledge & Kegan Paul, London, 1988).

Jameson, Fredric, *Postmodernism, or the Cultural Logic of Late Capitalism* (Verso, London, 1991).

Jameson, Fredric, *The Seeds of Time* (Columbia University Press, New York, 1994).

Jameson, Fredric, *The Cultural Turn: Selected Writings on the Postmodern* (Verso, London, 1998).

Jameson, Fredric, *The Jameson Reader*, ed. by Michael Hardt and Kathi Weeks (Blackwell, Oxford, 2000).

Jameson, Fredric, *A Singular Modernity* (Verso, London, 2002).

Lukács, Georg, *The Historical Novel* [1937], trans. by Hannah and Stanley Mitchell (Merlin Press, London, 1962).

Lukács, Georg, *Studies in European Realism* [1950], trans. by Edith Bone (Merlin Press, London, 1972).

Lukács Georg, *The Meaning of Contemporary Realism* [1957], trans. by John and Necke Mander (Merlin Press, London, 1963).

Macherey, Pierre, *A Theory of Literary Production* [1966], trans. by Geoffrey Wall (Routledge & Kegan Paul, London and Boston, 1978).

Macherey, Pierre and Balibar, Etienne, 'On Literature as an Ideological Form', in Robert Young (ed.), *Untying the Text: A Poststructuralist Reader* (Routledge & Kegan Paul, London and Boston, 1981) and Francis Mulhern (ed.) *Contemporary Marxist Literary Criticism* (Longman, London and New York, 1992).

Marcuse, Herbert, *One-Dimensional Man* (Beacon, Boston; Sphere, London, 1964).

Marcuse, Herbert, *Negations* (Allen Lane, London, 1968).

Marcuse, Herbert, *The Aesthetic Dimension* (Macmillan, London, 1979).

Pêcheux, Michel, *Language, Semantics and Ideology* [1975], trans. by Harbans Nagpal (Macmillan, Basingstoke, 1982).

Sartre, Jean-Paul, *What is Literature?* [1948; 1st trans. 1949; trans. by Bernard Frechtman; intro. by David Caute, 1967] (Routledge, London, 2001).

Willett, John (ed.), *Brecht on Theatre* (Methuen, London, 1964).

Williams, Raymond, *Culture and Society 1780–1950* (Chatto & Windus, London, 1958).

Williams, Raymond, *The Long Revolution* (Chatto & Windus, London, 1961).

Williams, Raymond, *Television: Technology and Cultural Form* (Fontana/Collins, London, 1974).

Williams, Raymond, *Marxism and Literature* (Oxford University Press, Oxford, 1977).

Williams, Raymond, *Politics and Letters: Interviews with New Left Review* (Verso, London, 1979).

Williams, Raymond, *Problems in Materialism and Culture* (New Left Books, London, 1980).

Williams, Raymond, *Keywords: A Vocabulary of Culture and Society* (Fontana/Collins, London, 1983).

Williams, Raymond, *Towards 2000* (Chatto & Windus, London, 1983).

Williams, Raymond, *Writing in Society* (Verso, London, 1984).

Williams, Raymond, *Resources of Hope* (Verso, London, 1988).

Williams, Raymond, *What I Came to Say* (Hutchinson Radius, London, 1989).

Williams, Raymond, *The Politics of Modernism: Against the New Conformists*, ed. by Tony Pinkney (Verso, London, 1989).

Williams, Raymond, *The Raymond Williams Reader*, ed. by John Higgins (Blackwell, Oxford, 2000).

Further reading

Belsey, Catherine, *Critical Practice* [1980] (2nd edn, Routledge, London, 2002).

Bennett, Tony, *Formalism and Marxism* [1979] (2nd edn, Routledge, London, 2003).

Brooker, Peter, *Bertolt Brecht: Dialectics, Poetry, Politics* (Croom Helm, London and New York, 1988).

Brooker, Peter and Thacker, Andrew (eds), *Geographies of Modernism: Cultures, Spaces* (Routledge, London and New York, 2005).

Donald, James, *Imagining the Modern City* (Athlone Press, London, 1999).

Donald, James, 'Flannery', in Peter Brooker and Andrew Thacker (eds, 2005), above.

Eagleton, Terry (ed.), *Raymond Williams: Critical Perspectives* (Polity Press, Oxford, 1989).

Friedberg, Anne, *Window Shopping. Cinema and the Postmodern* (California University Press, Berkeley, 1994).

Gibson, Nigel and Rubin, Andrew (eds), *Adorno: A Critical Reader* (Blackwell, Oxford, 2001).

Gilloch, Graeme, *Walter Benjamin: Critical Constellations* (Polity Press, Cambridge, 2001).

Hall, Stuart, *Critical Dialogues in Cultural Studies,* ed. by Dave Morley and Kuan-Hsing Chen (Routledge, London, 1996).

Haslett, Moyra, *Marxist Literary and Cultural Theories* (Palgrave Macmillan, Basingstoke, 1999).

Hawkes, David, *Ideology* (2nd edn, Routledge, 2003).

Higgins, John, *Raymond Williams: Literature, Marxism and Cultural Materialism* (Routledge, London, 1999).

Homer, Sean, *Fredric Jameson: Marxism, Hermeneutics, Postmodernism* (Polity Press, Cambridge, 1998).

James, C. Vaughan, *Soviet Socialist Realism: Origins and Theory* (Macmillan, London and Basingstoke, 1973).

Jameson, Fredric, *Late Marxism: Adorno or the Persistence of the Dialectic* (Verso, London, 1990).

Jarvis, Simon, *Adorno: A Critical Introduction* (Polity Press, Cambridge, 1998).

Jay, Martin, *The Dialectical Imagination: A History of the Frankfurt School* (Heinemann, London, 1973).

Kuhn, Tom and Giles, Steve (eds and trans.), *Brecht on Art and Politics* (London, Methuen, 2003).

Lunn, Eugene, *Marxism and Modernism* (Verso, London, 1985).

Montag, Warren, *Louis Althusser* (Palgrave Macmillan, Basingstoke, 2002).

Mulhern, Francis (ed.), *Contemporary Marxist Literary Criticism* (Longman, London and New York, 1992).

Nelson, Cary and Grossberg, Lawrence (eds), *Marxism and the Interpretation of Culture* (Macmillan, London, 1988).

Roberts, Adam, *Fredric Jameson* (Routledge, London, 2000).

Sinclair, Iain, *Lights Out For the Territory* (London, Granta 1997).

Soja, Edward W., *Thirdspace* (Blackwell, Oxford, 1996).

Thacker, Andrew, *Moving Through Modernity: Space and Geography in Modernism* (Manchester University Press, Manchester, 2003).

Wilson, Elizabeth, 'The Invisible *Flaneuse*', in Sophie Watson and Katherine Gibson (eds), *Postmodern Cities and Spaces* (Blackwell, Oxford, 1995), pp. 58–79.

Wolff, Janet, 'The Invisible *Flaneuse*: Women and the Literature of Modernity', *Theory, Culture and Society*, 2, 3 (1985), 37–46.

Wright, Elizabeth, *Postmodern Brecht: A Re-Presentation* (Routledge, London, 1988).

CHAPTER 6

Feminist theories

Women writers and women readers have always had to work 'against the grain'. Aristotle declared that 'the female is female by virtue of a certain lack of qualities', and St Thomas Aquinas believed that woman is an 'imperfect man'. When John Donne wrote 'Air and Angels' he alluded to (but did not refute) Aquinas's theory that form is masculine and matter feminine: the superior, godlike, male intellect impresses its form upon the malleable, inert, female matter. In pre-Mendelian days men regarded their sperm as the active seeds which give form to the waiting ovum, which lacks identity till it receives the male's impress. In Aeschylus's trilogy, *The Oresteia*, victory is granted by Athena to the male argument, put by Apollo, that the mother is no parent to her child. The victory of the male principle of intellect brings to an end the reign of the sensual female Furies and asserts patriarchy over matriarchy. Throughout its long history, feminism (for while the *word* may only have come into English usage in the 1890s, women's conscious struggle to resist patriarchy goes much further back) has sought to disturb the complacent certainties of such a patriarchal culture, to assert a belief in sexual equality, and to eradicate sexist domination in transforming society. Mary Ellman, for example, in *Thinking about Women* (1968), apropos the sperm/ovum nexus above, reverses male-dominated ways of seeing by suggesting that we might prefer to regard the ovum as daring, independent and individualistic (rather than 'apathetic') and the sperm as conforming and sheeplike (rather than 'enthusiastic'). Feminist *criticism*, in all its many and various manifestations, has also attempted to free itself from naturalized patriarchal notions of the literary and the literary-critical. As we implied in passing in the Introduction, this has meant a refusal to be incorporated by any particular 'approach' and to disturb and subvert all received theoretical praxes. In this respect, feminism and feminist criticism may be better termed a cultural *politics* than a 'theory' or 'theories'.

Indeed, some feminists have not wished to embrace theory at all, precisely because, in academic institutions, 'theory' is often male, even macho – the hard, abstract, *avant-gardism* of intellectual work; and as part of their general project, feminists have been at pains to expose the fraudulent objectivity of male 'science', such as Freud's theory of female sexual development. However, much recent feminist criticism – in the desire to escape the 'fixities and definites' of theory and to develop a female discourse which cannot be tied down as belonging to a recognized (and therefore probably male-produced) conceptual position – has found theoretical sustenance in post-structuralist and postmodernist thinking, not least because these seem to refuse the (masculine) notion of authority or truth. As we note in Chapter 7, psychoanalytic theories have been especially powerfully deployed by feminist critics in articulating the subversively 'formless' resistance of women writers and critics to male-formulated literary discourse.

But here, perhaps, we happen upon a central characteristic and also a problematic of contemporary feminist criticism: the competing merits – and the debate between them – on the one hand of a broad-church pluralism in which diverse 'theories' proliferate, and which may well result in the promotion of the experiential over the theoretical; and on the other of a theoretically sophisticated praxis which runs the risk of incorporation by male theory in the academy, and thereby of losing touch both with the majority of women and with its political dynamic. Mary Eagleton, in the introduction to her Critical Reader, *Feminist Literary Criticism* (1991; 2nd edn 1995), also draws attention to 'a suspicion of theory . . . throughout feminism' because of its tendency to reinforce the hierarchical binary opposition between an 'impersonal', 'disinterested', 'objective', 'public', 'male' *theory*, and a 'personal', 'subjective', 'private', 'female' *experience*. She notes that because of this there is a powerful element within contemporary feminist criticism which celebrates the 'personal' ('personal is political' has been a key feminist slogan, since it was coined in 1970 by Carol Hanisch), the 'experiential', the Mother, the Body, *jouissance* (see Chapter 7, pp. 150–1, and below under 'French Feminist Critical Theories'). However, she also notes that many feminists *are* engaged in debates with other critical theories – Marxism, psychoanalysis, poststructuralism, postmodernism, postcolonialism – because, simply, there is no 'free' position 'outside' theory, and to vacate the domain of theory on the assumption that there is such a position is at once to be embroiled in the subjectivism of an 'untheorized politics of personal experience', to disable oneself thereby, and 'unwittingly' to take up potentially reactionary positions. In this context, Eagleton cites Toril Moi's critique of Elaine Showalter's resistance to making her theoretical framework explicit (see below, p. 128).

What these alternative views amount to is a *position* within feminist critical debate, and this returns us to the key characteristic (and problematic) of feminist criticism (which is also the structuring device for Eagleton's book). Over the past twenty-five years or so, feminist critical theory has meant, *par excellence*, contradiction, interchange, debate; indeed it is based on a series of creative oppositions, of critiques and counter-critiques, and is constantly and innovatively in flux – challenging, subverting and expanding not only other (male) theories but its own positions and agenda. Hence there is no one 'grand narrative' but many '*petits récits*', grounded in specific cultural-political needs and arenas – for example, of class, gender and race – and often in some degree of contention with each other. This represents at once the creatively 'open' dynamic of modern feminist critical theories and something of a difficulty in offering a brief synoptic account of such a diverse, viviparous and self-problematizing field over what is, by now, a considerable period of time. What the present chapter attempts, then – while sharply conscious of the charge of ethnocentricity – is an overview of predominantly white, European and North American feminist theories from the pre-1960s so-called 'first-wave' critics through to the substantive achievements of the 'second-wave' theorists of the 1960s onwards. This identifies some of the central debates and differences which traverse the period – particularly those between the Anglo-American and French movements. In so doing, we strategically defer treatment of more recent 'Third-World'/'Third-Wave' feminist critical theorists to the last three chapters of the book, where they properly participate in the complex, interactive domain in which contemporary 'post-modern' theories deconstruct national, ethnic and sexual identities.

First-wave feminist criticism: Woolf and de Beauvoir

Feminism in general, of course, has a long *political* history, developing as a substantial force, in America and Britain at least, throughout the nineteenth and early twentieth centuries. The Women's Rights and Women's Suffrage movements were the crucial determinants in shaping this phase, with their emphasis on social, political and economic reform – in partial contradistinction to the 'new' feminism of the 1960s which, as Maggie Humm has

suggested in her book *Feminisms* (1992), emphasized the different 'materiality' of being a woman and has engendered (in two senses) both moral
solidarities created by feminist positions and identities, and a new 'knowledge' about the embodiment of women drawing on psychoanalytic, linguistic
and social theories about gender construction and difference. Feminist *criticism* of the earlier period is more a reflex of 'first-wave' preoccupations than
a fully fledged theoretical discourse of its own. But two significant figures
may be selected from among the many other feminists working and writing
in this period (e.g. Olive Schreiner, Elizabeth Robins, Dorothy Richardson,
Katherine Mansfield, Rebecca West, Ray Strachey, Vera Brittain and
Winifred Holtby): Virginia Woolf – in Mary Eagleton's phrase, 'the founding mother of the contemporary debate' – who 'announces' many of the
issues later feminist critics were to focus on and who herself becomes the
terrain over which some debates have struggled; and Simone de Beauvoir,
with whose *The Second Sex* (1949), Maggie Humm suggests, the 'first wave'
may be said to end.

Virginia Woolf's fame conventionally rests on her own creative writing as
a woman, and later feminist critics have analysed her novels extensively from
very different perspectives (see below, pp. 119, 125, 128, 136). But she also
produced two key texts which are major contributions to feminist theory,
A Room of One's Own (1929) and *Three Guineas* (1938). Like other 'first-wave'
feminists, Woolf is principally concerned with women's material disadvantages
compared to men – her first text focusing on the history and social context
of women's literary production, and the second on the relations between
male power and the professions (law, education, medicine, etc.). Although
she herself abjures the label 'feminist' in *Three Guineas*, Woolf nevertheless
promotes a wide-ranging slate of feminist projects in both books, from a
demand for mothers' allowances and divorce-law reform to proposals for
a women's college and a women's newspaper. In *A Room of One's Own*, she
also argues that women's writing should explore female experience in its
own right and not form a comparative assessment of women's experience in
relation to men's. The essay therefore forms an early statement and exploration of the possibility of a distinctive tradition of women's writing.

Woolf's general contribution to feminism, then, is her recognition that
gender identity is socially constructed and can be challenged and transformed,
but apropos of feminist criticism she also continually examined the problems facing women writers. She believed that women had always faced social
and economic obstacles to their literary ambitions, and was herself conscious
of the restricted education she had received (she was taught no Greek, for
example, unlike her brothers). Rejecting a 'feminist' consciousness, and

wanting her femininity to be unconscious so that she might 'escape from the confrontation with femaleness or maleness' (*A Room of One's Own*), she appropriated the Bloomsbury sexual ethic of 'androgyny' and hoped to achieve a balance between a 'male' self-realization and 'female' self-annihilation. In this respect, Virginia Woolf has been presented (in particular by Elaine Showalter) as one who accepted a passive withdrawal from the conflict between male and female sexuality, but Toril Moi advances a quite different interpretation of Woolf's strategy. Adopting Kristeva's coupling of feminism with *avant-garde* writing (see below, p. 128), Moi argues that Woolf is not interested in a 'balance' between masculine and feminine types but in a complete *displacement* of fixed gender identities, and that she dismantles essentialist notions of gender by dispersing fixed points of view in her modernist fictions. Woolf, Moi argues, rejected only that type of feminism which was simply an inverted male chauvinism, and also showed great awareness of the distinctness of women's writing.

One of Woolf's most interesting essays about women writers is 'Professions for Women', in which she regards her own career as hindered in two ways. First, she was imprisoned and constrained by the dominant ideologies of womanhood. Second, the taboo about expressing female passion prevented her from 'telling the truth about [her] own experiences as a body'. This denial of female sexuality was never consciously subverted in Woolf's own work or life, in that she thought women wrote differently not because they were different psychologically from men but because their social positioning was different. Her attempts to write about the experiences of women, therefore, were aimed at discovering linguistic ways of describing the confined life of women, and she believed that when women finally achieved social and economic equality with men, there would be nothing to prevent them from freely developing their artistic talents.

Simone de Beauvoir – French feminist, lifelong partner of Jean-Paul Sartre, pro-abortion and women's-rights activist, founder of the newspaper *Nouvelles féministes* and of the journal of feminist theory, *Questions féministes* – marks the moment when 'first-wave' feminism begins to slip over into the 'second wave'. While her hugely influential book *The Second Sex* (1949) is clearly preoccupied with the 'materialism' of the first wave, it beckons to the second wave in its recognition of the vast difference between the interests of the two sexes and in its assault on men's biological and psychological, as well as economic, discrimination against women. The book established with great clarity the fundamental questions of modern feminism. When a woman tries to define herself, she starts by saying 'I am a woman': no man would do so. This fact reveals the basic asymmetry between the terms 'masculine' and 'feminine': man defines the human, not woman, in an imbalance which goes back to the Old Testament. Being dispersed among men, women have no separate history, no natural solidarity; nor have they combined as other oppressed groups have. Woman is riveted into a lop-sided relationship with man: he is the 'One', she the 'Other'. Man's dominance has secured an ideological climate of compliance: 'legislators, priests, philosophers, writers and scientists have striven to show that the subordinate position of woman is willed in heaven and advantageous on earth', and, *à la* Virginia Woolf, the assumption of woman as 'Other' is further internalized by women themselves.

De Beauvoir's work carefully distinguishes between sex and gender, and sees an interaction between social and natural functions: 'One is not born, but rather becomes, a woman . . . it is civilization as a whole that produces this creature . . . Only the intervention of someone else can establish an individual as an *Other*.' It is the systems of interpretation in relation to biology, psychology, reproduction, economics, etc. which constitute the (male) presence of that 'someone else'. Making the crucial distinction between 'being female' and being constructed as 'a woman', de Beauvoir can posit the destruction of patriarchy if women will only break out of their objectification. In common with other 'first-wave' feminists, she wants freedom from biological difference, and she shares with them a distrust of 'femininity' – thus marking herself off from some contemporary feminists' celebration of the body and recognition of the importance of the unconscious.

Second-wave feminist criticism

One, perhaps over-simplifying, way of identifying the beginnings of the 'second wave' is to record the publication of Betty Friedan's *The Feminine Mystique* in 1963, which, in its revelation of the frustrations of white, heterosexual, middle-class American women – careerless and trapped in domesticity – put feminism on the national agenda, substantively and for the first time. (Friedan also founded NOW, the National Organisation of Women, in 1966.) 'Second-wave' feminism and feminist criticism are very much a product of – are shaped by and themselves help to shape – the liberationist movements of the mid-to-late 1960s. Although second-wave feminism continues to share the first wave's fight for women's rights in all areas, its focal emphasis shifts to the politics of reproduction, to women's 'experience', to sexual 'difference' and to 'sexuality', as at once a form of oppression and something to celebrate.

Five main foci are involved in most discussions of sexual difference: biology; experience; discourse; the unconscious; and social and economic conditions. Arguments which treat biology as fundamental and which play down socialization have been used mainly by men to keep women 'in their place'. The old Latin saying *'Tota mulier in utero'* ('Women is nothing but a womb') established this attitude early. If a woman's body is her destiny, then all attempts to question attributed sex-roles will fly in the face of the natural order. On the other hand, some radical feminists celebrate women's biological attributes as sources of superiority rather than inferiority, while others appeal to the special *experience* of woman as the source of positive female values in life and in art. Since only women, the argument goes, have undergone those specifically female life-experiences (ovulation, menstruation, parturition), only they can speak of a woman's life. Further, a woman's experience includes a different perceptual and emotional life; women do not see things in the same ways as men, and have different ideas and feelings about what is important or not important. An influential example of this approach is the work of Elaine Showalter (see below, pp. 126–9) which focuses on the literary representation of sexual differences in women's writing.

The third focus, discourse, has received a great deal of attention by feminists. Dale Spender's *Man Made Language* (1980), as the title suggests, considers that women have been fundamentally oppressed by a male-dominated language. If we accept Michel Foucault's argument that what is 'true' depends on who controls discourse (see Chapter 7, p. 178ff), then it is apparent that men's domination of discourse has trapped women inside a male 'truth'. From this point of view it makes sense for women writers to contest men's control of language rather than create a separate, specifically 'feminine' discourse. The opposite view is taken by the female socio-linguist Robin Lakoff (1975), who believes that women's language actually is inferior, since it contains patterns of 'weakness' and 'uncertainty', focuses on the 'trivial', the frivolous, the unserious, and stresses personal emotional responses. Male utterance, she argues, is 'stronger' and should be adopted by women if they wish to achieve social equality with men. Most feminists, however, consider that women have been brainwashed by this type of patriarchal ideology, which produces stereotypes of strong men and feeble women. The psychoanalytic theories of Lacan and Kristeva have provided a fourth focus – that of the unconscious. Some feminists have broken completely with biologism by associating the 'female' with those processes which tend to undermine the authority of 'male' discourse. Whatever encourages or initiates a free play of meanings and prevents 'closure' is regarded as 'female'. Female sexuality is revolutionary, subversive, heterogeneous and 'open' in that it refuses to define female sexuality: if there is a female principle, it is simply to remain outside the male definition of the female. As we have seen, Virginia Woolf was the first woman critic to include a sociological dimension in her analysis of women's writing. Since then, Marxist feminists in particular have related changing social and economic conditions to the changing balance of power between the sexes, thus underwriting feminism's rejection of the notion of a universal femininity.

Certain themes, then, dominate second-wave feminism: the omnipresence of patriarchy; the inadequacy for women of existing political organization; and the celebration of women's difference as central to the cultural politics of liberation. And these can be found running through many major second-wave writings, from popular interventions like Germaine Greer's *The Female Eunuch* (1970), which explores the destructive neutralization of women within patriarchy, through the critical reassessments of socialism (Sheila Rowbotham) and psychoanalysis (Juliet Mitchell), to the radical (lesbian) feminism of Kate Millett and Adrienne Rich (for Rich, see Chapter 10, pp. 248–9). In feminist literary theory more particularly, it leads to the emergence of so-called 'Anglo-American' criticism, an empirical approach fronted by the 'gynocriticism' of Elaine Showalter, which concentrates on the specificity of women's writing, on recuperating a tradition of women authors, and on examining in detail women's own culture. In dispute with this, however, is the slightly later and more theoretically driven 'French' feminist criticism, which draws especially on the work of Julia Kristeva, Hélène Cixous and Luce Irigaray, and emphasizes not the *gender* of the writer ('female') but the 'writing-effect' of the text ('feminine') – hence, *l'écriture féminine*. It is worth noting here that this distinction between 'Anglo-American' and 'French' feminist criticisms is a significant fault-line in second-wave developments, and distinguishes two dominant and influential movements in critical theory since the end of the 1960s. It is, however, problematical for four main reasons: one, it is not a useful *national* categorization (many British and American critics, for example, might be described as 'French'), and must be understood, therefore, to identify the informing intellectual tradition and not country of origin; two, set up as it is, it seems to exclude feminist critical input from anywhere else, and especially the 'Third World'; three, it reifies into too simple a binary opposition, suppressing at once the vast diversity of practices within both movements; four, it also masks their similarities. Both schools keep the idea of a 'feminine aesthetic' at the forefront of analysis and both run the risk of biological determinism: 'Anglo-American' criticism for its pursuit of works which, in Peggy Kamuf's words, are 'signed by biologically determined females of the species', and

'French Feminism' for its privileging of 'literal' rather than metaphorical female bodies. But before exploring these more recent developments, we must take note of a founding text from the late 1960s.

Kate Millett: sexual politics

Second-wave feminism in the United States took its impetus from the civil-rights, peace and other protest movements, and Kate Millett's radical feminism is of this order. First published in 1969, a year after Mary Ellmann's *Thinking About Women* and just before Germaine Greer's *The Female Eunuch*, Eva Figes's *Patriarchal Attitudes* and Shulamith Firestone's *The Dialectic of Sex* (all in 1970), Millett's *Sexual Politics* at once marks the moment when second-wave feminism becomes a highly visible, self-aware and activist movement, and when it itself became the *cause-célèbre* text of that moment. It has been – certainly in the significant legacy of its title – perhaps the best-known and most influential book of its period, and it remains (despite its inadequacies: see below) a ferociously upbeat, comprehensive, witty and irreverent demolition-job on male culture; and in this, perhaps, it is a monument to its moment.

Millett's argument – ranging over history, literature, psychoanalysis, sociology and other areas – is that ideological indoctrination as much as economic inequality is the cause of women's oppression, an argument which opened up second-wave thinking about reproduction, sexuality and representation (especially verbal and visual 'images of women', and particularly pornography). Millett's title, *Sexual Politics*, announces her view of 'patriarchy', which she sees as pervasive and which demands 'a systematic overview – as a political institution'. Patriarchy subordinates the female to the male or treats the female as an inferior male, and this power is exerted, directly or indirectly, in civil and domestic life to constrain women. Millett borrows from social science the important distinction between 'sex' and 'gender', where sex is determined biologically but 'gender' is a psychological concept which refers to *culturally* acquired sexual identity, and she and other feminists have attacked social scientists who treat the culturally learned 'female' characteristics (passivity, etc.) as 'natural'. She recognizes that women as much as men perpetuate these attitudes, and the acting-out of these sex-roles in the unequal and repressive relations of domination and subordination is what Millett calls 'sexual politics'.

Sexual Politics was a pioneering analysis of masculinist historical, social and literary images of women, and in our context here is a formative text in feminist literary criticism. Millett's privileging of *literature* as a source helped to establish writing, literary studies and criticism as domains especially appropriate for feminism. One crucial factor in the social construction of femininity is the way literary values and conventions have themselves been shaped by men, and women have often struggled to express their own concerns in what may well have been inappropriate forms. In narrative, for instance, the shaping conventions of adventure and romantic pursuit have a 'male' impetus and purposiveness. Further, historically the male writer has tended to address his readers as if they were men, while much contemporary advertising provides obvious parallel examples in mass culture. However, as we have noted in relation to Woolf and de Beauvoir, it is also possible for the female reader to collude (unconsciously) in this patriarchal positioning and read 'as a man'. In order to resist this indoctrination of the female reader, Millett exposes the oppressive representations of sexuality to be found in male fiction. By deliberately foregrounding the view of a *female* reader, she highlights the male domination which pervades sexual description in the novels of D. H. Lawrence, Henry Miller, Norman Mailer and Jean Genet, offering in the case of Lawrence, for example, often hilarious and devastatingly deflationary analyses of his phallocracy.

Millett's book provided a powerful critique of patriarchal culture, but other feminist critics believe that her sole selection of male authors was too unrepresentative and that she does not sufficiently understand the subversive power of the imagination in fiction. She misses, for instance, the deeply deviant and subversive nature of Genet's *The Thief's Journal*, and sees in the homosexual world depicted only an implied subjection and degradation of the female. It appears that, for Millett, male authors are compelled by their gender to reproduce the oppressive sexual politics of the real world in their fiction, an approach which would underestimate, say, James Joyce's treatment of female sexuality. Some feminists therefore have seen Millett as holding a one-dimensional view of male domination, treating sexist ideology as a blanket oppression which all male writers inevitably promote. Cora Kaplan, in a thoroughgoing critique of Millett, 'Radical Feminism and Literature: Rethinking Millett's *Sexual Politics*' (1979), has suggested that she sees 'ideology [as] the universal penile club which men of all classes use to beat women with'. Kaplan points to the crudity and contradictoriness of much of Millett's analysis of fiction, which sees it at once as 'true' and 'representative' of patriarchy at large, and simultaneously as 'false' in its representation of women. It fails, in its reductive reflectionism, to take account of the mediating 'rhetoric of fiction'.

Marxist feminism

Socialist/Marxist feminism was a powerful strand of the second wave during the late 1960s and 1970s, in Britain in particular. It sought to extend Marxism's analysis of class into a women's history of their material and economic oppression, and especially of how the family and women's domestic labour are constructed by and reproduce the sexual division of labour. Like other 'male' forms of history, Marxism had ignored much of women's experience and activity (one of Sheila Rowbotham's most influential books is entitled *Hidden from History*), and Marxist feminism's primary task was to open up the complex relations between gender and the economy. Juliet Mitchell's early essay, 'Women: The Longest Revolution' (1966), was a pioneering attempt, *contra* the ahistorical work of radical feminists like Millett and Firestone, to historicize the structural control patriarchy exerts in relation to women's reproductive functions; and Sheila Rowbotham, in *Women's Consciousness, Man's World* (1973), recognized both that working-class women experience the double oppression of the sexual division of labour at work and in the home, and that Marxist historiography had largely ignored the domain of personal experience, and particularly that of female culture.

In the literary context, Cora Kaplan's critique of the radical feminist Millett (above), especially in its concern with ideology, may be seen as an instance of socialist-feminist criticism, and Michèle Barrett, in *Women's Oppression Today: Problems in Marxist Feminist Analysis* (1980), presents a Marxist feminist analysis of gender representation. First, she applauds Virginia Woolf's materialist argument that the conditions under which men and women *produce* literature are materially different and influence the form and content of what they write: we cannot separate questions of gender-stereotyping from their material conditions in history. This means that liberation will not come merely from changes in culture. Second, the ideology of gender affects the way the writings of men and women are read and how canons of excellence are established. Third, feminist critics must take account of the *fictional* nature of literary texts and not indulge in 'rampant moralism' by condemning all male authors for the sexism of their books (*vide* Millett) and approving all women authors for raising the issue of gender. Texts have no fixed meanings: interpretations depend on the situation and ideology of the reader. Nevertheless, women can and should try to assert their influence upon the way in which gender is defined and represented culturally.

In the Introduction to *Feminist Criticism and Social Change* (1985), Judith Newton and Deborah Rosenfelt argue for a materialist feminist criticism which escapes the 'tragic' essentialism of those feminist critics who project an image of women as universally powerless and universally good. They criticize what they consider the narrow literariness of Gilbert and Gubar's influential *The Madwoman in the Attic* (1979: see below), and especially their neglect of the social and economic realities which play an important part in constructing gender roles. Penny Boumehla, Cora Kaplan and members of the Marxist-Feminist Literature Collective have instead brought to literary texts the kind of ideological analysis developed by Althusser and Macherey (see Chapter 5), in order to understand the historical formation of gender categories. However, Marxist feminism currently does not have the highest of profiles – no doubt because of the political 'condition' of postmodernity, but also perhaps because of the overriding effect of the 'debate' between Anglo-American and French feminisms.

Elaine Showalter: gynocriticism

Toril Moi's *Sexual/Textual Politics* (1985) is in two main sections: 'Anglo-American Feminist Criticism' and 'French Feminist Theory'. Not only does this bring into sharp focus one of the main debates in contemporary feminist critical theory, it also makes a statement. Moi's (conscious) slippage from 'criticism' to 'theory' indicates both a descriptive characterization *and* a value-judgement: for Moi, Anglo-American criticism is either theoretically naïve or refuses to theorize itself; the French, on the other hand, is theoretically self-conscious and sophisticated. In fact, as we noted on p. 122, there is much common ground and interpenetration between these two 'approaches' (not least in both tending to ignore class, ethnicity and history as determinants), and both continue to help define major modes of feminist critical address. The French we will consider a little more fully in a subsequent section.

The principal 'Anglo-Americans' are, in fact, Americans. As the 'images of women' criticism of the early 1970s (driven by Ellmann and Millett's work) began to seem simplistic and uniform, several works appeared which promoted both the study of *women* writers and a *feminist* critical discourse in order to discuss them. Ellen Moers's *Literary Women* (1976) was a preliminary sketching in or 'mapping' of the 'alternative' tradition of women's writing which separately shadows the dominant male tradition; but the major work of this kind, after Elaine Showalter's, is Sandra Gilbert and Susan Gubar's monumental *The Madwoman in the Attic* (1979), where they argue that key women writers since Jane Austen achieved a distinctive female 'duplicitous' voice by 'simultaneously conforming to and subverting patriarchal literary standards'. The female stereotypes of 'angel' and 'monster' (or 'mad-woman': their reading of Charlotte Brontë's *Jane Eyre* gives the book its title) are simultaneously accepted and deconstructed. However, as Mary Jacobus has pointed out, Gilbert and Gubar tend to limit women writers' freedom by constructing them as 'exceptionally articulate victims of a patriarchally engendered plot'; and Toril Moi adds that this continual retelling of the 'story' of female repression by patriarchy locks feminist criticism into a con-straining and problematical relation with the very authoritarian and patri-archal criticism it seeks to surmount.

Perhaps the most influential American critic of the second wave is Elaine Showalter, and especially her *A Literature of Their Own* (1977). Here Showalter at once outlines a literary history of women writers (many of whom had, indeed, been 'hidden from history'); produces a history which shows the configuration of their material, psychological and ideological determin-ants; and promotes both a feminist critique (concerned with women read-ers) and a 'gynocritics' (concerned with women writers). What the book does is to examine British women novelists since the Brontës from the point of view of women's experience. Showalter takes the view that, while there is no fixed or innate female sexuality or female imagination, there is never-theless a profound *difference* between women's writing and men's, and that a whole tradition of writing has been neglected by male critics: 'the lost continent of the female tradition has risen like Atlantis from the sea of English Literature'. She divides this tradition into three phases. The first, 'feminine', phase (1840–80) includes Elizabeth Gaskell and George Eliot, and is one where women writers imitated and internalized the dominant male aesthetic standards which required that female authors remain gentlewomen. The 'fem-inist' phase (1880–1920) includes such radical feminist writers as Elizabeth Robins and Olive Schreiner, who *protest* against male values and advocate separatist utopias and suffragette sisterhoods. The third, 'female', phase (1920 onwards) inherited characteristics of the former periods and developed the idea of specifically female writing and female experience in a phase of *self-discovery*. For Showalter, Rebecca West, Katherine Mansfield and Dorothy Richardson were its most important early 'female' novelists. In the same period that Joyce and Proust were writing long novels of subjective con-sciousness, Richardson's equally long novel *Pilgrimage* took as its subject *female* consciousness. Her views on writing (see 'Women in the Arts', 1925) anti-cipate recent feminist theories, in that she favoured a 'multiple receptivity' which rejects definite views and opinions (she called them 'masculine things'). Richardson consciously tried to produce elliptical and fragmented sentences in order to convey what she considered to be the shape and texture of the female mind. After Virginia Woolf, a new frankness about sexuality (adultery and lesbianism, for example) enters women's fiction, especially in Jean Rhys. Thereafter followed a new generation of university-educated women who no longer felt the need to express feminine discontents; this included A. S. Byatt, Margaret Drabble and Brigid Brophy. However, in the early seventies a shift once again towards a more angry tone occurs in the novels of Penelope Mortimer, Muriel Spark and Doris Lessing.

Showalter's title indicates her debt to Virginia Woolf, and as Mary Eagleton points out their projects are markedly similar: 'A passion for women's writing and feminist research . . . links both critics. Aware of the invisibility of women's lives, they are active in the essential work of retrieval, trying to find the forgotten precursors.' Showalter, however, criticizes Woolf for her 'retreat' into androgyny (denying her femaleness) and for her 'elusive' style. This, as Eagleton (1995) points out, is exactly where Toril Moi disagrees with Showalter, and where the focus of the opposition between Anglo-American and French critical feminisms may be sharply perceived. For the 'French' Moi, Woolf's refusal and subversion of the unitary self and her 'playful' textuality are her strengths, whereas the 'Anglo-American' gynocritic wishes to centre on the female author and character, and on female *experience* as the marker of authenticity – on notions of 'reality' (in particular of a collective understanding of what it means to be a woman) which can be represented, and experientially related to, by way of the literary work. Indeed, a further problem lies in the ethnocentric assumptions embedded in the ideas of 'authenticity' and 'female experience' perpetuated in the 'Anglo-American' tradition generally; as Mary Eagleton has pointed out, the white, heterosexual, middle-class woman is taken as the norm and the literary history produced is 'almost as selective and ideologically bound as the male tradition'. For Moi, Showalter's Anglo-American feminist criticism is also characterized both by being untheorized and by the shakiness, therefore, of its theoretical underpinning – most particularly in the connections it makes between literature and reality and between literary evaluation and feminist politics. A feature of Showalter's work is its reluctance to engage and contain French theoretical initiatives, for, almost by definition, it is deconstructed by them. Paradoxically, then, at the point when the gynocritics saw themselves as making women's experience and culture positively visible and empowering, poststructuralist feminism textualizes sexuality and regards the whole project of 'women writing and writing about women' as misconceived. It is to this more radically

theoretical analysis of women's difference, opened up by modern psychoanalysis, that we now turn.

French feminism: Kristeva, Cixous, Irigaray

Bearing in mind that the fallout from 'French' feminist critical theory is
constrained by no national boundary, it is nevertheless the case that this
other key strand of the 'second wave' originated in France. Deriving from
Simone de Beauvoir's perception of woman as 'the Other' to man, sexuality (together with class and race) is identified as a binary opposition
(man/woman, black/white) which registers 'difference' between groups of
people – differences which are manipulated socially and culturally in ways
which cause one group to dominate or oppress another. French feminist
theoreticians in particular, in seeking to break down conventional, male-
constructed stereotypes of sexual difference, have focused on language as
at once the domain in which such stereotypes are structured, and evidence
of the liberating sexual difference which may be described in a specifically 'women's language'. Literature is one highly significant discourse in
which this can be perceived and mobilized. (Black and lesbian feminists
in America and elsewhere have developed and/or critiqued these ideas in
relation to the ever more complex positionings of those whose 'difference'
is over-determined by race and/or sexual preference.)

French feminism has been deeply influenced by psychoanalysis, especially by Jacques Lacan's reworking of Freud (see Chapter 7), and in this
has overcome the hostility towards the latter hitherto shared by many feminists. Before Lacan, Freud's theories, especially in the United States (cf. Kate
Millett above), had been reduced to a crude biological level: the female child,
seeing the male organ, recognizes herself as female because she lacks the
penis. She defines herself negatively and suffers an inevitable 'penis envy'.
According to Freud, penis envy is universal in women and is responsible
for their 'castration complex', which results in their regarding themselves
as *'hommes manqués'* rather than a positive sex in their own right. Ernest
Jones was the first to dub Freud's theory 'phallocentric', a term widely adopted
by feminists when discussing male domination in general. Juliet Mitchell,
however, in *Psychoanalysis and Feminism* (1975), defended Freud, arguing
that 'psychoanalysis is not a recommendation *for* a patriarchal society
but an analysis *of* one'. Freud, she believes, is describing the *mental representation* of a social reality, not reality itself. Her defence of Freud helped
provide the basis for contemporary psychoanalytic feminism, along with

the more Lacanian-influenced work of Jacqueline Rose (*Sexuality in the Field of Vision*, 1986) and Shoshana Felman (*Literature and Psychoanalysis*, 1977), much of this work assisted by Mitchell and Rose's *Female Sexuality: Jacques Lacan and the École Freudienne* (1982). Inevitably feminists have reacted bitterly to a view of woman as, in Terry Eagleton's words, 'passive, narcissistic, masochistic and penis-envying'. However, some French feminists have emphasized that Freud's 'penis' or 'phallus' is a 'symbolic' concept and not a biological actuality, and Lacan's use of the term draws upon the ancient connotations of the phallus in fertility cults. The word is also used in theological and anthropological literature with reference to the organ's symbolic meaning as *power*.

One of Lacan's diagrams has been found useful by feminists in making clear the linguistic, and then social, arbitrariness of sexual difference:

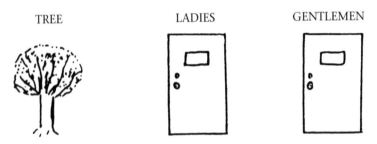

The first sign is 'iconic', describing the 'natural' correspondence between word and thing, and it sums up the old pre-Saussurean notion of language, according to which words and things appear naturally unified in a universal meaning. The second diagram destroys the old harmony: the signifiers 'ladies' and 'gentlemen' are attached to identical doors. The 'same' doors are made to enter the differential system of language, so that we are made to see them as 'different'. In the same way, the word 'woman' is a signifier, not the biological female: there is no simple correspondence between a specific body and the signifier 'woman'. However, this does not mean that if we remove the distorting inscription of the signifier, a 'real', 'natural' woman will come to light as she would have been before the onset of symbolization; we can never step outside the process of signification onto some neutral ground. Feminist resistance to phallocentrism (the dominance of the phallus as a signifier), then, must come from within the signifying process. As we will see in Chapter 7, the signifier is more powerful than the 'subject', who 'fades' and suffers 'castration'. 'Woman' represents a subject position banished to outer darkness ('the dark continent') by the castrating power of phallocentrism, and indeed, because such oppression works through discourse, by 'phallogocentrism' (Derrida's term for the domination exercised by patriarchal discourse). However, the black feminist critic Kadiatu Kanneh has pointed to the dangers inherent in any feminist reiteration of the 'dark continent' motif to suggest the subversive potential of all women (present in de Beauvoir's work and typified in Cixous's comments in 'The Laugh of the Medusa' that 'you are Africa, you are black. Your continent is dark. Dark is dangerous'). Kanneh writes: '[Cixous's] drive to unlock women from a history she labels as exclusively male manages to lock all women into a history of free-floating between images of black subjection and imperial domination' ('Love, Mourning and Metaphor: Terms of Identity', 1992). An understanding of the complex position of 'woman' as a dominated, compliant, but resistant subject under patriarchy is of course not new. Its ramifications are expressed in the telling concept of 'masquerade', first introduced in an essay of 1929 by the psychoanalyst, translator and colleague of Freud, Joan Rivière. Women, Rivière argued, adopt a public mask of 'womanliness' or 'femininity' in accordance with a male image of what a woman should be. Thus they conform to the stereotypes of patriarchy. In so far as this entails a role or performance, however (with no 'genuine womanliness' behind the mask, said Rivière), 'masquerade' implies a critique of a supposed or imposed female identity. To understand identity as constructed in this way lends a more positive aspect to 'masquerade' – one taken up by theories of performativity in queer theory and in the writings of Judith Butler (see Chapter 10).

For Lacan, the question of phallocentrism is inseparable from the structure of the sign. The signifier, the phallus, holds out the promise of full presence and power, which, because it is unobtainable, threatens both sexes with the 'castration complex'. Social and cultural factors, such as gender stereotypes, will accentuate or diminish the impact of this unconscious 'lack', but the phallus, being a signifier of full presence and not a physical organ, remains a universal source of 'castration complex'. Lacan sometimes calls this insistent signifier 'Name-of-the-Father', thus emphasizing its non-'real', non-biological mode of existence. The child arrives at a sense of identity by entering the 'symbolic' order of language, which is made up of relations of *similarity* and *difference*. Only by accepting the exclusions (if this, then not that) imposed by the Law of the Father can the child enter the gendered space assigned to it by the linguistic order. It is essential to recognize the *metaphoric* nature of the father's role: he is installed in the position of lawgiver not because he has a superior procreative function but merely as an effect of the linguistic system. The mother recognizes the speech of the father because she has access to the *signifier* of the paternal function

('Name-of-the-Father'), which regulates desire in a 'civilized' (i.e. repressed) manner. Only by accepting the necessity of sexual difference (either/or) and regulated desire can a child become 'socialized'.

However, feminists have objected that, even if we take a strictly 'symbolic' view of the phallus, the privileged position in signification accorded to it in Lacan's theories is quite disproportionate. According to Jane Gallop, the application of Lacan's categories to sexual difference seems inevitably to involve a subordination of female sexuality. The man is 'castrated' by not being the total fullness promised by the phallus, while the woman is 'castrated' by not being male. Nevertheless, the advantage of Lacan's approach is that it supersedes biological determinism and puts Freudian psychoanalysis in touch with the social system (through language). Further, as Gallop has also noted, Lacan tends to promote a 'feminist' anti-logocentric discourse: though not consciously feminist, he is 'coquettish', playful and 'poetic', refusing to assert conclusions or to establish truths. When he recalls Freud's unanswered question: 'What does Woman want?' (*Was will das Weib?*), he concludes that the question must remain open since the female is 'fluid', and fluidity is 'unstable'. 'Woman never speaks *pareil* [similar, equal, like]. What she emits is flowing [*fluent*]. Cheating [*Flouant*].' There is here a danger, once again, of slipping back into a phallocentric system which relegates women to the margin, dismissing them as unstable, unpredictable and fickle; but what appears to prevent such a recuperation of female 'openness' to the patriarchal system is the positive *privileging* of this openness. Female sexuality is directly associated with poetic productivity – with the psychosomatic drives which disrupt the tyranny of unitary meaning and logocentric (and therefore phallogocentric) discourse. The major proponents of this theory are Julia Kristeva and Hélène Cixous.

Kristeva's work (see also Chapter 7, pp. 161–2) has frequently taken as its central concept a polarity between 'closed', rational systems and 'open', disruptive, 'irrational' systems. She has considered poetry to be the 'privileged site' of analysis, because it is poised between the two types of system, and because at certain times poetry has opened itself to the basic impulses of desire and fear which operate outside the 'rational' systems. Her important distinction between the 'semiotic' and the 'symbolic' is the progenitor of many other polarities. In *avant-garde* literature, the primary processes (as described in Lacan's version of Freud's theory of dreams) invade the rational ordering of language and threaten to disrupt the unified subjectivity of the 'speaker' and the reader. The 'subject' is seen no longer as the source of meaning but as the site of meaning, and may therefore undergo a radical 'dispersal' of identity and loss of coherence. The 'drives' experienced by the child in the pre-Oedipal phase are like a language but not yet ordered into one. For this 'semiotic' material to become 'symbolic' it must be stabilized, and this involves repression of the flowing and rhythmic drives. The utterance which most approximates to a semiotic discourse is the pre-Oedipal 'babble' of the child. However, language itself retains some of this semiotic flux, and the poet is especially attuned to tapping its resonances. Because the psychosomatic drives are pre-Oedipal they are associated with the body of the mother; the free-floating sea of the womb and the enveloping sensuousness of the mother's breast are the first places of pre-Oedipal experience. This domain of oneness and plenitude experienced by the mother–child dyad, Kristeva names the 'semiotic chora' – the latter a term from Plato's *Timaeus* where it is used to designate a passage or bridge between worlds. This hybrid realm 'anterior to naming' is 'maternally connoted', writes Kristeva (1980), while the 'symbolic' is linked with the Law of the Father which censors and represses in order that discourse may come into being. Woman is the silence or incoherence of the pre-discursive: she is the 'Other', which stands outside and threatens to disrupt the conscious (rational) order of speech.

This thinking is linked to the concept of 'abjection' in Kristeva's work, a concept which names the horror of being unable to distinguish between the 'me' and 'not-me' – of which the first and primary instance is the embryo's existence within the mother (Kristeva, 1982). The 'abject' is what the subject seeks to expel in order to achieve an independent identity, but cannot, since the body is unable to cease both taking in and expelling 'waste' (body fluids, excrement, bile, vomit, mucus). The abject is therefore the troubled and recurrent marker bordering the clean and unclean, the self and other – including, primarily, the self and its mother. As Kelly Oliver (1993) comments, abjection is a way of 'denying the primal narcissistic identification with the mother, almost'. This border must be constantly patrolled by the individual subject and by societies which need to cleanse themselves of those at once repellent and seductive aspects of itself which threaten the maintenance of social order (as in religious observance, confession and burial rites). As such, the abject is to be distinguished from the Freudian notion of the repressed. Kristeva employs the concept to discuss literary works by Dostoevsky, Proust, Joyce, Borges and Artaud, and, principally, as a way of understanding the anti-Semitic beliefs of the French novelist, Louis Ferdinand Céline. Literature and the Bible she views as 'privileged signifiers' of the abject, as enacting 'an unveiling . . . a discharge and hollowing out of abjection' (1982). In a discussion which takes up Kristeva's ideas, Maud Ellman (1990) reads T. S. Eliot's *The Waste Land* as re-inscribing 'the horrors it is trying to repress': as 'fascinated by the femininity it reviles'. Eliot's poem is, she concludes, 'one of the most abject texts in English literature'. Elsewhere, the concept has been much used in recent studies of gothic literature and film (see Creed, 1993; Turcotte, 1995; Cavallaro, 2002) to demonstrate how the irrationality and psychic disturbance associated with the Other is regularly configured as female, or, in Creed's designation, as the 'monstrous-feminine'. 'Woman' is not simply marginalized to a position outside social-sexual norms in such texts, rather she is expelled and threatens from what is simultaneously an outer and inner realm.

We should note, however, that since the pre-Oedipal phase is undifferentiated sexually (although the semiotic is unequivocally 'feminine'), Kristeva does not identify the 'feminine' with the biological woman and 'masculine' with the biological man. She herself rejects the designation 'feminist'. Nevertheless, we might say that she does, indeed, stake a claim on behalf of women to this unrepressed and unrepressive flow of liberating energy. The *avant-garde* poet, man or woman, enters the Body-of-the-Mother and resists the Name-of-the-Father. Mallarmé, for example, by subverting the laws of syntax subverts the Law of the Father, and identifies with the mother through his recovery of the 'maternal' semiotic flux. In literature, the meeting of the semiotic and the symbolic, where the former is released in the latter, results in linguistic 'play'. The resultant '*jouissance*' enacts a 'rapture' that is close to 'rupture'. Kristeva sees this poetic revolution as closely linked with political revolution in general and feminist liberation in particular: the feminist movement must invent a 'form of anarchism' which will correspond to the 'discourse of the avant-garde'. Anarchism is inevitably the philosophical and political position adopted by a feminism determined to destroy the dominance of phallogocentrism. Kristeva, unlike Cixous and Irigaray, does not treat the oppression of women as different in principle from that of other marginalized or exploited groups, since initial feminism was part of a larger and more general theory of subversion and dissent. Indeed, the notion of 'abjection', mobilized in studies of literature and film as above, has an evident bearing, too, upon wider issues of power, prejudice, exclusion and subversion raised in Postcolonial Studies – specifically, in this context, in the forms of the 'Postmodern Gothic' (see Gelder, 2000; Taylor, Smith and Hughes (eds), 2003; Newman, 2004). Kristeva's reflections in *Strangers to Ourselves* (1991) are also relevant here, although it should be said that they have had a mixed reception. Thus, while Madan Sarup finds Kristeva's remarks on the 'foreigner' and 'foreignness' useful (1996), David Punter (2000) finds them 'curiously misguided', and judges her earlier generalizations in *About Chinese Women* (1977) as 'entirely reprehensible'. Gayatri Spivak had been critical of that work, too, pointing to Kristeva's 'primitivistic reverence' for the ' "classical" East' (1987; see also Chapter 9, p. 235, and for further discussion, Gelder and Jacobs, 1998).

A number of French feminists have argued that female sexuality is a subterranean and unknown entity which can nevertheless represent itself in literary writing. Hélène Cixous is a creative writer and philosopher who argues for a positive representation of femininity in a discourse she calls '*écriture féminine*', and her essay 'The Laugh of the Medusa' (1976) is a celebrated manifesto of 'women's writing' which calls for women to put their 'bodies' into their writing. While Virginia Woolf abandoned the struggle to speak of the female body, Cixous writes ecstatically of the teeming female unconscious: 'Write yourself. Your body must be heard. Only then will the immense resources of the unconscious spring forth.' The female imagination is infinite and beautiful; the truly liberated woman writer, when she exists, will say:

> I . . . overflow; my desires have invented new desire, my body knows unheard-of songs. Time and again . . . I have felt so full of luminous torrents that I could burst – burst with forms much more beautiful than those which are put up in frames and sold for a stinking fortune.

Since writing is the place where subversive thought can germinate, it is especially shameful that the phallocentric tradition has, for the most part, succeeded in suppressing woman's voice. Woman must uncensor herself, recover 'her goods, her organs, her immense bodily territories which have been kept under seal'; she must throw off her guilt (for being too hot or too frigid, too motherly or too unmaternal). But the heart of Cixous' theory is her rejection of theory: women's writing 'will always surpass the discourse that regulates the phallocentric system'. Always the 'Other' or negative of any hierarchies society may construct, *l'écriture féminine* will at once subvert 'masculine' symbolic language and create new identities for women, which, in their turn, will lead to new social institutions. However, her own work contains theoretical contradictions, whether strategic or not. Her concern for the free play of discourse rejects biologism, but her privileging of the female body seems to embrace it; she rejects the masculine/feminine binary opposition and embraces Derrida's principle of '*différance*' (her work on James Joyce – for example, 'The (R)use of Writing' (1970; trans. 1984) – represents her attempt to affirm the destabilizing nature of writing non-biologistically), but she connects 'feminine writing' with

Lacan's pre-Oedipal 'Imaginary' phase in which difference is abolished in a pre-linguistic, utopian unity of the child and the mother's body.

This liberating return to the 'Good Mother' is the source of Cixous' poetic vision of women's writing, and it opens the possibility of a new type of sexuality. She opposes the sort of neutral bisexuality espoused by Virginia Woolf, and advocates instead what she calls 'the *other bisexuality*' which refuses to 'annul differences but stirs them up'. Barthes' study of *Sarrasine* (see Chapter 7, pp. 151–3) is an excellent example of narrative bisexuality, and Cixous' account of female sexuality is often reminiscent of Barthes' description of the *avant-garde* text. 'A woman's body,' writes Cixous, 'with its thousand and one thresholds of ardor . . . will make the old single-grooved mother tongue reverberate with more than one language.' This is, of course, '*jouissance*' which, in Barthes and Kristeva, combines connotations of sexual orgasm and polysemic speech; the pleasure of the text, abolishing all repressions, reaches an intense crisis (the death of meaning). Such transgression of the laws of phallocentric discourse is the woman writer's special task, and having always operated 'within' male-dominated discourse, she needs 'to invent for herself a language to get inside of'.

Cixous' approach is essentially and strategically visionary, imagining a possible language rather than describing an existing one; but it runs the risk of driving women into a political and intellectual silence, interrupted only by 'uterine babble'. This danger is well understood by Kristeva, who sees women writers rather in the way that Virginia Woolf saw them, as caught between the father and the mother. On the one hand, as writers, they inevitably collude with 'phallic dominance, associated with the privileged father–daughter relationship, which gives rise to the tendency towards mastery, science, philosophy, professorships, etc.'. On the other, 'we flee everything considered "phallic" to find refuge in the valorisation of a silent underwater body, thus abdicating any entry into history'.

Luce Irigaray's *Spéculum de l'autre femme* (1974) develops, in more rigorously philosophical terms, ideas which resemble Cixous'. She considers that patriarchal oppression of women is founded on the type of negative constructions associated with Freud's theory of female sexuality. The concept of 'penis envy', for example, is based upon a view of woman as man's 'Other', lacking the penis which he possesses (precariously). She is not viewed as existing at all except as a negative mirror-image of a man. In this sense, women are invisible to the male gaze and can only achieve a sort of phantasmal existence in hysteria and in mysticism. Woman, like the mystic, is able to lose all sense of personal subjective being, and is therefore able to slip through the patriarchal net. While men are oriented to sight (they are scopophilic), women find pleasure in touch; and therefore woman's writing is connected with fluidity and touch, with the result that 'Her "style" resists and explodes all firmly established forms, figures, ideas, concepts.' Irigaray, in other words, promotes the radical 'otherness' of women's eroticism and its disruptive enactment in language. Only the celebration of women's difference – their fluidity and multiplicity – can rupture conventional Western representations of them.

Feminist theory's development and mobilization of critical positions which flow from such a 'poststructuralist' conception are dealt with in Chapters 8, 9 and 10. But it is worth signalling here that these kinds of criticism tend to recognize that 'Woman' is not a physical being but a 'writing-effect', that 'l'écriture féminine', in Mary Jacobus's phrase, 'asserts not the sexuality of the text but the textuality of sex'. They do not see writing as specifically 'gendered' but seek to disrupt fixed meaning; they encourage textual free-play beyond authorial or critical control; they are anti-humanist, anti-realist and anti-essentialist; and they represent, in effect, a potent form of political, cultural and critical deconstruction. In terms specifically of literary studies, they revalue and reshape (if not explode) literary canons, refuse a unitary or universally accepted body of theory, and overtly politicize the whole domain of discursive practice. They are fluid, multiplex, heteroglossic and subversive, and as such are at the centre of the contemporary poststructuralist and postmodernist assault on the 'master'-narratives which have governed Western – and hence colonial – cultures since the Enlightenment. It is to the originary development of such movements that we now turn.

Selected reading

Key texts

Abel, Elizabeth (ed.), *Writing and Sexual Difference* (University of Chicago Press, Chicago, 1982; Harvester Wheatsheaf, Hemel Hempstead, 1983).

Barrett, Michèle, *Women's Oppression Today: Problems in Marxist Feminist Analysis* (Verso, London, 1980).

Belsey, Catherine and Moore, Jane (eds), *The Feminist Reader: Essays in Gender and the Politics of Literary Criticism* (2nd edn, Palgrave Macmillan, Basingstoke, 1997).

Cixous, Hélène, 'The Laugh of the Medusa' [1975; revd 1976 version trans. by Keith and Paula Cohen], reprinted in Elaine Marks and Isabelle de Courtivron (eds), below.

Cixous, Hélène, *Writing Differences: Readings from the Seminar of Hélène Cixous*, Susan Sellers (ed.) (Open University Press, Milton Keynes, 1988).

Cixous, Hélène, *The Selected Plays of Hélène Cixous* (Routledge, London, 2003).

Cixous, Hélène and Mireille Calle-Gruber, *Hélène Cixous, Rootprints: Memory and Life Writing*, commentary by Jacques Derrida (Routledge, London, 1997).

de Beauvoir, Simone, *The Second Sex* [1949], trans. by H. M. Parshley (Bantam, New York, 1961; Penguin, Harmondsworth, 1974).

Eagleton, Mary (ed.), *Feminist Literary Theory: A Reader* (2nd edn, Blackwell, Oxford, 1995).

Ellmann, Mary, *Thinking About Women* (Harcourt Brace Jovanovich, New York, 1968).

Felman, Shoshana (ed.), *Literature and Psychoanalysis* (Johns Hopkins University Press, Baltimore, 1977).

Feminism: Critical Concepts in Literary and Cultural Studies, 4 vols, ed. by Mary Evans (Routledge, London, 2000).

Friedan, Betty, *The Feminine Mystique* (Dell, New York, 1963).

Gallop, Jane, *Feminism and Psychoanalysis: The Daughter's Seduction* (Macmillan, Basingstoke, 1982).

Gilbert, Sandra and Gubar, Susan, *The Madwoman in the Attic: The Woman Writer and the Nineteenth Century Literary Imagination* (Yale University Press, New Haven, 1979).

Gilbert, Sandra and Gubar, Susan, *No Man's Land: The Place of the Woman Writer in the Twentieth Century* (Yale University Press, New Haven, 1988).

Humm, Maggie, *The Dictionary of Feminist Theory* (Harvester Wheatsheaf, Hemel Hempstead, 1989).

Humm, Maggie (ed.), *Feminisms: A Reader* (Harvester Wheatsheaf, Hemel Hempstead, 1992).

Irigaray, Luce, *Speculum of the Other Woman* [1974], trans. by Gillian C. Gill (Cornell University Press, Ithaca, 1985).

Irigaray, Luce, *This Sex Which Is Not One* [1977], trans. by Catherine Porter with Carolyn Burke (Cornell University Press, Ithaca, 1985).

Irigaray, Luce, *The Irigaray Reader*, ed. and intro. by Margaret Whitford (Blackwell, Oxford, 1991).

Jacobus, Mary (ed.), *Women Writing and Writing About Women* (Croom Helm, London, 1979).

Jacobus, Mary, *Reading Woman: Essays in Feminist Criticism* (Methuen, London, 1986).

Johnson, Barbara, *A World of Difference* (Johns Hopkins University Press, Baltimore, 1987).

Kaplan, Cora, *Sea Changes: Culture and Feminism* (Verso, London, 1986).

Kauffman, Linda S., *American Feminist Thought at Century's End: A Reader* (Basil Blackwell, Oxford, 1993).

Kolodny, Annette, 'Dancing Through the Minefield: Some Observations on the Theory, Practice and Politics of a Feminist Literary Criticism', *Feminist Studies*, vol. 6 (1980), 1–25.

Kristeva, Julia, *About Chinese Women* [1977], trans. by Anita Barrows (Marion Boyars, New York and London, 1986).

Kristeva, Julia, *Desire in Language: A Semiotic Approach to Literature and Art*, trans. by Thomas Gora, Alice Jardine and Leon S. Roudiez; ed. by Leon. S. Roudiez (Columbia University Press, New York, 1980).

Kristeva, Julia, *Powers of Horror: An Essay on Abjection* (Columbia University Press, New York, 1982).

Kristeva, Julia, *The Kristeva Reader*, ed. by Toril Moi (Basil Blackwell, Oxford, 1986).

Kristeva, Julia, *Strangers to Ourselves*, trans. by Leon S. Roudiez (Columbia University Press, New York, 1991; also pub. by Harvester Wheatsheaf).

Marks, Elaine and de Courtivron, Isabelle (eds), *New French Feminisms: An Anthology* (Harvester Wheatsheaf, Hemel Hempstead, 1981).

(The) Marxist-Feminist Literature Collective, 'Women's Writing: *Jane Eyre, Shirley, Villette, Aurora Leigh*', *Ideology and Consciousness*, 3 (Spring, 1978), 27–48; pp. 27–34 are reprinted in ch. 3 of Peter Brooker and Peter Widdowson (eds), *A Practical Reader* (see Introduction, 'Selected Reading').

Millett, Kate, *Sexual Politics* (Doubleday, New York, 1970).

Mitchell, Juliet, *Psychoanalysis and Feminism* (Penguin, Harmondsworth, 1975).

Mitchell, Juliet, *Women: The Longest Revolution: Essays on Feminism, Literature and Psychoanalysis* (Virago, London, 1984).

Moers, Ellen, *Literary Women* (Anchor Press, Garden City, 1976).

Moi, Toril (ed.), *French Feminist Thought: A Reader* (Basil Blackwell, Oxford, 1987).

Newton, Judith and Rosenfelt, Deborah (eds), *Feminist Criticism and Social Change: Sex, Class, and Race in Literature* (Methuen, London, 1985).

Rivière, Joan, 'Womanliness as a Masquerade', *International Journal of Psycho-Analysis*, 10 (1929), 303–13.

Rose, Jacqueline and Mitchell, Juliet (eds), *Feminine Sexuality: Jacques Lacan and the École Freudienne* (Macmillan, Basingstoke, 1982).

Saguaro, Shelley (ed.), *Psychoanalysis and Woman* (Palgrave Macmillan, Basingstoke, 2000).

Showalter, Elaine, *A Literature of Their Own* (Princeton University Press, Princeton, NJ, 1977).

Showalter, Elaine (ed.), *Speaking of Gender* (Routledge, London, 1989).

Spender, Dale, *Man Made Language* (Routledge, London, 1980).

Spivak, Gayatri Chakravorty, *In Other Worlds: Essays in Cultural Politics* (Routledge, London, 1987). See also 'Selected Reading' for Chapter 9.

Wittig, Monique, *The Lesbian Body* [1973], trans. by David Le Vay (Peter Owen, London, 1975).

Woolf, Virginia, *A Room of One's Own* (Hogarth Press, London, 1929).

Woolf, Virginia, *Three Guineas* (Hogarth Press, London, 1938).

Woolf, Virginia, *On Women and Writing* [1979], selected and intro. by Michèle Barrett (The Women's Press, London, 2001).

Further reading

Belsey, Catherine, 'Critical Approaches', in Claire Buck (ed.), *Bloomsbury Guide to Women's Literature* (Bloomsbury, London, 1992).

Benstock, Shari, Ferriss, Suzanne and Woods, Susanne, *A Handbook of Literary Feminisms* (Oxford University Press, New York and Oxford, 2002).

Bronfen, Elisabeth, *Over Her Dead Body: Death, Femininity and the Aesthetic* (Manchester University Press, Manchester, 1992).

Bray, Abigail, *Hélène Cixous: Writing and Sexual Difference* (Palgrave Macmillan, Basingstoke, 2003).

Cavallaro, Dani, 'The Abject', in *The Gothic Vision: Three Centuries of Horror, Terror and Fear* (Continuum, London, 2002), pp. 199–206.

Célestin, Roger, DalMolin, Eliane and de Courtivron, Isabelle (eds), *Beyond French Feminisms: Debates on Women, Culture and Politics in France 1980–2001* (Palgrave Macmillan, Basingstoke, 2003).

Creed, Barbara, *The Monstrous Feminine: Film, Feminism and Psychoanalysis* (Routledge, London, 1993).

Culler, Jonathan, 'Reading as a Woman', in *On Deconstruction: Theory and Criticism after Structuralism* (Routledge, London, 1983).

de Lauretis, Teresa (ed.), *Feminist Studies/Critical Studies* (Indiana University Press, Bloomington, 1986).

Eagleton, Mary, *A Concise Companion to Feminist Theory* (Blackwell, Oxford, 2003).

Ellman, Maud, 'Eliot's Abjection', in John Fletcher and Andrew Benjamin (eds), *Abjection, Melancholia and Love: The Work of Julia Kristeva* (Routledge, London, 1990), pp. 178–98.

Felski, Rita, *Beyond Feminist Aesthetics: Feminist Literature and Social Change* (Hutchinson Radius, London, 1989).

Fullbrook, Edward and Kate, *Simone de Beauvoir: A Critical Introduction* (Polity Press, Cambridge, 2997).

Fuss, Diana, *Essentially Speaking: Feminism, Nature and Difference* (Routledge, London, 1989).

Gallop, Jane, *Around 1981: Academic Feminist Literary Theory* (Routledge, London, 1992).

Gates, Henry Louis, Jr (ed.), *Reading Black: Reading Feminist: A Critical Anthology* (Meridian, New York, 1990).

Gelder, Ken, 'Global/Postcolonial Horror' and 'Postcolonial Voodoo', *Postcolonial Studies*, 3, 1 (May, 2000), 35–8 and 89–98.

Gelder, Ken and Jacobs, Jane M., *Uncanny Australia: Sacredness and Identity in a Postcolonial Nation* (Melbourne University Press, Melbourne, 1998).

Grosz, Elizabeth, *Jacques Lacan: A Feminist Introduction* (Routledge, London, 1990).

Kamuf, Peggy, 'Writing Like a Woman', in Sally McConnell *et al.* (eds), *Women and Language in Literature and Society* (Praeger Publishers, New York, 1980).

Kanneh, Kadiatu, 'Love, Mourning and Metaphor: Terms of Identity', in Isobel Armstrong (ed.), *New Feminist Discourses: Critical Essays on Theories and Texts* (Routledge, London, 1992).

Kaplan, Cora, 'Feminist Literary Criticism: "New Colours and Shadows"', in *Encyclopaedia of Literature and Criticism*, Martin Coyle, Peter Garside, Malcolm Kelsall and John Peck (eds) (Routledge, London, 1990).

Kaplan, Cora, 'Radical Feminism and Literature: Rethinking Millett's *Sexual Politics*' [1979], reprinted in Mary Eagleton (ed., 1995), (see *Key texts* above).

Lakoff, Robin, *Language and Woman's Place* (Harper & Row, New York, 1975).

Laqueur, Thomas, *Making Sex: Body and Gender from the Greeks to Freud* (Harvard University Press, Cambridge, Mass. and London, 1990).

Lechte, John and Zournazi, Mary (eds), *The Kristeva Critical Reader* (Edinburgh University Press, Edinburgh, 2003).

McAfee, Nölle, *Julia Kristeva* (Routledge, London, 2003).

Miller, Nancy (ed.), *The Poetics of Gender* (Columbia University Press, New York, 1986).

Miller, Nancy, *Getting Personal: Feminist Occasions and Other Autobiographical Acts* (Routledge, London, 1991).

Mills, Sara, *Feminist Stylistics* (Routledge, London, 1995).

Mills, Sara, Pearce, Lynne, Spaull, Sue and Millard, Elaine, *Feminist Readings/Feminists Reading* (Harvester Wheatsheaf, Hemel Hempstead, 1989).

Modleski, Tania, *Feminism Without Women: Culture and Criticism in a 'Postfeminist' Age* (Routledge, London, 1991).

Moi, Toril, *Sexual/Textual Politics: Feminist Literary Theory* [1985] (2nd edn, Routledge, London, 2002).

Moi, Toril, *Feminist Literary Theory and Simone de Beauvoir* (Basil Blackwell, Oxford, 1990).

Moi, Toril, *What Is A Woman? And Other Essays* (Oxford University Press, Oxford, 2002).

Newman, Judie, 'Postcolonial Gothic: Ruth Prawer Jhabvala and the Sobhraj Case', in Fred Botting (ed.), *Gothic: Critical Concepts in Literary and Cultural Studies* (Routledge, London, 2004), pp. 293–307.

Oliver, Kelly, *Reading Kristeva: Unraveling the Double-Bind* (Indiana University Press, Bloomington, 1993).

Punter, David, *Postcolonial Imaginings: Fictions of a New World Order* (Edinburgh University Press, Edinburgh, 2000).

Robbins, Ruth, *Literary Feminisms* (Palgrave Macmillan, Basingstoke, 2000).

Rose, Jacqueline, *Sexuality in the Field of Vision* (Verso, London, 1986).

Sarup, Madan, *Identity, Culture and the Postmodern World* (Edinburgh University Press, Edinburgh, 1996).

Sellers, Susan (ed.), *Feminist Criticism: Theory and Practice* (Harvester Wheatsheaf, Hemel Hempstead, 1991).

Sellers, Susan, *Hélène Cixous: Authorship, Autobiography and Love* (Polity Press, Cambridge, 1996).

Taylor, Jonathan, Smith, Andrew and Hughes, William (eds), *Empire and the Gothic: The Politics of Genre* (Palgrave Macmillan, Basingstoke, 2003).

Tidd, Ursula, *Simone de Beauvoir* (Routledge, London, 2003).

Turcotte, Gerry, 'Sexual Gothic: Marian Engel's Bear and Elizabeth Jolley's The Well', in *ARIEL: A Review of International English Literature*, 26, 2 (1995), 65–91.

Waugh, Patricia, *Feminine Fictions: Revisiting the Modern* (Routledge, London, 1989).

Weedon, Chris, *Feminist Practice and Poststructuralist Theory* (2nd edn, Blackwell, Oxford, 1996).

Weedon, Chris, *Feminism, Theory and the Politics of Difference* (Blackwell, Oxford, 1999).

Whitford, Margaret, *Luce Irigaray: Philosophy in the Feminine* (Routledge, London, 1991).

CHAPTER 7

Poststructuralist theories

At some point in the late 1960s, structuralism gave birth to 'poststructuralism'. Some commentators believe that the later developments were already inherent in the earlier phase. One might say that poststructuralism is simply a fuller working-out of the implications of structuralism. But this formulation is not quite satisfactory, because it is evident that poststructuralism tries to deflate the scientific pretensions of structuralism. If structuralism was heroic in its desire to master the world of artificial signs, poststructuralism is comic and anti-heroic in its refusal to take such claims seriously. However, the poststructuralist mockery of structuralism is almost a self-mockery: poststructuralists are structuralists who suddenly see the error of their ways.

It is possible to see the beginnings of a poststructuralist counter-movement even in Saussure's linguistic theory. As we have seen, *langue* is the systematic aspect of language which works as the underpinning structure of *parole*, the individual instance of speech or writing. The sign is also bipartite: signifier and signified are like two sides of a coin. However, Saussure also notices that there is no necessary connection between signifier and signified. Sometimes a language will have one word (signifier) for two concepts (signifieds): in English 'sheep' is the animal and 'mutton' the meat; French has only one word for both signifieds ('mouton'). It is as though the various languages carve up the world of things and ideas into different concepts (signifieds) on the one hand, and different words (signifiers) on the other. As Saussure puts it, 'A linguistic system is a series of differences of sound combined with a series of differences of ideas.' The signifier 'hot' is able to work as part of a sign because it *differs* from 'hat', 'hit', 'hop', 'hog', 'lot', and so on. These 'differences' can be aligned with different signifieds. He concludes with his celebrated remark 'In language

there are only differences *without positive terms'*. However, before we jump
to the wrong conclusion, he immediately adds that this is only true if we
take signifiers and signifieds separately. There is a natural tendency, he assures
us, for one signified to seek its own signifier, and to form with it a *positive
unit*. Saussure's assertion of a certain stability in signification is to be expected in a 'pre-Freudian' thinker: while the signifier/signified relationship
is arbitrary, speakers in practice require particular signifiers to be securely
attached to particular concepts, and therefore they assume that signifier and
signified form a unified whole and preserve a certain identity of meaning.

Poststructuralist thought has discovered the essentially *unstable* nature
of signification. The sign is not so much a unit with two sides as a moment-
ary 'fix' between two moving layers. Saussure had recognized that signifier
and signified are two separate systems, but he did not see how unstable units
of meaning can be when the systems come together. Having established
language as a total system independent of physical reality, he tried to retain
a sense of the sign's coherence, even though his splitting of the sign into
two parts threatened to undo it. Poststructuralists have in various ways prised
apart the two halves of the sign.

Surely, we might ask, the unity of the sign is confirmed whenever we
use a dictionary to find a meaning (signified) of a word (signifier)? In fact,
the dictionary confirms only the relentless deferment of meaning: not only
do we find for every signifier several signifieds (a 'crib' signifies a manger,
a child's bed, a hut, a job, a mine-shaft lining, a plagiarism, a literal translation, discarded cards at cribbage), but each of the signifieds becomes yet
another signifier which can be traced in the dictionary with its own array
of signifieds ('bed' signifies a place for sleeping, a garden plot, a layer of
oysters, a channel of a river, a stratum). The process continues inter-
minably, as the signifiers lead a chameleon-like existence, changing their
colours with each new context. Much of the energy of poststructuralism
has gone into tracing the insistent activity of the signifier as it forms chains
and cross-currents of meaning with other signifiers and defies the orderly
requirements of the signified.

As we have noted in Chapter 4, structuralists attack the idea that language is an instrument for reflecting a pre-existent reality or for expressing
a human intention. They believe that 'subjects' are produced by linguistic
structures which are 'always already' in place. A subject's utterances belong
to the realm of *parole*, which is governed by *langue*, the true object of
structuralist analysis. This systematic view of communication excludes
all subjective processes by which individuals interact with others and with
society. The poststructuralist critics of structuralism introduce the concept

of the 'speaking subject' or the 'subject in process'. Instead of viewing language as an impersonal system, they regard it as always articulated with other systems and especially with subjective processes. This conception of language-in-use is summed up in the term 'discourse'.

The Bakhtin School (see Chapter 2) were probably the first modern literary theorists to reject the Saussurean notion of language. They insisted that all instances of languages had to be considered in a social context. Every utterance is potentially the site of a struggle: every word that is launched into social space implies a dialogue and therefore a contested interpretation. The relations between signifiers and signifieds are always fraught with interference and conflict. Language cannot be neatly dissociated from social living; it is always contaminated, interleaved, opaquely coloured by layers of semantic deposits resulting from the endless processes of human struggle and interaction.

Later, a parallel movement occurred in linguistic thought. In his celebrated distinction between *histoire* (narrative) and *discours* (discourse) Emile Benveniste tried to preserve the notion of a non-subjectivized region of language. He argued that a purely narrative use of language (characterized in French fiction by the use of the 'past historic' or 'aorist' tense) is quite devoid of intervention by the speaker. This appears to deny Bakhtin's belief that all language-in-use is 'dialogic'. The 'I–you' dimension is excluded in pure narrative, which seems to narrate itself without subjective mediation. The dialogues embedded in a fiction are situated and rendered manageable by the authority of the *histoire* which itself has no apparent subjective origin. As Catherine Belsey puts it, 'classic realism proposes a model in which author and reader are subjects who are the source of shared meanings, the origin of which is mysteriously extradiscursive' (*Critical Practice*, 1980). As has been demonstrated by Gérard Genette (see Chapter 4, pp. 71–2) and many others, the *histoire/discours* distinction does not hold water. Take the first sentence of the first chapter of George Eliot's *Middlemarch*: 'Miss Brooke had that kind of beauty which seems to be thrown into relief by poor dress.' At the level of *histoire* we are being told that Miss Brooke had a certain kind of beauty, and the impersonal syntax of the sentence seems to give it objectivity and truth. The locution 'that kind', however, immediately introduces a 'discursive' level: it refers to something which readers are expected to recognize and confirm. Roland Barthes would have said that George Eliot is here using the 'cultural code' (see the section on Barthes below). This underlines the fact that not only is the author endorsing a certain culturally specific assumption but that the 'I–you' relationship between author and reader is being invoked. Poststructuralists would agree that narrative can never escape the discursive level. The slogan 'there is only discourse' requires careful explication, but it sums up effectively the thrust of this chapter.

Poststructuralist thought often takes the form of a critique of empiricism (the dominant philosophical mode in Britain at least from the mid-seventeenth century onwards). It saw the subject as the source of all knowledge: the human mind receives impressions from without which it sifts and organizes into a knowledge of the world, which is expressed in the apparently transparent medium of language. The 'subject' grasps the 'object' and puts it into words. This model has been challenged by a theory of 'discursive formations', which refuses to separate subject and object into separate domains. Knowledges are always formed from discourses which pre-exist the subject's experiences. Even the subject itself is not an autonomous or unified identity, but is always 'in process' (see below on Kristeva and Lacan). There has been a parallel shift in the history and philosophy of science. T. S. Kuhn (see Chapter 3, p. 50) and Paul Feyerabend have challenged the belief in the steady progression of knowledge in the sciences, and have shown that science 'progresses' in a series of jumps and breaks, in a *discontinuous* movement from one discursive formation (or 'paradigm') to another. Individual scientists are not subjects apprehending objects through the blank mirror of the senses (and their technical extensions). They conduct and write up their research within the conceptual limits of particular scientific discourses, which are historically situated in relation to their society and culture.

The work of Michel Foucault (see below, pp. 178–80) has gone much further than this in mapping the discursive formations which, often in the name of science, have enabled institutions to wield power and domination by defining and excluding the mad, the sick, the criminal, the poor and the deviant. For Foucault discourse is always inseparable from power, because discourse is the governing and ordering medium of every institution. Discourse determines what it is possible to say, what are the criteria of 'truth', who is allowed to speak with authority, and where such speech can be spoken. For example, to take a degree in English literature we must study in or correspond with a validated institution. Only recognized teachers of the institution are allowed to determine the ways in which subjects are studied. In a given period only certain kinds of speaking and writing are recognized as valid. Marxist critics of Foucault have regarded his theory of discursive formations as unduly pessimistic and have suggested ways of theorizing discourse in terms of ideological formations which allow more readily for the possibility of resistance and subversion of dominant discourses (see below, 'New Historicism and Cultural Materialism').

Louis Althusser (see Chapter 5) made an important contribution to discourse theory in his 'Ideology and Ideological State Apparatuses' (1969). He argues that we are all 'subjects' of ideology which operates by summoning us to take our places in the social structure. This summoning (or 'interpellation') works through the discursive formations materially linked with 'state apparatuses' (religious, legal, educational and so on). The 'imaginary' consciousness which ideology induces gives us a representation of the way individuals relate to their 'real conditions of existence', but being merely an undisrupted and harmonious 'image' it actually represses the real relations between individuals and the social structure. By translating 'discourse' into 'ideology' Althusser gives a political charge to the theory by introducing a domination–subordination model. He adopts for his own purposes the psychoanalytic terminology of Jacques Lacan (see below), who questions the humanist notion of a substantial and unified subjectivity (an illusion derived from the pre-Oedipal 'imaginary' phase of childhood). However, Althusser's model of the subject's formation is more static. Lacan conceives the subject as a permanently unstable entity, split between the conscious life of the 'ego' and the unconscious life of 'desire'. Colin MacCabe has suggested that a more Lacanian model of interpellation can be envisaged:

> A Marxist reading of the division of the subject in the place of the Other would theorise the individual's assumption of the place produced for him or her by the complex of discursive formations and would insist that these places would be constantly threatened and undermined by their constitutive instability in the field of language and desire. ('*On Discourse*', in MacCabe 1981)

The work of Michel Pêcheux, which goes some way to providing a more elaborate account of the operation of ideological discourses in relation to subjectivity, will be discussed in the section on 'New Historicism', where Foucault's pessimism about the possibility of resistance to the discursive power of ideologies is countered by the arguments of Cultural Materialism.

Roland Barthes

Barthes (see also Chapter 4, pp. 65–6) was undoubtedly the most entertaining, witty and daring of the French theorists of the 1960s and 1970s. His career took several turns, but preserved a central theme: the conventionality of all forms of representation. He defines literature (in an early essay) as 'a message of the signification of things and not their meaning (by "signification" I refer to the process which produces the meaning and not this meaning itself)'. He echoes Roman Jakobson's definition of the 'poetic' as the 'set to the message', but Barthes stresses the *process* of signification, which appears less and less predictable as his work proceeds. The worst sin a writer can commit is to pretend that language is a natural, transparent medium through which the reader grasps a solid and unified 'truth' or 'reality'. The virtuous writer recognizes the artifice of all writing and proceeds to make play with it. Bourgeois ideology, Barthes' *bête noire*, promotes the sinful view that reading is natural and language transparent; it insists on regarding the signifier as the sober partner of the signified, thus in authoritarian manner repressing all discourse into a meaning. *Avant-garde* writers allow the unconscious of language to rise to the surface: they allow the signifiers to generate meaning at will and to undermine the censorship of the signified and its repressive insistence on one meaning.

If anything marks a poststructuralist phase in Barthes it is his abandoning of scientific aspirations. In *Elements of Semiology* (1967), he believed that structuralist method could explain all the sign-systems of human culture. However, in the very same text, he recognized that structuralist discourse itself could become the object of explanation. The semiological invest-igator regards his or her own language as a 'second-order' discourse which operates in Olympian fashion upon the 'first-order' object-language. The second-order language is called a metalanguage. In realizing that any metalanguage could be put in the position of a first-order language and be interrogated by another metalanguage, Barthes glimpsed an infinite regress (an 'aporia'), which destroys the authority of all metalanguages. This means that, when we read as critics, we can never step outside discourse and adopt a position invulnerable to a subsequent interrogative reading. All discourses, including critical interpretations, are equally *fictive*; none stand apart in the place of Truth.

What might be called Barthes' poststructuralist period is best represented by his short essay 'The Death of the Author' (1968). He rejects the traditional view that the author is the origin of the text, the source of its mean-ing, and the only authority for interpretation. At first, this sounds like a restatement of the familiar New Critical dogma about the literary work's independence (autonomy) from its historical and biographical background. The New Critics believed that the unity of a text lay not in its author's inten-tion but in its structure (for discussion of the 'intentional fallacy', see Chap-ter 1, pp. 20–1). This self-contained unity, nevertheless, has subterranean connections with its author, because, in their view, it represents a complex verbal enactment (a 'verbal icon') corresponding to the author's intuitions about the world. Barthes' formula is utterly radical in its dismissal of such humanistic notions. His author is stripped of all metaphysical status and reduced to a location (a crossroad), where language, that infinite storehouse of citations, repetitions, echoes and references, crosses and recrosses. The reader is thus free to enter the text from any direction; there is no correct route. The death of the author is already inherent in structuralism, which treats individual utterances (*paroles*) as the products of impersonal systems (*langues*). What is new in Barthes is the idea that readers are free to open and close the text's signifying process without respect for the signified. They are free to take their pleasure of the text, to follow at will the defiles of the signifier as it slips and slides evading the grasp of the signified. Readers are also sites of language's empire, but they are free to connect the text with systems of meaning and ignore the author's 'intention'. The central character in Dennis Potter's *Blackeyes* (1987) is a photographic model who possesses the openness of a sign awaiting the mark of the observer's inscribing gaze. Blackeyes expresses the 'sensuality of the passive. Her perfectly formed oval of a face was a blank upon which male desire could be projected. Her luminous large, jet-like eyes said nothing, and so said everything. She was pliable. She was there to be invented, in any posture, any words, over and over again, in ejaculatory longing.' She is a poststructuralist text totally at the mercy of the reader's pleasure. (Other, earlier, examples of 'free' characters who are available for an observer's inscription – note, they are all female – might be: Widow Wadman in *Tristram Shandy*, where Sterne leaves a blank page for the reader to fill in their own ideal description of the most 'concupiscible' woman in the world in place of Sterne's characterization; Tess, in Hardy's novel, who is often regarded as composed of images set up by the male gaze she is constantly subject to; and Sarah Woodruff in John Fowles's *The French Lieutenant's Woman*, whom the author considers an 'enigma' he cannot know.)

In *The Pleasure of the Text* (1973) Barthes explores this reckless abandon of the reader. He begins by distinguishing between two senses of 'pleasure':

Pleasure

'pleasure'   'bliss'

Within Pleasure there is 'bliss' (*jouissance*, with its orgasmic connotation) and its diluted form, 'pleasure'. The general pleasure of the text is whatever *exceeds* a single transparent meaning. As we read, we see a connection, an echo, or a reference, and this disruption of the text's innocent, linear flow gives pleasure. Pleasure involves the production of a *join* (seam, fault or flaw) between two surfaces: the place where naked flesh meets a garment is the focus of erotic pleasure. In texts the effect is to bring something unorthodox or perverse into connection with naked language. Reading the realistic novel we create another 'pleasure' by allowing our attention to wander, or by skipping: 'it is the very rhythm of what is read and what is not read that creates the pleasure of the great narratives'. This is especially true of reading erotic writing (though Barthes insists that pornography has no texts of bliss because it tries too hard to give us the ultimate truth). The more limited reading of pleasure is a comfortable practice which conforms to cultural habits. The text of bliss 'unsettles the reader's historical, cultural, psychological assumptions . . . brings a crisis to his relation with language'. It is clear that such a text does not conform to the sort of easily enjoyed pleasure demanded in the market economy. Indeed, Barthes considers that 'bliss' is very close to boredom: if readers resist the ecstatic collapse of cultural assumptions, they will inevitably find only boredom in the modernist text. How many blissful readers of Joyce's *Finnegans Wake* have there been?

Barthes' *S/Z* (1970) is an impressive poststructuralist performance. He begins by alluding to the vain ambitions of structuralist narratologists who try 'to see all the world's stories . . . within a single structure'. The attempt to uncover *the* structure is vain, because each text possesses a 'difference'. This difference is not a sort of uniqueness, but the result of textuality itself. Each text refers back differently to the infinite sea of the 'already written'. Some writing tries to discourage the reader from freely reconnecting text and this 'already written' by insisting on specific meaning and reference. A realistic novel offers a 'closed' text with a limited meaning. Other texts encourage the reader to *produce* meanings. The 'I' which reads is 'already itself a plurality of other texts' and is allowed by the *avant-garde* text the maximum liberty to produce meanings by putting what is read in touch with this plurality. The first type of text allows the reader only to be a *consumer* of a fixed meaning, while the second turns the reader into a *producer*. The first type of text is called 'readerly' (*lisible*), the second 'writerly' (*scriptible*). The first is made to be read (consumed), the second to be written (produced). The writerly text exists only in theory, though Barthes' description of it suggests the texts of modernism: 'this ideal text is a galaxy of signifiers, not a structure of signifieds; it has no beginning . . . we gain access to it by several entrances, none of which can be authoritatively declared to be the main one; the codes it mobilizes extend as far as the eye can reach'.

What are the 'codes'? As the quotation above makes clear, they are not the structuralist systems of meaning we might expect. Whatever systems (Marxist, formalist, structuralist, psychoanalytic) we choose to apply to the text can only activate one or more of the virtually infinite 'voices' of the text. As the reader adopts different viewpoints the text's meaning is produced in a multitude of fragments which have no inherent unity. *S/Z* is a reading of Balzac's novella, *Sarrasine*, which Barthes divides into 561 lexias (reading units). The lexias are read in sequence through the grid of five codes:

Hermeneutic

Semic

Symbolic

Proairetic

Cultural

The hermeneutic code concerns the *enigma* which arises whenever discourse commences. Who is this about? What is happening? What is the obstacle? Who committed the murder? How will the hero's purpose be achieved? A detective story is sometimes called a 'whodunit', thus drawing attention to the special importance of enigma to this genre. In *Sarrasine* the enigma surrounds La Zambinella. Before the question 'Who is she?' is finally answered ('she' is a castrato dressed as a woman), the discourse is spun out with one delaying answer after another: 'she' is a 'woman' ('snare'), 'a creature outside nature' ('ambiguity'), 'no one knows' (a 'jammed answer'). The code of 'semes' concerns the connotations often evoked in characterization or description. An early account of La Zambinella, for example, sparks off the semes 'femininity', 'wealth' and 'ghostliness'. The symbolic code concerns the polarities and antitheses which allow multivalence and 'reversibility'. It marks out the patterns of sexual and psychoanalytic relations people may enter. For example, when we are introduced to Sarrasine, he is presented in the symbolic relation of 'father and son' ('he was the only son of a lawyer . . .'). The absence of the mother (she is unmentioned) is significant, and when the son decides to become an artist he is no longer 'favoured' by the father but 'accursed' (symbolic antithesis). This symbolic coding of the narrative is developed later when we read of the warm-hearted sculptor Bouchardon who enters the absent place of the mother and effects a reconciliation between father and son. The proairetic code (or code of actions) concerns the basic sequential logic of action and behaviour. Barthes marks such a sequence between lexias 95 and 101: the narrator's girl-friend touches the old castrato and reacts by breaking out in a cold sweat; when his relatives react in alarm, she makes for a side room and throws herself upon a couch in fright. Barthes marks the sequence as five stages of the coded action 'to touch': (1) touching; (2) reaction; (3) general reaction;

(4) to flee; (5) to hide. They form a sequence which the reader, unconsciously operating the code, perceives as 'natural' or 'realistic'. Finally, the cultural code embraces all references to the common fund of 'knowledge' (physical, medical, psychological, literary, and so on) produced by society. Sarrasine first reveals his genius 'in one of those works in which future talent struggles with the effervescence of youth' (lexia 174). 'One of those' is a regular formula for signalling this code (see above, p. 146 in relation to George Eliot). Barthes ingeniously notes a double cultural reference: 'Code of ages and code of Art (talent as discipline, youth as effervescence)'.

Why did Barthes choose to study a realistic novella and not an *avant-garde* text of *jouissance*? The cutting-up of the discourse and the dispersal of its meanings across the musical score of codes seem to deny the text its classic status as realistic story. The novella is exposed as a 'limit text' for realism. The elements of ambivalence destroy the unity of representation which we expect in such writing. The theme of castration, the confusion of sexual roles, and the mysteries surrounding the origins of capitalist wealth all invite an anti-representational reading. It is as if the principles of poststructuralism were already inscribed in this so-called realist text.

Psychoanalytic theories

The relationship between psychoanalysis and literary criticism spans much of the twentieth century. Fundamentally concerned with the articulation of sexuality in language, it has moved through three main emphases in its pursuit of the literary 'unconscious': on the author (and its corollary, 'character'), on the reader and on the text. It starts with Sigmund Freud's analysis of the literary work as a symptom of the artist, where the relationship between author and text is analogous to dreamers and their 'text' (literature = 'fantasy'); is modified by post-Freudians in a psychoanalytic reader-response criticism where the reader's transactive relation to the text is foregrounded (see Chapter 3); and is contested by Carl Jung's 'archetypal' criticism in which, *contra* Freud, the literary work is not a focus for the writer's or reader's personal psychology but a representation of the relationship between the personal and the collective unconscious, the images, myths, symbols, 'archetypes' of past cultures. More recently, psychoanalytic criticism has been remodelled in the context of poststructuralism by the work of Jacques Lacan and his followers, in which the coupling of a dynamic notion of 'desire' with a model of structural linguistics has been influentially innovative. This is especially the case in feminist psychoanalytical criticism (see Chapter 6, pp. 129–37), which, as Elizabeth Wright has said, is concerned with

> the interaction of literature, culture and sexual identity, emphasising the way that configurations of gender are located in history. The feminist psychoanalytic enquiry has perhaps the potential for becoming the most radical form of psychoanalytic criticism, since it is crucially concerned with the very construction of subjectivity. (Wright, 1990)

There has been a consistent interest in contemporary Literary Studies in the Unconscious (it was Freud who gave this term a capital letter and definite article) and the notion and effects of 'repression', linked often with debates on sexuality. Some other concepts (discussed below) – for example, 'Nachträglichkeit' (referring to the 'working through' of trauma) and the 'uncanny' – have come into renewed prominence, quite possibly because they are compatible with contemporary concerns and a readiness to accept and probe uncertainties of time, subjectivity and meaning. Concepts such as these have therefore gained a new critical currency in the context of poststructuralism and cognate tendencies in postcolonial studies where this interest in destabilized borders and identities is evident in the use of terms such as 'hybridity', 'syncretism' and 'liminality' (see Chapter 8). Also, where postcolonial literatures have confronted the repression of past pre- or anti-colonial histories they have often had recourse, too, to the tropes of gothic or horror stories in narratives of haunting, nightmare, phantasms, ghosts and spectres. Here again there are cross-overs between psychoanalysis and insights in poststructuralism (see below on Jacques Derrida, pp. 170–1).

Freud introduced the concept of 'Nachträglichkeit' in his case study of the so-called 'Wolf Man' (Freud, 1974, vol. 17: 3–122). The 'Wolf Man' is said to witness an act of sexual intercourse between his parents at the age of one-and-a-half, but the traumatic shock of this incident is deferred until he is capable of bringing some mature sexual understanding to it. The implication is that an event has in effect two occurrences: an original happening and a later interpretative construction of it, or, in a still more radical gloss on this concept, the event is seen only to acquire significance in so far as it is remembered. That is to say, there is no first event other than its construction at a later stage, since meaning is always the retrospective result of a process of 'working through'. This implies a radically non-linear notion of memory and individual history, effectively positing that a memory at a later date is the 'cause' rather than the 'effect' of the supposed earlier, original, incident. This suggests, as above, an unexpected affinity between Freud and later poststructuralist concepts of 'belatedness' and 'deferral', and is of relevance to the writing and study of autobiographies and historical fictions which problematize standard notions of historical sequence and causation. An example of a study which follows through these implications with reference to Freud's concept is Peter Nicholls's reading of Toni Morrison's *Beloved* (in Brooker and Widdowson (eds) 1996 (see 'Anthologies of Literary Theory' in 'Selected reading' for Introduction): 441–56). Morrison's *Beloved* is also a ghost story in which the dead daughter, named Beloved, returns as a young woman; the novel, along with other of Morrison's fiction, is discussed in relation to 'haunting' in David Punter's *Postcolonial Imaginings* (2000).

In his essay on 'the uncanny' (1919), Freud explores the etymologies of the German terms *unheimlich* (uncanny, unfamiliar, frightening) and *heimlich* (homely, familiar) to discover that at a certain point the meanings of these opposite terms are very close, if not identical, since the sense of *heimlich* as 'belonging to the house' also produces the associated meanings of being concealed, made secret, or kept from sight. '"Unheimlich"', Freud comments, 'is in some way or another a subspecies of "Heimlich"' (1974, vol. 17: 226). Freud further relates the uncanny, first to the survival in the unconscious of a 'primitive' and subsequently repressed animistic mythological and mystic view of the world; and second, to the occurrence of repetitions, coincidences and doubles. This latter he understands as the result of repressed experiences in infancy. The 'unheimlich', he concludes, 'is what was once "heimisch", familiar; the prefix "un" [un-] is the token of repression' (1974, vol. 17: 245).

The uncanny is clearly relevant, as this suggests, to literary narratives, especially science fiction, horror, fantastic and gothic genres (see Jackson, 1981; Botting, 1996), including instances of the postcolonial gothic, where the figure of the alien, or Other, proves to be the projection of a repressed inner self and unsettles notions of a unified personality. Indeed, if we think of literature as 'defamiliarizing' the familiar and taken-for-granted, then it is invariably an example of the uncanny (see Royle, 2003). Freud's main illustration in his essay is itself a literary one: the tale of 'The Sandman' by the German Romantic writer E. T. A. Hoffman. In this story a student fears losing his eyes. The source of his fear are the visits to his childhood home of a family lawyer. At these times his father sent him to bed threatening that the sandman would pull out his eyes if he disobeyed. The boy associates the lawyer, and subsequently other men (an oculist, an eye-glass salesman), with the sandman and goes to his death fearing he has been trapped by this figure. Freud reads the story in terms of the Oedipal complex, seeing the boy's fear of the loss of his eyes as a displaced expression of the fear of castration. The boy and the reader therefore experience the repressed but familiar anxiety over castration as a now displaced, 'uncanny' fear of the loss of eyes.

However, Freud's reading of this tale has been seen as a reductive and selective one. Hélène Cixous (1976: see 'Key texts' for Chapter 6) responded by pointing to the figure of a doll in the story, ignored by Freud, who is brought to life and is therefore a further example of the uncanny. Angela Carter's story, 'The Loves of Lady Purple', we might also note, is the story of just such an animated vampiric doll. Jane Marie Todd (1986) probes the connection between the fear of castration and the male sight of the female body. Re-readings and re-writings of this kind are an example of Feminism's continuing debate with the assumed male norms of Freud's theory and serve in this instance to introduce more woman-centred versions of the uncanny (see Wright, 1989).

Jacques Lacan

Western thought has for a long time assumed the necessity of a unified 'subject'. To *know* anything presupposes a unified consciousness which does the knowing. Such a consciousness is rather like a focused lens without which nothing can be seen as a distinct object. The medium through which this unified subject perceives objects and truth is *syntax*. An orderly syntax makes for an orderly mind. However, reason has never had things all its own way; it has always been threatened by the subversive noise of pleasure (wine, sex, song), of laughter, and of poetry. Ascetic rationalists such as Plato always keep a sharp eye on these dangerous influences. They can all be summed up in the one concept – 'desire'. Disruption can go beyond the merely literary to the social level. Poetic language shows how dominant social discourses can be undermined by the creation of new 'subject positions'. This implies that far from being a mere blank which awaits its social or sexual role, the subject is *'in process' and is capable of being other than it is.*

The psychoanalytic writings of Jacques Lacan have given critics a new theory of the 'subject'. Marxist, formalist and structuralist critics have dismissed 'subjective' criticisms as Romantic and reactionary, but Lacanian criticism has developed a 'materialist' analysis of the 'speaking subject' which has been more acceptable. According to the linguist Emile Benveniste, 'I', 'he', 'she', and so on, are merely subject positions which language lays down. When I speak, I refer to myself as 'I' and to the person I address as 'you'.

When 'you' reply, the persons are reversed and 'I' becomes 'you', and so on. We can communicate only if we accept this strange reversibility of persons. Therefore, the ego which uses the word 'I' is not identical with this 'I'. When I say 'Tomorrow I graduate', the 'I' in the statement is known as the 'subject of the enunciation', and the ego which makes the statement is the 'subject of the enunciating'. Poststructuralist thought enters the gap between these two subjects, while Romantic thought simply elides them.

Lacan considers that human subjects enter a pre-existing system of signifiers which take on meanings only within a language system. The entry into language enables us to find a subject position within a relational system (male/female, father/mother/daughter). This process and the stages which precede it are governed by the unconscious. According to Freud, during the earliest phases of infanthood the libidinal drives have no definite sexual object but play around the various erotogenic zones of the body (oral, anal, 'phallic'). Before gender or identity are established there is only the rule of the 'pleasure principle'. The 'reality principle' eventually supervenes in the form of the father who threatens the male child's Oedipal desire for the mother with the punishment of 'castration'. The repression of desire makes it possible for the male child to identify with the place of the father and with a 'masculine' role. The Oedipal voyage of the female is much less straight-forward, and Freud's endemic sexism has been attacked by some feminist critics (see Chapter 6). This phase introduces morality, law, and religion, symbolized as 'patriarchal law', and induces the development of a 'superego' in the child. However, the repressed desire does not go away and remains in the unconscious, thus producing a radically *split* subject. Indeed, this force of desire *is* the unconscious.

Lacan's distinction between the 'imaginary' and the 'symbolic' corresponds to Kristeva's between 'semiotic' and 'symbolic' (see Chapter 6, p. 132). This 'imaginary' is a state in which there is no clear distinction between subject and object: no central self exists to set object apart from subject. In the pre-linguistic 'mirror phase', the child – from within this 'imaginary' state of being – starts to project a certain unity into the fragmented self-image in the mirror (there does not have to be an actual mirror); he or she produces a 'fictional' ideal, an 'ego'. This specular (*speculum* = mirror) image is still partly imaginary (it is not clear whether it is the child or another), but also partly differentiated as 'another'. The imaginary tendency continues even after the formation of the ego, because the myth of a unified selfhood depends upon this ability to identify with objects in the world as 'others'. Nevertheless, the child must also learn to differentiate itself from others if it is to become a subject in its own right. With the father's prohibition the child is thrown headlong into the 'symbolic' world of differences (male/female, father/son, present/absent, and so on). Indeed, the 'phallus' (not the penis but its 'symbol') is, in Lacan's system, the privileged signifier, which helps all signifiers achieve a unity with their signifieds. In the symbolic domain phallus is king. As we shall see, feminist critics have had a good deal to say about this.

Neither the imaginary nor the symbolic can fully comprehend the Real, which remains out there somewhere, but beyond reach because beyond the subject and beyond representation. 'The Real', says Sarup (1992), 'is the domain of the inexpressible, of what cannot be spoken about, for it does not belong to language. It is the order where the subject meets with inexpressible enjoyment and death.' Our instinctive *needs* are shaped by the discourse in which we express our *demand* for satisfaction. However, discourse's moulding of needs leaves not satisfaction but *desire*, which runs on in the chain of signifiers. When 'I' express my desire in words, 'I' am always subverted by that unconscious which presses on with its own sideways game. This unconscious works on in metaphoric and metonymic substitutions and displacements which elude consciousness, but reveals itself in dreams, jokes and art.

Lacan restates Freud's theories in the language of Saussure. Essentially, unconscious processes are identified with the unstable *signifier*. As we have seen, Saussure's attempts to solder up the gap between the separate systems of signifiers and signifieds was in vain. For example, when a subject enters the symbolic order and accepts a *position* as 'son' or 'daughter', a certain linking of signifier and signified is made possible. However, 'I' am never where I think; 'I' stand at the axis of signifier and signified, a split being never able to give my position a full presence. In Lacan's version of the sign, the signified 'slides' beneath a signifier which 'floats'. Freud considered dreams the main outlet for repressed desires. His theory of dreams is reinterpreted as a textual theory. The unconscious hides meaning in symbolic images which need to be deciphered. Dream images undergo 'condensation' (several images combine) and 'displacement' (significance shifts from one image to a contiguous one). Lacan calls the first process 'metaphor' and the second 'metonymy' (see Jakobson, Chapter 4). In other words, he believes that the garbled and enigmatic dream-work follows the laws of the signifier. Freud's 'defence mechanisms', too, are treated as figures of speech (irony, ellipsis, and so on). Any kind of psychic distortion is restated as a quirk of the signifier rather than some mysterious pre-linguistic urge. For Lacan there never were any undistorted signifiers. His psychoanalysis is the scientific rhetoric of the unconscious.

Lacan's Freudianism has encouraged modern criticism to abandon faith in language's power to refer to things and to express ideas or feelings. Modernist literature often resembles dreams in its avoidance of a governing narrative position and its free play of meaning. Lacan himself wrote a much discussed analysis of Poe's 'The Purloined Letter', a short story containing two episodes. In the first, the Minister perceives that the Queen is anxious about a letter she has left lying exposed on a table unnoticed by the King who has entered her boudoir unexpectedly. The Minister replaces the letter with a similar one. The Queen cannot intervene for fear that the King will be alerted. In the second episode, following the Prefect of Police's failure to find the letter in the Minister's house, Dupin (a detective) immediately sees it openly thrust in a card-rack on the Minister's mantlepiece. He returns, distracts the Minister, and replaces the letter with a similar one. Lacan points out that the contents of the letter are never revealed. The story's development is shaped not by the character of individuals or the contents of the letter but by the *position* of the letter in relation to the trio of persons in each episode. These relations to the letter are defined by Lacan according to three kinds of 'glance': the first sees nothing (the King's and the Prefect's); the second sees that the first glance sees nothing but thinks its secret safe (the Queen's and, in the second episode, the Minister's); the third sees that the first two glances leave the 'hidden' letter exposed (the Minister's and Dupin's). The letter, then, acts like a signifier by producing subject positions for the characters in the narrative. Lacan considers that, in this, the story illustrates the psychoanalytic theory that the symbolic order is 'constitutive for the subject'; the subject receives a 'decisive orientation' from the 'itinerary of a signifier'. He treats the story as an allegory of psychoanalysis, but also considers psychoanalysis as a model of fiction. The repetition of the structure of scene one in scene two is governed by the effects of a pure signifier (the letter); the characters move into their places as the unconscious prompts. (For a fuller account not only of Lacan's essay but also of Jacques Derrida's critical reading of Lacan's reading, see Barbara Johnson's essay in Robert Young's *Untying the Text*, 1981. In a brilliant demonstration of poststructuralist thought she introduces a further displacement of meaning into the potentially endless sequence: Poe > Lacan > Derrida > Johnson.)

As part of the impetus of poststructuralist thinking, Lacan's psychoanalytic ideas (also mediated in the work of Althusser (p. 148, above), Kristeva, and Deleuze and Guattari (see below)) have enjoyed a central status in recent British literary theory. However, while the 'linguistic turn' continues to permeate the study of cultural forms in general, British School psychoanalysis – whose genealogy stems directly from Freud's London years, and includes such names as Melanie Klein, D. W. Winnicott, Wilfred Bion and R. D. Laing – has complicated the Freudian psychoanalytic scenario which Lacan had 'poststructuralized' much as it stood. The emphasis has been on extending practical psychoanalytic investigation – in particular, the study of the finally untheorizable phenomena encountered in transference/countertransference negotiations of all kinds (including group-work), which are seen as at the core of the Freudian method. In *The Good Society and the Inner World* (1991), for instance, Michael Rustin laments the 'routing of all messages via Paris' and comments on Lacan's lack of interest in psychoanalysis's 'proper base in clinical work' – a sentiment also summed up by R. W. Connell as: 'theorists debate the Law of the Father or the significance of sublimation without two cases to rub together.' The British School view appears to be that even theoretical 'paradigm shifts' require a background of careful 'normal science', and that post-Lacanian French psychoanalysis is more interested in cultural theorizing than in further analysing the dynamics of actual psychic phenomena.

However, British School psychoanalysis lacks a sophisticated bridge between its clinical work and the discourse in which it is expressed; and it can appear naïve and out-of-date in its interdisciplinary overtures towards literary theory (still haunted in its conception of this by F. R. Leavis and an unproblematized notion of the canon). Yet it could become highly productive for literary and cultural studies. Of particular interest are its post-Kleinian emphasis on the child–mother dyad (thought of as more fundamental than Oedipal and anti-Oedipal theories); the performative creativity of the developing mind (whatever its social structuration); and the extension beyond the psychoanalytic 'subject' to both small and larger group-work. The first issue is already implicit in the ideas of Kristeva (see below, and Chapter 6, pp. 131–3) and is taken up in much feminist theory; the second in Derrida's meditations on Artaud and *Hamlet*, which reveal his acquaintance with Klein's work – but there is scope for further cooperation here. The third emphasis constitutes a possible bridge between the personal and the political as potentially as fruitful as Althusser's arranged-marriage between the unconscious and ideology. Since Wilfred Bion's pioneering work, the psychoanalytic study of group interactions – at an existentially more primal level than discourse as such – is highly suggestive for understanding how literature is produced in intertextual emulation and rivalry; why critical and theoretical movements (including poststructuralism, New Historicism and postmodernism) have strong emotive, as well as intellectual, authority; and the psychoanalytic terms in which even 'hard science' actually develops. There remains the possibility, then, of an *entente cordiale* in which literary theory could benefit at once from Parisian theoretical and British School analytical advances to produce a fuller account of cultural understanding in the period since Freud's 'Copernican Revolution'.

Julia Kristeva

Kristeva's work has had a consistent bearing upon the study of literary texts (for her inflection of psychoanalytic theory into feminism, and her view of the revolutionary potential of women writers in society, see Chapter 6). Two key contributions that might be singled out here appeared in early essays, later collected in *The Revolution in Poetic Language* (1974) and *Desire in Language* (1980). In the latter, in two essays, 'The Bounded Text' and 'Word Dialogue and Novel', written in the late 1960s, Kristeva draws on the work of Mikhail Bakhtin and the Russian Formalists to propose the idea of 'intertextuality', later associated with developments in poststructuralism. Thus she writes of 'text' as comprising 'a permutation of texts, an intertextuality', and of how 'in the space of a given text, several utterances, taken from other texts, intersect and neutralise one another'. In addition, seeking to connect the linguistic with the ideological (in common with other members of the *Tel Quel* group in Paris with which she was then associated), she draws on Bahktin and Medvedev's *The Formal Method in Literary Scholarship* to introduce the concept of the 'ideologeme'. This she deploys to suggest the intersection of a given textual arrangement with a broader set of 'exterior texts', or what she terms the 'text of society and history' – again anticipating later, more developed, notions of narrative textuality, as in Fredric Jameson (1981: see 'Key texts' for Chapter 5).

In *The Revolution in Poetic Langage*, Kristeva gives us a complex account, based in psychoanalytic theory, of the relationship between the 'normal' (ordered and rational) and the 'poetic' (heterogeneous and irrational). Human beings are from the beginning a space across which physical and psychic impulses flow rhythmically. This indefinite flux of impulses is gradually regulated by the constraints of family and society (potty-training, gender-identification, separation of public and private, and so on). At the earliest, pre-Oedipal stage, the flow of impulses centres on the mother, and allows not the formulation of a personality but only a rough demarcation of parts of the body and their relations. A disorganized pre-linguistic flux of movements, gestures, sounds and rhythms lays a foundation which remains active beneath the mature linguistic performance of the adult. This unorganized pre-signifying process she calls the 'semiotic' (see Chapter 6, pp. 132–3). We become aware of this activity in dreams, in which images are processed in 'illogical' ways (see the discussion of Lacan, above, p. 158), and through literature. The 'semiotic' comes under the regulation of the logic, coherent syntax and rationality of what Kristeva, following Lacan, terms the 'symbolic'. Entry into the 'symbolic' confers identity upon subjects but its mastery over the 'semiotic' is never complete.

The word 'revolution' in Kristeva's title has been seen as limited to discursive innovation, but it is not simply metaphoric. The possibility of radical social change is, in her view, bound up with the disruption of authoritarian discourses. Poetic language, in particular, introduces the subversive openness of the semiotic 'across' society's 'closed' symbolic order: 'What the theory of the unconscious seeks, poetic language practices, within and against the social order.' Sometimes she considers that modernist poetry actually prefigures a social revolution which in the distant future will come about when society has evolved a more complex form. However, at other times she fears that bourgeois ideology will simply recuperate this poetic revolution by treating it as a safety valve for the repressed impulses it denies in society.

Deleuze and Guattari

Gilles Deleuze and Félix Guattari, in *Anti-Oedipus: Capitalism and Schizophrenia* ([1972], 1983) and *Kafka: Towards a Minor Literature* ([1975], 1986), offer at once a radical critique of psychoanalysis – drawing on, but going beyond, Lacan – and a close textual method for the reading of texts which they term 'schizoanalysis' (see especially the fourth section of *Anti-Oedipus*). Their attack on psychoanalysis primarily targets its representation of desire as based in lack or need, which Deleuze and Guattari see as a capitalist device that deforms the unconscious: the Oedipus complex, hijacked as an internalized set of power relations, is the result of repression by capitalism within the family. Schizoanalysis would, conversely, *construct* an unconscious in which desire constitutes an untramelled 'flow' – an energy which is not contained by Oedipal 'anxiety' but is a positive source of new beginnings. 'Schizoanalysis' means the liberation of desire; whereas paranoiac unconscious desire 'territorializes' – in terms of nation, family, church, school, etc. – a schizophrenic one 'deterritorializes', offering a subversion of these (capitalist) totalities. In this sense, as Elizabeth Wright has said, Deleuze and Guattari's '"material psychiatry" becomes a political factor in its attempts to release the libidinal flow from what they see as oppression rather than repression'.

The relationship of schizophrenia to literature is that the latter too can subvert, and free itself from, the system. But the author/text also needs a 'desire-liberating reader', a 'schizoanalyst', to activate its potentially revolutionary discourses. Deleuze and Guattari's analysis of Kafka, whom they find particularly suited to their project (his work, in a favourite concept of theirs, exemplifies the movement and erratic production of meaning of the 'rhizome' – 'a fertile tuber that sprouts unexpected plants out of concealment' [Wright]), is a bravura, close, textual, entirely anti-New-Critical, out-deconstructing-deconstruction analysis of his work, which exposes the 'gaps' and tensions in the text, the continuously fluid combinations of images, and the subversion of 'normal' notions of representation, symbol and text within both psychoanalytic and other literary-critical discourse. In regarding the work not as 'text' but as essentially uncoded, the practice of the 'revolutionary' schizoanalytic reader/writer will 'deterritorialize' any given representation: hence, in the case of Kafka, accounting for his 'revolutionary' force by exposing the unconscious discourses of desire as more powerful than those of family and state. Kafka also, in an important distinction, represents 'minor' literature. This, in one sense, recognizes his social position as a marginalized author: a Czech Jew who wrote in German. More generally, however, Deleuze and Guattari characterize 'minor' literature as non-conformist, innovatory and interrogative, and as such, opposed to a 'majoritarian' literature which aims to 'represent' a given world and to match established models. This is a distinction drawn throughout *A Thousand Plateaus* (1987). 'Minor literature' becomes, by implication, a description of great literature which is 'creative' of meaning and identity – it is a literature of 'becoming' – rather than an 'expression' of a pre-existing world and assumed common human identity. This aligns literature with 'difference' where the latter has the force of alternative or oppositional affects to dominant cultural modes and mentalities. Praise for Kafka, or 'minor literature' more generally, nevertheless foregrounds the paradox of Deleuze and Guattari's position, for a revolutionary 'minoritarian' *political* project and associated schizoanalysis can only find a displaced and, we might think, limited form in the domain of literature and a schizoid literary criticism. Students of literature, however, will be most interested in this application. Aside from the co-authored volume on Kafka and Deleuze's early study, *Proust and Signs* (1964, trans. 1973), the obvious and most pertinent resource is his collection, *Essays: Critical and Clinical* (1997).

Buchanan and Marks (eds, 2001) take up this aspect of Deleuze's thinking, while, amongst several advanced studies, Colebrook (2002) provides a clear and helpful account of the philosophical ideas informing the wider project.

Deconstruction: Jacques Derrida

Derrida's paper 'Structure, Sign, and Play in the Discourse of the Human Sciences', given at a symposium at Johns Hopkins University in 1966, virtually inaugurated a new critical movement in the United States. Its argument put in question the basic metaphysical assumptions of Western philosophy since Plato. The notion of 'structure', he argues, even in 'structuralist' theory has always presupposed a 'centre' of meaning of some sort. This 'centre' governs the structure but is itself not subject to structural analysis (to find the structure of the centre would be to find another centre). People desire a centre because it guarantees *being as presence*. For example, we think of our mental and physical life as centred on an 'I'; this personality is the principle of unity which underlies the structure of all that goes on in this space. Freud's theories completely undermine this metaphysical certainty by revealing a division in the self between conscious and unconscious. Western thought has developed innumerable terms which operate as centring principles: being, essence, substance, truth, form, beginning, end, purpose, consciousness, man, God, and so on. It is important to note that Derrida does not assert the possibility of thinking outside such terms; any attempt to undo a particular concept is to become caught up in the terms which the concept depends on. For example, if we try to undo the centring concept of 'consciousness' by asserting the disruptive counterforce of the 'unconscious', we are in danger of introducing a new centre, because we cannot choose but enter the conceptual system (conscious/unconscious) we are trying to dislodge. All we *can* do is to refuse to allow either pole in a system (body/soul, good/bad, serious/unserious) to become the centre and guarantor of presence.

This desire for a centre is called 'logocentrism' in Derrida's classic work, *Of Grammatology*. 'Logos' (Greek for 'word') is a term which in the New Testament carries the greatest possible concentration of presence: 'In the beginning was the Word.' Being the origin of all things, the 'Word' underwrites the full presence of the world; everything is the effect of this one cause. Even though the Bible is written, God's word is essentially *spoken*. A spoken word emitted from a living body appears to be closer to an originating thought than a written word. Derrida argues that this privileging of speech over writing (he calls it 'phonocentrism') is a classic feature of logocentrism. What prevents the sign from being a full presence? Derrida invents the term '*différance*' to convey the divided nature of the sign. In French the 'a' in '*différance*' *is* not heard, and so we hear only '*différence*'. The ambiguity is perceptible only in writing: the verb '*différer*' means both 'to differ' and 'to defer'. To 'differ' is a spatial concept: the sign emerges from a system of differences which are spaced out within the system. To 'defer' is temporal: signifiers enforce an endless postponement of 'presence'. Phonocentric thought ignores '*différance*' and insists upon the self-presence of the spoken word.

Phonocentrism treats writing as a contaminated form of speech. Speech seems nearer to originating thought. When we hear speech we attribute to it a 'presence' which we take to be lacking in writing. The speech of the great actor, orator or politician is thought to possess 'presence'; it incarnates, so to speak, the speaker's soul. Writing seems relatively impure and obtrudes its own system in physical marks which have a relative permanence; writing can be repeated (printed, reprinted, and so on) and this repetition invites interpretation and reinterpretation. Even when a speech is subjected to interpretation it is usually in written form. Writing does not need the writer's presence, but speech always implies an immediate presence. The sounds made by a speaker evaporate in the air and leave no trace (unless recorded), and therefore do not appear to contaminate the originating thought as in writing. Philosophers have often expressed their dislike of writing; they fear that it will destroy the authority of philosophic Truth. This Truth depends upon pure thought (logic, ideas, propositions) which risk contamination when written. Francis Bacon believed that one of the main obstacles to scientific advance was the love of eloquence: 'men began to hunt more after words than matter; and more after . . . tropes and figures, than after the weight of matter . . . soundness of argument.' However, as the word 'eloquence' suggests, the qualities in writing to which he objected are those originally developed by orators. Thus, those very features of elaboration in writing which threaten to cloud the purity of thought were originally cultivated for speech.

This coupling of 'writing' and 'speech' is an example of what Derrida calls a 'violent hierarchy'. Speech has full presence, while writing is secondary and threatens to contaminate speech with its materiality. Western philosophy has supported this ranking in order to preserve presence. But, as the Bacon example shows, the hierarchy can easily be undone and reversed. We begin to see that both speech and writing share certain writerly features: both are signifying processes which lack presence. To complete the reversal of the hierarchy, we can now say that speech is a species of writing. This reversal is the first stage of a Derridean 'deconstruction'.

Derrida's questioning of the distinction between speech and writing is paralleled by his interrogation of those between 'philosophy' and 'literature', and between the 'literal' and the 'figurative'. Philosophy can only be philosophical if it ignores or denies its own textuality: it believes it stands at a remove from such contamination. 'Literature' is regarded by philosophy as mere fiction, as a discourse in the grip of 'figures of speech'. By reversing the hierarchy philosophy/literature, Derrida places philosophy *sous rature* or 'under erasure' (~~philosophy~~) – philosophy is itself governed by rhetoric and yet is preserved as a distinct form of 'writing' (we still see 'philosophy' under the mark of erasure). Reading philosophy as literature does not prevent us from reading literature as philosophy; Derrida refuses to assert a new hierarchy (literature/philosophy), although some Derrideans are guilty of this partial deconstruction. Similarly, we discover that 'literal' language is in fact 'figurative' language whose figuration has been forgotten. However, the concept of the 'literal' is not thereby eliminated but only deconstructed. It remains in effect, but 'under erasure'.

Derrida uses the term 'supplement' to convey the unstable relationship between couplets such as speech/writing. For Rousseau writing is merely a supplement to speech; it adds something inessential. In French, *'suppléer'* also means 'to substitute' (to take the place of), and Derrida shows that writing not only supplements but also takes the place of speech, because speech is always already written. All human activity involves this supplementarity (addition-substitution). When we say that 'nature' preceded 'civilization', we are asserting another violent hierarchy in which a pure presence lauds itself over a mere supplement. However, if we look closely, we find that nature is always already contaminated with civilization; there is no 'original' nature, only a myth which we desire to promote.

Consider another example. Milton's *Paradise Lost* may be said to rest on the distinction between good and evil. Good has the original fullness of being. It originated with God. Evil is a second comer, a supplement, which contaminates his original unity of being. However, if we look more closely, we begin to see reversal taking place. For example, if we seek a time when good was without evil, we find ourselves caught in an abysmal regression. Was it before the Fall? Before Satan's? What caused Satan's fall? Pride. Who created pride? God, who created angels and humans free to sin. We never reach an original moment of pure goodness. We may reverse the hierarchy and say that there are no 'good' acts by humans until after the Fall. Adam's first act of sacrifice is an expression of love for the fallen Eve. This 'goodness' comes only after evil. God's prohibition itself presupposes evil. In *Areopagitica* Milton opposed the licensing of books because he believed that we can be virtuous only if we are given the opportunity to struggle against evil: 'that which purifies us is trial, and trial is by what is contrary'. Thus, good comes *after* evil. There are many critical and theological strategies which can sort out this mess, but there remains a basis for deconstruction. Such a reading begins by noting the hierarchy, proceeds to reverse it, and finally resists the assertion of a new hierarchy by displacing the second term from a position of superiority too. Blake believed that Milton was on Satan's side in his great epic, and Shelley thought that Satan was morally superior to God. They simply reverse the hierarchy, substituting evil for good. A deconstructive reading would go on to recognize that the couplet cannot be hierarchized in either direction without 'violence'. Evil is both addition *and* substitution. Deconstruction can begin when we locate the moment when a text *transgresses the laws it appears to set up for itself*. At this point texts go to pieces, so to speak.

In 'Signature Event Context', Derrida gives writing three characteristics:

1   A written sign is a mark which can be repeated in the absence not only of the subject who emitted it in a specific context but also of a specific addressee.

2   The written sign can break its 'real context' and can be read in a different context regardless of what its writer intended. Any chain of signs can be 'grafted' into a discourse in another context (as in a quotation).

3   The written sign is subject to 'spacing' (*espacement*) in two senses: first, it is separated from other signs in a particular chain; second, it is separated from 'present reference' (that is, it can refer only to something not actually present in it).

These characteristics appear to distinguish writing from speech. Writing involves a certain irresponsibility, because if signs are repeatable out of context, then what authority can they possess? Derrida proceeds to deconstruct the hierarchy by, for example, pointing out that when we interpret oral signs, we have to recognize certain stable and identical forms (signifiers), whatever accent, tone or distortion may be involved in the utterance. It appears that we have to exclude the accidental phonic (sound) substance and recover a pure form. This form is the repeatable signifier, which we had thought characteristic of writing. Once again, we conclude that speech is a species of writing.

J. L. Austin's theory of 'speech acts' was developed to supersede the old logical-positivist view of language which assumed that the only meaningful statements are those which describe a state of affairs in the world. All other sorts of statements are not real ones but 'pseudo-statements'. Austin uses the term 'constative' to cover the first (referential statements), and 'performative' to cover those utterances which actually perform the actions they describe ('I swear to tell the whole truth and nothing but the truth' *performs* an oath). Derrida acknowledges that this makes a break with logocentric thought by recognizing that speech does not have to represent something to have a meaning. However, Austin also distinguishes between degrees of linguistic force. To make a merely linguistic utterance (say, to speak an English sentence) is a *locutionary* act. A speech act which has *illocutionary* force involves performing the act (to promise, to swear, to argue, to affirm, and so on). A speech act has *perlocutionary* force if it brings about an effect (*I persuade* you by arguing; I *convince* you by swearing; and so on). Austin requires that speech acts must have contexts. An oath can occur only in a court within the appropriate judicial framework or in other situations in which oaths are conventionally performed. Derrida questions this by suggesting that the repeatability ('iterability') of the speech act is more fundamental than its attachment to a context.

Austin remarks in passing that to be performative a statement must be spoken 'seriously' and not be a joke or used in a play or poem. An oath in a Hollywood court scene is 'parasitic' upon a real-life oath. John Searle's reply to Derrida, 'Reiterating the Differences', defends Austin's view and argues that a 'serious' discourse is logically prior to fictional, 'parasitic' citations of it. Derrida probes this and neatly demonstrates that a 'serious' performative cannot occur unless it is a repeatable sign-sequence (what Barthes called the 'always-already-written'). A real courtroom oath is just a special case of the game people play in films and books. What Austin's pure performative and the impure, parasitic versions have in common is that they involve repetition and citation, which are typical of the 'written'.

After his 1966 paper, Derrida became an academic celebrity in the United States and took up a teaching post at Yale University. Since 1984 he has been Professor at the École des Hautes Études en Sciences Sociales in Paris and has held Visiting Professorships at a number of European and American universities. In 1992 he was awarded an honorary doctorate at Cambridge University – but only after much controversy and the protests of over 200 dons. He died in October 2004 after a prolific late phase when his writing had turned more openly to questions of ethics and politics, including religion. Although versions of his thinking in the United States

and elsewhere had sometimes maligned or digressed from Derrida's own practice, his influence over the last three and more decades, as was recognized
at his death, has been wide and profound. His writing, it has to be said,
has also consistently frustrated and annoyed some readers, although it has
gone some way to satisfy some of his critics on the left, especially since the
early 1990s when it has often consisted of short interventions on questions
of ethics and politics. Of several relevant items in this later period, those
in translation have included the essay, 'Force of Law' (1994), *Politics of
Friendship* (1997), *Of Hospitality* (2000), *On Cosmopolitanism and Forgiveness*
(2001), and the longer study, *Spectres of Marx* (1994).

From the outset one of the difficulties of Derrida's work has been the
way it has moved across philosophy, linguistics, psychoanalysis, literature,
art, architecture and ethics, and thus evaded traditional discipline and subject boundaries. Not only does Derrida seem not to belong definitively to
any one of these areas, his work persistently questions the assumptions and
protocols on which they, or their canonic representatives, depend. This is
why, though it is common to term his work 'poststructuralist' (and this does
usefully signal an association with a broader intellectual trend), it is more
accurate to describe it as 'deconstruction', since the rigorous questioning of
assumed binary divisions and supposed unities which characterizes this *modus
operandi* describes the very relation Derrida has to those disciplines. As Derrida
typically writes, 'the task of deconstruction' is 'to discover . . . the "other"
of philosophy'. The result is a questioning, now common practice in radical sections of the Humanities, of notions of identity, origin, intention, and
the production of meaning.

One of the most contentious and important issues during this period
has concerned the 'politics' of deconstruction. For many, the apparent implication of Derrida's ideas on textuality and on the decentred, rather
than self-determining, coherent human subject has been to deny the reality of material reference in the world and a conception of human agency
necessary to an engaged ethical or political project. Some of Derrida's own
statements – most notably his often quoted comment: 'il n'y a pas de
hors-texte' (compounded by the English translation, 'there is nothing outside the text') – have fuelled this reaction. An alternative translation of the
phrase, suggested by Derek Attridge (Derrida, 1992), as 'there is no outside
text' would imply, for many more persuasively, that there is no escape from
narrative or textuality. However, deconstruction has witnessed a long
struggle against the charge of formalism and political quietism. The most
significant encounter along these lines has probably been with Marxism.
Terry Eagleton ([1983], 1996: see 'Key texts' for Chapter 5), for example,

posed the issue of deconstruction's political evasion and intent early on, and Alex Callinicos (1989, 1995) has been one of the most stringent critics of poststructuralism's 'depoliticisation of radical theory'. A contrary *rapprochement* between the two was proposed in Michael Ryan's *Marxism and Deconstruction* (1982) on the grounds that both encouraged 'plurality' rather than 'authoritarian unity', criticism rather than obedience, 'difference' rather than 'identity', and a general scepticism about absolute or totalizing systems. Derrida's own direct address to deconstruction's relation to Marxism came with the volume *Spectres of Marx* (1994). Deconstruction and all it entails, he writes, would have been unthinkable without Marxism. Further, 'Deconstruction has never had any sense of interest . . . except as a radicalisation, which is to say also in the *tradition* of a certain Marxism, in a certain *spirit of Marxism*.' What is important here is that deconstruction is not simply 'Marxist', or governed, in the end, by Marxist orthodoxy, but that it is an 'attempted radicalization' which follows in 'a' and not 'the' spirit of Marxism.

Derrida's use of the notion of 'spirit' in *Spectres of Marx* has also initiated a new analytical vocabulary. Spectres, spirits, apparitions, revenants and ghosts undo oppositions, Derrida argues, between the actual or present reality and its others, whether this is conceived of as absence, non-presence or virtuality. Such terms or phenomena thereby express what he terms the 'spectrality effect' or the logic of 'hauntology'. Marx and Engels' *The Communist Manifesto* opened with the famous declaration, 'A spectre is haunting Europe – the spectre of communism', and Derrida combines this idea of a spectre yet to come with the example of the ghost in Shakespeare's *Hamlet*. Hamlet reacts to the sight of his dead father's ghost with the words: 'The time is out of joint: Oh cursed spite/ that ever I was born to set it right'. Derrida expounds on this sense of disjoined time, expressed in the very figure of the ghost, who though appearing, as it seems, for the first time in the present, has returned (is a revenant) from the past and from the dead. The spectre always returns – 'it begins by coming back', as Derrida puts it.

These ideas are consistent with deconstruction's founding critique of the 'metaphysics of presence' and the ideas of a divided or decentred subjectivity, together with the many ways deconstruction has questioned and overturned binary oppositions (including the real and unreal, and, here, the living and the dead) in favour of the ongoing production of 'différance'. A number of literary studies have also taken up the theme of 'spectrality' which Derrida has opened up (Bennett and Royle, 2004, ch. 15; Buse and Stott (eds), 1998). Along with other work on 'friendship', 'cosmopolitanism' and 'hospitality', *Spectres of Marx* underlines, too, how much Derrida's theme has been alterity and difference – the relation of the self and other – in philosophy, language, literature and ethics (hence his characterization of deconstruction, noted above, as 'discover[ing] . . . the "other" of philosophy'). Works which pursue these themes by 'followers' of Derrida (amongst them, Docherty, 1996, and Attridge, 2004: see 'References' for Conclusion) can themselves be said to proceed 'in a certain spirit' of deconstruction.

American deconstruction

American critics flirted with a number of alien presences in their attempts to throw off the long-cherished formalism of the New Critics. The scientific 'myth criticism' of Northrop Frye, the Hegelian Marxism of Lukács, the phenomenology of Georges Poulet and the rigours of French structuralism each had its day. It is something of a surprise that Derrida won over many of America's most powerful critics. Several of them are Romantic specialists. Romantic poets are intensely concerned with experiences of timeless illumination ('epiphanies') which occur at certain privileged moments in their lives. They try to recapture these 'spots of time' in their poetry, and to saturate their words with this absolute presence. However, they also lament the loss of 'presence': in Wordsworth's words, 'there hath passed away a glory from the earth'. It is not surprising, therefore, that Paul de Man and others have found Romantic poetry an open invitation to deconstruction. Indeed de Man argues that the Romantics actually deconstruct their own writing by showing that the presence they desire is always absent, always in the past or future.

De Man's *Blindness and Insight* (1971) and *Allegories of Reading* (1979) are impressively rigorous works of deconstruction. Their debt to Derrida is evident, but de Man develops his own terminology. The first book circles around the paradox that critics only achieve insight through a certain blindness. They adopt a method or theory which is quite at odds with the insights it produces: 'All these critics [Lukács, Blanchot, Poulet] seem curiously doomed to say something different from what they meant to say.' The insights could be gained only because the critics were 'in the grip of this peculiar blindness'. For example, the American New Critics (see Chapter 1) based their practice upon the Coleridgean notion of organic form, according to which a poem has a formal unity analogous to that of natural form. However, instead of discovering in poetry the unity and coherence of the natural world, they reveal multi-faceted and ambiguous meanings: 'This unitarian criticism finally becomes a criticism of ambiguity.' This ambiguous poetic language seems to contradict their idea of an object-like totality.

De Man believes that this insight-in-blindness is facilitated by an unconscious slide from one kind of unity to another. The unity which the New Critics so frequently discover is not in the text but in the act of interpretation. Their desire for total understanding initiates the 'hermeneutic circle' of interpretation. Each element in a text is understood in terms of the whole, and the whole is understood as a totality made up of all the elements. This interpretative movement is part of a complex process which produces literary 'form'. Mistaking this 'circle' of interpretation for the text's unity helps them sustain a blindness which produces insight into poetry's divided and multiple meaning (the elements do not form a unity). Criticism must be ignorant of the insight it produces.

In *Allegories of Reading*, de Man develops a 'rhetorical' type of deconstruction already begun in *Blindness and Insight*. 'Rhetoric' is the classical term for the art of persuasion. De Man is concerned with the theory of 'tropes' which accompanies rhetorical treatises. 'Figures of speech' (tropes) allow writers to say one thing but mean something else: to substitute one sign for another (metaphor), to displace meaning from one sign in a chain to another (metonymy), and so on. Tropes pervade language, exerting a force which destabilizes logic, and thereby denies the possibility of a straightforwardly literal or referential use of language. To the question 'Tea or coffee?', I reply 'What's the difference?' My rhetorical question (meaning 'It makes no difference which I choose') contradicts the logic of my question's 'literal' meaning ('What is the difference between tea and coffee?'). De Man shows that, just as critical insights result from critical blindness, so passages of explicit critical reflection or thematic statement in literary texts seem to depend on the suppression of the implications of the rhetoric used in such passages. He grounds his theory in close readings of specific texts, and considers that it is the effects of language and rhetoric that prevent a direct representation of the real. De Man thus follows Nietzsche in believing that language is essentially figurative and not referential or expressive; there is no original unrhetorical language. This means that 'reference' is always contaminated with figurality.

De Man applies these arguments to criticism itself. Reading is always necessarily 'misreading', because 'tropes' inevitably intervene between critical and literary texts. Critical writing conforms essentially to the literary figure we call 'allegory'; it is a sequence of signs which stands at a distance from another sequence of signs, and seeks to stand in its place. Criticism is thus returned, like philosophy, to the common textuality of 'literature'. What is the point of this 'misreading'? De Man thinks that some misreadings are correct and others incorrect. A correct misreading tries to include and not repress the inevitable misreadings which all language produces. At the centre of this argument is the belief that literary texts are *self-deconstructing*: 'a literary text simultaneously asserts and denies the authority of its own rhetorical mode'. The deconstructor appears to have little to do except to collude with the text's own processes. If he or she succeeds, a correct misreading can be achieved.

De Man's refined critical procedure does not involve an actual denial of language's referential function (reference is merely placed 'under erasure'). However, since texts never seem to emerge from their textuality, there may be something in Terry Eagleton's view that American (and especially de Man's) deconstruction perpetuates by another means New Criticism's dissolution of history. While the New Critics cocooned the text in 'form' to protect it from history, the deconstructors swallow up history in an expanded empire of literature, 'viewing famines, revolutions, soccer matches and sherry trifle as yet more undecidable "text"'. Deconstruction cannot in theory establish a hierarchy text/history, but in practice it sees only text as far as the eye can reach.

The rhetorical type of poststructuralism has taken various forms. In historiography (the theory of history), Hayden White has attempted a radical deconstruction of the writings of well-known historians. In *Tropics of Discourse* (1978) he argues that historians believe their narratives to be objective, but because it involves structure their narration cannot escape textuality: 'Our discourse always tends to slip away from our data towards the structures of consciousness with which we are trying to grasp them.' Whenever a new discipline arises it must establish the adequacy of its own language to the objects in its field of study. However, this is done not by logical argument but by a '*pre*-figurative move that is more tropical than logical'. When historians order the material of their study, they render it manageable by the silent application of what Kenneth Burke called the 'Four Master Tropes': metaphor, metonymy, synecdoche, and irony. Historical thinking is not possible except in terms of tropes. White agrees with Piaget in thinking that this figurative consciousness may be part of normal psychological development. He goes on to examine the writings of major thinkers (Freud, Marx, E. P. Thompson and others) and shows that their 'objective knowledge' or 'concrete historical reality' is always shaped by the master tropes.

In literary criticism Harold Bloom has made spectacular use of tropes. Despite being a Yale professor, he is less radically 'textual' than de Man or

Geoffrey Hartman (see below), and still treats literature as a special field of study. However, his combination of the theory of tropes, Freudian psychology and cabbalistic mysticism is a daring one. He argues that since Milton, the first truly 'subjective' poet, poets have suffered an awareness of their 'belatedness': coming late in poetic history they fear that their poetic fathers have already used up all the available inspiration. They experience an Oedipal hatred of the father, a desperate desire to deny paternity. The suppression of their aggressive feelings gives rise to various defensive strategies. No poem stands on its own, but always in relation to another. In order to write belatedly, poets must enter a psychic struggle, to create an imaginative space. This involves 'misreading' their masters in order to produce a new interpretation. This 'poetic misprision' creates the required space in which they can communicate their own authentic inspiration. Without this aggressive wrenching of predecessors' meaning, tradition would stifle all creativity.

Cabbalistic writings (Jewish rabbinical texts which reveal hidden meanings in the Bible) are classic examples of *revisionary* texts. Bloom believes that Isaac Luria's sixteenth-century version of cabbalistic mysticism is an exemplary model of the way poets revise earlier poets in post-Renaissance poetry. He develops from Luria the three stages of revision: *limitation* (taking a new look), *substitution* (replacing one form by another), and *representation* (restoring a meaning). When a 'strong' poet writes, he repeatedly passes through the three stages in a dialectical manner, as he grapples with the strong poets of the past (we intentionally leave Bloom's masculine idiom exposed).

In *A Map of Misreading* (1975), he charts how meaning is produced in 'Post-Enlightenment images, by the language strong poets use in defence against, and response to, the language of prior strong poets'. The 'tropes' and 'defenses' are interchangeable forms of 'revisionary ratios'. Strong poets cope with the 'anxiety of influence' by adopting separately or successively six psychic defences. These appear in their poetry as tropes which allow a poet to 'swerve' from a father's poems. The six tropes are irony, synecdoche, metonymy, hyperbole/litotes, metaphor and metalepsis. Bloom uses six classical words to describe the six kinds of relationship between the texts of fathers and sons (revisionary ratios): *clinamen, tessera, kenosis, daemonization, askesis* and *apophrades. Clinamen* is the 'swerve' a poet makes in order to justify a new poetic direction (a direction which, it is implied, the master would or should have taken). This involves a deliberate misinterpretation of an earlier poet. *Tessera* is 'fragment': a poet treats the materials of a precursor poem as if they were in pieces, and required the finishing touch of the successor. *Clinamen* (revisionary ratio) has the rhetorical form of 'irony' (the figure of speech, not of thought), and is the psychic defence called 'reaction-formation'. Irony says one thing and means something different (sometimes the opposite). The other ratios are similarly expressed as both trope and psychic defence (*tessera* = synecdoche = 'turning against the Self', and so on). Unlike de Man and White, Bloom does not privilege rhetoric in his readings. It would be more accurate to call his method 'psychocritical'.

Bloom pays particular attention to the Romantic 'crisis-poems' of Wordsworth, Shelley, Keats and Tennyson. Each poet struggles to misread his predecessors creatively. Each poem passes through the stages of revision and each stage works through the pairs of revisionary ratios. Shelley's 'Ode to the West Wind', for example, struggles with Wordsworth's 'Immortality' ode as follows: stanzas I–II, *clinamen/tessera*; IV, *kenosis/ daemonization*; V, *askesis/apophrades*. It is necessary to study Part III of *A Map of Misreading* to grasp the full working of Bloom's method.

Geoffrey Hartman, having emerged from New Criticism, plunged into deconstruction and left behind him a scattered trail of fragmentary texts (collected in *Beyond Formalism*, 1970, *The Fate of Reading*, 1975, and *Criticism in the Wilderness*, 1980). Like de Man, he regards criticism as inside rather than outside literature. He has used this licence to justify his seemingly eclectic use of other texts (literary, philosophical, popular) to underpin his own discourse. For example, at one point he writes about the harshness and strangeness of Christ's parables, which were smoothed over by the 'older hermeneutics' which 'tended to be incorporative or reconciling, like Donne's "spider love that transubstantiates all"'. Donne's phrase is drawn in by association. 'Transubstantiation' is used metaphorically in a poem about love, but Hartman activates its religious connotations; his 'incorporative' picks up the incarnational connotations of 'transubstantiation', thus suppressing or ignoring the poisonous implication (in Donne's period) of 'spider'. His critical writings are frequently interrupted and complicated by such 'imperfect' references. This imperfection reflects Hartman's view that critical reading should aim not to produce consistent meaning but to reveal 'contradictions and equivocations' in order to make fiction 'interpretable by making it less readable'. Since criticism is inside literature, it must be equally unreadable.

Hartman rebels against the scholarly common-sense criticism of the Arnoldian tradition ('sweetness and light'). More generally, he adopts a poststructuralist rejection of science's 'ambition to master . . . its subject (text, psyche) by technocratic, predictive, authoritarian formulas'. However, he also questions the speculative and abstract 'sky-flying' of the philosopher-critic, who flies too high to keep in touch with actual texts. His own brand of speculative but densely textual criticism is an attempt at reconciliation (Wordsworth's poetry has been one of Hartman's principal sites of practice). He both admires and fears Derrida's radical theory – welcoming criticism's newly found creativity, but hesitating before the yawning abyss of indeterminacy which threatens it with chaos. As Vincent Leitch has written, 'he emerges as a voyeur of the border, who watches or imagines crossover and warns of dangers'. And yet, one cannot help thinking that Hartman's philosophical doubts are lulled by the lure of textual pleasure – well seen in the following extract from his discussion of Derrida's *Glas*, which incorporates passages from Genet's *Journal du voleur* (*The Thief's Journal*):

> *Glas*, then, is Derrida's own Journal du voleur, and reveals the vol-onto-theology of writing. Writing is always theft or bricolage of the logos. The theft redistributes the logos by a new principle of equity . . . as the volatile seed of flowers. Property, even in the form of the nom propre, is non-propre, and writing is an act of crossing the line of the text, of making it indeterminate, or revealing the midi as the mi-dit.

During the 1960s, J. Hillis Miller was deeply influenced by the Geneva School's 'phenomenological' criticism (see Chapter 3, p. 49). His work since 1970 has centred on the deconstruction of fiction (especially in *Fiction and Repetition: Seven English Novels*, 1982). This phase was inaugurated with a fine paper on Dickens given in 1970, in which he takes up Jakobson's theory of metaphor and metonymy (see Chapter 4, pp. 72–3). He begins by showing how the realism of *Sketches by Boz* is not a mimetic effect but a figurative one. Looking at Monmouth Street, Boz sees 'things, human artefacts, streets, buildings, vehicles, old clothes in shops'. These things metonymically signify something which is absent: he infers from the things 'the life that is lived among them'. However, Miller's account does not end with this relatively structuralist analysis of realism. He shows how the metonymic dead men's clothes come to life in Boz's mind as he imagines their absent wearers: 'waistcoats have almost burst with anxiety to put themselves on'. This metonymic 'reciprocity' between a person and his surroundings (house, possessions, and so on) 'is the basis for the metaphorical substitutions so frequent in Dickens's fiction'. Metonymy asserts an *association* between clothes and wearer, while metaphor suggests a *similarity* between them. First, clothes and wearer are linked by context, and second, as context fades, we allow clothes to substitute for wearer. Miller perceives a further self-conscious fictionality in Dickens's fondness for theatrical metaphor. He frequently describes the behaviour of individuals as an imitation of theatrical styles or of works of art (one character goes through 'an admirable bit of serious pantomime', speaks in 'a stage whisper', and appears later 'like the ghost of Queen Anne in the tent scene in Richard'). There is an endless deferment of presence: everyone imitates or repeats some-one else's behaviour, real or fictional. The metonymic process encourages a literal reading (this *is* London), while at the same time it acknowledges its own figurality. We discover that metonymy is as much a fiction as metaphor. Miller in effect deconstructs Jakobson's original opposition between 'realistic' metonymy and 'poetic' metaphor. A 'correct interpreta-tion' of them sees the 'figurative as figurative'. Both 'invite misinterpreta-tion which takes as substantial what are in fact only linguistic fictions'. Poetry, however metaphorical, is liable to be 'read literally', and realistic writing, however metonymic, is open to 'a correct figurative reading which sees it as fiction rather than *mimesis*'. It can be argued that Miller here falls into the vice of incomplete reversal of a metaphysical hierarchy (literal/figura-tive). By talking about a 'correct interpretation' and a 'misinterpretation', he exposes himself to the anti-deconstructive arguments of Gerald Graff (*Literature Against Itself*, 1979), who objects that Miller 'forecloses the very possibility of language's referring to the world' and therefore implies that every text (not just Dickens's) calls its own assumptions into question.

Barbara Johnson's *The Critical Difference* (1980) contains subtle and lucid deconstructive readings of literature and criticism. She shows that both literary and critical texts set up 'a network of differences into which the reader is lured with a promise of comprehension'. For example, in *S/Z* Barthes identifies and dismantles the masculine/feminine 'difference' in Balzac's *Sarrasine* (see above, pp. 151–3). By cutting up the novella into lexias, Barthes appears to resist any total reading of the text's meaning in terms of sexu-ality. Johnson shows that Barthes' reading nevertheless privileges 'castra-tion', and, further, that his distinction between the 'readerly' and the 'writerly' text corresponds to Balzac's distinction between the ideal woman (Zambinella as conceived by Sarrasine) and the castrato (Zambinella in actu-ality). Thus Zambinella resembles both the perfect unity of the readerly text and the fragmented and undecidable writerly text. Barthes' method of reading evidently favours 'castration' (cutting up). Sarrasine's image of Zambinella is based upon narcissism: her perfection (perfect woman) is the symmetrical counterpart of Sarrasine's masculine self-image. That is, Sarrasine loves 'the image of the lack of what he thinks he himself possesses'. Oddly enough, the castrato is 'simultaneously outside the difference between the sexes as well as representing the literalization of its illusory symmetry'. In this way Zambinella destroys Sarrasine's reassuring masculinity by showing that it is based on castration. Johnson's essential point about Barthes' reading of Balzac is that Barthes actually spells out the fact of castration where Balzac leaves it unspoken. In this way Barthes reduces a 'difference' to an 'identity'. Johnson makes this point not as a criticism of Barthes but as an illustration of the inevitable blindness of critical insight (to use de Man's terms).

Michel Foucault

There is another strand in poststructuralist thought which believes that the world is more than a galaxy of texts, and that some theories of textuality ignore the fact that discourse is involved in *power*. They reduce political and economic forces, and ideological and social control, to aspects of signifying processes. When a Hitler or a Stalin seems to dictate to an entire nation by wielding the power of discourse, it is absurd to treat the effect as simply occurring within discourse. It is evident that real power is exercised through discourse, and that this power has real effects.

The father of this line of thought is the German philosopher, Nietzsche, who said that people first decide what they want and then fit the facts to their aim: 'Ultimately, man finds in things nothing but what he himself has imported into them.' All knowledge is an expression of the 'Will to Power'. This means that we cannot speak of any absolute truths or of objective knowledge. People recognize a particular piece of philosophy or scientific theory as 'true' only if it fits the descriptions of truth laid down by the intellectual or political authorities of the day, by the members of the ruling elite, or by the prevailing ideologues of knowledge.

Like other poststructuralists Michel Foucault regards discourse as a central human activity, but not as a universal 'general text', a vast sea of signification. He is interested in the historical dimension of discursive *change* – what it is possible to say will change from one era to another. In science a theory is not recognized in its own period if it does not conform to the power consensus of the institutions and official organs of science. Mendel's genetic theories fell on deaf ears in the 1860s; they were promulgated in a 'void' and had to wait until the twentieth century for acceptance. It is not enough to speak the truth; one must be 'in the truth'.

In his early work on 'madness' Foucault found it difficult to find examples of 'mad' discourse (except in literature: de Sade, Artaud). He deduced that the rules and procedures which determine what is considered normal or rational successfully silence what they exclude. Individuals working within particular discursive practices cannot think or speak without obeying the unspoken 'archive' of rules and constraints; otherwise they risk being condemned to madness or silence (Foucault's relevance to feminism, to postcolonial theory and to gay and lesbian theory is apparent here). This discursive mastery works not just by exclusion, but also by 'rarefaction' (each practice narrows its content and meaning by thinking only in terms of 'author' and 'discipline'). Finally, there are the social constraints, especially the formative power of the education system which defines what is rational and scholarly.

Foucault's books, especially *Madness and Civilization* (1961), *The Birth of the Clinic* (1963), *The Order of Things* (1966), *Discipline and Punish* (1975) and *The History of Sexuality* (1976), show that various forms of 'knowledge' about sex, crime, psychiatry and medicine have arisen and been replaced. He concentrates on the fundamental shifts occurring between epochs. He offers no period generalizations, but traces the overlapping series of discontinuous fields. History is this disconnected range of discursive practices. Each practice is a set of rules and procedures governing writing and thinking in a particular field. These rules govern by exclusion and regulation. Taken together the fields form a culture's 'archive', its 'positive Unconscious'.

Although the policing of knowledge is often associated with individual names (Aristotle, Plato, Aquinas, Locke, and so on), the set of structural rules which informs the various fields of knowledge is quite beyond any individual consciousness. The regulation of specific disciplines involves very refined rules for running institutions, training initiates and transmitting knowledge. The Will-to-Knowledge exhibited in this regulation is an impersonal force. We can never know our own era's archive because it is the Unconscious from which we speak. We can understand an earlier archive only because we are utterly different and remote from it. For example, when we read the literature of the Renaissance, we often notice the richness and exuberance of its verbal play. In *The Order of Things*, Foucault shows that in this period *resemblance* played a central role in the structure of all knowledges. Everything echoed everything else; nothing stood on its own. We see this vividly in the poetry of John Donne, whose mind never rests on an object but moves back and forth from spiritual to physical, human to divine, and universal to individual. In his *Devotions*, Donne describes in cosmic terms the symptoms of the fever that almost killed him, linking the microcosm (man) and the macrocosm (universe): his tremblings are 'earthquakes', his faintings are 'eclipses' and his feverish breath 'blazing stars'. From our modern standpoint we can see the various kinds of

correspondence which shape Renaissance discourses, but the writers themselves saw and thought *through* them and therefore could not see them as
we see them.

Following Nietzsche, Foucault denies that we can ever possess an objective knowledge of History. Historical writing will always become entangled
in tropes; it can never be a science. Jeffrey Mehlman's *Revolution and
Repetition* (1979) shows how Marx's *Eighteenth Brumaire* presents the 'revolution' of Louis Napoleon as a 'farcical repetition' of his uncle's revolution.
Marx's historical account, according to Mehlman, acknowledges the
impossibility of knowledge; there is only the absurd trope of 'repetition'.
However, Foucault does not treat the strategies writers use to make sense
of History as merely textual play. Such discourses are produced within a
real world of power struggle. In politics, art and science, power is gained
through discourse: discourse is 'a violence that we do to things'. Claims to
objectivity made on behalf of specific discourses are always spurious: there
are no absolutely 'true' discourses, only more or less powerful ones.

New Historicism and Cultural Materialism

During the 1980s, the dominance of deconstruction in the United States
was challenged by a new theory and practice of literary history. While most
poststructuralists are sceptical about attempts to recover historical 'truth',
the New Historicists believe that Foucault's work opens the way to a new
and non-truth-oriented form of historicist study of texts. A parallel development has occurred in Britain, but the influence of Foucault is there enriched
by Marxist and feminist accents.

Throughout the nineteenth century there ran side by side two contradictory approaches to literary history. One presented it as a series of
isolated monuments, achievements of individual genius. The other was
'historicist', and saw literary history as part of a larger cultural history.
Historicism was the offspring of Hegelian idealism, and, later, of the evolutionary naturalism of Herbert Spencer. Several major 'historicists' studied
literature in the context of social, political and cultural history. They saw
a nation's literary history as an expression of its evolving 'spirit'. Thomas
Carlyle summed up their view when he wrote: 'The history of a nation's
poetry is the essence of its history, political, scientific, religious' (*Edinburgh
Review*, 53, no. 105, 1831).

In 1943, E. M. W. Tillyard published an extremely influential historicist
account of the culture of Shakespeare's period – *The Elizabethan World Picture*.

He argued, in Hegelian fashion, that the literature of the period expressed the spirit of the age, which centred on ideas of divine order, the chain of being, and the correspondences between earthly and heavenly existences. For Tillyard, Elizabethan culture was a seamlessly unified system of meanings which could not be disturbed by unorthodox or dissenting voices. He believed that the Elizabethans regarded 'disorder' as completely outside the divinely ordained norm, and that deviant figures such as Christopher Marlowe never seriously challenged the settled world-view of the age.

The New Historicists, like Tillyard, try to establish the interconnections between the literature and the general culture of a period. However, in all other respects they depart from Tillyard's approach. The poststructuralist intellectual revolution of the 1960s and 1970s challenges the older historicism on several grounds and establishes a new set of assumptions:

1   There are two meanings of the word 'history': (a) 'the events of the past' and (b) 'telling a story about the events of the past'. Poststructualist thought makes it clear that history is always 'narrated', and that therefore the first sense is problematic. The past can never be available to us in pure form, but always in the form of 'representations'; after poststructuralism, history becomes textualized.

2   Historical periods are not unified entities. There is no single 'history', only discontinuous and contradictory 'histories'. There was no single Elizabethan world-view. The idea of a uniform and harmonious culture is a myth imposed on history and propagated by the ruling classes in their own interests.

3   Historians can no longer claim that their study of the past is detached and objective. We cannot transcend our own historical situation. The past is not something which confronts us as if it were a physical object, but is something we construct from already written texts of all kinds which we construe in line with our particular historical concerns.

4   The relations between literature and history must be rethought. There is no stable and fixed 'history' which can be treated as the 'background' against which literature can be foregrounded. All history (histories) is 'foreground'. 'History' is always a matter of telling a story about the past, using other texts as our intertexts. 'Non-literary' texts produced by lawyers, popular writers, theologians, scientists and historians should not be treated as belonging to a different order of textuality. Literary works should not be regarded as sublime and

transcendent expressions of the 'human spirit', but as texts among other texts. We cannot now accept that a privileged 'inner' world of 'great authors' is to be set against the background of an 'outer' world of ordinary history.

The New Historicists in America and their counterparts in Britain, the 'Cultural Materialists' (the term was borrowed from Raymond Williams by Jonathan Dollimore), have produced a substantial body of work on Renaissance literature and society, on Romanticism and – differently inflected – on 'transgressive' sexuality and aesthetics (see below, pp. 186–8, and Chapter 10, pp. 246–7). A common influence on both movements was Michel Foucault's understanding of discourses, or discursive formations, as rooted in social institutions and as playing a key role in relations of power (see preceding section). Beyond this there is a commonly acknowledged divergence, for while New Historicism, seeking a 'touch of the real', learned – notably from the anthropologist, Clifford Geertz – to extend literary critical strategies to the discussion of hitherto unregarded cultural texts (see Gallagher and Greenblatt, 2001), Cultural Materialism adopted the more politicized notion of ideology developed in the writings of Louis Althusser. Althusser's theory (see above, p. 148, and Chapter 5) abandons the orthodox interpretation of ideology as 'false consciousness' in favour of a theory which situates ideology firmly within material institutions (political, juridical, educational, religious, and so on), and conceives ideology as a body of discursive practices which, when dominant, sustain individuals in their places as 'subjects' (subjects them). Every individual is 'interpellated' (or 'hailed') as a subject by a number of ideological discourses, which together serve the interests of the ruling classes. Foucault had similarly emphasized how social and political power works through the discursive regimes by which social institutions maintain themselves. For example, certain dichotomies are imposed as definitive of human existence and are operated in ways which have direct effects on society's organization. Discourses are produced in which concepts of madness, criminality, sexual abnormality, and so on are defined in relation to concepts of sanity, justice and sexual normality. Such discursive formations massively determine and constrain the forms of knowledge, the types of 'normality', and the nature of 'subjectivity' which prevail in particular periods. For example, Foucauldians talk about the emergence of the 'soul' or the 'privatization of the body' as 'events' produced by the bourgeois culture which arose during the seventeenth century. The discursive practices have no universal validity but are historically dominant ways of controlling and preserving social relations of exploitation.

These ideas have revolutionized the study of Romantic and especially Renaissance literature. New Historicists such as Stephen Greenblatt, Louis Montrose, Jonathan Goldberg, Stephen Orgel and Leonard Tennenhouse explore the ways in which Elizabethan literary texts (especially drama, masque and pastoral) act out the concerns of the Tudor monarchy, reproducing and renewing the powerful discourses which sustain the system. They see the monarchy as the central axis governing the power structure. While some have dissented from this rather 'functionalist' version of Foucault, American New Historicists have been widely associated with a pessimistic understanding of discursive power in literary representations of the Elizabethan and Jacobean social order. They suggest that, even though many of Shakespeare's plays give voice to subversive ideas, such questionings of the prevalent social order are always 'contained' within the terms of the discourses which hold that social order in place. Falstaff's resistance to monarchic order, for example, is in the end a valuable negative model for Hal, who is thereby enabled more effectively to reject Falstaff's disorderly challenge to normality and to assume kingly power. Greenblatt often thinks of subversion as an expression of an inward necessity: we define our identities always in relation to what we are not, and therefore what we are not (our Falstaffs) must be demonized and objectified as 'others'. The mad, the unruly and the alien are internalized 'others' which help us to consolidate our identities: their existence is allowed only as evidence of the rightness of established power. Greenblatt concludes pessimistically in his 'Epilogue' to *Renaissance Self-Fashioning* (1980): 'In all my texts and documents, there were, so far as I could tell, no moments of pure, unfettered subjectivity; indeed, the human subject itself began to seem remarkably unfree, the ideological product of the relations of power in a particular society.' Such a view, in the context of contemporary American society, is an expression of the 'politics' of cultural despair.

In the 1980s and 1990s, a further inflection of New Historicism emerged which focused primarily on the favourite hunting-ground of American Deconstruction, Romanticism – thus signalling its strategic challenge to the work of Bloom, de Man, Hartman *et al*. Critics on both sides of the Atlantic are associated with its general project, including John Barrell, David Simpson, Jerome McGann, Marilyn Butler, Paul Hamilton and Marjorie Levinson. Influenced in part by the work of Althusser, Macherey, Jameson and Eagleton, this New Historicism – according to Levinson, 'at once materialist and deconstructive' – deploys the 'historical imagination' to restore to a literary work those contemporary meanings which inscribe the matrix in which it is shaped, but which are not consciously 'in' the work as written. Such 'meanings' will be ideological 'trouble-spots' beyond the cognition of the writer; but in taking up a position within, but not of, the writer's ideological frame of reference, New Historicist criticism acquires 'the capacity to know a work as neither it, nor its original readers nor its author could know it' (*Wordsworth's Great Period Poems: Four Essays*, 1986). Re-situating texts in the complex discursive frame of their originating period by way of a detailed allusive reading of them in their intertextual relations with other contemporary political, cultural and 'popular' discourses takes this New Historicism way beyond the older crudely historicist juxtapositioning of 'text and context'. But it has itself been criticized for effectively depoliticizing literature by locking it away in its 'own' past – unable, as it were, to 'speak' to the present – and for effacing the interpretative (ideological) stance and role of the critic who is indeed reading in the present.

British 'Cultural Materialists', under the influence of Althusser and Mikhail Bakhtin (see Chapters 5 and 2 respectively, and pp. 146–8 above), have developed a more politically radical type of historicism, and have challenged the 'functionalism' of Greenblatt. They see Foucault as implying a more precarious and unstable structure of power, and they often aim to derive from his work a history of 'resistances' to dominant ideologies. Jonathan Dollimore, Alan Sinfield, Catherine Belsey, Francis Barker and others have adopted some of the theoretical refinements to be found in Raymond Williams's *Marxism and Literature* (1977; see Chapter 5, pp. 99–101), especially his distinction between 'residual', 'dominant' and 'emergent' aspects of culture. By replacing the Tillyardian concept of a single spirit of the age with Williams's more dynamic model of culture, they have freed a space for the exploration of the complex totality of Renaissance society, including its subversive and marginalized elements. They assert that every history of subjection also contains a history of resistance, and that resistance is not just a symptom of and justification for subjection but is the true mark of an ineradicable 'difference' (see Derrida above) which always prevents power from closing the door on change. A further important concern of Dollimore and others is with the 'appropriations' of Renaissance cultural representations which occurred at the time and subsequently. The meanings of literary texts are never entirely fixed by some universal criterion, but are always in play, and subject to specific (often politically radical) appropriations, including those of the Cultural Materialists themselves. Catherine Belsey has used the more neutral term 'cultural history' to describe her lively and political view of the task ahead. She urges the new history to adopt the perspective of 'change, cultural difference and the relativity of truth', and to give priority to the 'production of alternative knowledges' and 'alternative subject positions', something she seeks to do in such works as *The Subject of Tragedy* (1985) and *Desire: Love Stories in Western Culture* (1994). In her more recent book, *Shakespeare and the Loss of Eden: The Construction of Family Values in Early Modern Culture* (1999), Belsey critiques the construction in the sixteenth and seventeenth centuries of the normative and ultimately oppressive ideology of patriarchal family values and the reinforcement of heterosexual monogamy. Her practice of Lacanian 'cultural history' ('history at the level of the signifier') tracks the enactments of ideology in scenes from Genesis and Shakespeare's plays (but also in illustrations of such scenes) so as to expose the subversive rifts and instabilities of this norm. Thus the first family of Genesis, she argues, was marked by deceit and banishment, while Shakespeare shows how families repeatedly fall foul of jealousy and sibling rivalry. The period's conformist idealization of romantic love and marriage can only be maintained, more-over, in an uneasy coexistence with the Catholic ideal of celibacy and the courtly celebration of adultery. Some of the theoretical tools appropriate to Belsey's programme were developed in Michel Pêcheux's *Language, Semantics and Ideology* (1975). He combined Althusserian Marxism, modern linguistics and psychoanalysis in an attempt to develop a new theory of discourse and ideology. Althusser had described the process of 'interpella-tion' by which subjects identify with the discourses embedded in particu-lar ideological state apparatuses. Pêcheux recognized the need to develop the theory in ways which allow for the subject's possible *resistance* to the discursive formations which transmit ideological positions. It may be true that religious ideology works by interpellating individuals as God's subjects. However, we also need terms to describe the negative or subversive response of atheists and new religionists. Pêcheux solves this problem by proposing three types of subject:

1   The 'good subject', who 'freely' accepts the image of self which is projected by the discourse in question in an act of total 'identification' ('At last I have found my true self').

2   The 'bad subject', who refuses the identity offered by discourse in an act of 'counter-identification' ('Sorry, I don't believe any of that').

3   The subject who adopts a 'third modality' by transforming the subject position which is offered in an act of 'disidentification' ('I don't believe in that sort of god').

American New Historicists tend to see power structures as permitting only identification and counter-identification. British exponents belong to a politically more radical tradition, and they are much more interested in the possibility of subjects not only refusing offered subject positions but actually producing new ones.

The work of Mikhail Bakhtin (see Chapter 2) has been used by some New Historicists as a way of escaping the apparent structural closure of Foucault's historical theory. Michael Bristol's *Carnival and Theater: Plebeian Culture and the Structure of Authority in Renaissance England* (1985) used Bakhtin's concept of 'Carnival' in order to introduce a more open model of cultural production. He argued that Greenblatt and Dollimore fail to recognize the vitality and power of popular culture in the Elizabethan period. Bakhtin regards 'Carnival' as a 'second culture', which was opposed to the official culture, and which was carried on by the common people throughout the middle ages and well into the early modern period. Bakhtin's idea that Carnival inserts into official structures 'an indeterminacy, a certain semantic open-endedness' could well provide one way of describing how subjects might respond to dominant discourses through the modalities of 'counter-identification' or even 'disidentification'. Bristol summarized the potentially subversive mode of Carnival as follows: 'By bringing privileged symbols and officially authorized concepts into a crudely familiar relationship with common everyday experience, Carnival achieves a transformation downward or "uncrowning" of de jure relations of dependency, expropriation and social discipline.' Of course, some Foucauldians would reply that Carnival is also an officially permitted and carefully controlled expression of subversion which by its ritualized form only confirms the power of the authority it mocks.

As we have seen, the terms 'New Historicism' and 'Cultural Materialism' cover a wide range of approaches to the study of literature and history, and not unexpectedly they have questioned the received canon of literary works in orthodox literary histories, often in conjunction with feminist, postcolonialist and gay/lesbian criticism (see Chapters 9 and 10). Subsequently, this challenge has been made in the area of American Studies in works by Sacvan Bercovitch, Myra Jehlen, Philip Fisher and Henry Louis Gates, Jr (see Chapter 9, pp. 230–1, for an outline of Gates's work). In discussing the canon of nineteenth-century American literature, New Historicists such as Jane Tompkins and Cathy Davidson have drawn attention to popular and genre fiction. The sentimental novel, for example, says Tompkins, 'offers a critique of American society far more devastating than any delivered by better-known critics such as Hawthorne and Melville'. At the same time, however, it has been argued that in much New Historicist criticism challenges to the canon have involved 'less the detection of its "others" . . . than a repeated challenging of the familiar privileged texts which, while throwing them into a new perspective, leaves the canon itself pretty much intact'. Once again, British Cultural Materialism is thought to present a more decisive challenge, opening up post-war British popular culture and society to a politicized analysis in areas where such historicist techniques are enlisted by Cultural Studies. The British tradition has tried to differentiate itself from what it sees as a limited American reading of Foucault, but the fusion of radical currents of historicist thought in the Anglo-American streams remains an enticing prospect. The development of the new literary history has also meant that the former dominance of Deconstruction in the United States is no longer the case, and a great deal of interesting work (for example, by the 'new' New Historicists, as we have seen, and by such Poststructuralist theorists as Jonathan Culler and Christopher Norris) recognizes that Deconstruction must respond to the challenge of the Foucauldian and Althusserian types of new history. Structuralist critics set out to master the text and to open its secrets. Poststructuralists believe that this desire is in vain because there are unconscious, or linguistic, or historical forces which cannot be mastered. The signifier floats away from the signified, *jouissance* dissolves meaning, the semiotic disrupts the symbolic, *différance* inserts a gap between signifier and signified, and power disorganizes established knowledge. Poststructuralists ask questions rather than give answers; they seize upon the differences between what the text says and what it thinks it says. They set the text to work against itself, and refuse to force it to mean one thing only. They deny the separateness of 'literature', and deconstruct non-literary discourses by reading them as themselves rhetorical texts. We may be frustrated by the poststructuralists' failure to arrive at conclusions, but they are only being consistent in their attempts to avoid logocentrism. However, as they often admit, their desire to resist assertions is itself doomed to failure because only by saying nothing could they prevent us from thinking that they mean something. Even to summarize their views itself implies their failure in this respect.

Nevertheless, Foucault and the New Historicists initiate a new kind of intertextual historical theory which is inevitably an interventionist one since it assists in remaking the past. In Cultural Materialism, a commitment to transgressive and oppositional voices becomes more explicit. As such, while it draws upon poststructuralism, it questions the claims of some of its versions to liberate an innocent free play of meanings. The re-issue in 2003 of the third edition of Jonathan Dollimore's ground-breaking *Radical Tragedy,* first published in the mid-1980s, and now with a Foreword by Terry Eagleton and a searching new Introduction, shows how this consciously interventionist approach has acquired both a 'classic' status and main-tained its continuing relevance. What was particularly impressive about Dollimore's original argument, as John Brannigan (1998) has pointed out, was how his demystifying critique of the centred concept of the human individual extended from the Jacobean period to the reactionary political regime of Thatcherite Britain. *Radical Tragedy*, Eagleton confirms, ranks as a *'necessary* . . . critical intervention', not least because it thrust tragedy 'firmly back within the complex cross-currents of actual historical life'. Dollimore's new introduction, part retrospect and part an address to changed circumstances, tracks the demise of humanist ideology and aes-thetics in the face of new theory, global capitalism and the antipathy of non-Western cultures and religions to Western hegemony, which found a terrible expression in what the world shorthands as '9/11'. Dollimore looks for a new aesthetic, latent within the ruins of the Western canon and the twentieth century: an 'aesthetic where dangerous knowledge crosses with dissident desire and may well exacerbate conflict rather than transcend it'. He has in mind pornography, gothic fiction, the literature of sexual dissid-ence and Jacobean tragedy – the subjects of his own critical writings from *Radical Tragedy* itself to *Sex, Lies and Censorship* (2001). In the scope and boldness of this project, the politicized challenge of cultural materialism is clear.

Selected reading

Key texts

Barthes, Roland, *S/Z* [1970], trans. by Richard Miller (Jonathan Cape, London, 1975). For earlier work by Barthes, see Chapter 4, 'Selected Reading'.

Barthes, Roland, *The Pleasure of the Text* [1973], trans. by Richard Miller (Jonathan Cape, London, 1976).

Barthes, Roland, 'The Death of the Author' [1967], in *Image-Music-Text*, trans. by Stephen Heath (Fontana, London, 1977).

Barthes, Roland, *A Barthes Reader*, trans., ed. and intro. by Susan Sontag (Jonathan Cape, London, 1982). Also pub. as *Selected Writings* (Fontana, London, 1983).

Belsey, Catherine, *Critical Practice* [1980] (2nd edn, Routledge, London, 2002).

Belsey, Catherine, *The Subject of Tragedy: Identity and Difference in Renaissance Drama* (Methuen, London, 1985).

Belsey, Catherine, *Desire: Love Stories in Western Culture* (Blackwell, Oxford, 1994).

Belsey, Catherine, *Shakespeare and the Loss of Eden: The Construction of Family Values in Early Modern Culture* (Palgrave Macmillan, Basingstoke, 1999).

Belsey, Catherine, *Culture and the Real: Theorising Cultural Criticism* (Routledge, London, 2004).

Bloom, Harold, *The Anxiety of Influence: A Theory of Poetry* (Oxford University Press, New York, 1973).

Bloom, Harold, *A Map of Misreading* (Oxford University Press, New York, 1975).

Bloom, Harold, *The Western Canon* (Macmillan, Basingstoke, 1995).

Deconstruction: Critical Concepts in Literary and Cultural Studies, 4 vols, ed. with intro. by Jonathan Culler (Routledge, London, 2002).

Deleuze, Gilles, *Essays: Critical and Clinical* [1997], trans. by Daniel W. Smith and Michael A. Greco (Verso, London, 1998).

Deleuze, Gilles and Guattari, Félix, *Anti-Oedipus: Capitalism and Schizophrenia* [1972], trans. by Richard Hurley, Mark Seem and Helen R. Lane (Athlone Press, London, 1983).

Deleuze, Gilles and Guattari, Félix, *Kafka: Towards a Minor Literature* [1975], trans. by Dana Polan (University of Minnesota Press, Minneapolis and London, 1986).

de Man, Paul, *Blindness and Insight: Essays in the Rhetoric of Contemporary Criticism* [1971] (2nd revd edn, Methuen, London, 1983).

de Man, Paul, *Allegories of Reading: Figural Language in Rousseau, Nietzsche, Rilke, and Proust* (Yale University Press, New Haven, 1979).

de Man, Paul, *The Resistance to Theory* (Manchester University Press, Manchester, 1986).

Derrida, Jacques, *Of Grammatology* [1967], trans. by Gayatri Chakravorty Spivak (Johns Hopkins University Press, London, 1976).

Derrida, Jacques, *Writing and Difference* [1967; trans., with intro. and notes, by Alan Bass, 1978] (Routledge, London, 2001).

Derrida, Jacques, *Positions* [1972], trans. and annotated by Alan Bass (University of Chicago Press, Chicago, 1981).

Derrida, Jacques, *Dissemination* [1972], trans., with intro. and notes, by Barbara Johnson (Athlone Press, London, 1981).

Derrida, Jacques, *A Derrida Reader: Between the Blinds*, ed., with intro. and notes, by Peggy Kamuf (Harvester Wheatsheaf, New York and London, 1991).

Derrida, Jacques, 'Force of Law: The "Mystical Foundation of Authority"', in Michel Rosenfeld and David Gray Carlson (eds), *Deconstruction and the Possibility of Justice* (Routledge, London, 1992).

Derrida, Jacques, *Acts of Literature*, ed. by Derek Attridge (Routledge, London and New York, 1992).

Derrida, Jacques, *Spectres of Marx: The State of the Debt, The Work of Mourning and the New International* [1993], trans. by Peggy Kamuf (Routledge, London 1994).

Derrida, Jacques, *Politics of Friendship* [1994], trans. by George Collins (Verso, London, 1997).

Derrida, Jacques, *On Cosmopolitanism and Forgiveness* [1997], trans. by Mark Dooley and Michael Hughes (Routledge, London, 2001).

Derrida, Jacques, 'following theory' interview in Michael Payne and John Schad (eds) *life.after.theory.* (Continuum, London, 2003).

Derrida, Jacques and Dufourmantelle, Anne, *Of Hospitality* [1997], trans. by Rachel Bowlby (Stanford University Press, Stanford, 2000).

Dollimore, Jonathan, *Sexual Dissidence: Augustine to Wilde, Freud to Foucault* (Oxford University Press, Oxford, 1991).

Dollimore, Jonathan, *Death, Desire and Loss in Western Culture* (Penguin, London, 1994).

Dollimore, Jonathan, *Sex, Lies and Censorship* (Polity, Cambridge, 2001).

Dollimore, Jonathan, *Radical Tragedy: Religion, Ideology and Power in the Drama of Shakespeare and his Contemporaries* [1984] (3rd edn, with a new introduction and Foreword by Terry Eagleton, Palgrave Macmillan, Basingstoke, 2003).

Dollimore, Jonathan and Sinfield, Alan (eds), *Political Shakespeare: Essays in Cultural Materialism* (2nd edn, Manchester University Press, Manchester, 1994).

Foucault, Michel, *Language, Counter-Memory, Practice, Selected Essays and Interviews*, trans. by Donald F. Bouchard and Shierry Simon; ed. by D. F. Bouchard (Basil Blackwell, Oxford, 1977).

Foucault, Michel, *The Foucault Reader* [1984], ed. by Paul Rabinov (Penguin, Harmondsworth, 1986).

Gallagher, Catherine and Greenblatt, Stephen, *Practising New Historicism* (University of Chicago Press, Chicago, 2001).

Geertz, Clifford, *The Interpretation of Cultures: Selected Essays* [1973] (Basic Books, New York, 2000).

Greenblatt, Stephen, *Renaissance Self-Fashioning: From More to Shakespeare* (University of Chicago Press, Chicago, 1980).

Greenblatt, Stephen, *Representing the English Renaissance* (California University Press, Berkeley, 1991).

Greenblatt, Stephen, *Shakespearean Negotiations: The Circulation of Social Energy in Renaissance England* (California University Press, Berkeley, 1991).

Greenblatt, Stephen, *The Greenblatt Reader*, ed. by Michael Payne (Blackwell, Oxford, 2004).

Harari, Josué V. (ed.), *Textual Strategies: Perspectives in Post-Structuralist Criticism* (Cornell University Press, Ithaca, 1979).

Hartman, Geoffrey H., *Criticism in the Wilderness* (Johns Hopkins University Press, Baltimore and London, 1980).

Hartman, Geoffrey, *Saving the Text: Literature/Derrida/Philosophy* (Johns Hopkins University Press, Baltimore, 1981).

Hartman, Geoffrey, *Easy Pieces* (Columbia University Press, New York, 1985).

Hartman, Geoffrey and Daniel O'Hara (eds), *The Geoffrey Hartman Reader* (Edinburgh University Press, Edinburgh, 2004).

Johnson, Barbara, *The Critical Difference: Essays in the Contemporary Rhetoric of Reading* (Johns Hopkins University Press, Baltimore and London, 1980).

Kristeva, Julia, *The Revolution in Poetic Language* [1974], trans. by Margaret Waller, with intro. by Leon S. Roudiez (Columbia University Press, New York, 1984). For further works by Kristeva, see Chapter 6, 'Selected Reading'.

Kristeva, Julia, *Desire in Language: A Semiotic Approach to Literature and Art*, trans. by Thomas Gora, Alice Jardine and Leon S. Roudiez; ed. by Leon S. Roudiez (Columbia University Press, New York, 1980).

Kristeva, Julia, *The Kristeva Reader*, ed. by Toril Moi (Blackwell, Oxford, 1986).

Lacan, Jacques, *Ecrits: A Selection*, trans. by Alan Sheridan [1977] (Routledge, London, 2001).

Lacan, Jacques, *Jacques Lacan: Critical Evaluations in Cultural Theory*, 4 vols, ed. with intro. by Slavoj Žižek (Routledge, London, 2002).

Levinson, Marjorie, *Wordsworth's Great Period Poems: Four Essays* (Cambridge University Press, Cambridge, 1986).

Levinson, Marjorie, Butler, Marilyn, McGann, Jerome and Hamilton, Paul (eds), *Rethinking Historicism* (Blackwell, Oxford, 1989).

McGann, Jerome, *Romantic Ideology: A Critical Investigation* (Chicago University Press, Chicago, 1980).

McGann, Jerome, *The Textual Condition* (Princeton University Press, Princeton, 1991).

McQuillan, Martin (ed.), *Deconstruction: A Reader* (Edinburgh University Press, Edinburgh, 2001).

Miller, J. Hillis, *Fiction and Repetition: Seven English Novels* (Harvard University Press, Cambridge, Mass., 1982).

Miller, J. Hillis, *The Ethics of Reading: Kant, de Man, Eliot, Trollope, James and Benjamin* (Columbia University Press, New York, 1987).

Miller, J. Hillis, *Tropes, Parables and Performatives: Essays on Twentieth Century Literature* (Harvester Wheatsheaf, Hemel Hempstead, 1990).

Miller, J. Hillis, *The J. Hillis Miller Reader*, ed. by Julian Wolfreys (Edinburgh University Press, Edinburgh, 2004).

Pêcheux, Michel, *Language, Semantics and Ideology* [1975] trans. by Harbans Nagpal (Macmillan, Basingstoke, 1982).

Ryan, Kiernan (ed.), *New Historicism and Cultural Materialism: A Reader* (Arnold, London, 1996).

Ryan, Michael, *Marxism and Deconstruction: A Critical Articulation* (Johns Hopkins University Press, Baltimore and London, 1982).

Sim, Stuart (ed.), *Post-Marxism: A Reader* (Edinburgh University Press, Edinburgh, 1998).

Simpson, David, *Wordsworth's Historical Imagination* (Methuen, London, 1987).

Sinfield, Alan (see also with Jonathan Dollimore, above), *Faultlines: Cultural Materialism and the Politics of Dissident Reading* (Clarendon Press, Oxford, 1992).

Sinfield, Alan, *Cultural Politics – Queer Reading* (Routledge, London, 1994).

Vice, Sue (ed.), *Psychoanalytic Criticism: A Reader* (Polity Press, Cambridge, 1995).

White, Hayden, *Tropics of Discourse: Essays in Cultural Criticism* (Johns Hopkins University Press, Baltimore, 1978).

Young, Robert (ed.), *Untying the Text: A Post-Structuralist Reader* (Routledge & Kegan Paul, Boston and London, 1981).

Further reading

Aers, Lesley and Wheale, Nigel, *Shakespeare and the Changing Curriculum* (Routledge, London, 1991).

Allen, Graham, *Roland Barthes* (Routledge, London, 2003).

Bennett, Andrew and Royle, Nicholas, *Introduction to Literature, Criticism and Theory* (3rd edn, Pearson Education, Harlow, 2004).

Bercovitch, Sacvan (ed.), *Reconstructing American Literary History* (Harvard University Press, Cambridge, Mass., 1986).

Bogue, Ronald, *Deleuze and Guattari* (Routledge, London, 1989).

Botting, Fred, *Gothic* (Routledge, London and New York, 1996).

Brannigan, John, *New Historicism and Cultural Materialism* (Palgrave Macmillan, Basingstoke, 1998).

Bristol, Michael, *Carnival and Theater: Plebeian Culture and the Structure of Authority in Renaissance England* (Methuen, London and New York, 1985).

Buchanan, Ian and Marks, John, *Deleuze and Literature* (Edinburgh, Edinburgh University Press, 2001).

Burke, Sean, *The Death and Return of the Author: Criticism and Subjectivity in Barthes, Foucault and Derrida* (2nd edn, Edinburgh University Press, Edinburgh, 1998).

Buse, Peter and Stott, Andrew (eds), *Ghosts: Deconstruction, Psychoanalysis, History* (Palgrave, London, 1998).

Callinicos, Alex, *Against Postmodernism* (Polity, Cambridge, 1989).

Callinicos, Alex, *Theories and Narratives* (Polity, Cambridge, 1995).

Colebrook, Claire, *Gilles Deleuze* (London, Routledge, 2002).

Coward, Rosalind and Ellis, John, *Language and Materialism: Developments in Semiology and the Theory of the Subject* (Routledge & Kegan Paul, London, 1977).

Critchley, Simon, *The Ethics of Deconstruction* (Blackwell, Oxford, 1992).

Culler, Jonathan, *On Deconstruction: Theory and Criticism after Structuralism* (Routledge & Kegan Paul, London, 1983).

Curry, Mark, *Difference* (Routledge, London, 2004).

Dews, Peter, *Logics of Disintegration: Post-Structuralist Thought and the Claims of Critical Theory* (New Left Books, London, 1987).

Docherty, Thomas, *Alterities: Criticism, History, Representation* (Clarendon Press, Oxford, 1996).

Drakakis, John (ed.), *Alternative Shakespeares* (2nd edn, Routledge, London, 2002).

During, Simon, *Foucault and Literature: Towards a Genealogy of Writing* (Routledge, London, 1992).

Easthope, Antony, *British Post-Structuralism: Since 1968* (Routledge, London, 1991).

Easthope, Antony, *The Unconscious* (Routledge, London, 1999).

Egglestone, Robert, *Ethical Criticism: Reading After Levinas* (Edinburgh University Press, Edinburgh, 1997).

Felman, Shoshana (ed.), *Literature and Psychoanalysis: The Question of Reading – Otherwise* (Johns Hopkins University Press, Baltimore, 1982).

Fisher, Philip (ed.), *The New American Studies* (California University Press, Berkeley, 1991).

Freud, Sigmund, 'From the History of an Infantile Neurosis', in *The Standard Edition of the Complete Psychological Works of Sigmund Freud*, vol. 17, trans. by James Strachey (Hogarth Press and the Institute of Psycho-Analysis, London [1918], 1974, 3–122).

Grosz, Elizabeth, *Jacques Lacan: A Feminist Introduction* (Routledge, London, 1990).

Hamilton, Paul, *Historicism* (2nd edn, Routledge, London, 2003).

Hawkes, Terence (ed.), *Alternative Shakespeares: Volume 2* (Routledge, London, 1996).

Healy, Thomas, *New Latitudes: Theory and English Renaissance Literature* (Arnold, London, 1992).

Homer, Sean, *Jacques Lacan* (Routledge, London, 2004).

Howard, Jean E. and O'Connor, Marion F. (eds), *Shakespeare Reproduced: The Text in History and Ideology* (Methuen, New York, 1987).

Howells, Christina, *Derrida: Deconstruction from Phenomenology to Ethics* (Polity Press, Cambridge, 1998).

Jackson, Rosemary, *Fantasy: The Literature of Subversion* (Routledge, London, 1981).

Lechte, John, *Julia Kristeva* (Routledge, London, 1990).

Lechte, John and Zournazi, Mary (eds), *The Kristeva Critical Reader* (Edinburgh University Press, Edinburgh, 2003).

Lucy, Niall, *A Derrida Dictionary* (Blackwell, Oxford, 2004).

MacCabe, Colin, *The Talking Cure: Essays in Psychoanalysis and Language* (Macmillan, Basingstoke, 1981).

McQuillan, Martin, *Paul de Man* (Routledge, London, 2001).

McQuillan, Martin, *Roland Barthes* (Palgrave Macmillan, Basingstoke, 2003).

Mapp, Nigel, 'Deconstruction', in *Encyclopaedia of Literature and Criticism*, Martin Coyle *et al.* (eds) (Routledge, London, 1990).

Mills, Sara, *Michel Foucault* (Routledge, London, 2003).

Mills, Sara, *Discourse* (Routledge, London, 2004).

Mitchell, Juliet and Rose, Jacqueline (eds and trans.), *Femininity and Sexuality: Jacques Lacan, the École Freudienne* (Macmillan, London, 1982).

Norris, Christopher, *Derrida* (Fontana, London, 1987).

Norris, Christopher, *Deconstruction: Theory and Practice* [1982] (3rd revd edn, Routledge, London, 2002).

Rabaté, Jean-Michel, *Jacques Lacan: Psychoanalysis and the Subject of Literature* (Palgrave Macmillan, Basingstoke, 2001).

Rand, Nicholas, *Psychoanalysis and Literature* (Palgrave Macmillan, Basingstoke, 2003).

Royle, Nicholas (ed.), *Deconstructions: A User's Guide* (Palgrave Macmillan, Basingstoke, 2000).

Royle, Nicholas, *Jacques Derrida* (Routledge, London, 2003).

Royle, Nicholas, *The Uncanny* (Routledge, New York, 2003).

Rylance, Rick, *Roland Barthes* (Harvester Wheatsheaf, Hemel Hempstead, 1993).

Salusinsky, Imre, *Criticism in Society* (Methuen, New York and London, 1987). Interviews with Derrida, Hartman, Said and others.

Sarup, Madan, *Jacques Lacan* (Harvester Wheatsheaf, Hemel Hempstead, 1992).

Sarup, Madan, *An Introductory Guide to Post-Structuralism and Postmodernism* (2nd edn, Pearson Education, 1993).

Sturrock, John, *Structuralism* [1979] (2nd edn, with intro. by Jean-Michel Rabaté, Blackwell, Oxford, 2003).

Textual Practice, vol. 3 (1989), 159–72 and vol. 4 (1990), 91–100, features a debate on Cultural Materialism between Catherine Belsey, Alan Sinfield and Jonathan Dollimore.

Thurschwell, Pauline, *Sigmund Freud* (Routledge, London, 2000).

Todd, Jane Marie, 'The Veiled Woman in Freud's "Das Unheimliche"', *Signs*, 2, 3 (1986), 519–28.

Veeser, H. Aram (ed.), *The New Historicism* (Routledge, London, 1989).

Wayne, Don E., 'New Historicism', in *Encyclopaedia of Literature and Criticism*, Martin Coyle *et al.* (eds) (Routledge, London, 1990).

Wilson, Richard and Sutton, Richard (eds), *New Historicism and Renaissance Drama* (Longman, London, 1991).

Wilson, Scott, *Cultural Materialism in Theory and in Practice* (Blackwell, Oxford, 1995).

Wolfreys, Julian, *Deconstruction: Derrida* (Palgrave Macmillan, Basdingstoke, 1998).

Wright, Elizabeth, 'The Uncanny and Surrealism', in Peter Collier and Judith Davies (eds), *Modernism and the European Unconscious* (Polity Press, Cambridge, 1989).

Wright, Elizabeth, 'Psychoanalytic Criticism', in *Encyclopaedia of Literature and Criticism*, Martin Coyle *et al.* (eds) (Routledge, London, 1990).

Wright, Elizabeth, *Psychoanalytic Criticism: A Reappraisal* (Polity Press, Cambridge, 1998).

Wright, Elizabeth, *Speaking Desires Can Be Dangerous: The Poetics of the Unconscious* (Polity Press, Cambridge, 2000).

CHAPTER 8

Postmodernist theories

The term 'postmodernism' has been the subject of much debate, especially during the 1980s and 1990s. Some see it as simply the continuation and development of modernist ideas; others have seen in postmodern art a radical break with classical modernism; while others again view past literature and culture retrospectively through post-modern eyes, identifying texts and authors (de Sade, Borges, the Ezra Pound of *The Cantos*) as 'already' postmodern. Yet another argument, associated principally with the philosopher and social theorist Jürgen Habermas, claims that the project of modernity – which here designates the philo-sophical, social and political values of reason, equality and justice derived from the Enlightenment – is as yet unfulfilled and should not be relinquished. This position also relates to the debate over the continuing relevance (or redundancy) of Marxism, as well as that of modernist art works. Where the project of modernity is defended (with or without an accompanying defence of artistic modernism), this is in the face of the leading contentions of postmodernism: first, that the 'grand narratives' of social and intellectual progress initiated by the Enlightenment are discredited; and second, that any political grounding of these ideas in 'history' or 'reality' is no longer possible, since both have become 'textualized' in the world of images and simulations which characterize the contemporary age of mass consumption and advanced technologies.

These latter positions comprise the two major 'narratives' of what con-stitutes postmodernism, and which other commentators concur with or refute to varying degrees. They connect with what has been said in Chapter 7 on the relations between structuralism and poststructuralism, and have raised broad philosophical, aesthetic and ideological questions of interest to literary theory and criticism, as well as to a range of other academic disciplines (philosophy, social and political theory, sociology, art history, architecture, urban, media and cultural studies) and to forms of cultural production (architecture, film and video, pop and rock music). Despite the diversity of trends within each movement, there is no doubt that post-structuralist thought represents a body of reflection upon the same issues that concern commentators on postmodern literature and culture. We will elaborate on some of these commentaries below.

An additional problem, however, lies in the uses of the term 'post-modernism' as both a descriptive and an evaluative term. The three terms, 'postmodern', 'postmodernity' and 'postmodernism' are in fact often used interchangeably: as a way of periodizing post-war developments in advanced media societies and capitalist economies; to describe developments within or across the arts – which frequently do not synchronize with the first set of developments or with each other; and to signal an attitude to or position on these developments. For many, the best solution is to employ the term 'postmodern' or 'postmodernity' for general developments in the period of the later twentieth century, and to reserve the term 'post-modernism' for developments in culture and the arts – although this too can seem to suggest an over-simple distinction between the economic and cultural realms. A further problem of definition then arises because *post-modernism* is a relational term which is seen to denote: either, a continua-tion of dominant features in an earlier modernism and in *avant-garde* movements; or, a radical break with them. Not surprisingly, there is much debate also about the identity and boundaries of these earlier movements, and hence the significance of their being subsumed or superseded. For some, postmodernism signals a deplorable commodification of all culture, and the loss of tradition and value crucially embodied in the twentieth century in modernist works; for others, it has brought a release from the hidebound orthodoxies of high culture and a welcome dispersal of creativity across the arts and new media, open now to new social groups.

Several theorists draw attention to the way in which postmodern crit-ics reject the elitism, sophisticated formal experimentation and tragic sense of alienation to be found in the modernist writers. Ihab Hassan, for example, contrasts modernist 'dehumanization of Art' with the post-modernist sense of the 'dehumanization of the Planet, and the End of Man'. While James Joyce is 'omnipotent' in his impersonal mastery of art, Samuel Beckett is 'impotent' in his minimalist representations of endgames. Modernists remain tragically heroic, while postmodernists express exhaus-tion and 'display the resources of the void'. Hassan, in *Paracriticisms* (1975), provides suggestive lists of postmodernist footnotes on modernism. They include the following: 'Anti-elitism, anti-authoritarianism. Diffusion of the

ego. Participation. Art becomes communal, optional, anarchic. Acceptance
. . . At the same time, irony becomes radical, self-consuming play, entropy
of meaning.' As opposed to modernist experimentation, postmodernists
produce 'Open, discontinuous, improvisational, indeterminate, or aleatory
structures'. They also reject the traditional aesthetics of 'Beauty' and of
'uniqueness'. Echoing a famous essay by Susan Sontag, Hassan adds that
they are 'Against interpretation'. (All these positions, as we have seen in
Chapter 7, are to be found in the various poststructuralist theorists.) For
if there is a summarizing idea, it is the theme of the absent centre. The
postmodern experience is widely held to stem from a profound sense of
ontological uncertainty, a conception especially explored by Brian McHale in
his *Postmodernist Fiction* (1987). Human shock in the face of the unimaginable (pollution, holocaust, the death of the subject) results in a loss
of fixed points of reference. Neither the world nor the self any longer
possesses unity, coherence, meaning. They are radically 'decentred'.

This does not mean that postmodern fiction is all as disconsolate as
Beckett's. As some theorists have seen, the decentring of language itself
has produced a great deal of playful, self-reflexive and self-parodying
fiction. Jorge Luis Borges is a master of this manner, and his writings parallel the poststructuralist verbal exuberance of Roland Barthes or J. Hillis
Miller. The American authors, John Barth, Thomas Pynchon and Ishmael
Reed, for example, and the European writers, Italo Calvino, Umberto Eco,
Salman Rushdie and John Fowles, are also invariably discussed as postmodernist. In some of these cases, and especially that of Eco, there is an
explicit connection between critical theory and fiction. For Eco (semiotician,
novelist and journalist), postmodernism is defined by its intertextuality and
knowingness, and by its relation to the past – which postmodernism re-
visits at any historical moment with irony. His best-selling 'novel', *The
Name of the Rose* (1980), is at once an example of the interpenetration of
previously separated categories of fiction and non-fiction, and vertiginously
historical: a detective thriller which mixes gothic suspense with chronicle
and scholarship, intersects the medieval with the modern, and has a Chinese-
box-like narrative structure, to produce a self-reflexively comic mystery about
the suppression and recuperation of the 'carnivalesque' power of the comic
itself. Other examples of self-reflexive postmodernist metafiction where there
is a convergence between fiction and the assumptions of poststructuralist theory would include John Fowles's *The French Lieutenant's Woman*,
Graham Swift's *Waterland*, Paul Auster's *New York Trilogy*, and much of the
writing of E. L. Doctorow. Just as poststructuralists critique distinctions
between the traditional orders of discourse (criticism, literature, philosophy,
politics) in the name of a general textuality, so postmodernist writers break

down conventional boundaries of discourse, between fiction and history, or autobiography, realism and fantasy, in a *bricolage* of forms and genres.

Linda Hutcheon's work on contemporary fiction, for instance, has explored the parodic but still critical mode that postmodernist literature can adopt in this broad textual or narrative universe: at once complicit *and* subversive. The self and history, she argues, are not lost in postmodernist fiction (or what she terms 'historiographic metafiction'), but newly problematized there. This self-conscious problematization of the making of fiction and history is a prime characteristic of the postmodern: a productive intertextuality which neither simply repudiates the past nor reproduces it as nostalgia. Postmodernist irony and paradox, in this view, signals a critical distance *within* the world of representations, raising questions about the ideological and discursive construction of the past, and about not so much *the* truth as *whose* truth is at stake in these narrative constructions. Hutcheon can retain a political function for this kind of fiction (*contra* many cultural commentators who see postmodernism as unalterably compromised or penned in a world of apolitical play), in so far as it simultaneously inscribes itself, and intervenes, in a given discursive and ideological order. Patricia Waugh, in *Metafiction* (1984) and *Feminine Fictions: Revisiting the Postmodern* (1989), also explores these issues – in the latter case explicitly in reference to feminism and the potential for the representation of a new gendered social subject in contemporary fiction. In a later work, *Practising Postmodernism/ Reading Modernism* (1992), Waugh approaches postmodernism itself as an aesthetic and philosophical category which we can learn from and be critical of. Like many others, she seeks here to redefine rather than jettison modernist works and assumptions in the elaboration of what she calls a 'New Humanism'.

These, and other, critics have continued invariably to respond, however, to the two most influential theories of postmodernism indicated above: the dominance of the sign or image and consequent loss of the real, and a scepticism towards the 'grand narratives' of human progress. These are associated respectively with the French philosophers Jean Baudrillard and Jean-François Lyotard.

Jean Baudrillard

Baudrillard's early work questioned the tenets of both Marxism and structuralism. Having argued for the dominance in modern capitalist societies of consumption over production and of the signifier over the signified,

he turned his attention to a critique of technology in the era of media reproduction, and has come to repudiate all models which distinguish between
surface and depth or the apparent and the real. Hence, Baudrillard's reworking of the themes of poststructuralism and of the French Situationists
in the late 1970s and 1980s signalled a 'retreat from politics' by left intellectuals and brought him cult status. His increasingly provocative and
apocalyptic writings of this period announced the reign of the 'simulacra'
(the copy without an original) and the world of 'hyperreality' (a notion he
shares with Umberto Eco; see Eco's *Travels in Hyperreality*, 1987), in which
imitations or 'fakes' take precedence over and usurp the real.

Baudrillard's first influential work, *Simulacra et Simulation* (1981, translated in 1983 and 1994), explores this depthless world of unreflecting
images. According to Baudrillard, signs no longer correspond to, or mask,
their 'real-life' referent but replace it in a world of autonomous 'floating
signifiers'; there has been 'an implosion of image and reality'. This implosion, as Neville Wakefield comments, leads 'into the simulated non-space
of hyperreality. The "real" is now defined in terms of the media in which
it moves.' It is the image-creating postmodern communication technologies
– especially television – which for Baudrillard stimulate this proliferation
of self-generating images across the postmodern surface. Experience everywhere is now derivative and literally superficial, and has achieved its
final 'utopian' form in the instantaneous abundance and banality of the
'cultureless' society of the United States, quintessentially in Disneyland.

Baudrillard's writings through the late 1980s and into the 1990s
(including *America, Fatal Strategies, The Illusion of the End*) have been
increasingly nihilistic. He sees postmodernity repeatedly in terms of the
disappearance of meaning, of inertia, exhaustion and endings, whether of
history or subjectivity. (A number of other contemporary writings bear
similarly on the theme of the 'end of history', most noticeably Francis
Fukuyama's reflections on the implications of the fall of Communism.) For
Baudrillard, everything is 'obscenely' on display, moving endlessly and trans-
parently across a surface where there is no control or stabilizing reference,
or any prospect of transformation. Perhaps his most provocative statement along these lines was that the Gulf War of 1991 was not a real but a
television war, a media event or spectacle: 'it is unreal,' he wrote, 'war without the symptoms of war.' He saw in this episode the working out of a 'logic
of deterrence', from hot to cold war, and so to fighting over 'the corpse
of war'. War cannot escape the net of postmodern simulation for 'TV is our
strategic site, a gigantic simulator' which creates war as a virtual reality. This
view was attacked for its irresponsible sophistry by Christopher Norris,

one of Baudrillard's most serious critics. His riposte appeared as the leading chapter in the volume *Uncritical Theory: Postmodernism, Intellectuals and the Gulf War* (Norris (ed.), 1992). Here as elsewhere, Norris argues – via the philosophical tradition of Frege, Donald Davidson and Habermas – for an alternative to the structuralist paradigm and the consequent scepticism of poststructuralism and postmodernism. Aside from his refutation of Baudrillard's exclusive world of signs, Norris proposes – through an appeal to the commonsensical assurance that inequality, oppression, unemployment, urban decay, destruction and death in war are manifestly real forms of social experience – that presuppositions of truth and right reason are present in human discourse and conduct at all levels, and that these provide a basis for morality and political judgement.

More recently, Baudrillard has commented on the events of 9/11 in terms recalling his earlier comments on the Gulf War. In his essay, *The Spirit of Terrorism* (2003), he views the attack on the twin towers of the World Trade Center as confirming the 'virtual' mediated nature of reality and as undermining other received binary distinctions. America and 'we' of the West, he argues, are complicit with the attacks, since the hijackers plotted from inside the United States, like a virus within its host, and because we all harbour a dream, says Baudrillard, of striking at the global power embodied in United States hegemony and its symbolic expression in an edifice like the World Trade Center. The event has, moreover, confounded the conventional rules of military engagement, since the US has no answer to suicide attacks, and has confused any former clear identification of the enemy. We need to rethink, therefore, conventional categories and distinctions. 'Terrorism is immoral,' writes Baudrillard. 'The World Trade Center event, that symbolic challenge, is immoral, and it is a response to a globalization which is itself immoral. So let us be immoral; and, if we want to have some understanding of all this, let us go and take a little look beyond Good and Evil.'

The common perception that the attack of 9/11 was a calculated, media-savvy act in a symbolic war has given renewed currency to Baudrillard's analysis of trends in contemporary culture, though many at the same time would want to resist the view that this and other terroristic acts are matters of pure spectacle. His comment that the collapse of the World Trade Center towers, while 'unimaginable', was 'not enough to make it a real event' – alongside Karlheinz Stockhausen's infamous outburst that the attack was 'the greatest work of art there has ever been!' – have, unsurprisingly, been met with dismay. Noam Chomsky's commentary in his best-selling booklet, *9–11*, of the long history of Western state terrorism and of the United States' support for terrorist wars has brought a more throughgoing economic and political analysis to the supposed differences between Islam and the West. However, Baudrillard's questioning of the conventional distinctions of the real and the virtual, and of 'them' and 'us', poses its own difficult challenge at the levels of ethical and political as well as of philosophical understanding.

The Spirit of Terrorism is unusual in Baudrillard's later writings in referring to a specific event. More often he has avoided the specifics of social and cultural or artistic forms while pronouncing on them in a mode that blends telling aperçus with alarming hyperbole. In this world of simulation, spectacle and 'unreality', art itself cannot hope to innovate in any absolute sense but only repeat and recombine the recycled fragments of a (lost) past. The implicit Baudrillardian aesthetic mode is therefore that of pastiche, a feature of postmodern society emphasized by Fredric Jameson (see below), though this is countered by Linda Hutcheon in the terms sketched out above. In literature, there are close correlations with – even anticipations of – Baudrillard's thought in the early 1960s novel, *Crash*, by the science fiction novelist J. G. Ballard (on which Baudrillard wrote a later admiring essay: see *Simulacra and Simulation*, 1994), and the science fiction of Philip K. Dick. More recently, the implications of hyperreality and the simulacra have been explored in the cyberpunk fiction of William Gibson, Bruce Sterling and others – for Jameson 'the supreme *literary* expression' of postmodernism or late-capitalism – as well as in a generation of feature films, from *Blade Runner* to the *Terminator* and *Matrix* films (see Brooker and Brooker, 1997). In such examples, in tandem but not necessarily in entire agreement with Baudrillard's view that humankind can only surrender to a world of images and simulations, human protagonists are set the task of redefining the 'human' in new relations with invasive postmodern technologies. This theme is taken up most interestingly, and again not always pessimistically, in both theory and fiction in relation to the figure of the cyborg (see Haraway, 1985, below, pp. 211–12, and Wolmark, 1993). Indeed, as Best and Kellner have suggested, perhaps the best way still to read Baudrillard's work is as itself an example of 'speculative fiction'. His own thoughts along these lines (in *Fatal Strategies*, 1983 and *The Illusion of the End*, 1994) provide a melancholy extreme against which to judge these other contemporary speculations in literature and elsewhere about the end-of-millennium and the fate of human agency.

Jean-François Lyotard

For fifteen years a member of the revolutionary Marxist group, 'Socialisme ou Barbarie', Jean-François Lyotard came in the 1960s to question Marxism and to seek other terms for the investigation of philosophy and the arts. In *Discours, figure* (1971), he distinguished between the *seen*, the visual and three-dimensional (the 'figural'), and the *read*, the textual and two-dimensional (the 'discursive'). Lyotard thus identifies two regimes and sets of laws which structuralist and semiotic paradigms had ignored, rendering the spatial and visual realm of things too automatically or immediately into the flatness of text. In *Economie libidinale* (1974), Lyotard extended this critique to Marxism, advocating an alternative philosophy of desire, intensities and energetics indebted to Nietzsche. In its assumption that history is available to consciousness, Marxism is seen as emptying history of its materiality, filling the void thus created with a totalizing narrative. Discursive consciousness is seen as submerging the figural world and its associated nexus of desire (in a theory close to that of Deleuze and Guattari: see Chapter 7). This repression represents the mark of the 'modern', consequent upon the procedures of rationality and associated with the models of justice and civilization which characterize modernity. As summarized by Thomas Docherty:

> Capital, masculinism and so on – all the forms of a dominant ideological thought which characterises the modern world – depend upon the erasure of figurality and its premature transliteration into the form of discursivity. Modernity itself is based upon the foreclosure of the figure, of the depth of a reality, of the materiality of a historicity which is resistant to the categories of our understanding, but which we force or forge into the shapes of our discursive mental world. (Docherty, 1990)

As Docherty adds, what in modernity passes for understanding (the particular discursive mode of rational thinking) is, in this view, 'itself really a mastery or domination, not an understanding at all'.

Lyotard believes, therefore, that there is a level – the figural, marked by the flow and intensities of desire and its libidinal effects – which is plural, heterogeneous and forced into unitary meaning by totalizing reason. He is led to a valorization of difference, of contrary repressed impulses, open to the multiple and incommensurable. This he then develops beyond a philosophy of vitalism to a philosophy of language and justice in texts of the 1980s (*Just Gaming*, 1985 and *The Differend*, 1983). Art which participates in this postmodern awareness of difference and heterogeneity will therefore critique and destabilize the closures of modernity. It will explore the 'unsayable' and 'invisible'.

It is Lyotard's *The Postmodern Condition* (1979), however, which has proved the major focus for debates on cultural postmodernism. Drawing first on

Nietzsche's critique of the totalizing claims of reason as being without moral or philosophical grounds (or 'legitimation'), and second on Wittgenstein, Lyotard argues that the criteria regulating the 'truth claims' of knowledge derive from discrete, context-dependent 'language games', not absolute rules or standards. In its 'modern' phase, for example, science sought legitimation from one of two narrative types: either that of human liberation associated with the Enlightenment and the revolutionary tradition, or that of the prospective unity of all knowledge associated with Hegelianism.

According to Lyotard, neither of these legitimating 'metanarratives' or 'grands récits' now has credibility. In this critique, echoing the pessimism of the Frankfurt School – though Lyotard's focus is more narrowly upon forms of modern and postmodern knowledge – the Enlightenment project is seen as having produced a range of social and political disasters: from modern warfare, Auschwitz and the Gulag to nuclear threat and severe ecological crisis. The results of modernization have been bureaucracy, oppression and misery as the Enlightenment narrative of liberation and equality has ground into its opposite. Jürgen Habermas, as indicated earlier, has resisted this view and maintains that a commitment to the operation of an intersubjective 'communicative reason' will make the goals of justice and democracy realizable. In Lyotard's view the 'truth claims' and assumed consensus of such a universalizing history are repressive and untenable. Deprived of these premises, 'postmodern' science pursues the technical and commercial aims of optimal performance: a change reinforced by new, computerized technologies which make information a political quantity. However, this technocratic order is at odds with an internal experimental drive which questions the paradigms of 'normal science'. What Lyotard calls the activity of 'paralogism' – exercised in illogical or contradictory reasoning – produces a breakthrough into the unknown of new knowledge. There thus emerges a new source of legitimation, invested in more modest 'petits récits' and indebted to the radical avant-garde imperative to experiment and 'make it new'.

The postmodern aesthetic that emerges from Lyotard's work, therefore (most conveniently examined in the appendix to The Postmodern Condition: 'Answering the Question: What is Postmodernism?'), can be thought of as an investigative aesthetic of the 'sublime'. It should be noted, moreover, that this does not sequentially follow modernism so much as comprise its founding conditions. Here Lyotard departs from Baudrillard, Jameson and other postmodern commentators who see a decisive break between the modern and postmodern periods. For Lyotard, the postmodern is not an epoch, and less a periodizing concept than a mode: 'The postmodern is undoubtedly part of the modern', as he puts it: 'it would be that which, in the modern, puts forward the unpresentable in presentation itself'. Similarly, the 'figural' and 'discursive' are not to be thought of as sequential or as exclusively identified with the postmodern and modern, since the postmodern and figural can appear within the modern and discursive. This then presents a way of identifying postmodern writers and tendencies in the strictly 'modern' period (the Joyce of *Finnegans Wake*, for instance), and for recovering distinctions between forms of more closed and terroristic and more open and experimental modernism (between high modernism and the radical *avant-garde*, for example, or between T. S. Eliot, William Carlos Williams and Gertrude Stein).

In addition, the postmodern mode proceeds without predetermined criteria or rules, since these are discovered rather than assumed. By analogy this will also apply in the political arena, and to a working through to notions of 'postmodern' justice. It is here, however, in the consideration of social and political complexities, that Lyotard's thought is found by some to be at its weakest or most ambiguous. For while on the one hand, in common with deconstruction generally, it can be said to authorize a consciously decentred 'postmodern' micro-politics, alert to heterogeneity, the local, provisional and pragmatic in ethical judgements and conduct, it can be read, on the other hand, as sponsoring an unconnected relativism, high on rhetoric and low on proposals for concrete social action (see Fredric Jameson's Foreword to *The Postmodern Condition*, and essays in Nicholson, 1990, and Readings, 1990). At the same time, this issue is not limited to interpretations of Lyotard and might be said to comprise the most pressing and on-going theme in postmodern debates.

Postmodernism and Marxism

Two significant articles on postmodernism from within the Anglo-American tradition which responded to the positions presented by Baudrillard and Lyotard, and to the challenge postmodernism offers to Marxism in particular, were published in *New Left Review* by Fredric Jameson in 1984 and Terry Eagleton in 1985 (for further treatment of both critics, see Chapter 5). Jameson has consistently explored questions of social, economic and cultural change raised by postmodernism, and thus its relation to the changing nature of capitalism and the place of Marxism within it. The title of his 1984 essay, now itself a key document in debates on postmodernism, and reproduced in its most extended version as the title-essay of his later volume, *Postmodernism, or the Cultural Logic of Late Capitalism* (1991), highlights the symbiotic relationship between post-modernism and what Jameson sees as the expansion and consolidation of capitalist hegemony. Jameson believes that postmodernism is not merely one period style among others but the dominant style which takes its particular significance from the context of late capitalist society. He sees a profound connection between the 'electronic and nuclear-powered' technology of the multinational global economy and the depthless, frag-mented and randomly heterogeneous images of postmodernist culture. This culture has effaced the frontier (strongly defended by modernist art) between high culture and mass culture. Jameson points to the postmodern fascination with the 'whole "degraded" landscape of schlock and kitsch, TV soaps and *Readers' Digest*, advertising, motels, the late show, grade-B Hollywood film and pulp fiction'. This commercial culture is no longer held at bay or parodied in modernist fashion, or in the double-coded manner described by Linda Hutcheon (see above), but incorporated directly, Jameson believes, into postmodern art. Andy Warhol's work, for example, reveals the total interpenetration of aesthetic and commodity production. The char-acteristic mode of this culture, says Jameson, is 'pastiche' or 'blank parody': the 'disappearance of the subject' deprives the artist of an individual style, just as the 'loss of history' deprives art of originality. The artist can resort only to mimicry of past styles without purpose, irony or satire. Jameson summarizes his view of the resulting 'nostalgia mode' as follows: 'The approach to the present by way of the art language of the simulacrum, or of the pastiche of the stereotypical past, endows present reality and the openness of present history with the spell and distance of a glossy mirage.' Postmodernist art can no longer represent a real past but only our ideas and stereotypes about the past in the form of 'pop' history.

The central problem of Jameson's position lies in squaring his accept-ance of postmodernism as our cultural condition and his commitment to a Hegelian Marxism. For while he would accept Baudrillard's view of pre-sent society as a society of the 'imploded image' or simulacrum, detached from reference, reality, and authentic history, he wishes to retain a distinction between surface and depth within a dialectical materialism which, however embattled, still seeks to grasp the 'totality' of a fragmented society bereft of 'grand narratives' and to effect social and cultural transformation.

Eagleton, in his article, further pursues the idea of the convergence of art and commodity in late capitalism. Marx's analysis of money and exchange value included the concept of 'commodity fetishism'. This refers to the mystifying process by which human labour is transposed into its products: the value which labour time bestows upon products is seen as an independent and objective property of the products themselves. This inability to see products for what they are is at the root of social alienation and exploitation. Eagleton treats 'fetishism' as an aesthetic category: the process of commodity fetishism is an *imaginary* one which insists on the independent reality of the fictively conceived commodity, and the alienated human mind accepts the objective independence of its own imaginary creation. In view of this profound 'unreality' of both art and commodity, Eagleton asserts the 'historical truth that the very autonomy and brute self-identity of the postmodernist artefact is the effect of its thorough *integration* into an economic system where such autonomy, in the form of the commodity fetish, is the order of the day'.

Linda Hutcheon disputes the implication she finds in both Jameson and Eagleton that postmodernist intertextuality merely reproduces the past in the form of a shallow and compromised nostalgia rather than revealing its construction in discourse and ideology. In *The Politics of Postmodernism* (1989), she replies to Eagleton – 'a Marxist critic who has accused postmodern fiction of being ahistorical' – by way of an analysis of his own historical novel, *Saints and Scholars* (1987). She argues that this novel 'works towards a critical return to history and politics *through*, not despite, metafictional self-consciousness and parodic intertextuality'. Here lies the paradox of postmodernism's '"use and abuse" of history'.

Other Marxist critics who understand postmodernism as an intensification of capitalism – an extension of privilege and disadvantage on a global scale – and argue therefore for the continued relevance of class politics, follow Eagleton in their antagonism, or at best deep caution, towards theories of postmodernism. At the same time, many on the left have sought to revise their cultural politics, and the ideals of the Enlightenment or of modernity from which they derive, so as to respond to the altered conditions of the globalized media and information society postmodernism describes. Often this debate, and the attempt to ground a new postmodern ethics or politics, has been conducted in philosophy, social theory or cultural studies rather than literary theory or criticism (see Bauman, 1993; Squires, 1993; Nicholson and Seidman, 1995; and Hall, 1996). And indeed this discussion is critical of the more textualist models of postmodernism often found in literary studies. However, a committed 'worldly' postmodernism is also mobilized, in an alignment with trends in poststructuralist thought and deconstruction, to critique essentialist and exclusive models of the subject and elitist notions of literature and culture. Its leading arguments aim to 'decentre' unitary and normative conceptions of sexual, ethnic, racial or cultural identity, and in this guise a 'radical' or 'social postmodernism' connects with some of the most challenging contemporary ideas in feminism, postcolonialism, African American, gay, lesbian and queer theory and writing (see below, and Chapters 9 and 10).

Postmodern feminisms

As Linda Nicholson has pointed out, postmodernism's critique of a supposed academic neutrality and the claims of rationality would seem to make it 'a natural ally' of feminism's opposition to a normative masculinity which operates in league with the ideals of the Enlightenment project (*Feminism/ Postmodernism*, 1990). While some would wish to defend the Enlightenment universals of social progress, justice and equality as of continuing relevance to feminism (Lovibond, 1990), few would accept these in unrevised form, or deny the challenge of postmodern arguments, both to the gendered cultural and intellectual assumptions of modernity and to feminism's own universalizing or essentialist positions. Postmodernism, says Nicholson, can help to avoid 'the tendency to construct theory that generalizes from the experiences of Western, white middle-class women'.

Along similar lines, Patricia Waugh (*Feminine Fictions*, 1989) views feminism as having 'passed through a *necessary* stage of pursuing unity', but as more recently producing alternative conceptions of the subject and of subjectivity which 'emphasize the provisionality and positionality of identity, the historical and social construction of gender, and the discursive production of knowledge and power'. In a particularly influential example of non-essentializing theory, also of the late 1980s, Alice Jardine coined the term 'gynesis' in opposition to 'gynocriticism', or female-centred criticism, associated especially with the work of Elaine Showalter (see Chapter 6, pp. 126–9). Gynesis describes the mobilization of a poststructuralist analysis of the category 'woman'. Jardine observes that the crises experienced by the major Western narratives are not gender neutral. By probing the originary gendered relationships of Greek philosophy, Jardine argues that the fundamental 'dualistic oppositions that determine our ways of thinking' are those between *techne* or *time* (male) and *physis* or *space* (female). Thus a key aspect of the postmodernist questioning of the master narratives of the West is an 'attempt to create a new space or spacing within themselves for survival (of different kinds)'.

For Jardine, the condition of postmodernity (or the 'crisis-in-narrative that is modernity', as she prefers to think of it) is marked by the 'valorization of the feminine, woman' as 'intrinsic to new and necessary modes of thinking, writing, speaking'. Concerned with the 'non-knowledge' or feminine 'space' which the master narratives always contain but cannot control, gynesis is the *process* of putting into discourse that 'Other': 'woman'. The object produced by this process is a *gynema*: not woman as a person but a 'reading effect', a 'woman-in-effect' that is 'never stable and has no identity' (and might be produced in texts by male writers).

As with other versions of *l'ecriture féminine*, gynesis asserts, in Mary Jacobus's phrase, 'not the sexuality of the text but the textuality of sex'. This, then, is a kind of writing which is not specifically gendered but disrupts fixed meaning and encourages textual free play beyond authorial or critical control. Jardine's opposition to gynocentric feminist theory forms an important questioning of the core concepts which gynocentrism takes to be self-evidently meaningful. Gynesis also counters the inability of Anglo-American criticism to theorize adequately the significance and significations of *avant-garde* and modernist literary texts. Though Jardine's model is anti-humanist, anti-realist and anti-essentialist, she still wants to hold on to a working model of feminist politics. As Catherine Belsey suggests ('Critical Approaches', 1992), postmodernism for Jardine is 'incompatible with feminism to the degree that feminism is the single story of Woman'. Gynesis is a potent form of political, cultural and critical deconstruction. It revalues and reshapes (if not explodes) literary canons, refuses unitary or universally accepted meanings, and overtly politicizes the whole domain of discursive practice. Gynesis does not see 'woman' as empirically provable: rather, 'woman' is a gap or absence that troubles and destabilizes the master narratives.

The different claims of empirical and poststructuralist traditions in feminist criticism is a matter of continuing debate, but has been taken in a more pronounced postmodernist direction in Judith Butler's account of gender (for more on Butler, see Chapter 10, pp. 248, 255–6). Butler recognizes that branches of feminism informed by poststructuralism have been attacked for losing sight of a stable concept of identity, but argues that 'contemporary feminist debates over the meanings of gender lead time and again to a sense of trouble, as though the indeterminacy of gender might eventually culminate in the failure of feminism'. For Butler, the feminist 'we' is a 'phantasmatic construction' which 'denies internal complexity and indeterminacy' and 'constitutes itself only through the exclusion of some part of the constituency that it simultaneously seeks to represent'.

Butler takes identity-based feminism to be restrictive and limiting because it has a tendency, however minimally, to produce gendered identities as 'real' or 'natural'. Butler's thesis is that 'there is no gender identity *behind* the expressions of identity', 'identity is performatively constituted by the very "expressions" that are said to be its results'. Gendered behaviour is not the consequence of a prior identity: 'there need not be a "doer behind the deed", rather, the "doer" is variably constructed in and through the deed.' In this sense, Butler differs from existential theories of the self (such as de Beauvoir's – see Chapter 6) which maintain a 'prediscursive structure for both the self and its acts', and from Cixous who upholds the view that women occupy a pre-cultural or pre-civilizational world which is closer to the rhythms of nature. Instead, Butler urges us to consider identity as a *signifying practice*: gender is something we 'do', and, like all signifying practices, is dependent on *repetition* – the repetition of words and acts which make the subject culturally intelligible. The result is that not only are categories of identity such as femininity recognized as varied and contested (rather than fixed), but a subversion of identity also becomes possible.

Thus Butler's privileged model of subversion in action is the practice of parody in which gender is produced as a 'failed copy', as fundamentally flawed and split. Her argument runs close at this point to Linda Hutcheon's version of postmodern parody and to Homi Bhabha's account of colonial mimicry in which the mimic men, who are obliged to internalize the laws of the colonizing nations, do so only imperfectly: 'almost the same but not quite'; an imperfect repetition or imitation which signifies the flaws and fissures of the colonial project (see Chapter 9). For Butler, the parodic repetition of gender exposes the 'illusion of gender identity as an intractable depth and inner substance'. The 'loss of gender norms would have the effect of *proliferating* gender configurations, destabilizing substantive identity, and depriving the naturalizing narratives of compulsory heterosexuality of their central protagonists: "man" and "woman"'.

Donna Haraway's essay 'A Manifesto for Cyborgs' (1985, in Nicholson, ed., 1990) is relevant here and has been of continuing interest. Haraway's view of the 'cyborg' as a 'creature in a postgender world' marks another radical critique of the dualisms and polarities (such as nature/culture, public/private, organic/technological) which are constantly rearticulated as the fundamental organizing structures of subjectivity in the West. Haraway's openness to technology allows her to question the strengths of myths of origin and fulfilment. The 'twin potent myths' of individual development and of history, 'inscribed most powerfully for us in psychoanalysis and Marxism', depend on the 'plot of original unity out of which difference must be produced and enlisted in a drama of escalating domination of woman/nature'. The radicalism of the cyborg is that it 'skips the step of original unity, of identification with nature in the Western sense'; it is oppositional, utopian and 'has no truck with bisexuality, pre-Oedipal symbiosis, unalienated labor, or other seductions to organic wholeness'.

Haraway's argument picks up from contemporary feminist and post-colonial views that the struggle for the meanings of writing is an important form of political struggle. For Haraway, writing is 'pre-eminently the technology of cyborgs', and cyborg politics is the 'struggle for language and the struggle against perfect communication, against the *one code* that translates all meaning perfectly, the central dogma of phallogocentrism'. Haraway finds equivalents of cyborg identities in the stories of 'outsiders': defined as those groups (such as 'women of colour' in the United States – see 'Race and Ethnicity' in Chapter 9) with no available original dream of a common language (a notion associated with Adrienne Rich, on whom see Chapter 10, pp. 248–9). In retelling origin stories or exploring themes of identity when one never possessed the original language or never 'resided in the harmony of legitimate heterosexuality in the garden of culture', cyborg authors celebrate illegitimacy and work to subvert the central myths of Western culture.

Selected reading

Key texts

Baudrillard, Jean, *For a Critique of the Political Economy of the Sign* [1972], trans. and intro. by Charles Levin (Telos Press, St Louis, 1981).

Baudrillard, Jean, *The Mirror of Production* [1973], trans. by Mark Poster (Telos Press, St Louis, 1975).

Baudrillard, Jean, *Symbolic Exchange and Death* [1976], trans. by Iain Hamilton Grant (Sage, London, 1993).

Baudrillard, Jean, *Simulacra and Simulation* [1981], trans. by Sheila Faria Glaser (University of Michigan Press, Ann Arbor, 1994).

Baudrillard, Jean, *Fatal Strategies* [1983], trans. by Philip Beitchman and W. G. J. Nieluchowski; ed. by Jim Fleming (Pluto, London, 1990).

Baudrillard, Jean, 'The Ecstasy of Communication' [1985], in Hal Foster (ed.), below.

Baudrillard, Jean, *America* [1986], trans. by Chris Turner (Verso, London, 1988).

Baudrillard, Jean, *The Illusion of the End* [1992], trans. by Chris Turner (Polity Press, Oxford, 1994).

Baudrillard, Jean, *The Spirit of Terrorism* [2001], trans. by Chris Turner (Verso, London, 2002).

Baudrillard, Jean, *Jean Baudrillard: Selected Writings*, ed. by Mark Poster (2nd enlarged edn, Polity Press, Cambridge, 2001).

Brooker, Peter (ed.), *Modernism/Postmodernism* (Longman, London, 1992).

Butler, Judith, *Gender Trouble: Feminism and the Subversion of Identity* (Routledge, London and New York, 1992).

Butler, Judith, *Bodies That Matter: On the Discursive Limits of 'Sex'* (Routledge, London and New York, 1993).

Butler, Judith, *The Judith Butler Reader*, ed. by Sara Salih (Blackwell, Oxford, 2003).

Connor, Steven, *Postmodernist Culture: An Introduction to Theories of the Contemporary* (2nd edn, Blackwell, Oxford, 1996).

Connor, Steven (ed.), *The Cambridge Companion to Postmodernism* (Cambridge University Press, Cambridge, 2004).

Docherty, Thomas (ed.), *Postmodernism: A Reader* (Harvester Wheatsheaf, Hemel Hempstead, 1992).

Eagleton, Terry, 'Capitalism, Modernism and Postmodernism' [1985], in *Against the Grain: Selected Essays, 1975–85* (Verso, London, 1986).

Eagleton, Terry, *The Illusions of Postmodernism* (Blackwell, Oxford, 1996).

Eco, Umberto, *Travels in Hyperreality* [1986], trans. by William Weaver (Picador, London, 1987).

Encyclopedia of Postmodernism, ed. by Victor E. Taylor and Charles E. Winquist (Routledge, London, 2000).

Foster, Hal (ed.), *Postmodern Culture* (Pluto, London, 1985).

Habermas, Jürgen, 'Modernity – An Incomplete Project' [1985; in Hal Foster (ed.), above], reprinted in Peter Brooker (ed.), above.

Haraway, Donna, 'A Manifesto for Cyborgs: Science, Technology, and Socialist Feminism in the 1980s', *Socialist Review*, 15, 18 (1985), reprinted in Linda Nicholson (ed.), below.

Hassan, Ihab, 'POSTmodernISM', in *Paracriticisms: Seven Speculations of the Times* (Illinois University Press, Urbana, 1975).

Hassan, Ihab, *The Postmodern Turn: Essays in Postmodern Theory and Culture* (Illinois University Press, Urbana, 1975).

Hutcheon, Linda, *A Poetics of Postmodernism: History, Theory, Fiction* (Routledge, London, 1988).

Hutcheon, Linda, *The Politics of Postmodernism* [1989] (2nd edn, Routledge, London, 2002).

Huyssen, Andreas, *After the Great Divide: Modernism, Mass Culture, Postmodernism* (Macmillan, Basingstoke, 1988).

Jameson, Fredric, 'Postmodernism, or the Cultural Logic of Late Capitalism', *New Left Review*, 146 (1984).

Jameson, Fredric, 'Postmodernism and Consumer Society', in Hal Foster (ed.), above.

Jameson, Fredric, *Postmodernism, or the Cultural Logic of Late Capitalism* (Verso, London, 1991).

Jameson, Fredric, *A Singular Modernity* (Verso, London, 2002).

Jardine, Alice, *Gynesis: Configurations of Women in Modernity* (Cornell University Press, Ithaca, 1985).

Lovibond, Sarah, 'Feminism and Postmodernism', in Roy Boyne and Ali Rattansi (eds), *Postmodernism and Society* (Macmillan, Basingstoke, 1990).

Lucy, Niall (ed.), *Postmodern Literary Theory: An Anthology* (Blackwell, Oxford, 1999).

Lyotard, Jean-François, *Discours, figure* (Klincksieck, Paris, 1971).

Lyotard, Jean-François, *The Postmodern Condition: A Report on Knowledge* [1979], trans. by Geoff Bennington and Brian Massumi (Manchester University Press, Manchester, 1984).

Lyotard, Jean-François, *The Differend* [1983], trans. by Georges Van Den Abbeele (Manchester University Press, Manchester, 1988).

Lyotard, Jean-François, *The Lyotard Reader*, ed. by Andrew Benjamin (Basil Blackwell, London and Cambridge, Mass., 1989).

Nicholson, Linda (ed.), *Feminism/Postmodernism* (Routledge, London and New York, 1990).

Waugh, Patricia (ed.), *Postmodernism: A Reader* (Arnold, London, 1992).

Further reading

Alexander, Marguerite, *Flights from Realism: Themes and Strategies in Postmodernist British and American Fiction* (Arnold, London, 1990).

Bauman, Zygmunt, *Postmodern Ethics* (Blackwell, Oxford, 1993).

Bertens, Hans, *The Idea of the Postmodern: A History* (Routledge, London, 1995).

Bertens, Hans and Natoli, Joseph (eds), *Postmodernism: The Key Figures* (Blackwell, Oxford, 2002).

Belsey, Catherine, 'Critical Approaches', in Claire Buck (ed.), *Bloomsbury Guide to Women's Literature* (Bloomsbury, London, 1992).

Best, Steven and Kellner, Douglas, *Postmodern Theory: Critical Interrogations* (Macmillan, Basingstoke, 1991).

Brooker, Peter, *New York, Fictions: Modernity, Postmodernism, The New Modern* (Longman, London, 1995).

Brooker, Peter and Brooker, Will (eds), *Postmodern After-Images: A Reader in Film, TV and Video* (Arnold, London, 1997).

Caesar, Michael, *Umberto Eco: Philosophy, Semiotics and the Work of Fiction* (Polity Press, Cambridge, 1999).

Callinicos, Alex, *Against Postmodernism* (Polity/Basil Blackwell, Cambridge, 1989).

Chomsky, Noam, *9–11* (Seven Stories Press, New York, 2001).

Debord, Guy, *The Society of the Spectacle* (Black & Red, Detroit, 1970).

Debord, Guy, *Comments on the Society of the Spectacle*, trans. by Malcolm Imrie (Verso, London, 1998).

Docherty, Thomas, *After Theory: Postmodernism/Postmarxism* (Routledge, London, 1990).

Docherty, Thomas, review of *The Lyotard Reader* (Andrew Benjamin (ed.) above), *Paragraph*, vol. 15 (1992), 105–15.

Docherty, Thomas, *After Theory* (Edinburgh University Press, Edinburgh, 1996).

Hall, Stuart, *Critical Dialogues in Cultural Studies*, ed. by David Morley and Kuan-Hsing Chen (Routledge, London and New York, 1996).

Kaplan, E. Ann (ed.), *Postmodernism and its Discontents: Theories, Practices* (Verso, London, 1988).

Kellner, Douglas, *Jean Baudrillard: From Marxism to Postmodernism and Beyond* (Polity/Basil Blackwell, Cambridge, 1988).

Kellner, Douglas, *Postmodernism/Jameson/Critique* (Maisonneuve Press, Washington, DC, 1990).

Lane, Richard J., *Jean Baudrillard* (Routledge, London, 2000).

Lee, Alison, *Realism and Power: Postmodern British Fiction* (Routledge, London, 1990).

McHale, Brian, *Postmodernist Fiction* (Routledge, London, 1987).

McHale, Brian, *Constructing Postmodernism* (Routledge, London, 1993).

Malpas, Simon (ed.), *Postmodern Debates* (Palgrave Macmillan, Basingstoke, 2001).

Malpas, Simon, *Jean-François Lyotard* (Routledge, London, 2002).

Malpas, Simon, *The Postmodern* (Routledge, London, 2004).

Nicholson, Linda and Seidman, Steven (eds), *Social Postmodernism: Beyond Identity Politics* (Cambridge University Press, Cambridge, 1995).

Norris, Christopher, *What's Wrong with Postmodernism: Critical Theory and the Ends of Philosophy* (Harvester Wheatsheaf, Hemel Hempstead, 1991).

Norris, Christopher, *Uncritical Theory: Postmodernism, Intellectuals and the Gulf War* (Lawrence & Wishart, London, 1992).

Readings, Bill, *Introducing Lyotard: Art and Politics* (Routledge, London, 1990).

Sarup, Madan, *An Introductory Guide to Post-Structuralism and Postmodernism* (2nd edn, Harvester Wheatsheaf, Hemel Hempstead, 1993).

Silverman, Hugh J. (ed.), *Postmodernism, Philosophy and the Arts* (Routledge, London, 1990).

Sim, Stuart (ed.), *The Routledge Companion to Postmodernism* (Routledge, London, 2001).

Squires, Judith (ed.), *Principled Positions: Postmodernism and the Rediscovery of Value* (Lawrence & Wishart, London, 1993).

Wakefield, Neville, *Postmodernism: The Twilight of the Real* (Pluto, London, 1990).

Waugh, Patricia, *Metafiction: The Theory and Practice of Self-Conscious Fiction* (Routledge, London, 1984).

Waugh, Patricia, *Feminine Fictions: Revisiting the Postmodern* (Routledge, London, 1989).

Waugh, Patricia, *Practising Postmodernism/Reading Modernism* (Arnold, London, 1992).

Williams, James, *Lyotard: Towards a Postmodern Philosophy* (Polity Press, Cambridge, 1998).

Wolmark, Jenny, *Aliens and Others: Science Fiction, Feminism and Postmodernism* (Prentice Hall/Harvester Wheatsheaf, Hemel Hempstead, 1993).

Woods, Tim, *Beginning Postmodernism* (Manchester University Press, Manchester, 1999).

CHAPTER 9

Postcolonialist theories

A further movement which draws on the more radical implications of poststructuralism is the study of colonial discourse, or what is usually termed 'postcolonial criticism' – although we should offer a caveat about settling too neatly on a name for this internally diverse cluster of writers and writings. Analysis of the cultural dimension of colonialism/imperialism is as old as the struggle against it; such work has been a staple of anti-colonial movements everywhere. It entered the agenda of metropolitan intellectuals and academics as a reflex of a new consciousness attendant on Indian independence (1947) and as part of a general leftist reorientation to the 'Third-World' struggles (above all in Algeria) from the 1950s onwards. Frantz Fanon's *The Wretched of the Earth* (1961) was and remains an inspirational key text (it had an important preface by the metropolitan 'convert', Jean-Paul Sartre). Thereafter, 'postcolonial studies' overtook the troublesome ideological category of 'Commonwealth literature' to emerge in the 1980s as a set of concerns marked by the decentredness otherwise associated, philosophically, with poststructuralism and particularly deconstruction (see Chapter 7).

The appearance of postcolonial criticism has therefore overlapped with the debates on postmodernism, though it brings, too, an awareness of power relations between Western and 'Third World' cultures which the more playful and parodic, or aestheticizing postmodernism has neglected or been slow to develop. From a postcolonial perspective, Western values and traditions of thought and literature, including versions of postmodernism, are guilty of a repressive ethnocentrism. Models of Western thought (derived, for example, from Aristotle, Descartes, Kant, Marx, Nietzsche and Freud) or of literature (Homer, Dante, Flaubert, T. S. Eliot) have dominated world culture, marginalizing or excluding non-Western traditions and forms of cultural life and expression.

Jacques Derrida has described Western metaphysics as 'the white mythology which reassembles and reflects the culture of the West: the white man takes his own mythology, Indo-European mythology, his own *logos*, that is, the *mythos* of this idiom, for the universal form of that he must still wish to call Reason', and the methods of deconstruction have proved a major inspiration for postcolonial critics. Some of the other theoretical arguments discussed elsewhere in this book – derived, for example, from Bakhtin's dialogics, theories of ideology, Lacanian psychoanalysis and Foucault's writings on power and knowledge – have also been relevant to post- or anti-colonial ways of thinking and reading, and Lyotard's 'postmodern' critique of the universalizing historical narratives and strategies of Western rationality has clearly been influential too. The fact that these models find their source in Western intellectual traditions, however, makes them somewhat problematical. In Lyotard's case, for example, there is ironically a totalizing thrust to his 'war on totality' and to his 'incredulity towards master narratives' and, for some, an arrogance all too characteristic of the blindnesses of Western *avant-gardist* paradigms.

Linda Hutcheon (1989, and see Chapter 8, pp. 200, 208) attempts to clarify some of these matters by drawing a distinction between respective aims and political agendas. Thus, postmodernism and poststructuralism direct their critique at the unified humanist subject, while postcolonialism seeks to undermine the imperialist subject. The first, she says, must 'be put on hold' in order for postcolonial and feminist discourses 'first to assert and affirm a denied or alienated subjectivity'. But this is to commit non-Western cultures (as it commits women) to a form of subjectivity and a (repressed) narrative of individual and national self-legitimation characterizing Western liberal-humanism. The danger, evidently, is that 'colonial subjects' are confirmed in their subjection to Western ideological modes whose hegemonic role is at the same time reinforced. This is the perspective of 'Orientalism' explored and exposed by Edward Said (*Orientalism*, 1978), a principal influence upon postcolonial criticism, whose work is shaped fundamentally by his position as an Arab-American and political commitment to the Palestinian cause. Foucault's most distinguished American adherent, especially in his early work, Said is attracted to Foucault's version of poststructuralism because it allows him to link the theory of discourse with real social and political struggles. By challenging Western discourse, Said follows the logic of Foucault's theories: no discourse is fixed for all time;

it is both a cause and an effect. It not only wields power but also stimulates resistance and opposition.

Edward Said

Said's *Orientalism* (1978) is his most celebrated and debated work. In a full account, it belongs in a trilogy with the more polemical works, *The Question of Palestine* (1980) and *Covering Islam* (1982), the first of a series of writings dealing principally with the Israeli–Palestinian conflict. The phenomenon of 'Orientalism', Said reasons, occupies three overlapping domains. It designates first the 4000-year history of and cultural relations between Europe and Asia; second the scientific discipline producing specialists in Oriental languages and culture from the early nineteenth century; and third the long-term images, stereotypes and general ideology about 'the Orient' as the 'Other', constructed by generations of Western scholars. A key outcome has been the familiar, long-term myths about the laziness, deceit and irrationality of orientals reproduced – and rebutted – in current debates on the Arab-Islamic world and its exchanges, particularly, with the United States. 'Orientalism' depends, in all these aspects, on a culturally constructed distinction between 'the Occident' and 'the Orient' (a fact less of nature than of 'imaginative geography', as Said terms it) and is inescapably political, as is its study. This then raises the crucial issue for postcolonialism of the position of the critic; the question, as Said puts it in 'Orientalism Reconsidered' (1986), of 'how knowledge that is non-dominative and non-coercive can be produced in a setting that is deeply inscribed with the politics, the considerations, the positions and the strategies of power'. Said rejects any assumption of a 'free' point outside the object of analysis, and rejects too the assumptions of Western historicism which has homogenized world history from a privileged and supposedly culminating Eurocentricity. Said's work draws to some extent upon Marxism, and more markedly, as we have noted, on Foucault's analysis of discourse as power, which Said extends to elucidate the function of cultural representations in the construction and maintenance of 'First'/'Third-World' relations. Analysis, he says, must be understood 'as in the fullest sense being *against* the grain, deconstructive, utopian'. He calls for a critical 'decentred consciousness' and for interdisciplinary work committed to the collective libertarian aim of dismantling systems of domination. At the same time he warns against the obstacle to this goal of 'possessive exclusivism'; the danger that anti-dominant critiques will demarcate separatist areas of resistance and struggle. The critic's credentials do not reside in the presumed authenticity of ethnic or sexual identity or experience, or in any purity of method, but elsewhere. Where and what this elsewhere is, is the major problem of postcolonial criticism, and of other differently directed forms of radical 'ideology critique'. Said's own *Orientalism* has been criticized in this respect – not always fairly – for its under-theorized and unproblematic appeal to humanist values (see Childs and Williams, 1996: 115–18); but while the stronger echoes of deconstruction in Said's later writing help to answer this charge, deconstruction in itself does not ground the kinds of political practice and change Said wishes to see.

In fact, Said's orientation has always been more materialist than deconstruction conventionally allows. The title essay of the early *The World, the Text and the Critic* (1983), for example, explored the 'worldliness' of texts. Here, Said rejects the view that speech is in the world and texts are removed from the world, possessing only a nebulous existence in the minds of critics. He believes that recent criticism overstates the 'limitlessness' of interpretation because it cuts the connections between text and actuality. The case of Oscar Wilde suggests to Said that all attempts to divorce text from actuality are doomed to failure. Wilde tried to create an ideal world of style in which he would sum up all existence in an epigram. However, writing finally brought him into conflict with the 'normal' world. An incriminating letter signed by Wilde became a key document in the Crown's case against him. Texts are therefore profoundly 'worldly': their use and effects bound up with 'ownership, authority, power and the imposition of force'.

But what, once more, of the position and power of the critic? Said argues that when we write a critical essay, we may enter one or more of several relations with text and audience. The essay may stand *between* literary text and reader, or on the side of one of them. Said puts an interesting question concerning the real historical context of the essay: 'What is the quality of the essay's speech, toward, away from, into the *actuality*, the arena of non-textual historical vitality and presence that is taking place simultaneously with the essay itself?' Said's terms (actuality, non-textual, presence) challenge the scepticism towards all such concepts in poststructuralist thought. He goes on to direct this question of context towards the more familiar monolithic meaning of a past text. The critic, however, must always write within his/her present time. Said, for example, can only speak of Wilde in terms which are sanctioned now by a prevailing discourse, which in turn is produced impersonally from the 'archive' of the present. He claims no authority for what he says, but nevertheless tries to produce *powerful* discourse.

The issue here is the more general one of the role and discursive strategy of the political intellectual, and it has run as a persistent theme through Said's work. In *Orientalism*, he is concerned overwhelmingly with conformist administrators and scholars who express an uncritical affiliation with the dominant mode of Western representation of the non-Western world. This emphasis, too, omitting dissenting, resistant voices, has given rise to criticisms of Said's work. In the later *Culture and Imperialism* (1993), he turns directly to 'Third World' or postcolonial intellectuals who have either critiqued the West from within, in its own terms (C. L. R. James is a favourite example), or worked strategically through the semi-autonomous sphere of the academy. The postcolonial intellectual is, implicitly for Said, the type of the modern intellectual, existing simultaneously inside and outside the dominant regime. This argument emerged strongly in his 1993 Reith Lectures, 'Representations of the Intellectual', as did his resilient – and again, for some, unsatisfactory – humanism and concomitant belief in the individual and universal values.

Said's lasting interest in the works of the Western canon is consistent with this position. A key example is Joseph Conrad, whom he has often returned to since his first critical work, *Joseph Conrad and the Fiction of Autobiography* (1966). Unlike the Nigerian novelist, Chinua Achebe – who, in his discussion of Conrad's novella, 'The Heart of Darkness', famously declared Conrad a 'thoroughgoing racist' – Said sought to elucidate its 'two visions' (see *Culture and Imperialism*). He sets the story in an opening account of late-twentieth-century political and economic culture, in which 'remorselessly selfish and narrow interests' suppress an awareness of 'the actual and often productive traffic . . . among states, societies, groups identities'. Conrad's novella captures the imperialist attitude at its height, but allows us also to see that the imperialist venture was circumscribed within a larger history. Two narratives or visions become evident: one of the official imperialist enterprise and a second of an unsettling, non-western world associated with the 'darkness' of the story and with Africa, which 'can reinvade and reclaim what imperialism has taken for *its* own'. Said's essay is an example of his 'contrapuntal reading' which calls for 'a simultaneous awareness' of both dominating and dominated, resistant histories. Conrad shows – but limited to his own time, cannot fully see – these alternatives. Now, in the present, Said argues, these second histories are more apparent. As examples, he cites the anti-Western political activism which inspired the Islamic Revolution in Iran, and the counter-texts of non-European novelists who tend to appropriate the forms of colonial culture for their own postcolonial purposes. One such is the Sudanese writer, Tayib Salih, whose *Season of Migration to the North* tells of a black man's journey into white territory, thereby reversing the Kurz and Marlow story of a white man's voyage into the unknown.

Said died in 2003. Late essays and tributes alike confirmed him as the very type of the political intellectual he had described: a resilient and critical humanist in exile – one who believed, as the title of his 1999 memoir has it, that he was always 'out of place'.

Gayatri Chakravorty Spivak

A leading postcolonial critic who closely follows the lessons of deconstruction and whose work raises once more the difficult politics of this enterprise is Gayatri Chakravorty Spivak, also translator and author of the important translator's preface to Derrida's *Of Grammatology* (1976). In addition to a defiantly unassimilated 'ethics' of deconstruction, Spivak draws, too, on Marxism and feminism, and this stringently 'anti-foundationalist', hybridized eclecticism is itself significant, since she aims not to synthesize these sources but to preserve their discontinuities – the ways they bring each other to crisis. She realizes she appears as 'an anomaly': sometimes regarded as a 'Third-World Woman' and thus as a convenient marginal or awkward special guest, the eminent but 'visiting' American Professor; sometimes as the Bengali middle-class exile; sometimes as a success story in the star system of American academic life. She cannot be simply or singly positioned, or 'centred', biographically, professionally or theoretically; and yet she *is*, and much of her thought and writing attends scrupulously to this process, to the conditions and rationale of the ways she herself is named by her others, as an 'other', or as the same. This gives rise to a patient, seemingly backward-moving or suspended procedure of questioning and statement which elicits the taken-for-granted in the positioning of the subject, and the naming, or 'worlding' in her term, of 'The Third World' under that very description. Spivak's methods, in other words, are above all deconstructive. Like Derrida she is interested in 'how truth is constructed rather than in exposing error', and as she confirms: 'Deconstruction can only speak in the language of the thing it criticizes . . . The only things one really deconstructs are things into which one is intimately mired.' This makes it very different from ideology critique; as she puts it on another occasion, deconstructive investigation allows you to look at 'the ways in which you are complicit with what you are so carefully and cleanly opposing'.

Postcolonial criticism in general draws attention to questions of identity in relation to broader national histories and destinies; and Spivak's work is of special interest because she has made the unsynchronized and contradictory factors of ethnicity, class and gender that compose such identities her own 'subject'. She traces this 'predicament of the postcolonial intellectual' in a neo-colonized world in her own case as well as in the texts of the Western or Indian traditions she examines. What seems to join these aspects of her work is the strategy of 'negotiating with the structures of violence' imposed by Western liberalism: to intervene, question and change the system from within. This can mean showing both how a label like 'Third-World' or 'Third-World Woman' expresses the desire of peoples in the 'First World' for a manageable other, and how a master text of English literature needs an 'other' to construct itself, but does not know or acknowledge this need. A striking example of the latter analysis appears in Spivak's discussion of the novels *Jane Eyre, Wide Sargasso Sea* and *Frankenstein* in the essay 'Three Women's Texts and a Critique of Imperialism'. Spivak sees in *Jane Eyre* – otherwise a classic text for Anglo-American feminism – 'an allegory of the general epistemic violence of imperialism'; and in her central observation she reads the last section of Jean Rhys's *Wide Sargasso Sea*, where Rochester's creole bride Antoinette is brought to England and imprisoned there as the renamed Bertha, as an enactment of the unwritten narrative of *Jane Eyre*. 'Rhys makes Antoinette see her *self* as her Other, Brontë's Bertha . . . In this fictive England she must play out her role, act out the transformation of her "self" into that fictive Other, set fire to the house and kill herself, so that Jane Eyre can become the feminist individualist heroine of British fiction.'

Antoinette/Bertha therefore comes to represent the figure of the 'subaltern', an important category in Spivak's writings adapted from the Italian Marxist, Antonio Gramsci, who used it to refer to those of inferior rank without class consciousness. The problem is that this colonized non-elite, in Spivak's usage, cannot speak. That is to say, the oppressed and silenced cannot, by definition, speak or achieve self-legitimation without ceasing to be that named subject under neo-colonialism. But if the oppressed subalterns cannot be spoken for by Western intellectuals – because this would not alter the most important fact of their position – nor speak for themselves, there can apparently be no non- or anti-colonial discourse. Deconstructive postcolonialism is brought to an impasse having achieved its political limit, complicit at last with the systems it opposes but in which it is 'intimately mired'.

This is something like Terry Eagleton's conclusion in his cutting review of Spivak's *A Critique of Postcolonial Reason: Toward a History of the Vanishing*

Present (1999). Complicity (and obscurantist prose), he argues, befuddles any intended clear or 'clean' opposition on Spivak's part (see Chapter 5, p. 104). His review was entitled 'The Gaudy Supermarket' – a reference to the (for him) plethora of intellectual goods on sale in American academia to which he believes Spivak has sold out at the price of incoherence and a failure to stage any meaningful political critique. Like other 'imports known as third-world intellectuals', she had served instead to salve America's guilt. Eagleton poses two related questions: of style and position. Spivak's aware-ness of the subaltern who cannot speak makes the question of clarity all the more pertinent: as one commentator on this debate has put it, 'to whom, in light of her knotted, baffling style, is Spivak speaking?' (Wright, 2002). The question of position concerns, more broadly, the efficacy of the crit-ical intellectual as a public figure – a question as relevant to Edward Said, as we have seen, as it is to Spivak and to other *non*-postcolonial theorists such as Eagleton himself. None, surely, can take a position which steps free of the constraints of academic institutions and the structures of social and political power. And this, in turn, will affect matters of language, style and audience. If Spivak's prose can be ungracious and convoluted, therefore, we should bear in mind the problematics of her own position and her very evident awareness of its intricacies.

We might view this self-reflexivity and inwardness as a consequence of accepting deconstruction's notion of 'textuality', although Spivak insists that this means, in Derrida, more a weave of constituting traces and conditions than simply an endless verbal textuality. Even so, the post-colonial critic is held within textuality, committed, as she puts it, to the 'deconstructive problematization of the positionality of the subject of investigation'. At one moment at least, however, in a discussion of 'New Historicism' (see Chapter 7), Spivak appears to accept that there is 'something else' identi-fying reality beyond the production of signs. This has to do with the 'pro-duction narrative' of capitalism for which Marxism offers a global account. Yet Spivak calls for a moratorium on global solutions and instructively describes Marxism as 'a critical philosophy' without a positive politics. 'The mode of production narrative in Marx', she says, 'is not a master narrat-ive and the idea of class is not an inflexible idea.' Marx's texts can be read, that is to say, in other ways than in the fundamentalist interpretations of the Marxist tradition. This is to read Marx through Derrida perhaps, but together with her opposition to liberal/individual feminism and her de-cisive anti-sexism, it offers a purchase on questions of capitalist power and patriarchy which extends the deconstruction of privileged Western intel-lectual subject positions.

Throughout, Spivak remains centrally interested in literary texts. Her essay, 'Reading *The Satanic Verses*', from the volume, *Outside in the Teaching Machine* (1993: 219–38), provides an interesting example, precisely in the terms of her title, of the procedures Spivak adopts in deploying a deconstructionist-feminist-Marxist reading of an important and controversial contemporary text. She first raises questions about authorship, by way of Barthes and Derrida, and in two sections of the body of the essay, posits: first a 'reading of the novel' – as 'after all a novel' as if the crisis that followed its publication had not happened; and second, assembles a selective dossier of different readerships so as to investigate the 'cultural politics' of how it was indeed read in the months following publication. She directs attention in this discussion, and at the end of the essay, to the marginalized role of women, the female prophets in Rushdie's novel, and to a case concerning the award of maintenance to a divorced woman, Shahbano, which was obscured by the public attention given to the male 'authors', the Ayatollah Khomeni and Rushdie. The essay clearly communicates the terms of Spivak's principled critique, but leaves unresolved the distinction which structures its sections between textual reference and meaning and the place and effect of the text in the world. It returns us, in other words, to the problematic distinction drawn above – if it is a meaningful distinction after all – between the language (or text) and public role of the author as postcolonial critic.

Homi K. Bhabha

Homi Bhabha's mode of postcolonial criticism also deploys a specifically poststructuralist repertoire (Foucault, Derrida, Lacanian and Kleinian psychoanalysis) for his explorations of colonial discourse. Bhabha's primary interest is in the 'experience of social marginality' as it emerges in non-canonical cultural forms or is produced and legitimized within canonical cultural forms. The writings collected as *The Location of Culture* (1994) are characterized by his promotion of the ideas of 'colonial ambivalence' and 'hybridity' and by his use of aesthetic terms and categories (mimesis, irony, parody, *trompe l'œil*) to mobilize an analysis of the terms of (inter-) cultural engagement within the context of empire. For Bhabha, the 'rich text' of the civilizing mission is remarkably split, fissured and flawed. The project of domesticating and civilizing indigenous populations is founded on ideas of repetition, imitation and resemblance, and in the essay 'Of Mimicry and Man: The Ambivalence of Colonial Discourse' (1984, in 1994) Bhabha probes the (psychic) mechanisms of this process of 're-presentation' to tease out the 'ambivalence' of a project that produces colonial subjects which are *almost the same but not quite*' (and later, '*almost the same but not white*'): from the 'colonial encounter between the white presence and its black semblance, there emerges the question of the ambivalence of mimicry as the problematic of colonial subjection'. The obligation on the part of the colonized to mirror back an image of the colonizer produces neither identity nor difference, only a version of a 'presence' that the colonized subject can only assume 'partially'. Thus the 'mimic man' who occupies the impossible space between cultures (a figure that can be 'traced through the works of Kipling, Forster, Orwell, Naipaul') is the 'effect of a flawed colonial mimesis in which to be Anglicized, is emphatically not to be English'. Occupying also the precarious 'area between mimicry and mockery', the mimic man is therefore iconic both of the enforcement of colonial authority and its 'strategic failure'.

Bhabha's interest in these figures or figurings of the 'in-between' of colonial discourse is evident also in his invocation and transformation of the Bakhtinian notion of 'hybridity'. In Bakhtin, hybridization destabilizes univocal forms of authority. Bhabha sees hybridity as a 'problematic of colonial representation' which 'reverses the effects of the colonialist disavowal [of difference], so that other "denied" knowledges enter upon the dominant discourse and estrange the basis of its authority'. Once again, the 'production of hybridization' not only expresses the condition of colonial enunciation but also marks the possibility of counter-colonial resistance: hybridity 'marks those moments of civil disobedience within the discipline of civility: signs of spectacular resistance'. Such a theory of resistance is further extended in his theorization of the 'Third Space of enunciation' as the assertion of difference in discourse: the 'transformational value of change lies in the rearticulation, or translation, of elements that are *neither the One* (unitary working class) *nor the Other* (the politics of gender) *but something else besides* which contests the terms and territories of both'.

The radicalism of Bhabha's work lies in its deployment of the idea of *différance* (internal dissonance – see Derrida, Chapter 7, p. 165) within an analysis of colonialism as a 'cultural text or system of meaning' and his emphasis on the performative dimension of cultural articulation; for, as he writes, 'the representation of difference must not be hastily read as the reflection of *pre-given* ethnic or cultural traits'. A guiding concern throughout this thinking is the development of a postcolonial critical practice which recognizes that the 'problem of cultural interaction emerges only at the significatory boundaries of cultures, where meanings and values are (mis)read or signs are misappropriated'. Bhabha's clearest statement of the 'postcolonial perspective' is outlined in the essay 'The Postcolonial and the Postmodern: The Question of Agency' (1992, in 1994), which also forms a defence of his interest in 'indeterminacy' against charges of the formalist orientation of his work (see Thomas, Parry and McClintock below).

A key problem remains in the actual naming of all such criticism as 'postcolonial', for the prefix 'post-' raises questions similar to those arising from its attachment to the term 'modernism'. Does 'post-' signal a break into a phase and consciousness of newly constructed independence and autonomy 'beyond' and 'after' colonialism, or does it imply a continuation and intensification of the system, better understood as neo-colonialism? The second understanding authorizes the strategies of the 'postcolonial' critic (inside, but critical of, neo-colonialism) adopted by Gayatri Spivak. This is not an anticolonialist or anti-imperialist criticism, however, of the kind that can be attributed to Frantz Fanon, or to the author and critic Chinua Achebe (1988), who finds Joseph Conrad's story 'The Heart of Darkness', for example, 'racist' and therefore unacceptable (where others might defend its value by historicizing its combined complicity in, and critique of, colonialism). Indeed, the example of Achebe points out that 'postcolonial criticism' is often used as an umbrella term to identify a range of distinct and diverse disciplines such as Colonial Discourse Analysis, Subaltern Studies, British Cultural Politics, Third Worldist Theory, African American Cultural Studies. A rich body of work is now developing from these sources which contests the analytical strategies of 'canonical' postcolonial 'theory' (Said, Spivak, Bhabha), arguing against accounts of colonial discourse which present it as a 'global and transhistorical logic of denigration' which is impervious to the voice and presence of the colonized. Benita Parry (1987), Nicholas Thomas (*Colonialisms Culture*, 1994) and Anne McClintock (1995) have all argued that postcolonial 'theory' occludes both the historically contingent aspects of signification and the 'native as historical subject and agent of an oppositional discourse'.

A further move, suggested in these debates, is the adoption of the idea of a newly founded comparative world literature, or the use of terms such as 'multiculturalism' or 'cosmopolitanism' as an advance on the ambiguities and limitations of 'postcolonialism'. Any singular, essentialist or totalizing term will now, however, be problematic. All of these suggested new terms, as well as the terms 'poststructuralism', 'postmodernism' and 'postcolonialism', bear witness to a contemporary crisis of signification and power relations, at least within literary and cultural criticism. These debates can seem hermetic and dilatory, to suspend rather than to promote change, but at the same time they show a readiness to interrogate and work through issues of language and meaning towards a new discourse of global literary and cultural relations.

Race and ethnicity

'The experience of migrant or diasporic people', writes Marie Gillespie (1995), 'is central to contemporary societies.' Responding to this development, studies of race and ethnicity have been at the forefront of recent discussion seeking to articulate the lived experience of postmodernity. Literary theory and criticism have taken their lead here from cultural studies, though the boundaries between these areas are symptomatically blurred. Often this work is keen, first of all, to distinguish between the concepts of race and ethnicity and to deconstruct the assumptions in the use of both terms of a fixed, naturally given, or unified national identity. To this end it has developed concepts also deployed in postcolonial theory: one such is the concept of hybridity used by the British sociologist of culture, Stuart Hall (1990). Hybridity is an enabling metaphor which assists theorization of the 'black experience' as a 'diaspora experience' (both in Britain and the Caribbean) and brings to the fore the doubleness or double-voiced structures which he sees as constitutive of this experience.

Hall's analysis of black diasporic cultural and aesthetic practices utilizes the concept-metaphor 'hybridity' both to signify the complexity of the 'presence/absence of Africa' ('nowhere to be found in its pure, pristine state' but 'always-already fused, syncretised, with other cultural elements') and to highlight the 'dialogue of power and resistance, of refusal and recognition', with and against the dominance of European cultures. Hall does not use the term 'diaspora' in the 'imperialising', 'hegemonising' sense of 'scattered tribes whose identity can only be secured in relation to some sacred homeland to which they must at all costs return, even if it means pushing other people into the sea.' Instead, the diaspora experience is defined 'not by essence or purity, but by the recognition of a necessary heterogeneity and diversity; by a conception of "identity" which lives with and through, not despite, difference; by hybridity'. Hall has always seen cultural studies as an interventionist practice and the important essays 'Minimal Selves' (1988) and 'New Ethnicities' (1996) introduce the notion of a provisional, politicized ethnic identity (comparable to Spivak's concept of 'strategic essentialism' – see below, p. 235) to combat at once the free-floating, politically quietist implications of more textualist conceptions of difference, and the conventional, reactionary nationalist associations of the concept of ethnicity. Hall's redefinition of ethnic identity and his account of a 'diaspora aesthetic' and 'diasporic intellectual' have been accompanied by related work in other areas of cultural studies (bell hooks, 1991; Gilroy, 1993; Mercer, 1994; Brah, 1996; Bromley, 2000) which sometimes include, but do not prioritize, literature alongside a range of other cultural representations, notably film and music.

Paul Gilroy's analyses of 'modern black political culture' focus on the doubleness or 'double consciousness' of black subjectivity, emphasizing that the constitutive experience of modern diasporic identities is that of being 'in the West but not of it'. Gilroy, like Hall, points out that 'the contemporary black English' stand 'between (at least two) great cultural assemblages, both of which have mutated through the course of the modern world that formed them and assumed new configurations'. Gilroy is consistently anti-essentialist, but like Hall seeks to avoid a modish, unhistoricized post-structuralism: 'European' and 'black' are 'unfinished identities' which for modern black people in the West are not 'mutually exclusive'. For Gilroy, cultures do not 'always flow into patterns congruent with the borders of essentially homogeneous nation states', but his critical practice questions the popularity of theorizations of the 'space between' or of 'creolization', 'mestizaje' or 'hybridity', not only because such terms keep in view ideas of cultural boundedness and of common cultural conditions, but also because they are 'rather unsatisfactory ways of naming the processes of cultural mutation and restless (dis)continuity that exceed racial discourse and avoid capture by its agents'. 'Doubleness' and 'cultural *intermixture*' distinguish the 'experience of black Britons in contemporary Europe' and Gilroy sees black artistic expression as having 'overflowed from the containers that the modem nation state provides for them'.

The idea of 'doubleness' (derived from theorizations of the pioneering African American historian, W. E. B. Du Bois) is also a pivotal concept in the work of the influential African American critic, Henry Louis Gates, Jr. Gates's collection of essays, *Black Literature and Literary Theory* (1984), was critically ground-breaking and much of his work in the 1980s (such as *The Signifying Monkey: A Theory of Afro-American Literary Criticism*, 1988) offered an innovative, deconstruction-influenced analysis of African American literature. In these studies, Gates draws attention to the 'complex double formal antecedents, the Western and the black' of African American literatures, and argues for recognition of the continuities between black vernacular and literary traditions. In the 1980s, Gates's work developed a critical approach which saw black literature as 'palimpsestic' and which released the 'black voice' to speak for itself, returning to the 'literariness' of the black text. Gates advocated the close reading of black literature at a time when 'theorists of European and Anglo-American literature were offering critiques of Anglo-American formalism', because critical methodologies had 'virtually blocked out the "literariness" of the black text'. As Gates argues in his Introduction to the important collection of essays, *'Race', Writing, and Difference* (1985), 'I once thought it our most important gesture to master the canon of criticism, to initiate and apply it, but I now believe that we must turn to the black tradition itself to develop theories of criticism indigenous to our cultures.'

In a further move, however, Gates has emphasized the dialogic inter-textuality both of black writing 'signifying' on itself in the making of a common symbolic geography (a notion he shares with Houston A. Baker, Jr and Toni Morrison) and on mainstream white literature. This is linked to a deconstructive notion of identities, beyond the sheer binaries of black and white. 'No longer', he writes, 'are the concepts of "black" and "white" to be thought to be preconstituted; rather they are mutually constitutive and socially produced' (1990c). 'We are all ethnics,' he concludes in a further essay, 'the challenge of transcending ethnic chauvinism is one we all face' (1991). To be American, therefore, is to possess a hyphenated, ethnic identity, to be part of 'a cultural complex of travelling culture', but this is not to say it is free of the regulatory effects of power and privilege. For if American culture is best thought of as 'a conversation among different voices', this is a conversation, says Gates, 'some of us weren't able to join until recently'.

The problematics of identity are also taken up by Cornel West. West is a key theorizer of the formation of (minority) postmodern cultural subjects (a 'fragmented subject pulling from past and present, innovatively producing a heterogeneous product'), and he shares with Stuart Hall and Paul Gilroy the desire to create a discourse of cultural difference that struggles against ethnic fixity and represents a wider minority discourse that incorporates issues of sexuality, religion and class. West's key contribution to such debates has been his construction of a 'prophetic pragmatic tradition' (Du Bois, Martin Luther King, James Baldwin, Toni Morrison are cited in *The Future of the Race*, 1996), arguing that 'it is possible to be a prophetic pragmatist and belong to different political movements, e.g. feminist, Black, chicano, socialist, left-liberal ones' (*The American Evasion of Philosophy*, 1990).

In the Black American tradition of feminist scholarship, critical landmarks include Barbara Smith's pioneering collection of essays, *Towards a Black Feminist Criticism* (1977), which sketches out the contours and difference of black women's writing. In proposing a black feminist aesthetic, it also importantly exposes and critiques the silencing of the black lesbian writer in both black male and white feminist criticism. Alice Walker, in *In Search of Our Mothers' Gardens* (1983), is similarly committed to a black feminist literary criticism, but rejects the racial and relational phrase 'black feminism' in favour of the concept of 'womanism'. Also in the early 1980s, bell hooks (*Ain't I A Woman*, 1981) was among a number of black feminist writers and critics who pointed to the 'double invisibility' suffered by black women: 'No other group in America has so had their identity socialized out of existence as have black women . . . When black people are talked about the focus tends to be on black men; and when women are talked about the focus tends to be on white women.' In *Talking Back: Thinking Feminist, Thinking Black* (1989), hooks questions the feminist slogan 'the personal is political' and suggests that dwelling on the personal at the expense of the political is dangerous. She advocates instead the need for coalitions, of working together across differences. To this extent her political vision (and her vision of the politics of writing) is similar to that advanced by Cornel West. Both also argue, along these lines, for politicized forms of postmodernism (West, 1988; hooks, 'Postmodern Blackness', 1991).

Hazel Carby's *Reconstructing Womanhood: The Emergence of the Afro-American Woman Novelist* (1987) takes issue with any simple attempt to reconstruct a homogenous African American literary tradition which articulates 'shared' experience, and stresses the need to look at historical and locational differences in African American women's writing. Here too, Toni Morrison's work is of importance. Her essay, 'Rootedness: The Ancestor as Foundation' (1984), is concerned with the exclusions of women from writing, but examines also the relationship of the artist to the community 'for whom they speak'. Morrison explores these issues, including the relation of black writing to the hegemonic white tradition or canon, in both her fiction and later essays. Notably, in *Playing in the Dark* (1992), she exposes the double exclusion or marginalization of black culture from a dominant white literary sensibility for which blackness has been a denied, but defining, 'presence'. Like Gates and others, therefore, her work explores the 'doubleness' or 'hybridity' of African American identity in a project committed to recovering its suppressed histories and 'the words to say it': at once an artistic discourse and an engaged cultural politics.

June Jordan's collection of essays, *Civil Wars* (1981), had outlined the perils of 'appropriating' and reconstructing the voices of those women who cannot speak for themselves. During the 1980s, the visibility and growing political confidence of Latina, Native American and Asian American writers and critics led to assertions and explorations of the distinctiveness of these literatures, particularly as writings which encourage a blurring of boundaries and a mixing of genres (see Asunción Horno-Delgado, *Breaking Boundaries: Latina Writings and Critical Readings*, 1989; Paula Gunn Allen, *The Sacred Hoop; Recovering the Feminine in American Indian Traditions*, 1986; Shirley Geok-lin Lim and Amy Ling (eds), *Reading the Literatures of Asian America*, 1992).

Much feminist work on the English and French-speaking Caribbean is similarly concerned to restore the presence of women writers who have been submerged and obliterated by the critical privileging of their male peers. The theme of women's 'double colonization' (voiced so eloquently in Gayatri Spivak's essay 'Can the Subaltern Speak?', 1996) runs through and links various traditions of postcolonial feminist criticism and attempts to develop 'new ethnic' cultural and national identities. Irish feminist critics have pointed out that Irish women writers are forced to negotiate the mediations and violations of both patriarchy and colonialism upon subjectivity and sexuality. In Canada, certain feminist critics have expressed the view that the conventional designation 'ethnic women's writing' (given to writers whose first language is not English or French) enforces a double marginalization: on the grounds of both gender and ethnicity. The task of negotiating a way out of this 'double burden' informs the feminist projects of indigenous women in Australia, New Zealand, the Pacific region, East and West Africa, and of feminist movements in Southern Africa – confronted additionally by the damage done to political identities and affiliations by the legacy of apartheid.

In each of these cases, it might appear that the cultural or national identity of particular writers and critics is being asserted as a pre-established position or a primary identity to the exclusion of other constitutive features. But questions of identity and position are consistently problematized in international feminism, as in the other areas considered above, and rarely is there an unselfconscious or uncompromised appeal to essentialist identities. These are patently crucial issues for black, postcolonial and cultural feminists like Trinh T. Minh-ha (*Woman Native, Other*, 1989), who are concerned that the generic category 'woman' not only 'tends to efface difference within itself' but frequently assures white privilege. Chandra Talpade Mohanty ('Under Western Eyes', 1991) has pointed out that feminist discourse does not have clean hands when it comes to power, and Western feminism's construction of the 'third world difference' frequently appropriates and 'colonizes' the 'constitutive complexities which characterize the lives of women in these countries'. The demand that feminism confront its own heterosexist and racist hegemonies and recognize that culturally and polit- ically constituted identities are complex and multiple has long been a driving force of black and anti-colonial feminist criticism. *Contra* white feminists, race (and indeed age, class, religion, nation) is not an 'added' problem where racial and cultural articulations are 'mapped onto' sexual difference. Emphasis is placed on the 'interarticulations' of race, class and sexuality, and notions of 'multiple identities' form a common link between many Asian, African-American, Black British, Aboriginal Australian, 'women of colour' and working-class writers.

One basic strategy here has been to establish identifiable and separate discursive traditions in order to give voice to the particular experience of black, and other, women (as in Alice Walker's *In Search of Our Mothers' Gardens*, 1983). For women who have been 'hidden from history', simply putting on the record and valuing such experience is a major political initiative. Equally, drawing on 'other' cultural traditions (stories, songs, domestic practices), a 'poetics' of difference (such as the poetry of Sonia Sanchez and the novels of Bharati Mukherjee) at once questions Western notions of the autonomy of the aesthetic and establishes and celebrates a non-incorporated women's discourse.

Donna Haraway's proposition (see Chapter 8, pp. 211–12) that ' "women of color" might be understood as a cyborg identity' is a further contribution to a poetics and politics of difference. Haraway's model of the cyborg as 'a potent subjectivity synthesized from fusions of outsider identities' approx- imates, at certain key points, to Gloria Anzaldúa's notion of *la mestiza* (*Borderlands/La Frontera: The New Mestiza*, 1987), an unbounded and flex- ible figuring of femininity which is at once 'cultured' and 'cultureless'. For Anzaldúa, a Chicana writer and teacher and self-identified 'border woman', the new *mestiza* tolerates contradictions and ambiguities and 'learns to jug- gle cultures': she has a 'plural personality' and 'operates in a pluralistic mode'. The work of *mestiza* consciousness is to transcend dualities: the 'answer to the problem between the white race and the colored, between males and females, lies in healing the split that originates in the very foundation of our lives, our culture, our languages, our thoughts'. Anzaldúa's resistance to theorizing the subject as fixed and culturally bounded is enforced through her allusion to Virginia Woolf's famous model of international sisterhood: 'As a *mestiza* I have no country . . . yet all countries are mine because I am every woman's sister or potential lover.' (See also Chapter 10, on lesbian and queer theory, p. 250.)

The idea of women's transcultural unity has received significant and in- sistent questioning by feminists who do not regard themselves as part of

Eurocentric cultural and political traditions. Gayatri Spivak's important positioning of French feminism within an 'international frame' (1987; on Spiviak, see also pp. 223–6 above) enables her to voice a deep criticism not only of Anglo-American ('First-World', white) feminist criticism in its ethnocentricity, but also of French theory (particularly Kristeva's *About Chinese Women*, 1977) in its willingness to export its analysis to different political contexts without investigating either its own relation to other feminisms or its tendency to espouse a belief in the revolutionary potential of the metropolitan *avant-garde*. In asking the vital questions: 'not merely who am I? but who is the other woman? How am I naming her? How does she name me? Is this part of the problematic I discuss?', Spivak launches a debate about positionality which Cora Kaplan sees ('Feminist Literary Criticism', 1990: see 'Further reading' for Chapter 6) as resulting in Western feminist criticism becoming 'more aware than ever that the critic and text both need to be understood in relation to their position within culture – any new reading practice . . . must first locate itself and in doing so must reflect on its limitations and possibilities for the reader'.

This necessary self-consciousness is joined by Spivak's notion of 'strategic essentialism' ('Subaltern Studies', 1987: see 'Key texts' for Chapter 6, and see Stuart Hall on identity, above, p. 229). While an unrelenting self-critique might seem disabling, this concept enables a recognition of politically constituted identities as a 'strategic use of positivist essentialism in a scrupulously visible political interest'. As Diana Fuss has similarly argued (*Essentially Speaking*, 1989), there is an 'important distinction' between ' "deploying" or "activating" essentialism and "falling into" or "lapsing into" ' essentialism: ' "Deploying" or "activating" implies that essentialism may have some strategic or interventionary value.' Perhaps the characteristic feature of contemporary feminist theory in this postmodern 'international frame' is analogous to Gloria Anzaldúa's '*mestiza* consciousness' once more: the 'continual creative motion that keeps breaking down the unitary aspect of each new paradigm'. If so, this is a strategy which deploys the breaking-down of universalizing notions not only of 'woman' but also of 'feminism'.

Selected reading

Key texts

Anzaldúa, Gloria, *Borderlands/La Frontera: The New Mestiza* (Spinsters/Aunt Lute, San Francisco, 1987).

Bhabha, Homi K., 'The Other Question: Difference, Discrimination and the Discourse of Colonialism' [1986], in Francis Barker *et al.* (eds), see *Further reading*, below.

Bhabha, Homi K., 'Remembering Fanon: Self, Psyche and the Colonial Condition', Foreword to Fanon (1986), below.

Bhabha, Homi K. (ed.), *Nation and Narration* (Routledge, London, 1990).

Bhabha, Homi K., *The Location of Culture* [1994] (Routledge, London, 2004).

Braziel, Jana Evans and Mannur, Anita (eds), *Theorizing Diaspora: A Reader* (Blackwell, Oxford, 2002).

Castle, Gregory (ed.), *Postcolonial Discourses: An Anthology* (Blackwell, Oxford, 2001).

Derrida, Jacques, 'White Mythology' [1971], in *Margins of Philosophy*, trans. by Alan Ball (Chicago University Press, Chicago, 1982).

Derrida, Jacques, 'Racism's Last Word', in Henry Louis Gates, Jr (ed., 1985), below.

Essed, Philomena and Goldberg, David (eds), *Race Critical Theories: Text and Context* [anthology] (Blackwell, Oxford, 2001).

Fanon, Frantz, *Black Skin, White Masks* [1952], trans. by C. L. Markmann, with Foreword by Homi Bhabha (Pluto, London, 1986).

Fanon, Frantz, *The Wretched of the Earth* [1961], trans. by Constance Farrington, with Preface by Jean-Paul Sartre (Penguin, London, 2001).

Gates, Henry Louis, Jr (ed.), *Black Literature and Literary Theory* (Routledge, London, 1984).

Gates, Henry Louis, Jr (ed.), *'Race', Writing and Difference* (Chicago University Press, Chicago and London, 1985). Contains essays by Bhabha, Derrida and Spivak.

Gates, Henry Louis, Jr, *Figures in Black: Words, Signs and the 'Racial' Self* [1987] (Oxford University Press, Oxford, 1990a).

Gates, Henry Louis, Jr, *The Signifying Monkey: A Theory of Afro-American Literary Criticism* [1988] (Oxford University Press, Oxford, 1990b).

Gates, Henry Louis, Jr, 'Introduction: Tell me, Sir, . . . What is "Black" Literature?', *PMLA*, 105 (January, 1990c).

Gates, Henry Louis, Jr, 'Goodbye Columbus? Notes on the Culture of Criticism', *American Literary History*, 4 (Winter, 1991).

Gates, Henry Louis, Jr, *The Third World of Theory* (Oxford University Press, Oxford, 2004).

Gilroy, Paul, *There Ain't No Black in the Union Jack: The Cultural Politics of Race and Nation* (Hutchinson, London, 1987).

Gilroy, Paul, *The Black Atlantic: Modernity and Double Consciousness* (Verso, London, 1993).

Gilroy, Paul, *Small Acts: Thoughts on the Politics of Black Cultures* (Serpent's Tail, London and New York, 1993).

Gilroy, Paul, *Between Camps: Nations, Cultures and the Allure of Race* (Penguin, London, 2001).

Goldberg, David Theo and Quayson, Ato (eds), *Relocating Postcolonialism* (Blackwell, Oxford, 2002).

Gramsci, Antonio, 'History of the Subaltern Classes: Some Methodological Criteria', excerpts in Quintin Hoare and Geoffrey Nowell Smith (eds), *Selections from the Prison Notebooks of Antonio Gramsci* (Lawrence & Wishart, London, 1971).

Hall, Stuart, 'Minimal Selves', in *The Real Me: Postmodernism and the Question of Identity* (ICA Documents, London, 1988).

Hall, Stuart, 'Cultural Identity and Diaspora', in Jonathan Rutherford (ed.), *Identity: Community, Culture, Difference* (Lawrence & Wishart, London, 1990).

Hall, Stuart, *Critical Dialogues in Cultural Studies*, ed. by David Morley and Kuan-Hsing Chen (Routledge, London and New York, 1996).

Harris, Wilson, *Selected Essays of Wilson Harris*, ed. by A. J. M. Bundy (Routledge, London, 1999).

hooks, bell, *Ain't I A Woman: Black Women and Feminism* (Pluto, London, 1981).

hooks, bell, *Talking Back: Thinking Feminist, Thinking Black* (Pluto, London, 1989).

hooks, bell, *Yearning: Race, Gender and Cultural Politics* (South End Press, Boston; Turnaround Press, London, 1991).

James, Joy and Sharpley-Whiting, T. Denean (eds), *The Black Feminist Reader* (Blackwell, Oxford, 2000).

Lewis, Reina and Mills, Sara (eds), *Feminist Postcolonial Theory: A Reader* (Edinburgh University Press, Edinburgh, 2003).

Memmi, Albert, *Racism* [1982], trans. and intro. by Steve Martinot (University of Minnesota Press, Minneapolis and London, 2000).

Mercer, Kobena, *Welcome to the Jungle: New Positions in Black Cultural Studies* (Routledge, London and New York, 1994).

Morrison, Toni, 'Rootedness: The Ancestor as Foundation', in Mari Evans (ed.), *Black Women Writers 1950–1980: A Critical Evaluation* (Pluto, London, 1984).

Morrison, Toni, *Playing in the Dark: Whiteness and the Literary Imagination* (Harvard University Press, Cambridge, Mass., and London, 1992).

Postcolonialism: Critical Concepts in Literary and Cultural Studies, 5 vols, ed. by Diana Brydon (Routledge, London, 2000).

Said, Edward, *Orientalism* (Routledge, London, 1978).

Said, Edward, *The World, the Text and the Critic* (Harvard University Press, Cambridge, Mass., 1983).

Said, Edward, 'Orientalism Reconsidered' [1986], in Francis Barker *et al.* (eds), see *Further reading*, below.

Said, Edward, *Culture and Imperialism* (Chatto & Windus, 1993).

Said, Edward, *Out of Place: A Memoir* (Granta, London, 1999).

Said, Edward, *Reflections on Exile and Other Literary and Cultural Essays* (Granta, London, 2001).

Said, Edward, *The Edward Said Reader*, ed. by Moustafa Bayoumi and Andrew Rubin (Granta, London, 2001).

Smith, Barbara, *Toward a Black Feminist Criticism* (Out and Out Press, New York, 1977).

Smith, Barbara (ed.), *Home Girls: A Black Feminist Anthology* (Kitchen Table Women of Color Press, New York, 1983).

Spivak, Gayatri Chakravorty, 'Three Women's Texts and a Critique of Imperialism', in Henry Louis Gates, Jr (ed.), 1985. Partly reprinted in Peter Brooker and Peter Widdowson (eds), *A Practical Reader* (1996): see Introduction, 'Selected reading'.

Spivak, Gayatri Chakravorty, *In Other Worlds: Essays in Cultural Politics* (Routledge, London, 1987).

Spivak, Gayatri Chakravorty, in Sarah Harasym (ed.), *The Post-Colonial Critic: Interviews, Strategies, Dialogues* (Routledge, London, 1990).

Spivak, Gayatri Chakravorty, *Outside in the Teaching Machine* (Routledge, London, 1993). Includes the essay on Salman Rushdie, 'Reading *The Satanic Verses*', a substantial excerpt from which is reprinted in Brooker and Widdowson (eds), *A Practical Reader* (1996): see Introduction, 'Selected reading'.

Spivak, Gayatri Chakravorty, *A Critique of Post-Colonial Reason: Toward a History of the Vanishing Present* (Harvard University Press, Cambridge, Mass., 1999).

Spivak, Gayatri Chakravorty, *Death of a Discipline* (Columbia University Press, New York, 2003).

Spivak, Gayatri Chakravorty, *The Spivak Reader: Selected Writings of Gayatri Chakravorty Spivak*, ed. by Donna Landry and Gerald MacLean (Routledge, London, 1996).

Trinh T. Minh-ha, *Woman, Native, Other: Writing Postcoloniality and Feminism* (Indiana University Press, Bloomington, 1989).

Walker, Alice, *In Search of Our Mothers' Gardens: Womanist Prose* (Harcourt Brace Jovanovich, New York, 1983).

Walker, Alice, *Living By the Word: Selected Writings, 1973–1987* (Harcourt Brace Jovanovich, New York, 1988).

West, Cornel, 'Interview with Cornel West', in Andrew Ross (ed.), *Universal Abandon? The Politics of Postmodernism* (Edinburgh University Press, Edinburgh, 1988).

West, Cornel, *The American Evasion of Philosophy* (Macmillan, Basingstoke, 1990).

Further reading

Ansell-Pearson, Keith, Parry, Benita and Squires, Judith (eds), *The Gravity of History: Reflections on the Work of Edward Said* (Lawrence & Wishart, London, 1996).

Ashcroft, Bill, *Edward Said* (Routledge, London, 2000).

Ashcroft, Bill, *Post-Colonial Transformation* (Routledge, London, 2001).

Ashcroft, Bill, Griffiths, Gareth and Tiffin, Helen (eds), *The Empire Writes Back: Theory and Practice in Post-Colonial Literature* [1985] (2nd edn, Routledge, London, 2002).

Ashcroft, Bill, Griffiths, Gareth and Tiffin, Helen (eds), *The Post-Colonial Studies Reader* (Routledge, London and New York, 1995).

Ashcroft, Bill, Griffiths, Gareth and Tiffin, Helen, *Postcolonial Studies: The Key Concepts* (Routledge, London, 2000).

Baker, Houston A., Jr, *Afro-American Poetics: Revisions of Harlem and the Black Aesthetic* (University of Wisconsin Press, Madison, 1988).

Barker, Francis, Hulme, Peter, Loxley, Diana and Iverson, Margaret (eds), *Literature, Politics, Theory: Papers from the Essex Conference, 1974–6* (Routledge, London, 1986).

Bassnett, Susan (ed.), *Studying British Cultures* (2nd edn, Routledge, London, 2003).

Bassnett, Susan and Trivedi, Harish (eds), *Postcolonial Translation* (Routledge, London, 1998).

Bobo, Jacqueline (ed.), *Black Feminist Cultural Criticism* (Blackwell, Oxford, 2001).

Bowers, Maggie Ann, *Magic(al) Realism* (Routledge, London, 2004).

Boyce-Davies, Carole, *Black Women, Writing and Identity: Migrations of the Subject* (Routledge, London, 1994).

Brah, Avtar, *Cartographies of Diaspora* (Routledge, London, 1996).

Bromley, Roger, *Narratives for a New Belonging: Diasporic Cultural Fictions* (Edinburgh University Press, Edinburgh, 2000).

Carby, Hazel V., *Reconstructing Womanhood: The Emergence of the Afro-American Woman Novelist* (Oxford University Press, Oxford, 1987).

Childs, Peter (ed.), *Post-Colonial Theory and English Literature: A Reader* (Edinburgh University Press, Edinburgh, 1999).

Childs, Peter and Williams, Patrick, *Introduction to Post-Colonial Theory* (Pearson Education, Harlow, 1996).

Christian, Barbara, *Black Feminist Criticism: Perspectives on Black Women Writers* (Pergamon, New York, 1985).

Eagleton, Terry, 'The Gaudy Supermarket', *London Review of Books*, 21, 10 (1999), 3–6.

Gates, Henry Louis, Jr and West, Cornel, *The Future of the Race* (Alfred A. Knopf, New York, 1996).

Gillespie, Marie, *Television, Ethnicity and Cultural Change* (Routledge, London and New York, 1995).

Hodge, Bob and Mishra, Vijay, *The Dark Side of the Dream: Australian Literature and the Postcolonial Mind* (Allen & Unwin, Sydney, 1991).

Huddart, David, *Homi Bhabha* (Routledge, London, 2004).

Hull, Gloria *et al.* (eds), *All the Women Are White, All the Blacks Are Men, But Some of Us Are Brave: Black Women's Studies* (The Feminist Press, New York, 1982).

Hulme, Peter, *Colonial Encounters: Europe and the Native Caribbean 1492–1797* (Routledge, London, 1992).

Hutcheon, Linda, 'Circling the Downspout of Empire: Post-Colonialism and Postmodernism', *Ariel*, vol. 20: 4 (1989), 149–75. Reprinted in Ian Adam and Helen Tiffin (eds), *Past the Last Post: Theorizing Post-Colonialism and Post-Modernism* (Harvester Wheatsheaf, Hemel Hempstead, 1991).

Jump, Harriet Devine (ed.), *Diverse Voices: Twentieth-Century Women's Writing from Around the World* (Harvester Wheatsheaf, Hemel Hempstead, 1991).

Kennedy, Valerie, *Edward Said* (Polity Press, Cambridge, 2000).

Loomba, Ania, *Colonialism/Postcolonialism* (Routledge, London, 1998).

Loomba, Ania and Orkin, Martin (eds), *Post-Colonial Shakespeares* (Routledge, London, 1998).

McClintock, Anne, *Imperial Leather: Race, Gender and Sexuality in the Colonial Context* (Routledge, New York and London, 1995).

McLeod, John, *Beginning Postcolonialism* (Manchester University Press, Manchester, 2000).

Mohanty, Chandra Talpade, 'Under Western Eyes: Feminist Scholarship and Colonial Discourses', in Mohanty *et al.* (eds), *Third World Women and the Politics of Feminism* (Indiana University Press, Bloomington, 1991).

Morton, Stephen, *Gayatri Chakravorty Spivak* (Routledge, London, 2002).

Parry, Benita, 'Problems in Current Theories of Colonial Discourse', *Oxford Literary Review*, 9, 1–2 (1985); reprinted in Ashcroft *et al.* (eds, 1995), above.

Parry, Benita, *Postcolonial Studies: A Materialist Critique* (Routledge, London, 2004).

Proctor, James, *Stuart Hall* (Routledge, London, 2004).

Pryse, Marjorie and Spillers, Hortense (eds), *Conjuring: Black Women's Fiction and the Literary Tradition* (Indiana University Press, Bloomington, 1985).

Quayson, Ato, *Postcolonialism: Theory, Practice or Process* (Polity Press, Cambridge, 1999).

Schwarz, Henry and Ray, Sangeeta (eds), *A Companion to Postcolonial Studies* (Blackwell, Oxford, 2000).

Walder, Dennis, *Post-Colonial Literatures in English: History, Language, Theory* (Blackwell, Oxford, 1998).

Wall, Cheryl A. (ed.), *Changing Our Own Words: Essays on Criticism, Theory and Writing by Black Women* (Rutgers University Press, New Brunswick, 1989).

Williams, Patrick and Chrisman, Laura (eds), *Colonial Discourse and Postcolonial Theory: A Reader* (Prentice Hall/Harvester Wheatsheaf, Hemel Hempstead, 1993).

Willis, Susan, *Specifying: Black Women Writing the American Experience* (Routledge, London, 1990).

Wright, Colin, 'Centrifugal Logics: Eagleton and Spivak on the Place of "Place" in Postcolonial Theory', *Culture Theory and Critique*, vol. 43: 1 (April, 2002), 67–82.

Yancy, George (ed.), *Cornel West: A Critical Reader* (Blackwell, Oxford, 2001).

Young, Robert, *White Mythologies: Writing, History and the West* [1990] (2nd edn, Routledge, London, 2004).

Young, Robert, *Colonial Desire: Hybridity in Theory, Culture and Race* (Routledge, London and New York, 1995).

Young, Robert, *Postcolonialism: An Historical Introduction* (Blackwell, Oxford, 2001).

CHAPTER 10

Gay, lesbian and queer theories

esbian and gay theories originate, like feminist and Black criticism, not in academic institutions, but in the radical movements of the 1960s. The birth of the Gay Liberation Movement can be traced to the Stonewall Riot in New York in 1969 when occupants of a gay bar resisted a police raid. The event had a radicalizing effect on Homosexual Rights groups throughout the United States and Europe. Thereafter, Gay Liberation in the 1970s had two main goals: to resist persecution and discrimination against a sexual minority, and to encourage gay people themselves to develop a pride in their sexual identities. The movement utilized two main strategies: 'consciousness-raising', borrowed from Black and women's movements, and 'coming out' – publicly affirming gay identity – which is unique to gay communities whose oppression partly lies in their social invisibility. Gay Liberation activists saw themselves as part of a more general move towards the liberalization of sexual attitudes in the 1960s, but in particular challenged the homophobic prejudices and repressive character of mainstream heterosexual society.

Since then, gay and lesbian activists have employed the term 'heterosexism' to refer to the prevailing social organization of sexuality which privileges and mandates heterosexuality so as to invalidate and suppress homosexual relations. Whereas 'homophobia' – the irrational fear or hatred of same-sex love – implies an individualized and pathological condition, 'heterosexism' designates an unequal social and political power relation, and has arguably proved the more useful theoretical term in lesbian and gay theories. It clearly owes a debt to the feminist concept of sexism: the unequal social organization of gender, and in this respect has been of more importance to lesbian feminist theory than to gay theory which developed in overlapping but distinct ways in the 1970s and 1980s.

Gay theory and criticism

The diversity of gay and bisexual research since the 1970s reflects the efforts to reclaim literary texts, cultural phenomena and historical narratives which had remained hidden from critical attention. At the same time (largely as a product of psychoanalysis and feminism), there has been an explosion in the diversity of strategies for exploiting these materials. While there have been a number of attempts to provide explanatory models which posit defining moments in the history of sexuality (Bray, 1988; Cohen, 1989), this research generally concludes that past constructions of sexuality cannot be exhaustively understood, either in their own terms or in ours. For many critics the past offers alien constructions of sexuality in a contrasting relation to the present, rather than possible identifications or celebratory moments. Jonathan Katz (1994) draws such a lesson from his history of sodomitical sin:

> our own contemporary social organization of sex is as historically specific as past social-sexual forms. Studying the past, seeing the essential differences between past and present social forms of sex, we may gain a fresh perspective on our own sex as socially made, not naturally given.

A shared interest in recent gay and historicist studies (Cohen, Katz, Trumbach) has been the construction of sexuality in a network of power relations, exercised both through the regulatory practices of church and state and the less overt yet manifold ways in which Western culture has circumscribed interpersonal relations.

Two main influences on gay theory have been Freud and Michel Foucault. Already in the nineteenth and early twentieth century, detailed psychological case-studies appeared to complicate and infinitely expand the range of sexualities. Karl Heinrich Ulrichs published twelve volumes on homosexuality between 1864 and 1879 (the term was first used by Karl Benkert in 1869), and Krafft-Ebing's *Pyschopathia Sexualis* (in its 1903 edition) included 238 case histories (see Weeks, 1985). Such works were important to Freud in exploding the notion that heterosexuality was safely grounded in nature. In *Three Essays on the Theory of Sexuality*, for instance, he noted that it was not a self-evident fact that men should find a sexual interest in women. Psychoanalytic theory therefore appeared to promise a new plurality of possible classifications. Yet in certain respects Freud's work proved to have a strictly normative effect in that of his followers, whose goal appeared to be to return the patient to an integrated, healthy state, purged of the disorienting 'illness' of homosexuality. Jeffrey Weeks's criticism of

Freud focuses on the notion that desire 'cannot be reduced to primeval biological urges, beyond human control, nor can it be seen as a product of conscious willing and planning. It is somewhere ambiguously, elusively, in between, omnipotent but intangible, powerful but goal-less' (1985). In so far as desire is inherently unstable, the individual's procreative goal (or more specifically, genital sex) is threatened by perverse, transgressive forces. Freud had noted in an *Outline of Psychoanalysis* that sexual life was concerned primarily with obtaining pleasure from the body, often beyond the needs of reproduction. If this is the case, heterosexuality supports bourgeois ideologies to the extent that procreation mirrors production. Gay sex, in contrast, is desire deprived of this goal; it is the very negation of productive work.

The second major influence upon gay theory, which has returned some critics to a re-reading of Freud, has been Michel Foucault (see Chapter 7, pp. 178–80), who has inspired the study of the multiple operations of power and set the problematics of defining homosexuality within discourse and history. In *The History of Sexuality* (1976), Foucault sees late-nineteenth-century homosexuality as characterized 'by a certain quality of sexual sensibility, a certain way of inverting the masculine and the feminine in oneself'. Homosexuality appeared as one of the forms of sexuality when it was transposed from the practice of sodomy onto a kind of interior androgyny, a hermaphroditism of the soul. 'The sodomite', he concludes, 'had been a temporary aberration; the homosexual was now a species.' Foucault explored how sodomy was largely determined by civil or canonical codes as 'a category of forbidden acts' which accordingly defined their perpetrator as no more than their judicial subject. However, the nineteenth century, Foucault argues, saw the emergence of the homosexual as 'a personage, a past, a case history, and a childhood . . . Nothing that went into his total composition was unaffected by his sexuality.' This model has been broadly accepted, if elaborated or sometimes disputed in its details (Cohen, 1989). Nevertheless, a general problem lies in how Foucault theorizes the transition from one mode to another. As noted by Eve Kosofsky Sedgwick (1985 – and see below, pp. 256–9), in Foucault's discontinuous profile 'one model of same-sex relations is superseded by another, which may again be superseded by another. In each case the supposed model then drops out of the frame of analysis.' None the less, historians of sexuality have assembled models of shifting sexual categories across time influenced by Foucault, although more scholarly and less rigid or polemical than his own. The historian Randolph Trumbach, for instance, has been much more open than Foucault to the emergence of lesbianism in the eighteenth century, while

Weeks, Greenberg and Bray, though accepting the constructedness of sexuality, have resisted the extreme position on the dating of the category of homosexuality which was characteristic of Foucault's work.

Foucault's influence upon gay studies, however, extends beyond the above debates to work done within the areas of New Historicism and Cultural Materialism (see Chapter 7, pp. 182, 187–8). Most noticeably in Great Britain in the work of Jonathan Dollimore and Alan Sinfield, gay theory became part of a wider cultural poetics and cultural politics, focused within literary studies, and as such had affinities with the work of others pursuing a similar general project (for example, Stallybrass and White, 1986).

A number of categories have been mobilized in this criticism to discuss the inscription of homosexuality in texts and to reclaim aspects of gay life: 'effeminacy', 'drag' and 'camp', for example, or the categories of 'the homoerotic', 'male bonding' or 'homosociality', which have been used in the reading of non- or anti-gay texts. In this connection, the theory of 'homophobia' has also given rise to the concepts of 'panic' and of 'internalized homophobia'. Alan Sinfield (1989), for instance, has shown how anti-effeminacy operated in 'The Movement' writing of John Wain and Kingsley Amis (among others), and how effeminacy was used as a signifier of perversion. Yet he also demonstrates that the muscular, down-to-earth writing of 'The Movement' was subverted in the poetry of Thom Gunn, who constructed figures of rough young men which shifted towards homoerotic identification. The construction of masculinities has been explored further in the essay by Sinfield and Dollimore on Shakespeare's *Henry V* (Drakakis, ed., [1985] 2002: see 'Further reading' for Chapter 7) and in Gregory Woods' work on Ernest Hemingway. Here Woods shows how writers who have functioned as emblems of machismo need to be reassessed. What the 'struggle against effeminate eloquence' in this writing expresses, he argues, 'is the nagging anxiety which is the true condition (in both senses) of masculinity'. The voice of heterosexual masculinity is 'to be compared with that of closeted gay men, to the extent that it is terrified of indiscretion. To say too much might be to sound queer' (Still and Worton, 1993). In the related study, *Articulate Flesh* (1987), Woods explores the expression of homoeroticism in D. H. Lawrence, Hart Crane, W. H. Auden, Allen Ginsberg and Thom Gunn.

Gay criticism of this kind both borrows the techniques of cultural poetics and explores the relations between culture, history and text in an increasingly politicized version of literary studies. Nicholas F. Radel, in his essay 'Self as Other: The Politics of Identity in the Works of Edmund White', for example (in Ringer, ed., 1994), has argued that White's novels help reveal 'a gay subject as it responds to political pressure from the culture at large.

Far from being mere aesthetic products, these novels about gay life both confirm and interrogate their historical milieu and its construction of sexual orientation as gender difference.' David Bergman's analysis of James Baldwin's *Giovanni's Room* serves to illustrate its deployment of 'internalized homophobia'. He seeks to position Baldwin 'within a line he nowhere acknowledges – a line of both gay and African-American writers' (in Bristow, ed., 1992). Increasingly, too, critics have been exploring the relationship between nationalism, anti-imperialism and sexuality – in Parker *et al.*, *Nationalisms and Sexualities* (1992), for example, and Rudi C. Bleys's *The Geography of Perversion* (1996).

In Foucault's work, multiplying configurations of power are shown to be central to the production and control of sexuality. In developing this insight, Jonathan Dollimore, in particular, has explored the complex involvement of power with pleasure: 'pleasure and power do not cancel or turn back against one another', he writes in *Sexual Dissidence* (1991), 'they seek out, overlap, and reinforce one another. They are linked together by complex mechanisms and devices of excitation and incitement.' In this way, Dollimore has effectively returned gay theory to Freud's concept of 'polymorphous perversity' – the theory that the child enjoys multiple sexualities before it moves to the reductive primacy of genital sex. But Dollimore moves beyond Freud, and arguably beyond Foucault, in remapping a politically subversive programme for perversity. He argues that we should think in terms of the 'paradoxical perverse or the perverse dynamic', which he claims is 'a dynamic intrinsic to social process'. Both Sinfield and Dollimore, and others working within a tradition of gay cultural materialist criticism, have drawn attention, in new ways, to the example of Oscar Wilde. In Wilde, Dollimore discovers a transgressive aesthetics:

> Wilde's experience of deviant desire . . . leads him not to escape the repressive ordering of society, but to a reinscription within it, and an inversion of the binaries upon which that ordering depends; desire, and the transgressive aesthetic which it fashions, reacts against, disrupts, and displaces from within.
> (Dollimore, 1991)

Such a shift beyond binary oppositions marks the transition from gay to queer theory.

Lesbian feminist theory and criticism

Lesbian feminist theory emerged as a response both to the heterosexism of mainstream culture and radical subcultures, and to the sexism of the male-dominated Gay Liberation Movement. Its focus is the interlocking structures of gender and sexual oppression. In particular, lesbian feminist theory has consistently problematized heterosexuality as an institution central to the maintenance of patriarchy and women's oppression within it. Lesbian feminist theory, like lesbian feminism, is a diverse field which draws on a wide range of other theories and methods. While it cannot be reduced to a single model, several features stand out: a critique of 'compulsory heterosexuality', an emphasis on 'woman identification', and the creation of an alternative women's community. Whether taking a Black feminist, a radical feminist or a psychoanalytic approach, lesbian feminist theory foregrounds one or all of these elements.

The concept of 'compulsory heterosexuality' was first articulated by Gayle Rubin (1975), and subsequently given wide circulation by Adrienne Rich in her essay 'Compulsory Heterosexuality and Lesbian Existence' (1980). The concept challenges the common-sense view of heterosexuality as natural and therefore requiring no explanation, unlike lesbian and gay sexuality. Rich argues that heterosexuality is a social institution supported by a range of powerful sanctions. The fact of lesbian existence, notwithstanding such sanctions, is evidence of a powerful current of woman-bonding which cannot be suppressed. Rich locates the source of lesbianism in the fact that girl children are 'of woman born' and have an original same-sex attachment to their mothers.

Monique Wittig's analogous concept of 'the straight mind' (1980, reprinted 1992) views heterosexuality as an ideological construct which is almost completely taken for granted, yet institutes an obligatory social relationship between men and women: 'as an obvious principle, as a given prior to any science, the straight mind develops a totalizing interpretation of history, social reality, culture, language and all subjective phenomena at the same time.' The discourses of heterosexuality work to oppress all those who attempt to conceive of themselves otherwise, particularly lesbians. In contrast to Rich, Wittig rejects the concept of 'woman identification', arguing that it remains tied to the dualistic concept of gender which lesbians challenge. She claims that in an important sense lesbians are not women, 'for what makes a woman is a specific social relation to a man' and so 'woman' acquires 'meaning only in heterosexual systems of thought and heterosexual economic systems'.

Judith Butler (1992), drawing on the work of both Wittig and Rich, uses the term 'heterosexual matrix' to 'designate that grid of cultural intelligibility through which bodies, genders, and desires are naturalized'. Butler ceases to use the term in her later work (see below, pp. 255–6) but continues to argue for the subversion of sexual identities and for a distinction between sex, sexuality and gender in the social 'performances' that constitute them.

The concepts of 'woman identification' and 'lesbian feminist community' were introduced by Radicalesbians in their influential essay, 'The Woman-Identified Woman' (1970), and further developed once more by Adrienne Rich. Rich (1980) depicts woman-bonding as an act of resistance to patriarchal power, and advances the concept of 'lesbian continuum' to describe 'a range – through each woman's life and throughout history – of woman-identified experience'. Her definition encompasses not simply sexual experience but all forms of 'primary intensity' between and among women, including relationships of family, friendship and politics. Rich's own 1976 essay, 'The Temptations of a Motherless Girl', perfectly illustrates the concepts of 'lesbian continuum' and the related lesbian critical 'revisioning'. It offers a lesbian reading of *Jane Eyre* which changes the focus from a heterosexual romance plot to a narrative of loving female pedagogy in which Jane is nurtured and educated by a succession of female mother/mentors. Rich convincingly demonstrates and denaturalizes the ideological hegemony of heterosexuality in our reading and interpretative strategies.

Barbara Smith's essay, 'Towards a Black Feminist Criticism' (reprinted in Showalter, 1986), adopts a critical model similar to Rich's in order to argue that Toni Morrison's *Sula* can be productively reread as a lesbian novel, 'not because the women are "lovers", but because they . . . have pivotal relationships with one another'. 'Whether consciously or not,' she adds, 'Morrison's work poses both lesbian and feminist questions about Black women's autonomy and their impact on each other's lives.' The French feminist, Luce Irigaray, explores an analogous concept of autonomous female sexuality in *This Sex Which Is Not One* (1985). She redefines women's sexuality as based on difference rather than sameness, arguing that it is multiple: 'Woman does not have a sex. She has at least two of them . . . Indeed she has more than that. Her sexuality, always at least double, is in fact plural.'

Irigaray further attempts to combine a psychoanalytic and political approach to lesbianism. In 'When the Goods Get Together', she advances the concept of 'hom(m)osexuality – punning on the signifiers of both maleness and sameness – to capture the dual nature of hetero-patriarchal culture. 'Hom(m)osexual' discourse privileges male homosocial relations and a male sexuality of the same (whether hetero- or homosexual). Her work links critiques of both gender and sexual power relations and in its anti-essentialism chimes with the political aims of lesbian feminism.

The concept of 'woman-identification' has been challenged by some lesbian feminists, especially Black and Third World critics. Cherrie Moraga and Gloria Anzaldúa (1981), for example, draw attention to the way the concept has been used to mask power relations among women. Rejecting a universal model of identity, they create more flexible concepts of lesbian identity – such as Anzaldúa's (1987) concept of the new *mestiza* – able to encompass the connections between women of different cultures and ethnicities (see Chapter 9, p. 234).

Representation – in both the political and the literary senses – is a key issue for lesbian criticism. In 1982, Margaret Cruikshank identified the crucial role literature has played in the development of lesbian criticism. In the thirty and more years since its emergence, lesbian literary criticism has developed from being largely polemical – calling for the acknowledgement of lesbian writers, readers and texts, and the definition of these – to a sophisticated and diverse body of politically informed theoretical work which aims to explore the multiple articulations of the sign 'lesbian'.

The early agenda for lesbian criticism was set by Virginia Woolf's analysis of the relationship between women and writing in *A Room of One's Own* (1929 – see Chapter 6) which showed how literary power relations result in a textual effacement of relationships among women. It was not until Jane Rule's *Lesbian Images* (1975), however, that a critical text sought to delineate a lesbian literary tradition. Here Rule analyses the life and work of a group of twentieth-century lesbian writers, including Gertrude Stein, Ivy Compton-Burnett, Maureen Duffy and May Sarton. Despite its focus on individual writers, Rule's text goes beyond a celebratory biographical approach and anticipates the multigeneric and intertextual style of much later lesbian literary criticism.

Lesbian literary criticism of the 1970s and early 1980s was concerned to identify a lesbian literary tradition and a lesbian literary aesthetic, whether this was based on textual content, characters, themes, or the identification of the author as herself lesbian. This was aided by a number of reference works (Grier, 1981; Cruikshank, 1982; Wittig and Zeig, 1979) which continue to provide invaluable source materials for lesbian teachers, students and researchers. Work of this kind also performed the valuable '(re)discovery' of writers assumed to be heterosexual (Judith Fetterley's essay on Willa Cather (1990) is a later example), or, in Alison Hennegan's 1984 essay, 'What is a Lesbian Novel?', identified a lesbian 'sensibility' in a text's 'necessarily oblique vision of the world'. Related to this is the 'encodement' approach advanced by Catharine Stimpson (1988) which analyses the strategies of concealment (the use of an obscure idiom, gender and pronoun ambiguity, or a male pseudonym), or of internal censorship and silence necessarily employed by woman-identified writers in a homophobic and misogynistic culture. One example of this approach is Stimpson's analysis of the sexual codes, use of silence, and experimentation with syntax in the writings of Gertrude Stein. Other critics have used the approach to interpret the work of Angelina Weld Grimke, Emily Dickinson, H.[ilda] D.[oolittle], and Willa Cather.

Given the historical difficulty of writing lesbian, however, as well as the changing definitions of the sign 'lesbian', lesbian critics have progressively moved away from this search for a single lesbian identity or discourse. Mandy Merck (1985), for instance, takes issue with Hennegan's view that lesbians share a common perspective. What Hennegan calls lesbian 'sensibility', says Merck, can be found in works by other writers who don't identify as lesbian. She also questions an emphasis, such as there is in Hennegan's 'On Becoming a Lesbian Reader', on the importance of textual representations in the formation of readers' lesbian identities. A more radical approach, Merck argues, lies in the application of perverse readings which rely neither on the author's or text's concealment or disclosure of sexual identity but on the queer perspective of the reader who subverts the dominant interpretative frameworks. Bonnie Zimmerman (1986) also, in her essay 'What Has Never Been: An Overview of Lesbian Feminist Literary Criticism', offers a more sophisticated model of lesbian textuality. She cautions against reductive and essentialist models of the lesbian text, and proposes the notion of lesbian 'double vision' drawn from the dual perspectives of lesbians as members of mainstream and minority cultures simultaneously. In a later study, *The Safe Sea of Women* (1991), Zimmerman advances a historically based definition of lesbian fiction, grounding this category in the cultural and historical contexts in which it is produced and read.

Rather than seek an autonomous lesbian tradition, distinctive aesthetic, lesbian author or reader, therefore, more recent lesbian criticism has addressed the question of how texts internalize heterosexism and how lesbian literary strategies can subvert its norms. One such strategy is intertextuality. In an early essay, Elaine Marks (1979) argued that lesbian writing is fundamentally intertextual, and that it has drawn on historical figures such as Sappho in the rnaking of its discursive history and the production of 'challenging counterimages': lesbian texts 'written exclusively by women for women, careless of male approval'. More recently, some of the most exciting lesbian criticism has been produced by bilingual and postcolonial/Third World lesbian writers who similarly foreground the intertextual, dialogic aspects of their texts. The Quebequoise writer, Nicole

Brossard, and the Chicana writer, Cherrie Moraga, produce lyrical, polemical writings which interweave theory, politics and poetry. In *Amantes* (1980, translated as *Lovhers*, 1987), Brossard practises 'writing in the feminine' which like *écriture féminine* deconstructs the opposition body/text. Similarly, Moraga and Anzaldúa's concept of 'theory in the flesh' (1981) elides the gap between the Chicana lesbian body and text.

Teresa de Lauretis, in her article 'Sexual Indifference and Lesbian Representation' (1993), also draws on French theory, using Irigaray's concept of 'hom(m)osexuality' to discuss the invisibilizing of the lesbian body/text. Her essay subverts dominant interpretations of Radclyffe Hall's famous lesbian novel, *The Well of Loneliness* (1928), by reading against the grain of sexology and drawing out the text's 'other' lesbianism. In common with lesbian and queer theory, de Lauretis plays on the distinction between sex/gender and sexuality, celebrating the diversity of lesbian writing, both critical and creative, and the ways in which lesbian writers 'have sought variously to escape gender, deny it, transcend it, or perform it in excess, and to inscribe the erotic in cryptic, allegorical, realistic, camp, or other modes of representation'.

These various strategies and the resulting intersection of postmodern discourses and lesbian criticism have led to the textualization of lesbian identity, whereby lesbianism is seen as a position from which to speak 'otherwise' and thus 'queer' heterosexist discourse.

Queer theory and criticism

During the 1980s, the term 'queer' was reclaimed by a new generation of political activists involved in Queer nation and protest groups such as ActUp and Outrage, though some lesbian and gay cultural activists and critics who adopted the term in the 1950s and 1960s continue to use it to describe their particular sense of marginality to both mainstream and minority cultures. In the 1990s, 'Queer Theory' designated a radical rethinking of the relationship between subjectivity, sexuality and representation. Its emergence in that decade owes much to the earlier work of queer critics such as Ann Snitow (1983), Carol Vance (1984) and Joan Nestle (1988), but also to the allied challenge of diversity initiated by Black and Third World critics. In addition, it gained impetus from postmodern theories with which it overlapped in significant ways. Teresa de Lauretis, in the Introduction to the 'Queer Theory' issue of *differences* (1991), traced the emergence of the term 'queer' and described the impact of postmodernism on lesbian and gay theorizing.

Further examples which explore this intersection, and the way both discourses operate to decentre foundationalist narratives based on 'sex' or 'reason', would include Judith Roof's *A Lure of Knowledge* (1990), Laura Doan's
The Lesbian Postmodern (1994), and essays in the volume *Sexy Bodies* (Grosz
and Probyn (eds), 1995). Queer theory's foregrounding of a politics of difference and marginality has assisted gay and lesbian critiques of heterosexual
hegemony and patriarchy while the development of a postmodern aesthetic
has helped inspire the expression of sexual plurality and gender ambivalence in the area of cultural production: a dynamic dialogue which has placed
lesbian and gay theories at the forefront of work in the increasingly cross-
disciplinary field of critical theory.

Signs of this development have since appeared in the academic rise of
Gender Studies and the dialogues in Gay Studies with the emerging discipline of Men's Studies, which aims to build on feminism and gay theory
so as to provide a critique and reconstruction of men's sexualities and
lifestyles. There has been anxiety over and opposition to both these tendencies, and there remains in some quarters an unsettled, even antagonistic, relationship between gay theory and feminism. In Joseph Bristow's view
in 1992, 'lesbian and gay criticism does not comprise a coherent field', but
this, he argued was 'its strength'. Bristow's exploration of what lesbian and
gay mean involves a sense of their sameness and difference: they 'designate
entirely different desires, physical pleasures, oppressions, and visibilities
. . . But both subordinated groups share parallel histories within a sexually
prohibitive dominant culture . . . '. As new areas of theoretical enquiry
emerge it becomes less clear how to maintain academic boundaries. Are
transvestitism or cross-dressing, for example, topics for lesbian, gay or
bisexual studies, or for Men's, Women's or Gender Studies, or for Shakespeare, theatre or performance studies? Queer studies 'queries' orthodoxies
and promotes or provokes such uncertainties, moving beyond lesbian and
gay sexualities to include a range of other sexualities that disrupt such fixed
or settled categorization altogether.

Some of the figures and arguments influencing the transition from gay
to queer theory have been referred to above. Jeffrey Weeks, for example,
while arguing that sexualities are historically constructed, sees them as none
the less refusing to yield up a stable cognitive core, but 'only changing
patterns in the organization of desire' (1985). Yet if this is true of homosexuality, surely heterosexuality too is also a recent construction and not a
naturally grounded identity. As we have seen, the notion that sexual desire
naturally and necessarily involves a gravitation towards a person of the opposite biological sex was already challenged by Freud (see also Laqueur, 1990).

In a postmodern, postcolonial world, in which the object of knowledge has itself become a problematic space, queer theory seeks further to question all such essentializing tendencies and binary thinking. An elusive sexuality, fragmented into local, perverse particularities, is celebrated in all its deviant versions. Such 'perversions' are mobilized in resistance to the bourgeois construction of self modelled upon a rigid, patriarchal heterosexuality which has exercised its hegemony for over two centuries.

In repoliticizing gay theory along these lines, queer theory has drawn on Foucault, as discussed earlier in this chapter, and in its inflection in Great Britain especially towards cultural materialism, on the work of Althusser and Raymond Williams. Here some tension has emerged between queer positions and more traditional Marxist approaches. In Jeffrey Weeks's view, for instance, capitalist social relations have an effect on sexualities (as on many other matters), 'but a history of capitalism is not a history of sexuality' (1985). His own work demonstrates that power should not be treated as single and unitary but as itself diverse, shifting and unstable, and hence as open to resistance in a variety of ways. This argument makes possible the formation, in Foucault's terms, of a '"reverse" discourse' in which 'homosexuality began to speak in its own behalf, to demand that its legitimacy or "naturality" be acknowledged, often in the same vocabulary, using the same categories by which it was medically disqualified' (1976).

Theorists and critics following this Marxist or post-Marxist tradition must negotiate the situation summarized by Raymond Williams in *Marxism and Literature* (1977 – see Chapter 5) as one in which 'all or nearly all initiatives and contributions, even when they take on manifestly alternative or oppositional forms, are in practice tied to the hegemonic'. Queer theory would question the implication, apparent here and in Foucault's work, that alternative or oppositional meanings are fully appropriated by the state. As Dollimore (1991) writes, 'Thinking history in terms of the perverse dynamic begins to undermine that binary opposition between the essentialist and the anti-essentialist.' As he discovers in the multiple resistances to Renaissance ideologies, marginality is not simply marginal. Dollimore's and Sinfield's work, in theoretical tandem with other examples in Cultural Materialism and New Historicism (Stallybrass and White, 1986; Bredbeck, 1991; Goldberg, 1992, 1994, progressing again beyond Foucault, especially in the area of Renaissance studies. See also Chapter 7), shows that binary oppositions become unstable in the subversive moment of queer writing. A key instance here, once more, is Oscar Wilde. Identifying a series of oppositions between Wilde and his culture, such as 'surface/depth'; 'lying/ truth'; 'abnormal/normal'; 'narcissism/maturity', Dollimore concludes:

'That which society forbids, Wilde reinstates through and within some of its most cherished and central cultural categories – art, the aesthetic, art criticism, individualism.' Wilde, he argues, appropriates dominant categories in the same gesture that he 'transvalues them through perversion and inversion', demonstrating how 'abnormality is not just the opposite, but the necessarily always present antithesis of normality'.

Two further figures of special importance to the emergence of queer theory are Judith Butler and Eve Kosofsky Sedgwick. At the same time, their influence extends beyond this category, Butler in fact claiming that in the first instance she wrote *Gender Trouble* (1992), her most influential book in this field, primarily as a feminist for feminist readers. Also, queer theory itself, certainly in versions indebted to Butler, contests the categorization which would limit it to questions of gay or lesbian sexual identities. In this view, queer theory does not name a separatist movement claiming an essence of gayness, but on the contrary emphasizes the constructedness, ambivalence and potential plurality of all gendered and sexual identities. As David Halperin has said in emphasizing the critical 'querying' aspect of queer theory, 'Queer is by definition whatever is at odds with the normal, the legitimate, the dominant. *There is nothing in particular to which it necessarily refers.* It is an identity without an essence' (Halperin, 1990). Butler accordingly uses the (non)category of queer to disrupt not only the authority of the hom(m)osexual economy but also the attribution of identity *per se*. In 'Imitation and Gender Insubordination' (1991), she calls for a rejection of the essentialism of the hetero/homosexual binary opposition, and for the queering of heterosexist master narratives. Unlike lesbian feminists such as Wittig, she refuses to identify lesbian as a positive oppositional term, arguing that it is the absence of a defined lesbian counter-identity that enables the postmodern lesbian to queer the master discourse. As Butler puts it, 'I would like to have it permanently unclear what precisely that sign signifies.' In this way, queer theory proposes a disruption of normative sexual identities and a conception of agency linked to the 'performance' which installs those identities. Butler's work is known above all for her association of the idea of 'performativity' with sexual or gendered identities. Often this is taken to posit a theatrical self, able to freely select from a range of possible identities. Moe Meyer, for example, argues that queer theory is 'an ontological challenge that displaces bourgeois notions of the Self as unique, abiding, and continuous while substituting instead a concept of the Self as performative, improvisational, discontinuous, and processually constituted by repetitive and stylized acts' (Meyer, 1994).

While recognizing that there is an evident popular desire for a conception of improvised identity and that her own work has been seen to endorse this, Butler has explained that she intends a more philosophically rigorous and more limited popular notion of performativity which makes plain that gender is constructed, or 'contoured', through 'repetition and recitation', is the subversive 're-signification' of normative identities – but is not a matter of free choice (Butler, 1994). Liz Grosz (1996) concurs with Butler that it is the indeterminacy of the sign 'lesbian' which gives it its radical potential, but she also offers a critique of queer theory's elision of systematic structures of power and its celebration of deviant sexual practices of whatever kind. Other lesbian feminists are critical of queer theory's tendency to downplay the significance of gender difference. Many would argue that, although distinct, gender and sexuality cannot be completely disarticulated. It makes no sense to claim that lesbians' oppression, while being specific, is not connected to their oppression as women. The tendency for lesbian existence to be marginalized in the new queer discourses is no doubt indicative of the continuing power relations between the sexes. Nevertheless, there exists a productive tension between lesbian, gay male and feminist theory in the development of textual and intertextual strategies which undermine both literary norms and everyday sexual stereotypes (Humm, 1994).

Butler's recent work, in the meantime, while revisiting the themes of performativity and regulative social-sexual norms, has confirmed the breadth of her theoretical sources (Freud, Foucault, Derrida), and sought to address broader political themes. *Excitable Speech: A Politics of the Performative* (1997) is a study of racist 'hate speech', pornography, and the discourse about gays in the military. What Butler argues, however, is that an inevitable disjuncture between intent and effect, or speech and conduct, means that injurious terms can be appropriated and re-deployed for counter purposes (the term 'queer', used to reverse its intended meanings, would be a case in point). *The Psychic Life of Power*, also produced in 1997, argues that the psyche is crucial to the formation of normative sexual identities in that it is constrained to adopt the exclusionary prohibitions – upon homosexuality, for example – determined by the hegemonic social order. The result is a 'melancholy' loss of what is forbidden but cannot be avowed. But here again, Butler argues that this experience may be countered through the unpredictable, and therefore resistant, ways in which norms might be adopted or performed.

Butler's reputation rests primarily on her earlier works. Eve Kosofsky Sedgwick, similarly, made her most significant contribution to gender and queer theory in two key early studies, *Between Men* (1985) and *Epistemology of the Closet* (1990). Like Butler, she draws in these works on deconstructive postmodern theory but with a more evident political intent or implication and also with more direct reference to literary texts. The supposed opposition between sex and gender, she argues, seems 'only to delineate a problematical space rather than a crisp distinction' (1990). Sexuality has often been confused with sex, she says, adding that other categories such as race or class might themselves be important in the construction of sexuality. Just as there is no single sexuality, so there is no privileged narrative of nation. Sexualities, like nationalities, are therefore simply shaped by their differences, not by something innately grounding them. Sexual boundaries are no more fixed than national ones, though they may, for a period, serve to delineate a particular discursive space. More recent work in this area has shown how sexology and colonial anthropology were linked but that one nation's sexual classifications do not neatly equate with those of another. This has coincided with a move away from the black denunciation of homosexuality as something alien to black culture. At the same time, though the existence of cross-dressing and a homosexual rite of passage into manhood in other cultures have been sometimes exoticized and misunderstood, a critical reading of ethnographic literatures (such as that of Rudi C. Bleys, 1996) can provide a sense of the larger narratives involved in the construction of gay identities.

Sedgwick has also deployed the concept of 'homosociality' as an interpretative tool to demonstrate 'the usefulness of certain Marxist-feminist historical categories for literary criticism'. In her *Between Men: English Literature and Male Homosocial Desire* (1985), she begins to distance herself from determinate notions of patriarchy; male and female homosociality none the less have different historical shapes and they remain 'articulations and mechanisms of the enduring inequality of power between women and men'. She acknowledges a debt to feminism, but increasingly, in a move typical of the deconstructive tendencies of queer theory, considers the multiple constructedness of sex, gender and sexuality. Her study of Shakespeare's *Sonnets*, Wycherley's play, *The Country Wife*, Tennyson, George Eliot and Dickens illustrates the paradoxically historicizing and dehistoricizing tendencies of this kind of work. The book is also notable for its discussion of the Gothic as 'Terrorism and Homosexual Panic'. In particular (building on Freud), she explores the theory that 'paranoia is the psychosis that makes graphic the mechanisms of homophobia'.

Queer theory views the traditional and prescriptive essentialist model of sexuality as failing to do the conceptual work involved in the adequate description of how desires function, and how sexualities are made. The range of critical terminologies, models and strategies outlined above confirms that it is no longer viable to think in terms of a single, coherent 'sexuality' and has effected the transition from the 'natural' homosexual individual, to whom rights could be attached, to the disorienting notion that all sexualities are perverse and can be reclaimed and celebrated as such. If gay or lesbian theory has often been defensively grounded in liberal rights, queer theory is a deeper philosophical challenge to the status quo, which at the same time aims to provide readings which at once subvert sameness and celebrate otherness.

In consequence, queer theory is mobile and varied in its assault upon privileged, stable, heterosexual 'origins'. While some, in a mood of holiday fun, seek to celebrate the carnival of style, artifice, performance and play discovered in perverse sexualities, others seek a more politicized stance, moving beyond Foucault or adopting a more materialist response to post-structuralist textualism. Jeffrey Weeks sees the 'flux of desire' as itself too much for capitalist society to endure, for it simultaneously encourages and abhors this chaos, and cannot live with the infinite variety of potential interconnections and relationships. Sedgwick has similarly attacked the assumption that homosexuality today 'comprises a coherent definitional field rather than a space of overlapping, contradictory, and conflicting definitional forces'. In questioning stable, unproblematic classifications of sexuality, this seems to remove any common platform for action. However, Sedgwick urges a less systematic approach: surely, she argues, it would be sensible to work from 'the relation enabled by the unrationalized coexistence of different models during the times they do exist'.

Accordingly, the starting-point for 'queer theory' is, in Moe Meyer's words, 'an ontological challenge to dominant labelling philosophies'. This strategy takes up Weeks's 'whirlwind of deconstruction' by contesting the binary opposition between (among other things) homosexuality and heterosexuality, and has taken important effect in gay and academic communities. In the 1980s, it was feared that the spectre of AIDS would unleash homophobic repression, that gay men would be marginalized, and the right to a diversity of sexual pleasure be strictly limited. Yet the message that sex must simply be safer, not less varied, has led to the recovery and reinvention of erotic possibilities. Gay groups are working with sex-workers (male and female), forcing a concern with sexuality to return to questions of class, economics and inequality. The appearance of AIDS and HIV shifted notions of identity, and brought with it new challenges, discourses and forms of representation. In a more theoretical direction, Lee Edelman, taking up the associations of AIDS and plague mapped by Susan Sontag (1989), argues in his 'The Plague of Discourse: Politics, Literary Theory, and Aids' (in Butters, *AIDS and its Metaphors*, 1989), for the placing of literary theory between 'politics' and 'AIDS', since 'both of those categories produce, and are produced as, historical discourses susceptible to analysis by the critical methodologies associated with literary theory'. His essay questions the ideological opposition between the biological, literal and real on the one hand, and on the other, the literary, figural and fictive, and concludes that a deconstructive queer theory must make its case on AIDS through a necessarily 'diseased' discourse.

Queer critics continued in this same period to mobilize the 'coming out' of theory in the academic world. Silence in this regard was seen as a species of closetedness. Writing in 1990, Eve Kosofsky Sedgwick recalled that, 'in a class I taught at Amherst College, fully half the students said they had studied *Dorian Gray* in previous classes, but no one had ever discussed the book in terms of any homosexual content'. As this tells us, much has had to be done in learning to speak and write about literature's and our own sexual constructedness. Fifteen years on, what would teachers and students of *Dorian Gray* now have to say?

Selected reading

Key texts

Abelove, Henry *et al.* (eds), *The Lesbian and Gay Studies Reader* (Routledge, London, 1993).

Adams, Rachel and Savran, David (eds), *The Masculinity Studies Reader* (Blackwell, Oxford, 2002).

Anzaldúa, Gloria, *Borderlands/La Frontera: The New Mestiza* (Aunt Lute Books, San Francisco, 1987).

Bristow, Joseph (ed.), *Sexual Sameness: Textual Difference in Lesbian and Gay Writing* (Routledge, London, 1992).

Bristow, Joseph, *Effeminate England: Homoerotic Writing after 1885* (Open University Press, Milton Keynes, 1995).

Bristow, Joseph, *Sexuality* (Routledge, London, 1997).

Bristow, Joseph and Wilson, Angela R. (eds), *Activating Theory: Lesbian, Gay and Bisexual Politics* (Lawrence & Wishart, London, 1996).

Butler, Judith, 'Imitation and Gender Subordination', in Diana Fuss (ed., 1991), below.

Butler, Judith, *Gender Trouble: Feminism and the Subversion of Identity* (Routledge, London and New York, 1992).

Butler, Judith, *Bodies That Matter: On the Discursive Limits of 'Sex'* (Routledge, London and New York, 1993).

Butler, Judith, 'Gender as Performance: An Interview with Judith Butler', conducted by Peter Osborne and Lynne Segal, *Radical Philosophy*, 67 (Summer, 1994).

Butler, Judith, *Excitable Speech: A Politics of the Performative* (Routledge, London, 1997).

Butler, Judith, *The Psychic Life of Power: Theories in Subjection* (Stanford University Press, California, 1997).

Butler, Judith, *Undoing Gender* (Routledge, London, 2004).

Butler, Judith, *The Judith Butler Reader*, ed. by Sara Salih (Blackwell, Oxford, 2003).

Cohen, Ed., 'Legislating the Norm: From Sodomy to Gross Indecency', *South Atlantic Quarterly*, 88 (1989), 181–217.

Corber, Robert J. and Valocchi, Stephen J. (eds), *Queer Studies: An Interdisciplinary Reader* (Blackwell, Oxford, 2003).

Cruikshank, Margaret (ed.), *Lesbian Studies: Present and Future* (The Feminist Press, New York, 1982).

Daly, Mary, *Gyn/Ecology: The Metaethics of Radical Feminism* (Beacon Press, Boston, 1978).

de Lauretis, Teresa, 'Introduction', *differences*: 'Queer Theory Issue', 3: 2 (Summer, 1991).

de Lauretis, Teresa, 'Sexual Indifference and Lesbian Representation', in Henry Abelove *et al.* (eds), above.

Doan, Laura (ed.), *The Lesbian Postmodern* (Columbia University Press, New York, 1994).

Dollimore, Jonathan, *Sexual Dissidence: Augustine to Wilde, Freud to Foucault* (Clarendon Press, Oxford, 1991).

Dollimore, Jonathan, *Sex, Literature and Censorship* (Polity Press, Cambridge, 2001).

Edelman, Lee, *Homographesis: Essays in Gay Literary and Cultural Theory* (Routledge, London, 1994).

Epstein, Julia and Straub, Kristina (eds), *Body Guards: The Cultural Politics of Gender Ambiguity* (Routledge, London and New York, 1991).

Fetterley, Judith, 'My Antonia! Jim Blunden and the Dilemma of the Lesbian Writer', in Karla Jay, Joanne Glasgow and Catharine R. Stimpson (eds), *Lesbian Texts and Contexts: Radical Revisions* (New York University Press, New York, 1990).

Foucault, Michel, *The History of Sexuality: Volume 1. An Introduction* [1976], trans. by Robert Hurley (Penguin, Harmondsworth, 1990).

Fuss, Diana (ed.), *Inside/Outside: Lesbian Theories, Gay Theories* (Routledge, London, 1991).

Gever, Martha, Parmar, Pratibha and Greyson, John, *Queer Looks* (Routledge, London, 1993).

Goldberg, Jonathan, *Sodometries: Renaissance Texts: Modern Sexualities* (University of California Press, Stanford, 1992).

Goldberg, Jonathan (ed.), *Reclaiming Sodom* (Routledge, London and New York, 1994).

Goldberg, Jonathan (ed.), *Queering the Renaissance* (Duke University Press, Durham, NC and London, 1994).

Greenberg, David F., *The Construction of Homosexuality* (University of Chicago Press, Chicago, 1988).

Grier, Barbara, *The Lesbian in Literature: A Bibliography* (The Naiad Press, Tallahassee, 1981).

Grosz, Elizabeth, *Space, Time, Perversion* (Routledge, London, 1996).

Grosz, Elizabeth and Probyn, Elsbeth (eds), *Sexy Bodies: The Strange Carnalities of Feminism* (Routledge, London, 1995).

Hennegan, Alison, 'What is a Lesbian Novel?', *Woman's Review*, no. 1 (1984).

Hennegan, Alison, 'On Becoming a Lesbian Reader', in Susannah Radstone (ed.), *Sweet Dreams: Sexuality, Gender and Popular Fiction* (Lawrence & Wishart, London, 1988).

Hocquenghem, Guy, *Homosexual Desire* (Allison & Busby, London, 1978).

Irigaray, Luce, *This Sex Which Is Not One* (Cornell University Press, Ithaca, 1985).

Jay, Karla and Glasgow, Joanne (eds), *Lesbian Texts and Contexts: Radical Revisions* (New York University Press, New York, 1990).

Johnstone, Jill, *Lesbian Nation* (Simon & Schuster, New York, 1973).

Kopelson, Kevin, *Love's Litany: The Writing of Modern Homoerotics* (University of California Press, Stanford, 1994).

Laqueur, Thomas, *Making Sex: Body and Gender from the Greeks to Freud* (Harvard University Press, Cambridge, Mass., 1990).

Lilly, Mark (ed.), *Lesbian and Gay Writing: An Anthology of Critical Essays* (Macmillan, Basingstoke, 1990).

Lorde, Audre, *Sister/Outsider* (Crossing Press, New York, 1984).

Marks, Elaine, 'Lesbian Intertextuality', in George Stamboulian and Elaine Marks (eds), *Homosexualities and French Literature* (Cornell University Press, Ithaca, 1979).

Merck, Mandy, Review of 'Girls Next Door', *Women's Review*, 1 (Nov. 1985), 40.

Merck, Mandy, *Perversions: Deviant Readings* (Virago, London, 1993).

Meyer, Moe (ed.), *The Politics and Poetics of Camp* (Routledge, New York and London, 1994).

Moraga, Cherrie and Anzaldúa, Gloria, *This Bridge Called My Back: Writings by Radical Women of Color* (Kitchen Table Press, New York, 1981).

Munt, Sally (ed.), *New Lesbian Criticism* (Harvester Wheatsheaf, Hemel Hempstead, 1992).

Parker, Andrew, *et al.* (eds), *Nationalisms and Sexualities* (Routledge, London and New York, 1992).

Radicalesbians, 'The Woman-Identified Woman', *The Ladder*, vol. 14, 11/12 (1970).

Rich, Adrienne, 'Compulsory Heterosexuality and Lesbian Existence', *Signs*, 5, 4 (Summer, 1980), 631–60.

Rich, Adrienne, 'The Temptations of a Motherless Girl', in *On Lies, Secrets and Silence* (Virago, London, 1980).

Roof, Judith, *A Lure of Knowledge: Lesbian Sexuality and Theory* (Columbia University Press, New York, 1990).

Rule, Jane, *Lesbian Images* (Crossing Press, Trumansberg, NY, 1975).

Sedgwick, Eve Kosofsky, *Between Men: English Literature and Male Homosocial Desire* (Columbia University Press, New York, 1985).

Sedgwick, Eve Kosofsky, *Epistemology of the Closet* (University of California Press, Berkeley and Los Angeles, 1990).

Sedgwick, Eve Kosofsky, *Tendencies* (Routledge, London, 1994).

Showalter, Elaine (ed.), *The New Feminist Criticism: Essays on Women, Literature and Theory* (Virago, London, 1986).

Sinfield, Alan, *Literature, Politics and Culture in Postwar Britain* (Basic Blackwell, Oxford, 1989).

Sinfield, Alan, *The Wilde Century* (Cassell, London, 1994).

Sinfield, Alan, *Cultural Politics – Queer Reading* (Routledge, London, 1994).

Smith, Barbara, 'Towards a Black Feminist Criticism', in Elaine Showalter (ed., 1986), above.

Stallybrass, Peter and White, Allon, *The Politics and Poetics of Transgression* (Methuen, London, 1986).

Still, Judith and Worton, Michael, *Textuality and Sexuality: Reading Theories and Practices* (Manchester University Press, Manchester, 1993).

Weeks, Jeffrey, *Sexuality and its Discontents: Meanings, Myths and Modern Homosexualities* (Routledge, New York and London, 1985).

Whitehead, Stephen M. and Barrett, Frank J. (eds), *The Masculinities Reader* (Polity Press, Cambridge, 2001).

Wittig, Monique, 'The Straight Mind' [1980], reprinted in *The Straight Mind and Other Essays* (Harvester Wheatsheaf, Hemel Hempstead, 1992).

Wittig, Monique, 'One Is Not Born a Woman', *Feminist Issues*, 1/2 (1981), 47–54.

Wittig, Monique and Zeig, Sandi, *Lesbian Peoples: Materials for a Dictionary* [French edn, 1976] (Avon, New York, 1979).

Woods, Gregory, *Articulate Flesh: Male Home-Eroticism in Modern Poetry* (Yale University Press, New Haven and London, 1987).

Zimmerman, Bonnie, 'What Has Never Been: An Overview of Lesbian Feminist Literary Criticism', in Elaine Showalter (ed., 1986), above.

Zimmerman, Bonnie, *The Safe Sea of Women: Lesbian Fiction 1969–1989* (Beacon Press, Boston, 1991).

Further reading

Bingham, C., 'Seventeenth-Century Attitudes Toward Deviant Sex', *Journal of Interdisciplinary History*, 1 (1971), 447–68.

Bleys, Rudi C., *The Geography of Perversion: Male-to-Male Sexual Behaviour Outside the West and the Ethnographic Imagination 1750–1918* (Cassell, London, 1996).

Bray, Alan, *Homosexuality in Renaissance England* (Gay Men's Press, London, 1988).

Bredbeck, Gregory W., *Sodomy and Interpretation: Marlowe to Milton* (Cornell University Press, Ithaca, 1991).

Bremner, Jeni, *From Sappho to de Sade: Moments in the History of Sexuality* (Routledge, London, 1989).

Burston, Paul and Richardson, Colin (eds), *A Queer Romance: Lesbians, Gay Men and Popular Culture* (Routledge, London, 1995).

Butters, Ronald R. *et al.* (eds), *Displacing Homophobia: Gay Male Perspectives in Literature and Culture* (Duke University Press, Durham, NC and London, 1989).

Clark, David and Barber, Stephen (eds), *Regarding Sedgwick: Essays on Queer Culture and Critical Theory* (Routledge, London, 2002).

Cleto, Fabio (ed.), *Camp: Queer Aesthetics and the Performing Subject: A Reader* (Edinburgh University Press, Edinburgh, 1999).

Davenport-Hines, R., *Sex, Death and Punishment: Attitudes to Sex and Sexuality in Britain Since the Renaissance* (Collins, London, 1990).

De Jean, Joan, *Fictions of Sappho 1565–1937* (University of Chicago Press, Chicago and London, 1989).

Donoghue, Emma, *Passions Between Women: British Lesbian Culture 1668–1801* (Scarlet Press, London, 1993).

Dynes, Wayne, *Homolexis: A Historical and Cultural Lexicon of Homosexuality* (Gai Saber Monograph, New York, 1985).

Ferris, Lesley (ed.), *Crossing the Stage: Controversies on Cross-Dressing* (Routledge, New York and London, 1993).

Garber, Marjorie, *Vested Interests: Cross-Dressing and Cultural Anxiety* (Routledge, New York and London, 1992).

Glover, David and Kaplan, Cora, *Genders* (Routledge, London, 2000).

Hall, Donald E., *Queer Theories* (Palgrave Macmillan, Basingstoke, 2002).

Halperin, David M., *One Hundred Years of Homosexuality and Other Essays on Greek Love* (Routledge, London, 1990).

Hamer, Diane and Budge, Belinda (eds), *The Good, The Bad and The Gorgeous: Popular Culture's Romance with Lesbianism* (Pandora, London, 1994).

Hawkes, Terence, *Alternative Shakespeares, Volume 2* (Routledge, London, 1996).

Humm, Maggie, *A Reader's Guide to Contemporary Feminist Theory* (Harvester Wheatsheaf, Hemel Hempstead, 1994).

Katz, J. N., 'The Age of Sodomitical Sin, 1607–1740', in Jonathan Goldberg (ed., 1994), see *Key texts*, above.

Lewis, Reina, 'The Death of the Author and the Resurrection of the Dyke', in Sally Munt (ed., 1992), see *Key texts*, above.

Maccubbin, Robert P., *'Tis Nature's Fault: Unauthorised Sexuality during the Enlightenment* (Cambridge University Press, Cambridge, 1985).

Nestle, Joan, *A Restricted Country: Essays and Short Stories* (Sheba, London, 1988).

Norton, Rictor, *Mother Clap's Molly House: The Gay Subculture in England 1700–1830* (The Gay Men's Press, London, 1992).

Palmer, Paulina, *Contemporary Lesbian Writing* (Oxford University Press, Oxford, 1993).

Ringer, R. Jeffrey (ed.), *Queer Words, Queer Images: Communication and the Construction of Homosexuality* (New York University Press, London and New York, 1994).

Rousseau, G. S. and Porter, Roy (eds), *Sexual Underworlds of the Enlightenment* (Manchester University Press, Manchester, 1992).

Rubin, Gayle, 'The Traffic in Women', in Rayna R. Reiter (ed.), *Toward an Anthropology of Women* (Monthly Review Press, New York, 1975).

Salih, Sara, *Judith Butler* (Routledge, London, 2002).

Saslow, James M., *Ganymede in the Renaissance: Homosexuality in Art and Society* (Yale University Press, New Haven and London, 1986).

Senelick, Laurence, 'Mollies or Men of Mode? Sodomy and the Eighteenth-Century London Stage', *Journal of the History of Sexuality*, 1 (1990), 33–67.

Smith, Bruce, R., *Homosexual Desire in Shakespeare's England: Cultural Poetics* (University of Chicago Press, Chicago and London, 1991).

Snitow, Ann *et al.* (eds), *Powers of Desire: The Politics of Sexuality* (New Feminist Library, New York, 1983).

Stimpson, Catharine, *Where the Meanings Are: Feminism and Cultural Spaces* (Routledge, London, 1988).

Sullivan, Nikki, *A Critical Introduction to Queer Theory* (Edinburgh University Press, Edinburgh, 2003).

Trumbach, Randolph, 'Sodomitical Subcultures, Sodomitical Roles, and the Gender Revolutions of the Eighteenth Century: The Recent Historiography', *Eighteenth-Century Life*, 9 (1985), 109–21.

Trumbach, Randolph, 'London's Sapphists: From Three Sexes to Four Genders in the Making of Modern Culture', in Julia Epstein and Kristina Straub (eds, 1991), see *Key texts*, above.

Vance, Carole S. (ed.), *Pleasure and Danger: Exploring Female Sexuality* (Routledge, London, 1984).

Whitehead, Stephen J., *Men and Masculinities* (Polity Press, Cambridge, 2002).

Conclusion: Post-theory

As the present Introduction has indicated, the first edition of *A Reader's Guide* opened in 1985 with comments on the likely resistance to theory from those who felt their assumptions about literature, ways of reading, and criteria of value were under challenge. While theory – sustained by its attendant Introductions, Guides, Readers and Glossaries – has since taken deep and pervasive root in Departments of English and related areas of study, the anxieties it has engendered have persisted. David Carroll and Jonathan Culler, for example, rehearsed such complaints during the 1990s as follows: if the status of the literary canon is in doubt; if the formal integrity of literature, of art and of textual evidence in general is ousted by ideas of inner contradiction, marginality and indeterminacy; if objective fact is replaced by an idea of narrative construction; if the normative unity of the reading subject is questioned – then 'it must be the fault of "theory"', which seems anyway not to be about literature at all (Carroll, 1990; Culler, 1997).

Other studies, however, appearing on the cusp of and into the new millennium, have taken on a new tone. For it seems now that the days of theory which gave rise to these anxieties are over. As a flurry of titles (some of which are discussed below) have told us, the present age has opened upon the 'End of Theory' or, more ambiguously, the moment of 'after-' or 'post-' Theory. Thus we are presented with Valentine Cunningham's *Reading After Theory* (2002), Jean-Michel Rabaté's *The Future of Theory* (2002) and Terry Eagleton's *After Theory* (2003), as well as the collections, *Post-Theory: New Directions in Criticism* (1999), *What's Left of Theory?* (2000) and *Life. After. Theory* (2003). Leaving aside any argument about whether we can ever meaningfully be 'post-theory', in the end we discover that what this portends is less a dramatic apocalypse than a reorientation. For what, by common consent, is thought to be over is the age of 'Theory', with its commanding capital letter and associated star names – especially that cast of (mostly) French intellectuals associated with varieties of structuralism, poststructuralism and postmodernism: Barthes, Althusser, Foucault, Lacan, Derrida, Baudrillard, Lyotard, Kristeva, Cixous, Spivak, Bhabha and Jameson, who dominated thinking in the 1970s and 1980s. Now there seems to be no single ortho-doxy; no new movement one must catch up with; no difficult, philoso-phically inclined, theory text one must read. Some newer figures might be nominated for the role of leading theorist – Slavoj Žižek or Judith Butler, for example – but Butler herself, at least, would reject such a role: 'I do not understand the notion of "theory"', she says, 'and am hardly interested in being cast as its defender, much less in being signified as part of an elite gay / lesbian theory crowd' (Rabaté, 2002: 1).

From one perspective this is a situation to be regretted. Where, in British or Western culture, asks Robert Clark (2003), is the public intellec-tual of the stature of Raymond Williams or Edward Said who will give a lead on major political issues? But then this concern too is a long-standing one, centred over the last two centuries – curiously enough, surely – upon the special place of literature and a literary education in the general cul-ture. The recourse to 'Theory' in the heyday of the 1980s (which appeared to mean not *literary* theory, but 'philosophy', 'psychoanalysis', 'feminism' or 'cultural theory') seemed to some to facilitate this broader role. To others, though, this was the heart of the problem. For the injunction to consult the theoretical canon or 'latest thing', could be felt as an intim-idating, modish or frustrating distraction from the proper business of literary study. The difference now, once more, is that these questions – including questions on the specific nature and role of literature or art – are being asked, not in the spirit of 'anti-theory', but of 'post-Theory' with its capital letter. For invariably the works on this theme tell us there can be no return to the days of pre-theory in lower case. Rather, it is felt that the high 'Theory' of the 1970s and 1980s is now superseded or thoroughly absorbed into theory or 'theories', understood less as a body of texts or positions than an activity: one which brings a critical scepticism to taken-for-granted assumptions about institutions, social, sexual, economic relations, and conceptions of subjective, cultural and transcultural identities. Thus theory is 'a pugnacious critique of common sense notions', says Jonathan Culler (1997), which 'offers not a set of solutions but the prospect of fur-ther thought'; David Carroll (1990) concurs: theory confronts 'the unex-amined aspects of the dominant critical strategies and analytical methods ... the contradictions and complexities inherent in traditional questions';

it seeks 'to ask different kinds of questions or to ask questions in a different way'; is committed to 'keeping the critical process open'. For Michael Payne (2003), 'theory is about how we self-reflectively see things'; for Terry Eagleton (2003), similarly: 'If theory means a reasonably systematic reflection on our guiding assumptions, it remains as indispensable as ever.' And Valentine Cunningham (2002) – dispensing with the consolations of innocent reading – confirms that 'We all – all of us readers – come after theory'. In this sense theory is here to stay; it is, as Culler says, 'endless'.

While there is this degree of common ground, the ideas of what comes next these authors present are nevertheless markedly different. We can understand such differences better with the help of Jean-Michel Rabaté (2002), himself a commentator on this scene. Theory, he writes, is always understood as being 'too one-sided, the mere half . . . of a whole in which the missing element is by definition truer, more vital, more essential . . . The problem with Theory seems to be that it is always accused of having missed something.' That (truer, more vital, more real) 'something' has been in the past and is again designated by those coming 'after Theory' as 'literature' or 'aesthetics', 'criticism' or 'reading', 'culture' or 'politics'. For Culler, in an essay in the volume *What's Left of Theory?* (2000), it is explicitly literature and the literary which have been neglected. In particular, what has been sidelined is the self-reflexiveness of the literary text, the 'poetic function' famously described by the linguist Roman Jackobson as 'the focus on the message for its own sake'. This distinctive mark of the literary has been overlaid by the imperatives of race, sexuality, gender. And where this occurs, Culler says in his 1997 book, literary studies and its modes of textual analysis defer to the 'symptomatic interpretation' of a sociologically inclined cultural studies. The volume in which Culler's essay of 2000 appears contains two essays directly on issues of race, sexuality identity politics and the law which make no mention of literature. This does not mean they are not valuable essays, but it does help make Culler's point that 'the question of literature', once 'at the heart of the theoretical project' (most evidently in structuralism), no longer occupies this place. Despite this, Culler means to keep 'the literary in theory', because from this position, the complexities and indeterminacies which comprise the 'thick description' of literary texts can complicate or challenge standard assumptions or reductive propositions on questions, for example, of identity, agency or kinship which also interest cultural studies. The difficulty, however, would seem to be in maintaining this textual emphasis. If theory, as above, is understood as an attitude of permanent critique, open to alterity and the other, then it is close cousin to the literary, and the signs, Culler says, are indeed that 'the literary has migrated into theory'. For some, on the contrary, the literary has spread even further – in fact, too far – to become the common idiom of a self-consciously fictionalizing postmodern culture. The price of this extension, for Culler, is the loss of distinctiveness and critical edge: 'perhaps it is time', he reasons therefore, 'to reground the literary in literature'. What beckons, then, is a return to 'poetics', the concerted study of the operation and reception of poetry and narrative developed in Culler's own earlier work.

Valentine Cunningham's *Reading After Theory* (2002) would also return us to literature. The 'Theory' first introduced in the 1960s has had an undoubted impact, he says, upon the teaching of English and other disciplines. But where do we go from here? Should we embark on a re-reading of the canon? Should we pick and mix, text by text, much as we select items from the supermarket shelves or from the 'gumbo' (the full and varied plate) of an exotic postmodernism? Cunningham's answer calls for a return to the traditional close reading of texts, which he believes theory has 'cast into outer . . . darkness'. We might wonder in passing to what extent this has been true of feminist or postcolonial criticism; and isn't deconstruction committed to a close engagement with texts? Terry Eagleton (2003), for one, states clearly that 'It is not true that cultural theory avoids close reading'. Cunningham remains unconvinced, while allowing that a number of critics and some theorists have kept to the path of close reading and that others have returned from the outer darkness of Theory, having seen the error of their ways. His exemplary case is Frank Kermode who holds firm to what Cunningham calls 'the old, and British, tradition of interest in truth and value and reference'. These virtues he contrasts with a postmodern scepticism towards truth, avoidance of value, and substitution of difference for reference. The ideal relation of a reader with a text depends in all this, says Cunningham, on 'tact': the 'gentle' 'caring', 'loving touch' of an 'unmanipulative reading' in 'close-up, hands-on-textual encounters', and showing 'a rational, proper, moral even, respect for the primacy of text over all theorizing about text'.

All reading and all readers come 'after theory'. So Cunningham reiterates, and so much is generally agreed. But when we go back to read the text, what theory do we take with us? The practice of close reading has had its own associated schools and exemplars from early in the 1920s and its own implied theoretical suppositions about literary form, meaning and value. However, Cunningham is not advocating a return to the supposed objectivity of Practical or New Criticism, though he shares the major assumption with these movements that the text has primacy – for if theory comes first, it should know its place, he says, as the 'lesser partner' and handmaiden to criticism. Beyond this, Cunningham's guiding terms and criteria – truth, reference, 'good sense', 'humanism and moralism' – evoke an older tradition whose core principles, he contends, were ignored or displaced by Theory. His response to the sceptical and pluralist ethos marking the aftermath of Theory raises a number of important and contentious issues. Of these, one of the most important – most obviously in debates on the literary canon – is the question of 'literary value'.

Frank Kermode, in fact, provides an interesting example here. Though he was one of the first to introduce and encourage discussion of the new theory in the late 1960s and 1970s, Kermode has remained more a literary critic than a theorist. While alert to theory's insights and supportive of the need, as he puts it in a recent discussion (2003), 'to think about what thinking about literature means', he is aware that this activity could not satisfy the desire 'to come into intimate contact with literary texts'. 'Since the aesthetic is out of fashion', he says, we have a self-reflexive theoretical discourse and some shaky classical and romantic ideas concerning literary value, coherence, wholeness and 'organic unity'. We remain confused, therefore, about what makes art or literature good for us. Cunningham has no such doubts, at least about how to approach literature: it comes down to 'what all tactful readers have known all along, namely that all good and true reading is close reading; that no reading can claim the name which is not like that'. One value Kermode does allude to strongly is that of 'general civility', something he finds in intellectual discussion, in Shakespeare, and in a style of criticism which seeks to address academic and general readers alike. Perhaps Cunningham, too, has such a double readership in mind, both as readers of literature and of his own study – hence its loosely conversational, openly combative tone. The result connects, or seeks to connect, good literature, good reading and an idea of good society: a humanist scenario whose sources (in an 'old, and British, tradition') lie as deep in 'pre-Theory' as in the moment of 'after Theory'.

Cunningham's call for a return to a traditional 'tactful' reading of literary texts finds at once a companion and contestant in another, reinvigorated older practice. Close reading, claims Jonathan Bate (2003), looked down on an interest in the 'facts' of an author's life or the scholarly editing of texts. 'We weren't very scientific in those days', he says – until 'Theory', that is, which as Structuralism (he mentions Culler admiringly) appeared to offer a 'new rigour and objectivity'. This was disturbed by Deconstruction, which seemed to endorse saying 'whatever we liked' as long as it now illustrated a text's self-deconstruction rather than its unity. 'Facts' were again ruled out of court. Even so, through this period and the turn to ideology, thinks Bate, 'literary scholarship – biographical, historical, bibliographic and textual' continued quietly on while theory made all the running and all the noise. Now, he proposes, critics, teachers and students need the 'basics' first, not of theoretical '-isms', but of literary biography and textual bibliography.

Textual bibliography examines the transition of a text from manuscript to book, in this way seeking the factual textual evidence of an author's intentions, forms of censorship, collaboration and revision. Often this procedure, which emerged strongly in the 1980s, is called 'genetic criticism'. The versions and revisions comprising the genesis of James Joyce's *Ulysses* or Ezra Pound's *Cantos*, for example, have received this kind of diligent treatment. 'Genetic Criticism', as Jean-Michel Rabaté (2002) suggests, is the key remaining example of literary study's relation to science. It has some affinities, too, with historical method – though much depends then on what we mean by 'history'. For although, on the one hand, 'genetic criticism' owes something to New Historicism or Cultural Materialism and to Deconstruction (displacing a reverential notion of the 'original' with the material evidence of textual difference), it can also sound like a reassertion of undisputed 'fact' anchored in the physical evidence of the textual archive. Bate encourages the latter view: fact has been branded, he recalls – evoking Charles Dickens's novel *Hard Times* and the character of its disciplinarian school-teacher, Thomas Gradgrind – as the sign of an oppressive industrialism. But in our own postmodern age of image and simulation, the coin is flipped over, says Bate, with the result that the subject of English now needs the Gradgrindery of sheer fact to critique the 'free for all' the discipline and society have become. The implication, too, is that with so much patient, textual deciphering to do, theoretical questions can be left on the shelf.

We might be forgiven for thinking that, for some of these authors, 'after Theory' in effect means a return either to the formalist or traditional reading of literary texts or to a reinvigorated literary scholarship which is in fact bored with or indifferent to Theory. John Brenkman (2000) implies that any invocation of the 'literary' will be nostalgic – and there is a degree of nostalgia surely in Culler's, Cunningham's and Bate's arguments. Brenkman adds usefully, however, that there can be 'formalist and non-formalist approaches to form'. But if he himself sides with the latter, it is with some aversion to the routine non-formalist analysis of the themes of race, class, gender and sexuality associated with a reductive version of cultural studies. Current criticism of this type ignores the dynamic of inner form, he says, and so weakens the connection of literature and politics where it should be strongest. Brenkman therefore calls for attention to be paid to inner form *and* to worldliness (the 'historical lifeworld' comprising the content of an artwork). Both the social practice of writing and aesthetic experience, he adds, belong to the public realm – the second in the sense that an experience of beauty depends upon the assent of others to that beauty. This public realm Brenkman sees as sustained by the liberal and republican traditions of Western thought, which – damaged though they are – 'cannot be superseded'. Broad consequences would thus follow from a new emphasis upon form: a revitalized linkage of literature and politics and a reaffirmation of the public realm and Western Enlightenment traditions upon which, for Brenkman, such a linkage depends.

We see how, advancing on the distinction made earlier by Rabaté between theory on one side and the 'something' which is missing on the other, that it matters what is meant not only by 'theory' but by these second terms ('the literary', 'reading', 'culture', 'politics') and how then the relations between these terms are understood. Some new criticism has also introduced other more specific domains, themes and issues having to do with the law, ecology, space and location (Garrard, 2004; Brooker, 2002). This work is also often linked with new interdisciplinary initiatives, between literary and legal studies or literature and social and cultural geography, for example, whose agenda is neither narrowly textual nor over-whelmingly theoretical, but is committed none the less to the subtleties of inner form and to present-day social and political issues. Much Feminist and Postcolonial criticism has also maintained what Brenkman describes as 'non-formalist approaches to form'. At this point, however, we want to look at two approaches – perhaps manifestos would be a better term – which urge us to look afresh to either end of this spectrum of form and worldli-ness, or, to put it differently again: art and politics.

One self-proclaimed new direction has been the 'New Aestheticism', announced under this title in the collection of essays by Joughlin and Malpas (2003). 'The rise of critical theory', the editors say on their first page, 'has all but swept aesthetics off the map.' What in this case has been lost, they claim, is 'the sense of art's specificity as an object of analysis . . . its specificity as an aesthetic phenomenon'. An initial problem with this pro-posal is that ideas of 'the aesthetic' and 'aestheticism' suggest a rearguard action rather than a new beginning: a return to a belief in artistic auto-nomy, individual genius, and transcendent universal values, or to the provocative formalism of the 'art for art's sake' movement of the late nine-teenth century. Harold Bloom, too, it is worth noting, founds his Western

Canon (1995) on aesthetic criteria rather than on moral values or cultural politics – for which he has only disdain. And Bloom also laments 'the flight from the aesthetic among so many of my profession'. However, there is a significant difference in intention between these authors. For Bloom, the aesthetic is 'an individual rather than a social concern' and a measure of art's autonomy – of which he tends to feel himself the lone defender. The editors, contributors and associated authors of the 'New Aestheticism' argue, in a quite different direction, that theirs is a social, indeed political, concern: that a 'turn' to the aesthetic implies a radical reorientation, vital, in Isobel Armstrong's account (2000), to a democratic founding of literary education.

The case made by Joughlin and Malpas is first that the 'New Aestheticism' inaugurates a conversation with philosophy which theory avoided. What theory in fact tended to pillory and reject, they argue, was an outmoded view of the aesthetic. This attitude assumed that the aesthetic stood for the idea of artistic autonomy and a universalizing humanist ideology, falsely derived, says Isobel Armstrong, from Immanuel Kant. Instead, the proponents of 'New Aestheticism' are advocating a new 'post-theoretical' phase, even a 'post-aestheticism', when theory becomes more reflective, but in ways which will have wide implications for art and culture. Above all this entails maintaining a dialectical view of works of art which recognizes that while 'Art is inexplicably tied to the politics of contemporary culture . . . the singularity of the work's "art-ness"' is not determined by surrounding political, historical or ideological discourses. As such, the 'new' or 'post-aesthetic' is strongly indebted to Theodor Adorno's '"defence of autonomous art as socially critical"' and his belief that '"art works bring forth another world, one opposed to the empirical world"'.

Isobel Armstrong's related proposal for a 'democratic aesthetic' argues for a broadened conception of what we mean by art, based on her belief that 'the components of aesthetic life . . . playing and dreaming, thinking and feeling . . . are common to everyone'. This emphasis on 'play', along with a range of other associated ideas – the 'new', the 'modern', the 'youthful', 'potential', 'hospitality' and 'alterity' – is also taken up by Thomas Docherty (2003). 'New Aestheticism' finds a home here in a newly conceived literary education and culture, a way of reading and a form of living in society which is open to the 'other'. This sets Docherty in clear opposition to a latter-day Gradgrindian philosophy which would stamp out play in schools, and to a general cultural philistinism ('Business Studies', Docherty notes provocatively at one point, 'has no place in a university'). Interestingly, too, Docherty turns explicitly in this argument, among much else, to the example of Dickens's *Hard Times*, as does Bate above. Where Bate, however, argues that we need more facts, Docherty evokes the contrasting knowledge and energies of the character, Sissy Jupe, and of the circus in Dickens's novel. Thus he ends his essay with an insistence on 'more dance, more love, more hospitality, more experience'.

Both textual bibliography or 'Genetic Criticism' and the 'New Aestheticism' present themselves as responses to the contemporary world, which is seen as standing in need either of more facts or of more play and transgressive openness. They show, once more, how diverse the positions taken up 'after theory' can be, but also how these differences depend on the way in which the wider world is perceived. That both Bate and Docherty use an example from literarary fiction is itself interesting; that they use the same example to quite different ends is also clearly revealing. We might ask, however, how relevant the symbolic figure and philosophy of Dickens's Thomas Gradgrind is. Is the present age a utilitarian age? Don't we hear more about 'spin' than 'facts', and hasn't market capitalism and globalization taken us a long way from the English industrial revolution?

In this connection, the editors of *The New Aestheticism* refer at one point to the significantly titled volume, *The Anti-Aesthetic* (1983). The introduction to this collection by Hal Foster, and the key essays it contained by Jürgen Habermas, Jean Baudrillard and Fredric Jameson, helped launch a decade of debate on postmodernism. For Joughlin and Malpas, this introduction of the postmodern spelt the simultaneous and premature rejection of the aesthetic. In the passage they quote, Foster himself recognizes the force of Adorno's conception of the aesthetic as a negative, subversive category: 'a critical interstice in an otherwise instrumental world'. This, he says, 'is hard to relinquish'. Foster's point, however, is that, 'Now [in postmodern times] we have to consider that this aesthetic space too is eclipsed'. It follows that 'New Aestheticism', in so far as it is *'new'*, must show how its arguments connect with the details of this changed world – or how literature can be reconnected to society and politics, to echo Brenkman's theme. To put this differently, the evident debt to Adorno in these arguments suggests how much the resources for a 'new aesthetic' lie in the modernist tradition and an associated aesthetic of 'estrangement' – that is, of art's own 'alienation', critical distance and potential. In hailing the 'new' and 'modern', Docherty refers, for example, to 'the defamilarising contact with the unknown'. Elsewhere, Joughlin reflects on the process of 'adaptation' as evidence of the potential and openness to otherness of exemplary art-works. To what purpose, we might ask, does this New Aestheticism 'adapt' an earlier modernist, *avant-garde* impulse to a world where art is enmeshed in contemporary commodity culture? Does a 'new aesthetic' of play and transgressive internal critique stand as a credible opponent to what in many accounts of the postmodern is described as an already thoroughly aestheticized world of simulation and the 'free play' of signs – or what Joughlin and Malpas call 'the rootless aesthetic contingencies of cultural studies or lit. crit. postmodernism'?

In his volume *After Theory* (2003), Terry Eagleton means to respond at the outset to the present world situation. For him, the 'other half' missing from theory is not literature or reading, culture or aesthetics, but politics. The theory Eagleton has in mind, however, is not so much the 'high theory' of Foucault, Derrida, Cixous and others, but 'postmodernism', which he generally also identifies with recent cultural theory. The problem confronting the present age, Eagleton argues, is fundamentalism: the West's 'implacable political enemy'. In the face of this challenge, a 'postmodern' theoretical and critical agenda focusing on gender, race and sexuality, along with its characteristic attitudes of scepticism and pluralism, is found seriously wanting. The latter's wariness of concepts of absolute truth and the universal – of fundamentals, in short – means that it lacks depth and ambition: 'where the political right acts globally', as Eagleton puts it, 'the postmodern left thinks locally', confined to the pragmatic and particular while the 'grand narrative' of capitalist globalization sweeps up everything in its path, including postmodern cultural theory itself, which emerges less as critique than accomplice of late capitalism, attached as it is – and as is capitalism – to the transgressive, hybrid and pluralistic. In the realm of value, Eagleton comments, a deconstruction of fixed hierarchies has 'merged effortlessly with the revolutionary levelling of all values known as the marketplace'.

Eagleton's alternative is an ambitious 'political criticism' (to borrow a description from his earlier *Literary Theory: An Introduction*) within a revitalized Marxist and socialist tradition. 'After theory' therefore means *more* theory, on a grander and more responsible scale, open to the large questions postmodernism has shied away from: of morality and metaphysics, love, biology, religion and revolution, evil, death and suffering, essences, universals, truth, objectivity and disinterestedness. This new project embraces, that is to say, both an expanded Marxism and a revaluation of some of the keystones of liberalism. Thus the concept of 'disinterestedness' Eagleton wants to understand not as 'impassivity' but as the opposite of 'self-interest'; similarly, 'objectivity' he interprets not as a spurious impartiality but as ensuring a recognition of the independent existence of 'the other'. It includes, too, a willingness to reflect on the legitimacy of Western values in the face of the fundamentalisms which reject this model. Fundamentalism seeks a 'non-being', argues Eagleton, which guarantees the purity of closure and unity. The result is dogmatism and, at its extreme, what he calls the 'brutally benighted state' of Islamic fundamentalism and the 'evil' of terrorism. Eagleton's answer is neither a simple defence of the West, nor of the present-day pluralism of Western left intellectuals. Rather it is to launch a critical rethinking of the West's 'enlightened values' in order to rescue it from its own benighted state and so engage in a struggle over 'fundamentals' on the global stage.

Eagleton urges theory to take risks and takes some himself in what is extremely sensitive political territory. One thing we can note, however, is that for all its sweep his new agenda lacks one main topic or category: 'Art' – and, in the present context, 'the literary'. In his hands 'cultural theory' seems to stretch away from the literary or the aesthetic just at the point when others are seeking to conjoin these, or to reconfigure their relationship. For the most part, these latter positions dismiss cultural theory and cultural studies, often along with a similarly rejected postmodernism. They share this with Eagleton, even though he does not take 'the literary' or 'the aesthetic' with him. Thus for many of the above, coming 'after theory' seems to mean coming after, or coming out of, the period when cultural studies and postmodernism took hold. The latter, or more generally the study of cultural texts (do these include the literary?) and theories of the contemporary, then drop out of the picture. That this entails the rejection of such a recent past is striking. Was so much in this period misconceived? Should the terms of this rejection be examined more closely? Should not one of the tasks of the present be to take up once more a theorization of the literary *and* of the cultural and the contemporary in order more fully to understand the terms of this transition – or, indeed, of another way forward?

References and suggested reading

Armstrong, Isobel, *The Radical Aesthetic* (Blackwell, Oxford, 2000).

Attridge, Derek, *The Singularity of Literature* (Routledge, London, 2004).

Bate, Jonathan, 'Navigate the Circus of Fancy with Fact', *THES* (1 August 2003).

Bissell, Elizabeth Beaumont, *The Question of Literature: The Place of the Literary in Contemporary Theory* (Manchester University Press, Manchester, 2002).

Bloom, Harold, *The Western Canon* (Macmillan, London, 1995).

Brenkman, John, 'Extreme Criticism', in Butler, Guillory and Thomas (eds), 2000, below, pp. 114–36.

Brooker, Peter, *Modernity and Metropolis: Writing, Film and Urban Formations* (Palgrave Macmillan, London, 2002).

Butler, Judith, Guillory, John and Thomas, Kendall (eds), *What's Left of Theory?* (Routledge, London, 2000).

Carroll, David (ed. with intro.), *The States of 'Theory': History, Art, and Critical Discourse* (Columbia University Press, 1990).

Clark, Robert, 'English Studies in the Current Crisis or: The Condition of the Subject and the War in Iraq', *European English Messenger*, XII/2 (Autumn, 2003), 46–9.

Coupe, Laurence (ed.), *The Green Studies Reader: From Romanticism to Ecocriticism* (Routledge, London, 2000).

Culler, Jonathan, *Literary Theory: A Very Short Introduction* (Oxford University Press, Oxford, 1997).

Cunningham, Valentine, *Reading After Theory* (Blackwell, Oxford, 2002).

Davis, Colin, *After Poststructuralism* (Routledge, London, 2003).

Docherty, Thomas, *After Theory* (Edinburgh University Press, Edinburgh, 1997).

Docherty, Thomas, 'Aesthetic Education and the Demise of Experience', in Joughlin and Malpas (eds), 2003, below, pp. 23–35.

Eagleton, Terry, *After Theory* (Basic Books, New York, 2003).

Foster, Hal (ed.), *The Anti-Aesthetic* [1983], pub. as *Postmodern Culture* (Pluto Press, London, 1985).

Garrard, Greg, *Ecocriticism* (Routledge, London, 2004).

Joughlin, John J. and Malpas, Simon (eds), *The New Aestheticism* (Manchester University Press, Manchester, 2003).

Kermode, Frank, *Pieces of My Mind: Writings 1958–2002* (Allen Lane, London, 2003).

McQuillan, Martin *et al.* (eds), *Post-Theory: New Directions in Criticism* (Edinburgh University Press, Edinburgh, 1999).

Miller, J. Hillis, *On Literature* (Routledge, London, 2002).

Payne, Michael and Shad, John (eds), *Life. After. Theory* (Continuum, London, 2003).

Rabaté, Jean-Michel, *The Future of Theory* (Blackwell, Oxford, 2002).

Singer, Alan and Dunn, Allen (eds), *Literary Aesthetics: A Reader* (Blackwell, Oxford, 2000).

Widdowson, Peter, *Literature* (Routledge, London, 1998).

Recommended glossaries of theoretical and critical terms and concepts

Baldick, Chris, *A Concise Dictionary of Literary Terms* (2nd edn, Oxford University Press, Oxford, 2004).

Bennett, Andrew and Royle, Nicholas, *An Introduction to Literature, Criticism and Theory* (3rd edn, Pearson Education, Harlow, 2004). Contains a brief 'Glossary'.

Brooker, Peter, *A Glossary of Cultural Theory* (2nd edn, Arnold, London, 2002).

Childs, Peter (ed.), *The Routledge Dictionary of Literary Terms* (Routledge, London, 2005).

Cudden, J. A. and Preston, C. E., *A Dictionary of Literary Terms and Literary Theory* (4th edn, Blackwell, Oxford, 1998).

Goring, Paul, Hawthorne, Jeremy and Mitchell, Domnhall, *Studying Literature: The Essential Companion* (Arnold, London, 2001). Contains a substantial 'Glossary of Literary and Theoretical Terms' – largely drawn from Hawthorne's 1998 *Glossary*, below.

Hawthorne, Jeremy, *A Glossary of Contemporary Literary Theory* (3rd edn, Arnold, London, 1998). There is also a *Concise* version: same publisher and date.

Murfin, Ross C. and Ray, Supryia, *The Bedford Glossary of Critical and Literary Terms* (2nd edn, Palgrave Macmillan, Basingstoke, 2003).

Peck, John and Coyle, Martin, *Literary Terms and Criticism* (3rd edn, Palgrave Macmillan, Basingstoke, 2002).

Stephen, Martin, *English Literature: A Student Guide* (3rd edn, Pearson Education, Harlow, 1999). Contains a brief 'Guide to Basic Literary Terms'.

Wolfreys, Julian (ed.), *Introducing Literary Theories: A Guide and Glossary* (Edinburgh University Press, Edinburgh, 2001).

Wolfreys, Julian, *Critical Keywords in Literary and Cultural Theory* (Palgrave Macmillan, Basingstoke, 2003).

Wolfreys, Julian, Robbins, Ruth and Womack, Kenneth, *Key Concepts in Literary Theory* (Edinburgh University Press, Edinburgh, 2001).

Literary, critical and cultural theory journals

Angelaki: journal of the theoretical humanities (Routledge).

Atlantic Studies (Routledge).

Auto/Biography (Arnold).

Comparative Critical Studies (Edinburgh University Press).

Critical Quarterly (Blackwell).

Critical Survey (Berghahn).

Culture, Theory and Critique (Routledge).

English (The English Association).

feminist review (Palgrave Macmillan).

Interventions: International Journal of Postcolonial Studies (Routledge).

Journal of Postcolonial Writing (Routledge).

New Formations (Lawrence & Wishart).

Paragraph: A Journal of Modern Critical Theory (Edinburgh University Press).

Postcolonial Studies (Routledge).

Pretexts: studies in writing and culture (Routledge).

Textual Practice (Routledge).

Translation and Literature (Edinburgh University Press).

The Year's Work in Critical and Cultural Theory [annual volumes] (Oxford University Press).

Wasafiri (University of London).

Index of names and titles

The indexes include the Introduction, Chapters 1–10 and the Conclusion but not the Preface or Appendices. Titles of books, journals and films are shown in *italic*, e.g. *Considerations on Western Marxism* (1976) 103; titles of journal articles and poems are shown in 'single speech marks', e.g. 'Death of the Author, The' (1968) 149–50. The filing order is word-by-word. Numbers are filed as if spelled out.

Index of topics